PRINCIPLES AND TYPES OF SPEECH COMMUNICATION

Thirteenth Edition

BRUCE E. GRONBECK
The University of Iowa

RAYMIE E. MCKERROW
Ohio University

DOUGLAS EHNINGER
ALAN H. MONROE

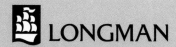 LONGMAN

An imprint of Addison Wesley Longman, Inc.

New York • Reading, Massachusetts • Menlo Park, California • Harlow, England
Don Mills, Ontario • Sydney • Mexico City • Madrid • Amsterdam

Senior Acquisitions Editor: Deirdre Cavanaugh
Project Coordination and Text Design: York Production Services
Cover Design: Kay Petronio
Cover Photo: Keith Tishken
Art Coordination: York Production Services
Photo Researcher: Julie Tesser
Electronic Production Manager: Valerie Zaborski
Manufacturing Manager: Helene G. Landers
Electronic Page Makeup: York Production Services
Printer and Binder: R. R. Donnelley and Sons Company
Cover Printer: The Lehigh Press, Inc.

Library of Congress Cataloging-in-Publication Data

Principles and types of speech communication/Bruce E. Gronbeck . . . [et al.]. — 13th ed.
    p.   cm.
  ISBN: 0-673-98047-2
  Includes bibliographical references and index.
  1. Public speaking.   I. Gronbeck, Bruce E.
PN4121.P72   1996
808.5'1—dc20   96–9037
                                      CIP

ISBN: 0-673-98047-2

12345678919—DOC—99989796

CONTENTS

Chapter 8

$\mathcal{B}$EGINNING AND ENDING THE SPEECH 209

Chapter 14

𝒮PEECHES TO PERSUADE AND ACTUATE   356

A NOTE TO STUDENTS AND TEACHERS

Principles and Types of Speech Communication has been a mainstay in the basic speech course, a celebrated leader in communication studies, for over half a century because it not only follows but also sets educational standards in this field. Longevity comes from adaptability to varied conditions. This book always has looked both backward and forward: backward to the timeless principles of speech that are central to the Euro-American cultural experience since the ancient Greeks, and forward to the latest research and the leading challenges of today and tomorrow. The thirteenth edition of this book follows in that tradition. The leading challenge of today is educational assessment, and this edition is at the forefront of those responding to the challenge.

As the twentieth century winds down, we are witnessing startling predictions not only about political, social, economic, and personal life in the next century (and millennium), but sharp evaluations of our educational institutions and systems as well. Public education—from K-12 through college and university—exploded onto the scene at the beginning of the century; the United States adopted many characteristics of the nineteenth-century German system of schooling, adapting that structure to the more democratic impulses of American citizens. We built schools on an educational philosophy that stressed basic skills acquisition followed by increasingly specialized studies as students moved up through the grades and into higher education. The philosophy was based on direct instruction and hard-nosed testing to demonstrate that the learning—especially of facts, procedures, and other ideas that could be assessed as "right" or "wrong" and "better" or "worse"—had occurred.

Hence it should come as no surprise that at the end of the twentieth century we are witnessing an increasing anxiety about how to demonstrate that students have learned what they ought to have learned in schools at all levels. Among the many end-of-the-century areas of evaluation and prediction are those centering on how to teach school in this country. In the 1960s, teachers were encouraged to relate better to their students, while in the 1970s teachers were encouraged to set behavioral objectives in order to "see" how much learning had occurred. There was a return to basics in the 1980s because we were, as a major educational report told us, *A Nation at Risk*. And in the 1990s, teachers were encouraged to stress local autonomy and accountability as a part of *Goals 2000*. Even as this preface is being written, a committee of the Speech Communication Association—the Committee for the Listening, Media Literacy, and Speaking Standards—is hammering out a series of content standards and proficiency levels that, it assumes, various states will use to assess instructional-learning outcomes of communication instruction. We thus live in a world where education-oriented governing agencies, from state departments of public instruction to local school boards, are attempting to create mechanisms to demonstrate that educational institutions are doing their jobs and that students are learning what they should, both in terms of content and performance.

Teachers who have used this book will find a dramatically expanded emphasis on assessment. To be sure, *content assessment* has been a part of this book for a long time; for the last twenty years, Bloom's Taxonomy of Education Outcomes has been a part of the testing machinery of the book. But with this new edition comes a concern for *proficiency assessment:* the need to identify key skills all speakers should possess and to specify various levels of skill proficiency. Students, too, must come to understand that acquiring a communication skill—say, offering an audience-sensitive introduction to a speech—is but one way to enter the arena of public talk with someone else's attention. To actually affect that person's knowledge, evaluations, and actions, a speaker must refine that skill, learning how to vary the strategies used in introducing a speech from situation to situation, from audience to audience. The refinement of speaking skills—increases in one's proficiency as an oral communication—can occur with the help of a textbook sensitive to the multiple levels on which such skills exist. This edition of *Principles and Types of Speech Communication* retains the qualities that will make it what it has always been: the flagship of communication studies, the most respected introduction to the field and adds coverage which will lead us into the next millennium.

NEW TO THIS EDITION

In this edition, we continue to offer the best advice the past has generated for speakers, but we've also looked forward. Several elements and perspectives stand out:

1. Introduction of proficiency assessment criteria. As has been suggested, assessment is central to today's college-level educational processes, and so it is to this book. New to this edition are the Assessment Previews opening each Chapter. The Assessment Previews provide a clear listing of some goals that beginning, average, and superior speakers should aspire to achieve. Assessment Checks, located within each chapter, allow students to stop for a moment and reflect on their acquisition of specific knowledge and skills. The Assessment Activities section at the end of each chapter links assessment to student experiences with a focus on particular speech preparation tasks: analytical skills, techniques for using the library, and exercises asking students to understand and evaluate their own habits and skills. While we've been careful to avoid constant talk about assessment and recognize that not every classroom is focused formally on an assessment philosophy of education, we've tried to provide the grounds for a speech course built around an assessment-based pedagogy.

2. Introduction of "how to" boxes. In keeping with the increased emphasis on oral communication skills—skills needed to both prepare and deliver effective speeches—has come a new feature: the "how to" box. Each of these boxes contains specific advice on how the concepts might be used in a specific illustration, thereby putting theory into practice. For example, "How To . . . Be an Active Listener, Improve Your Voice, and Avoid Sexist Language."

3. Expansion of materials on ethical issues facing speakers. Our "ethical moments" boxes were among the most positively received features of the twelfth edition. In this edition we have updated and revised the discussions of plagiarism, sexism, the ethics of credibility and hyperemotionalism, ghost writing, and statistical sleight-of-hand. The moral decisions speakers face are laid out.

4. Greater sensitivity to a culturally diverse world. The demands that the world places on the selection and use of effective communication strategies in order to successfully communicate in our diverse society has received greater emphasis in this edition. Throughout, we have increased the breadth and depth of examples drawn from various subcultures within this country, as well as examples reflecting the international community of which we are but a part. Beyond being rhetorically sensitive to gender differences and to ethnic, religious, and other cultural differences within this country, speakers also face a broader international community. *Principles and Types of Speech Communication* tries at every turn to assist you in refining your human relation skills. Chapters 1, 4, 12, and 13 are especially strong in this area.

5. Streamlined coverage for today's public speaking classroom. In response to reviewer suggestions, this edition has been streamlined to sixteen chapters from the previous edition's eighteen. Chapter 3, "Getting Started: Planning the Speech" includes material covered in chapters 3 and 4 of the last edition to provide a convenient overview of the early stages of speech preparation. Chapter 7 "Adapting the Speech Structure to Audiences: The Motivated Sequence" includes material covered in Chapters 8 and 9 of the last edition. As a result Motivated Sequence and its usefulness as a tool for more effective internal speech organization can be covered in a single chapter.

6. Continued pedagogical support. Both teachers and students need to be well supported in the educational process. *Principles and Types of Speech Communication,* thirteenth edition, continues to be a leader in pedagogical support. Among those ancillaries offered for instructors are multiple videos on topics such as speaker apprehension and audience analysis and a guide on how to use them; an Instructor's Manual that includes elements covered in the previous edition's Speaker's Resource Book as well as tips for teaching; bibliographies; chapter reviews for lecturing; and additional tested exercises prepared by the expert hand of Professor Kathleen German, Miami University, Ohio.

Accompanying these changes are revisions throughout the chapters. For example, you'll find a strengthened focus on cultural diversity and community building in Chapter 1; a simplified but more usable approach to listening in Chapter 2; a streamlined discussion of beginning steps to speech preparation in Chapter 3; a more accessible treatment of basic appeals in Chapter 5; an enhanced treatment of computer searches through the Internet in Chapter 6; tighter coordination between the Monroe's Motivated Sequence and the internal patterns of organization in Chapter 7; an enhanced treatment of computer-generated visual aids in Chapter 11; a new introduction to the importance of orality in Chapter 12; an updated treatment of the role of factual information in Chapter 13; a discussion of persuasion that provides the latest in research results undergirding the selection of effective strategies in chapter 14, and a new introduction focusing on social commitments made as an arguer in Chapter 15. Chapter 16, on special occasions, brings the text full circle, with a renewed emphasis on cultural diversity in relation to the importance of meeting the needs of audiences on socially significant and potentially memorable occasions.

$\mathscr{S}$TRENGTHS THAT CONTINUE FROM EDITION TO EDITION

Principles and Types of Speech Communication has earned its reputation because of traditional strengths, and we have been sure to retain those characteristics here.

1. Strong blend of theory and performance skills. The best textbooks strive both to conceptualize and, at the same time, teach practical skills. Although known for its solid grounding in rhetorical and communication research, this book also maintains a clear focus on the actual experience itself: creating and presenting an effective public speech. Our "How To" boxes coupled with our "Communication Research Dateline" boxes are examples of a dual focus on grounded knowledge and practical advice to speakers.

2. Focus on both speechmaking in society and student presentations in classrooms. This book has an obligation to compel communication studies' students to reflect seriously upon the electronic revolution and its implication for responsible dialogue between and among citizens. Throughout the text we utilize examples and illustrations that focus attention on contemporary political, economic, religious, and social issues. We ask students to analyze these issues in a manner that will help them construct arguments and appeals that reflect their own beliefs and resonate with their audience's beliefs, desires, and needs. Simultaneously, we recognize that as a reader, you are seeking to survive and grow in your own environment—the college communication classroom. Thus, you'll find many of our examples, illustrations, and sample speeches drawn from campus life as well as from student speakers. This book not only asks you to assess your skills where you are, but also to look ahead to the experience of building community through communication after your college years.

3. Emphasis on critical thinking and critical listening skills. This textbook always has been grounded in analysis: analysis of audiences, of the self, of one's purposes, and of the occasions on which one speaks. Our surveys clarify, however, that today's student needs more than that. The speech classroom is an excellent place in which to present the principles of critical thinking and critical listening—consumer-oriented techniques for examining messages, for assessing their characteristics, and for evaluating their claims in terms of logical and psychological criteria. Critical thinking is thus central to *Principles and Types of Speech Communication,* especially the chapters on listening (Chapter 2), gathering supporting materials (Chapter 6) and argumentation/critical thinking (Chapter 15).

4. Four-color presentation. The four-color design of this book will help you understand emphases on concepts and principles, locate special features, translate diagrams and figures into meaningful concepts and relationships, and come to grips with the "real world" of communication as presented in photographs. The treatment is as useful as it is aesthetically pleasing.

5. Chapter-end summaries and Key Terms. In addition to the Assessment Activities already mentioned, each chapter closes with a clear summary and a list of the key terms used in the chapter. These will be helpful in recalling concepts and building a vocabulary with which to discuss public communication events.

Overall, we know that this edition of the most popular public-speaking textbook of the twentieth century has merged traditional and innovative features to keep it at the forefront of communication studies. It is based on a speech skills tradition, which assures educators that course outcomes can be tested in concrete ways, and yet it lives and breathes the liberal arts tradition, which makes the basic speech course but an introduction to the world of communication studies—to the scientific, theoretical, historical, and critical study of public communication and social life. We are convinced that you will find *Principles and Types of Speech Communication* to be a solid yet malleable teaching and learning instrument.

$\mathscr{A}$CKNOWLEDGEMENTS

We owe a great debt to those instructors who took time to review the previous edition: Mike Allen, University of Wisconsin, Milwaukee; Thomas Harte, Southeast Missouri State University; Rita Hubbard, Christopher Newport University; Colleen Keough, University of Southern California; Nellie McCrory, Gaston College; Sherrie Sharp, Southwestern Oklahoma State University; James Stewart, Tennessee Technological University; and Aileen Sundstrom, Heny Ford Community College

Special thanks, once again, to Kathleen German, who transformed the Instructor's Manual into the most innovative manual in the field. Gratitude is owed to the University of Iowa Project on the Rhetoric of Inquiry, especially its administrative director, Kate Neckerman; the facilities provided by the Project during the year of revision made it go most smoothly. Thanks as well to Christopher, Jakob, and Ingrid Gronbeck, who continue to contribute their talents for library research and attempt to keep their father current. Gratitude is owed as well to Gayle McKerrow for her constant encouragement and continued support, especially during the long-distance move that interrupted the normally peaceful revision process.

We also thank Addison Wesley Longman for the resources and talents it invested in this project. This edition was executed under the careful watch of our Editor, Deirdre Cavanaugh, and our Developmental Editor, Leslie Taggart. The word-by-word manuscript preparation was overseen by Kevin Bradley, York Production Services. We also appreciate the assistance of the Permissions Department in keeping us legal. We were pleased with the efforts of marketing expert Peter Glovin and look forword to working with our new marketing manager, Jay O'Callaghan. And finally, we thank the group of talented sales representatives who carried this book onto the campuses and ultimately to you.

You, of course, are the bottom line. We thank you for examining and using this book. Your own personal commitment to excellence as a public communicator will be enhanced here and you will find new ways both to improve your own fortunes and to build a better community in a culturally diverse world. Your commitments are ours as well and we remain ever mindful of our obligation to enable you to succeed as ethical communicators.

Bruce E. Gronbeck
Raymie E. McKerrow

Part One
𝒫ROCESS

What other power [than eloquence] could have been strong enough either to gather scattered humanity into one place, or to lead it out of its brutish existence in the wilderness up to our present condition of civilization as [people] and as citizens, or, after the establishment of social communities, to give shape to laws, tribunals, and civic rights?

Cicero
De oratore I.33

CHAPTER
1

$\mathscr{B}$UILDING COMMUNITY, PRESERVING DIVERSITY: A CHALLENGE FOR SPEAKING IN PUBLIC

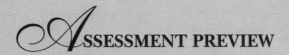

$\mathscr{A}$SSESSMENT PREVIEW

Measuring your understanding and ability to perform tasks will be a continuing feature of the chapters in this book. We will focus on the knowledge and skills a competent speaker should possess. After reading Chapter 1, the student with basic communication competencies will be able to

- list the basic elements in the speechmaking process.
- understand the role of specific skills and competencies in contributing to a successful speech.

The student with average communication competencies will also be able to

- recognize the relationship between the spoken word, the creation of community, and the preservation of cultural diversity.
- understand what constitutes an effective communication act: the interplay among the various speech elements—speaker, message, listener, feedback, channel, and social and cultural situation—and the speaker's skills and competencies, including integrity, knowledge, and ethics.

The student with superior communication competencies will also be able to

- evaluate the contribution of speakers to the creation of community, and critically examine the role of communication in preserving cultural diversity.
- evaluate the ethics underlying personal attempts to inform or persuade others as well as the attempts by others to influence belief and action.

Y *ou've arrived on this campus because of a scholarship. As a hockey player from Montreal, your first language is French. Your knowledge of English is fair, but speaking it in public, with your pronounced French accent, is a scary prospect.*

You've arrived on this campus from Bangkok, Thailand. You've studied English for a time, but you know the sounds are different from your native language. You're afraid students won't understand your accent or your pronunciation when you give your speech.

You've lived your life in Washington County, Maine, and now find yourself on a college campus in Arizona, in a speech class of all places. You are proud of your pronounced "Downeast" accent, and your new friends have teased you about how you say simple words like "car." As you prepare for your first speech, you know the subject well, but you aren't exactly looking forward to being teased about your—to these students—strange and almost incomprehensible pronunciation of words.

Born and raised in Harlem, you know the street talk of your brothers well; but now, you're in a speech class on campus, and the instructor is expecting you to talk in a different style from that of your social community. You know you can, as you've done it in high school. But what if you slip back into the street vernacular?[1]

From the time you spoke your first words, whether in English or in another language, people have been listening to what you have to say. Sometimes they've listened intently, sometimes only casually; sometimes they've agreed with you, sometimes not. So, you are used to talking to others, especially those who are your close friends, whether on the phone, in the coffee shop, before class starts, or in late night chats. Now you find yourself in a public speaking class. Some of you will identify with the experiences of those students profiled above. Preserving your cultural identity, while being understood, is a critical issue. Some of you will not be as concerned about how you will be understood, as English is your native language, and your accent is not demonstrably different from the "midwestern" accent you hear everyday on the news. One concern all of you will share, to one degree or another, is that speaking in public changes the rules: What you are comfortable doing in small gatherings among friends suddenly becomes much different when you are in front of a group (and a group that is made up of mostly strangers!). For most of us, "making a speech" is an activity that raises innumerable questions:

> What should I talk about?
> How should I start my speech?
> Why am I doing this? What do I want to achieve?
> How should I stand? What do I do with my hands?
> What if they can't understand my awkward English pronunciation?
> What if someone asks a question I can't answer?
> What if I forget what I want to say?

You were the high school commencement speaker, and you managed to get up there and say what you planned to say, and you didn't embarrass yourself in front of your parents and friends. Why all the concern now? One reason for the concern is that this is a new situation, and you want to make a good impression. Even if you've given speeches in other settings, preparing to get up and speak before a speech classroom brings up all of the anxiety and doubt represented in the above questions. In fact, you should worry more if you are *not* nervous, than if you are, as being nervous suggests that the adrenaline is flowing, the senses are heightened, and you will come across as alive, animated, and interested in conveying ideas to others.

While the prospect of speaking in public seems scary, learning to channel your natural nervousness so as to come across as poised, prepared, and even persuasive is why you are here. In addition, you're in this class because a lot of people in higher education believe that public speaking is something that well-educated, community-oriented people must be able to do well.

As the quotation from Cicero at the beginning of this unit indicates, the power of speech in building community is worthy of study. Preserving your own identity while creating that community is the special challenge we face as the next century looms before us.

ℬUILDING COMMUNITY THROUGH DIVERSITY

First and foremost, to speak in public is to declare yourself to be a member of a community. By "going public" with your ideas, you demand that others accept you and your suggestions as worthy of consideration. Asserting this right to be heard and taken seriously, especially when that right has been denied, is a vital part of our history. Without Frederick Douglass, a former slave who urged the abolition of slavery, we would be less than we are. In the language of his times, Douglass said: "Men may combine to prevent cruelty to animals, for they are dumb [mute] and cannot speak for themselves; but we are men and must speak for ourselves, or we shall not be spoken for at all."[2] Martin Luther King Jr.'s "Dream" may not yet be fully realized, but the legacy of Douglass lives on as African Americans continue to speak on behalf of their cultural heritage. Similarly, the women attending the Seneca Falls, New York, convention for women's rights in 1848 argued that they should be allowed to talk publicly; originally, they had been assigned to watch the proceedings from the gallery, but they were determined to define their own rights. The words of Elizabeth Cady Stanton give eloquent testimony to the need to speak:

> I should feel exceedingly diffident to appear before you at this time . . . did I not feel that woman herself must do this work. . . . Man cannot speak for her, because he has been educated to believe that she differs from him so materially, that he cannot judge of her thoughts, feelings, and opinions by his own.[3]

Speaking in public, then, is a personal declaration of your beliefs and values, or your right to be a representative of your community. Not to speak is to engage in silence. Silence can make you disappear, become invisible, a nonperson in the eyes of others: the Jews of Hitler's Germany were talked about as "silent animals" in *Mein Kampf;* American slaves were thought of as the personal property of slave owners; Native Americans were viewed as children, and treated as such; and whole segments of populations have been, and continue to be, treated as outcasts in their own land (and even "cleansed" in ethnic genocide, as in the Bosnia-Herzegovena tragedy). When whole peoples are silenced, through force or other forms of intimidation, they are in danger of elimination. The connection between the right to be heard publicly and being accepted as a human being with a distinct cultural heritage is trivialized at the expense of human freedom. If one can speak, what then of the community from which, or to which, one speaks? The words *community* and *communication* both derive from the common Latin root words *cum,* meaning "with," and *munis* denoting "public work." Communities are defined into existence by public talk; human conversation creates, sustains, and alters the sense of community one has with another. Such groups are created and maintained symbolically, as Boy Scouts or Girl Scouts who take their oaths together, as members of a church congregation who together recite the Lord's Prayer, as people stand and cease talking during the playing of the national anthem at the start of a hockey game.

Public speech, whether as part of a ritual performance or as a specific address to right social wrongs, has as a side benefit the maintenance or alteration of communities to which we belong. In our culturally diverse land, maintaining community is a special right of those whose culture differs from others. With maintenance comes the twin obligation of respecting differences between cultures, even in the same physical community.

In 1989 Henri Mann Morton, a member of the Cheyenne nation, addressed a multicultural conference and gave voice to the long-standing concern for preserving **cultural diversity** in these words:

> I am the granddaughter of those who welcomed many of our grandmothers and grandfathers—your grandparents—to this country. It is now our country.
>
> We were multi-tribal; heterogeneous as the indigenous people of America, and following Anglo contact exchanged the term "multi-tribal" for "multicultural," so we could embrace those who came to live with us. Prior to non-Indian contact, we as American Indians were culturally diverse. We were familiar with the concept of "cultural diversity," and recognized that those cultural differences made us strong. Cultural diversity made for strength— there was/is strength in cultural diversity. Cultural diversity makes our country strong. It has made us a great nation and we all have an opportunity to achieve the American dream.[4]

On the opening night of the 1992 Democratic National Convention in New York City, the third keynote speech was given by the late Barbara Jordan, the former congresswoman from Texas who had been, in 1976, the first female African American to keynote a national party convention. Dealing forthrightly with the issue of race relations in this country, she implored her listeners to recognize and value difference in the midst of unity:

> We are one, we Americans, and we reject any intruder who seeks to divide us on the bases of race and color. We honor cultural identity. We always have, we always will. But separateness is not allowed. Separateness is not the American way. We must not allow ideas like political correctness to divide us and cause us to reverse hard-won achievements in human rights and civil rights. Xenophobia has no place in the Democratic party. We seek to unite people, not divide them.
>
> As we seek to unite people, we reject both white racism and black racism. This party, this party, this party will not tolerate bigotry under any guise. Our strength, our strength in this country is rooted in our diversity. Our history bears witness to that fact. E pluribus unum. "From many, one." It was a good idea when our country was founded, and it's a good idea today.[5]

That two speeches by female members of minority groups would deal with matters of cultural diversity and racial divisions as well as with social unity was no accident. We were then, and continue to be, rocked by a series of incidents

In an age of diversity; it is important that you learn to speak publicly in order to build and maintain community.

In an age of diversity, it is important that you learn to speak publicly and to analyze the messages of public speakers from diverse cultural backgrounds.

that suggest the country has not escaped the danger of splitting apart along racial lines. From the "Rodney King incident," to the incendiary (to many) lyrics of rapper Ice-T's song "Cop Killer" to the sexual harassment allegations during the Hill/Thomas hearings, to Spike Lee's film *Malcolm X,* to the allegations surrounding the Fuhrman tapes and the Simpson trial, maintaining a sense of community while preserving diversity has been sorely tried.

Social division along racial lines is but one of the cleavages that shows itself nightly on television. Men battle women for elected office, for managerial and entry-level jobs, and over custody rights of children at the time of divorce and charges of sexual discrimination and harassment. College and university campuses are alive with debate over "political correctness": concern about giving members of the political left or right access to student audiences, about racial and gender quotas in faculty hiring, about what constitutes sexual or racial harassment, about what authors should be read in basic literature and history classes.[6]

The remarks of Morton and Jordan are signs that even mainstream public spokespersons have become frustrated by the divisions that threaten to crack open this country. The difficulty was clearly articulated by Jordan: We believe in and regularly affirm **cultural diversity,** even while we know it is essential that we maintain *social unity* to achieve common goals both locally and globally. Many have rejected the old notion of this country as the "melting pot"—a metaphor indicating that people's separate cultures were somehow assimilated into one homogeneous "American" culture. Jesse Jackson's "rainbow coalition" of many colors is one way of expressing the kind of tension articulated by Jordan: seen in the sky, the rainbow is at the same time "one" and "many." Achieving community while preserving diversity remains a challenge. That challenge can be met, in part, through common activity. People who work together, play together, fight a common enemy, or seek a common goal usually find out that people are people. When men and women teach together, they better appreciate each other's strengths; when Latinos and whites serve on community boards together, they generally discover shared hopes for their neighborhoods.

Sharing work and play can lead to shared views. But mere association is not enough. Most people need more than proximity to get to know and understand each other, and this fact gives rise to the second means, and the focus of this book. People need to talk. They need to chat about their teenage years, children, disgust with local government, favorite basketball teams, commitments. They need to argue over abortion or statehood for the District of Columbia or tax credits for kids in college. They need to verbally construct bridges between female and male, brown and white, immigrants and Native Americans. In their diversity, they must speak to become one.

Public speaking is a primary vehicle for recognizing individual identity even as a group of people seeks to share common ideas, values, action plans, and identities. If we had no need to share information and ideas, attitudes and values, plans and projects, or images of what we hold in common, we wouldn't have to talk. But we have those needs, we talk publicly, and we must become better at such talk.

$\mathcal{H}$OW PUBLIC SPEECH BUILDS COMMUNITY AND PRESERVES DIVERSITY

Both speaking and listening skills are important because *public communication* for centuries has been the glue that holds societies together. A sense of sharing, the *"with-ness"* part of the Latin root of the English word *communication,* bonds people together. More specifically, public speeches perform four important functions for a community:

1. *Speeches are used for self-definition.* Especially on such occasions as Memorial Day, the Fourth of July, dedications of community centers, and political conventions, communities define themselves, indicating what they stand for, what it means to be a member of the community, in speeches. That's why we all look to each other as we speak to sense who we are. ("As one speaks so she or he is" is an aphorism from the time of the Roman orator, Seneca.)
2. *Speeches are used to spread information through a community.* The president announces the latest plans for a European economic summit

through public talk; the surgeon general holds a press conference to update AIDS research findings; the mayor uses a radio interview to spread the word on next week's downtown jazz festival. Most information, of course, is distributed via print or electronic display, but spoken information is so much more personalized that important ideas are very often spoken directly to you. Even when offering ideas across national boundaries, world leaders still speak through translators, because of the personal nature of talk.

3. *Speeches are used to debate questions of fact, value, and policy in communities.* Human beings always have fought through their differences with each other. As civilizations advanced, verbal controversy replaced much of physical combat, and the art of public debate was born. From government to the workplace, arguing one's way through to a decision is an important function of talk.

4. *Speeches are used to bring about individual and group change.* For centuries persuasion has been the heart of public talk. The earliest books about public speaking dealt exclusively with persuasion as the most important kind of talk. Societies must adapt to changes in their environments, values, and practices; if change is to occur, most people must be persuaded to accept it.

Speechmaking, therefore, performs four broad social functions in communities. Whether one is talking about community broadly (as in a community of nations) or narrowly (as in a community of friends), collectivities simply could not exist and work without multiple forms of public communication.

𝒯HE NEED FOR SPEECH TRAINING IN THE AGE OF DIVERSITY

It is clear you need public-speaking skills to live productively in the Age of Diversity. Unless you have the speaking talents necessary to engage in committee discussions, presentations to clients, and interactions with your managers, you may be in trouble on the job. How important is it, really? In a recent study, over one thousand corporate leaders, from a variety of firms, named communication courses as those best preparing students for careers; in fact, communication courses were named more than courses within the students' majors. Put another way, far more people are fired due to an inability to communicate or handle basic human relations than are fired due to technical incompetence.[7] Your speechmaking skills also affect your ability to change people's minds at neighborhood meetings or coffee room gatherings, city or student councils, political conventions and public hearings, and the innumerable associations, clubs, and pressure groups that lobby the government. You will become a fully developed, thinking, and forceful human being to the degree that you've learned and practiced speechmaking and other oral communication skills. Ultimately, you speak not only to serve others but also to achieve your own goals on the job and in the public forum. You might even have fun doing it; human beings talk with others both to survive and to play a little.

Before you plunge into the activities that will improve your speaking skills, however, it is helpful to visualize the whole process, to think about the various elements that comprise communication in general and public speaking in particular. The rest of this chapter will examine those elements, the competencies they require of you, and matters of fear and ethics that you face as a speaker.

$\mathscr{B}$ASIC ELEMENTS IN THE SPEECHMAKING PROCESS

It's time you started thinking seriously and more technically about the speechmaking you are about to study and practice. Speechmaking is comprised of a number of elements: a *speaker,* the primary communicator, gives a speech, a continuous, purposive oral *message,* to the *listeners,* who provide *feedback* to the speaker. Their exchange occurs through various *channels* in a particular communication *situation* and *cultural context.* Consider each of these elements individually.

FIGURE 1.1   The Speech Communication Transaction

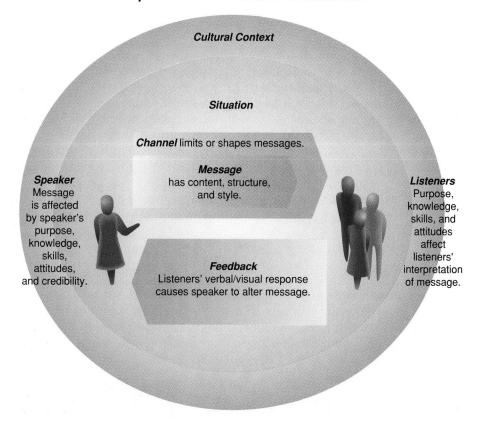

Cultural Context

Situation

Channel limits or shapes messages.

Message
has content, structure, and style.

Speaker
Message is affected by speaker's purpose, knowledge, skills, attitudes, and credibility.

Feedback
Listeners' verbal/visual response causes speaker to alter message.

Listeners
Purpose, knowledge, skills, and attitudes affect listeners' interpretation of message.

The Speaker

A speaker must consider four key elements in every speech exchange or trans-action[8]: *his or her purpose; knowledge of subject and communication skills; attitudes toward self, listeners, and subject; and degree of credibility.*

The Speaker's Purpose. Every speaker talks to achieve a goal. That goal can be as simple as a desire for social exchange or as complex as the desire to alter someone's ideas and actions. Your purpose or goal may be to entertain, call attention to a problem, refute an assertion, ward off a threat, or establish or maintain your status or power.

The Speaker's Knowledge. Your knowledge of the subject affects the character of your message and your effectiveness. If you have only surface knowledge of a topic, listeners feel cheated; they want you to say something important, new, relevant, interesting. You also need a knowledge of fundamental speaking skills. This book addresses both areas, with an emphasis on communication goals, finding and assembling relevant information, organizing messages in coherent and powerful ways, illustrating them visually, and delivering them with clarity and punch.

The Speaker's Attitudes. Your attitudes toward your self, your listeners, and your subject significantly affect what you say and how you say it. We all have mental pictures of ourselves—self-concepts or **self-images** of the kinds of individuals we are and of how others perceive us.[9]

Your self-image influences the way you speak in particular situations. Suppose you're giving a speech in class about your experience communicating with international students. If you have little confidence in your abilities and if you haven't done any research beyond your own limited experience, you'll tend to speak hesitantly; your voice will become weak, your body stiff, and you'll watch the walls rather than your audience. If you're convinced of your vast superiority over your listeners, you might move to the other extreme, becoming overbearing, disregarding listeners' needs, or riding roughshod over their feelings. Ideally, you'll find a middle way, balancing your personal experience with concrete research, and speaking with enough self-confidence to believe in your usefulness to your listeners and enough sensitivity to treat them with respect.

Part of your treatment of audiences comes from your *power relations* with them and the ways you perceive them—as instructors or fellow students, supervisors or employees, subordinates or equals. Giving a speech about cross-cultural communication in front of a teacher who's grading you involves an unequal power relationship; giving the same speech to a student research committee of which you're a member involves a relatively equal relationship. As power relations change, you adjust your speaking style accordingly. You have other attitudes that may affect your talk:

1. *Are you comfortable in the speaking situation, or does it make you feel strange?* For example, a speech classroom will make you feel

awkward at first, and that feeling will affect your speeches, but as you grow more at home your attitudes will improve—and so will your skills. Most people take a while to get used to speaking in church or synagogue, clubs, or civic groups.

2. *Are you comfortable with your subject and your mastery of it?* Is it interesting to you, or did you pick it because an article in *Time* or *USA Today* set it up for you? Does anyone else care about it? Can you make them care? Do you really know enough to speak about hiring quotas in front of a mixed-racial group? Your answers to these questions will be reflected in the ways you use your voice and body, in the intensity of your language and demeanor, and even in your selection of materials.

The Speaker's Credibility.　Your listeners' estimation of your credibility will affect their reception of your message. Speaker **credibility** is the degree to which an audience judges a communicator trustworthy, competent, sincere, attractive, and dynamic. The idea of credibility is rooted in the classical Greek concept of **ethos,** a word that means *character*. Research has repeatedly demonstrated that a speaker who can raise an audience's estimation of his or her trustworthiness, competency, sincerity, attractiveness, and dynamism will heighten the impact of any speech.

As these generalizations suggest, you and your message are inseparable in people's minds. Your audience's perception of you is the key—Aristotle called it the most important aspect of persuasion—to your effectiveness.

The Message

Your messages often are referred to as your *ideas* or *information*. In public speaking, three aspects of the message—content, structure, and style—are especially important.

The Content of the Message.　The message of a speech does not consist merely of facts and descriptions. A speech's **content** is the substantive and valuative materials that form your view of the issues that need to be covered. So, the content of a speech on notebook computers is more than a recitation of brands, model numbers, and features; the content is the way that the information is shaped for an audience's use. Such shaping often shows up in the central idea guiding the speech, such as "Three factors—price, preference in disk operating systems, and uses—should guide your decision on which notebook computer to purchase." In speeches, content is comprised of information plus the ways it is packaged for others.

The Structure of the Message.　Any message you transmit is of necessity structured in some way, simply because you say some words first, others second, and so on. Even if you ramble, listeners seek to impose their own pattern on your unstructured speech. It's important, therefore, to provide a pattern in order to guide their search for coherence. That structure may be as simple as

How TO
ENHANCE YOUR CREDIBILITY AS A SPEAKER

Research has verified the following generalizations, among others:

1. References to yourself and your experience—provided you're not boasting or excessive—tend to increase your perceived trustworthiness and competence. References to those acknowledged as authorities tends to increase your perceived trustworthiness and dynamism.

2. Using highly credible authorities to substantiate your claims increases your perceived fairness.

3. If you can demonstrate that you and your audience share common beliefs, attitudes, and values, your overall credibility will increase.

4. Well-organized speeches are more credible than poorly organized speeches.

5. The more sincere you are, the better chance you have of changing your listeners' attitudes.[10]

numbered points ("First I'll discuss, . . . next I will . . . and finally I'll . . . ") or as complex as a full outline with points and sub-points.

The Style of the Message. Just as you must select and arrange the ideas you wish to convey to listeners, so too must you select words, arranging them in sentences and using them to reveal your self-image to others. Selecting and arranging words and revealing yourself to be a certain kind of person are matters of style.

Given the innumerable words from which to choose, the great varieties of sentence structures, and even the many possible self-images available to speakers, many styles are possible. Styles can be personal or impersonal, literal or ironic, plain or elevated, philosophical or poetic. Such labels refer to particular combinations of vocabulary, syntax (sentence structure), and images of the speaker. What we call style, therefore, really has little to do with the elegance (stylishness) of language. Rather, it refers to those aspects of language that convey impressions of you, details of the world, and emotional overtones.

The Listener

Like speakers, listeners have purposes in mind; they are partners in speech transactions. The way they think about what is said is affected by their *purposes, knowledge of and interest in the subject, level of listening skills,* and *attitudes toward self, speaker, and the ideas presented.*

The Listener's Purposes. Listeners always have one or more purposes when they come to a speech. No less than speakers, they're looking for rewards. For example, you may attend a presentation by actor-activist Ted Danson in part to be entertained, in part to learn something about the environmental causes he champions, in part just to see what a star looks and sounds like in person. Such purposes might form your expectations; you'd be disappointed if he didn't refer to any of his movies or his long run in the TV show *Cheers,* or if he only talked about Hollywood without discussing the dangers to our oceans. Speakers must take listeners' purposes into account or risk rejection.

The Listener's Knowledge and Interest Levels. In speaking situations, listeners' knowledge of and interest in the subject significantly affect how they respond to the message. One of your jobs is to figure out how much listeners know about your topic and whether they have any personal stake in it. You can give only the most elementary speech on why bridges collapse to an audience that knows nothing about engineering principles; however, talking to a structural engineering class would allow you to get to the heart of the matter. Beyond assessing knowledge and interest, you also need to analyze cultural differences, if any, and how they will affect the audience's reception of your speech. For example, talking about "time" to a cultural group that does not place the same importance on "being on time" requires an awareness of the difference. What shared experiences can you call upon when talking with this audience?

The Listener's Command of Listening Skills. Listeners vary in their abilities to process oral messages. Some people were raised in homes in which complex oral exchanges occurred, while others were not. Some people have acquired the ability to follow long chains of reasoning, while others struggle to get the point. Most younger children cannot concentrate on difficult speeches, while most college students already have been taught to do so. What you must do is constantly scan your audience, looking for signs of comprehension and confusion.

The Listener's Attitudes. Listeners' attitudes toward themselves, the speaker, and the subject affect how they interpret and respond to speeches. Listeners with low self-esteem, for example, tend to be swayed more easily than those with stronger self-images. Listeners who feel their opinions are confirmed by the views of the speaker are also more easily influenced than those holding contrary ideas. Moreover, as a rule, people seek out speakers whose positions they already agree with and retain longer and more vividly those ideas of which they strongly approve.[11] **Audience analysis** is one of the keys to speaking success, because you need to know much about people's attitudes before you can reach them.

Feedback

You may think of public speaking as communication flowing in one direction, from speaker to listener. But information, feelings, and ideas flow the other way as well. **Feedback** is information that listeners return to you about the clarity and acceptability of your ideas.

Two kinds of information are provided by feedback. By looking for frowns or other signs of puzzlement, or, in a classroom, seeing how well students do on tests, speakers can learn whether their ideas have been comprehended clearly. Speakers also look for cues to the acceptability of their ideas; audiences can boo, look disgusted or antsy, or even leave the room. Being able to read feedback for signs of *comprehension* and *acceptability* is important, for this skill allows you to make mid-course adjustments in the speech.

Suppose you're giving a speech on child abuse. You might distinguish between punishment and abuse by referring to various modes of spanking. If you see wrinkled brows of puzzlement, you might elaborate by comparing grounding a child with chaining him or her to a bed (the latter has occurred). Each time, you'd try to show a difference between nonabusive and abusive discipline. Or, if you quote an expert on the subject and some listeners still look skeptical, you might add another authority as well as descriptions of such incidents of abuse. Throughout all this, you might not be able to convince everyone that your distinction between punishment and abuse is workable, but at least you might convert a few doubters. Feedback thus is a return message from audience members that tells you how much progress you've made and how far you've yet to go to reach your goals.

The Channels

The public communication transaction occurs across multiple channels. The **verbal channel** carries words, society's agreed-upon symbols for ideas. The **visual channel** transmits the gestures, facial expressions, bodily movements, and postures of the speakers and listeners; these tend to clarify, reinforce, or emotionalize the words or to transmit needed information about the audience's state of mind to the speaker. The visual channel sometimes is supplemented with a **pictorial channel**—visual aids such as diagrams, charts, graphs, sketches, and objects. The **aural channel**—also called the **paralinguistic channel**—carries the tone of voice, variations in pitch, loudness, and other vocal modulations; this channel carries cues to the emotional state of the speaker and the tone (ironic, playful, serious) of the speech.

Because these four channels are seen and heard simultaneously, the overall message is really a combination of several messages flowing through all of the pathways. Communication via multiple channels is what makes public speaking such a rich and subtle transactive experience. You must learn to shape and control the messages moving through all four channels.

The Situation

What you say and how you say it are affected significantly by the situations in which you're speaking. You don't talk the same way at work as you do at a party. Your speech is affected by the physical setting and the social context in which it occurs.

Physical Setting.   The physical setting influences listeners' expectations as well as their readiness to respond to your speech. People waiting at the convocation center for graduation ceremonies to begin have very different expectations from people attending a local politician's announcement of defeat at what was to be a victory party.

Even furniture and decor make a difference. Soft chairs and muted drapes help to put discussants at ease and to promote productive exchange. The executive who talks to an employee from behind a massive walnut desk in the middle of an opulently decorated room with large windows looking down from the twenty-fifth floor gains a communication advantage from that setting; it connotes power, authority, and command over others. The professor who has soft chairs and a lamp table in the corner of her office for interacting with students creates a different atmosphere than the professor who remains seated behind a desk while leaving the student standing.

Social Context.   Even more important to message reception than physical setting is the social context in which speeches are presented. A **social context** is a particular combination of people, purposes, and places interacting communicatively. In a social context, *people* are distinguished from each other by such factors as gender, age, occupation, power, degree of intimacy, ethnicity, and knowledge. These factors in part determine how you "properly" communicate with others. You've learned not to talk in class while the instructor is talking. In other settings, you're expected to speak deferentially to your elders, your boss, a judge, or a high status person in politics. Some settings have created formal conventions for engaging in

$\mathscr{C}$OMMUNICATION RESEARCH DATELINE

COMMUNICATION AND YOUR CAREER

In many chapters of this book, you will find a Communication Research Dateline highlighting a particular aspect of research on the public-speaking process. This first one centers on research dealing with communication and your career. Since the early 1970s, members of the Speech Communication Association, the national professional organization for speech communication teachers and scholars, have been interested in the relationship of speech training to postcollege employment. SCA's *Career Communication: Directions for the Seventies* (1972) discussed the applications of speech training for stu-

dents interested in particular careers—counseling, the ministry, police work, telephone company positions, retail sales, direct sales, teaching, and management (focusing on the Sears, Roebuck program). More recently, Al Weitzel's *Careers for Speech Communication Graduates* (1987) brings research findings to bear on the great variety of tracks in speech communication education; on the image that communication majors and the outside world have of speech students; on some career options (in particular, the skills needed for careers in training and development, public relations, law,

communication (as in the law court) while others are far more informal (a social gathering at a local restaurant).

Certain *purposes* or goals are more or less appropriately communicated in different social contexts. Thus a memorial service is not the context for attacking a political opponent; a "meet the candidates" night is. Some *places* are more conducive to certain kinds of exchanges than others. Public officials are often more easily influenced in their offices than in public forums, where they tend to be more defensive; sensitive parents scold their children in private, never in front of their friends.

Societies are governed by customs, norms, and traditions that become the bases for communication rules. **Communication rules** are guides to communication behavior, specifying who talks to whom about what in what style and under what conditions. Some communication rules tell you what to do: "An audience will better remember what you have to say if you break your subject into three to five main points." Others tell you what to avoid: "Don't wander aimlessly across the stage while talking because it will distract your audience." Such rules, of course, can be broken; some wandering speakers are nevertheless listened to, probably because they have so many other virtues. Occasionally, rule breaking is inconsequential; sometimes, however, it determines success or fail-

teaching, sales or marketing, and other positions); on some techniques for maximizing employability (including working at internships, joining professional organizations, improving communication skills, and the like); and on simple steps to find appropriate employment.

A point worth underscoring that comes from this career-related research is that, after completing your communication training, you can profitably pursue either (1) "communication" careers (the ministry, education, politics, advertising, sales, broadcasting, filmmaking, writing, editing, and so on) or (2) "noncommunication" careers (careers that emphasize other special skills, such as accounting, scientific research, insurance, computer science, engineering, nursing, and the like). That is, oral (and written) communication skills, as indicated by some

of the sources cited in reference note 7 in this chapter, are useful to virtually *any* entry-level position in American education, business, government work, service industries, or other occupations. No matter what you will do after graduation, think of communication skills training as training for your life's work.

For Further Reading

Richard Nelson Bolles, *What Color Is Your Parachute? A Practical Manual for Job-Hunters and Career Changers* (Berkeley, CA: Ten Speed Press; published annually); *Pathways to Careers in Speech Communication,* 4th ed. (Annandale, VA: Speech Communication Association, 1995).

Al R. Weitzel and Paul Gaske, "An Appraisal of Communication Career-Related Research," *Communication Education* 33 (April 1984): 181–94.

ure, and it always involves a certain amount of risk. The key is to determine the level of risk acceptable to you, and act accordingly.[12]

The Cultural Context

Finally, elements of communication may have different meanings depending upon the **culture,** or social understandings within which the communication is taking place. Each society has its own rules for interpreting communication signals. Some societies frown on taking second helpings of food, while in others, it's a supreme compliment to the host or hostess. Negotiating the price of a T-shirt is unheard of at Sears in Atlanta, yet it's a sign of active interest in an Istanbul bazaar or at a Cleveland garage sale. Communication systems operate within the confines of cultural rules and the expectations of members of any given society.

Cultural rules and expectations become important in two situations: during *intercultural contact* and *cross-cultural presentations.* When talking to members of other societies on your home turf, you might offend them by violating some rule that they bring with them to your speech. A common violation that occurs during intercultural contact is too much familiarity or informality with a new acquaintance. To call people by their first names in public, for example, is simply not acceptable in many countries.

Your problem may be even greater, of course, if you attempt to speak in public in another country. During such cross-cultural presentations, you risk violating not only personal standards of interaction but the rules of the situation operating at that time and place. Americans soon learn that they cannot joke publicly about royalty in Sweden in the same way that they can joke about the president's family in the United States. If you are going to speak in various countries, you have to learn the communication rules governing the ways to introduce a person to an audience, to quote appropriate authorities, and to refer to yourself and audience members correctly. Rules for such communication situations tend to vary from country to country. To tap into the cultural context for public speaking is to grapple with the most fundamental questions of diversity and sociality—how people in various countries interact with each other and transact public business.

The cultural context for public speaking is the ultimate source of the communication rules you've been taught. Because speeches almost always represent transactions whose appropriateness is determined by cultural rules or expectations, throughout this book you'll find explicit pieces of advice—do's and don'ts. It's not really "wrong," for example, to skip a summary at the end of your speech, but most audiences expect one. If you omit it, the audience might question your **communication competence**—your ability to construct a speech in accordance with audience expectations. These sorts of expectations do not have to be followed slavishly, because conditions and even speaker talents vary from situation to situation; however, you should follow the rules of communication most of the time because you want listeners to evaluate your ideas, not your communication skills. A consistent theme of this book is the supreme importance of developing communication competence—the possession and execution of speech skills.

Speakers and listeners, messages and feedback, channels, context, and culture are the primary elements of the public-speaking process. As you strive to refine your skills in managing all of them consider the following points:

1. *A change in one element usually produces changes in others.* During a speech on learning to use the campus computer system, for example, your attitude will affect your language and delivery, your listeners' attitudes toward you, and even the feedback that you receive from them.
2. *No single element controls the entire process.* You may think the speaker controls the entire process, but, of course, the speaker does not, because listeners can tune in or tune out, and because cultural expectations often affect the listeners' perceptions of the speaker's talents.

Overall, therefore, public speaking is a *transaction* or *exchange:* you prepare a speech to give your listeners, and, in turn, they give you their attention and reactions or feedback. From among all of the things you could say, you

*A*SSESSMENT CHECK

Think about a speech you heard recently or read one now from the collection in this book. Look analytically at the message the speech promotes or the way it is organized and presented for the audience. In particular, ask yourself:

- Does the speech foster the development of community?
- Does the speech promote cultural diversity?
- Does the speaker promote ideas in an ethical manner?
- What skills or competencies are particularly noteworthy in this instance? Which appear deficient?
- What can I learn about successful public speaking from hearing or reading this speech?

actually select only a few and tailor them to the listeners' interests, wants, and desires, so that they can absorb and accept them. And, just as you assert your right to speak, they assert their right to listen or not to listen. *Public speaking is a communication transaction, a face-to-face process of mutual give-and-take.*

*S*KILLS AND COMPETENCIES NEEDED FOR SUCCESSFUL SPEECHMAKING

Because public speaking is an interactive process through which people transact various kinds of business, you must acquire certain skills (psychomotor abilities) and competencies (mental abilities to identify, assess, and plan responses to communication problems). From the beginning of your coursework, four basic qualities merit your attention: *integrity, knowledge, sensitivity to both listener needs and speaking situations, and oral skills.*

Integrity

Your reputation for reliability, truthfulness, and concern for others is your single most powerful means of exerting rhetorical influence over others. Integrity is important, especially in an age of diversity, when various groups in a fragmented culture are wary of each other and each other's purposes. Listeners who haven't had personal experience with a particular subject or with representatives of particular social groups must be convinced of your trust and concern for them. You must earn their trust while speaking if you are to succeed.

Knowledge

No one wants to listen to an empty-headed windbag; speakers simply must know what they're talking about. So, even though you have a lot of personal experience with criterium bike-racing, take time to do some extra reading, talk with other bikers and shop owners, and find out what aspects of the topic interest your potential listeners before giving a speech about it.

Rhetorical Sensitivity

Sometimes we talk publicly for purely *expressive* reasons—simply to give voice to ourselves. Usually, however, we speak for *instrumental* reasons, to pass on ideas or to influence the way others think or act. The most successful speakers are "other directed," concerned with meeting their listeners' needs and solving their problems through public talk. These speakers are rhetorically sensitive to others.

Rhetorical sensitivity refers to speakers' attitudes toward the process of speech composition.[13] More particularly, rhetorical sensitivity is the degree to which speakers recognize that all people are different and complex, and hence must be considered individually; adapt their messages and themselves to particular audiences; consciously seek and react to audience feedback; understand that in some cases silence is better than speaking; and work at finding the right set of arguments and linguistic expressions to make particular ideas clear and attractive to particular audiences. Being rhetorically sensitive doesn't mean saying only what you think an audience wants to hear. Rather, it's a matter of careful self-assessment, audience analysis, and decision making. What are your purposes? To what degree will they be understandable and acceptable to others? To what degree can you adapt your purposes to audience preferences while maintaining your own integrity and self-respect? These questions demand that you be sensitive to listener needs, the demands of speaking situations, and the requirements for self-respect. Being a rhetorically sensitive speaker attests to your competence as a communicator.

Oral Skills

Fluency, poise, voice control, and coordinated body movements mark you as a skilled speaker. These skills don't come naturally; they're developed through attention to the advice offered in this textbook, and to putting advice into practice. As you practice inside and outside the classroom, your aim is to refine your skill as an animated, natural, and conversational speaker. Many competent public speakers—discounting those speaking in the highly ceremonial situations of politics and religion—seem to be merely *conversing* with their audiences. That should be your goal: to practice being yourself while engaging others in public conversation.[14]

*O*VERCOMING SPEECH ANXIETY

As you think about speaking publicly, you're likely to feel some anxiety because you don't want to fail. This fear of failure or embarrassment may be even stronger than your desire to speak, leading to speech anxiety.

Research distinguishes between two kinds of speech anxiety: state apprehension and trait apprehension.[15] **State apprehension** refers to the anxiety you feel in particular settings or situations. For example, perhaps you can talk easily with friends but are uncomfortable when being interviewed for a job. This sort of apprehension is also known as *stage fright* because it's the fear of performing that leads to your worries about embarrassing yourself. Extreme stage fright has physiological manifestations: clammy hands, weak knees, dry mouth, and a trembling or even cracking voice. Its psychological manifestations include mental blocks (forgetting what you're going to say), vocal hesitation and nonfluency, and an internal voice that keeps telling you that you're messing up your speech. The knowledge that you're being evaluated by others intensifies these anxious moments.

While some aspects of nervousness are characteristic of the situation, others are a part of your own personality. This kind of apprehension, called **trait apprehension,** refers to your level of anxiety as you face any communication situation. A high level of such anxiety may lead people to withdraw from any situation that requires interpersonal or public communication with others.

There are no shortcuts to developing self-confidence about speaking in public. For most of us, gaining self-confidence is partly a matter of psyching ourselves up and partly a matter of experience. The sick feelings in your stomach may well always be there, at least momentarily, but they needn't paralyze you. As you gain experience with each of the essential steps—from selecting a subject to practicing the speech—your self-confidence as a speaker will grow.

Shyness and Public Speaking

Do you think of yourself as shy? If so, does shyness affect your willingness and ability to speak in public? Many people think of themselves as shy, but some people suffer from heavy-duty speech fright to the point of paralysis. A leading psychologist, Stanford's Philip G. Zimbardo, defines shyness as "an apprehensiveness about certain social situations due to excessive preoccupation with being critically evaluated, resulting in a variety of behavioral, physical, cognitive, and emotional reactions." Shyness may vary from bashfulness to social paralysis, with the middle ground being a state in which the person lacks self-confidence and is easily embarrassed. About 40 percent of American college students describe themselves as shy, another 40 percent say that they used to be shy, and about 15 percent see themselves as shy in certain situations. To get at the roots of shyness, Zimbardo and his colleagues developed *The Stanford Shyness Survey,* a tool used to diagnose shyness and its sources in specific individuals. Using such instruments as the Shyness Survey, therapists can tailor treatment programs to individual needs. They can help individuals build new social skills, boost self-esteem, and utilize relaxation techniques and other strategies to manage shyness.

Shyness is probably at the base of what we usually call "speech fright" or "communication apprehension." If you are shy, one of the goals you ought to

How to
Manage Your Fear of Public Speaking

There are positive ways of reducing such apprehension in the classroom setting:

1. *Realize that tension and nervousness are normal and, in part, even beneficial to speakers.* Learning how to control fear and make it work for you is the key to reliev- ing tension. Tension can pro- vide you with energy and alert- ness. As adrenaline pours into your bloodstream, you experi- ence a physical charge that in- creases bodily movement and psychological acuity. A speaker who isn't pumped up may come across as dull and lifeless.

set for yourself in this classroom is the control and redirection of those feel- ings. Talk with your instructor, and perhaps other professionals on campus, if you want help.[16] ■

The Ethics of Public Speaking

Being perceived by listeners as a person with strong ethical principles is vital to your success as a speaker. In helping people define who they are, in assem- bling and packaging information for others, in seeking to persuade them to

2. *Take comfort that tension is physiologically reduced by the act of speaking.* As you talk and discover that your audience accepts and understands what you're saying, your nervousness will dissipate. Physiologically, your body is using up the excess adrenaline it generated; psychologically, your ego is getting positive reinforcement. The very act of talking aloud reduces fear.

3. *Talk about topics that interest you.* Speech anxiety arises in part because of self-centeredness; sometimes you're more concerned with your personal appearance and performance than with your topic. One means of reducing that anxiety is to select topics that thoroughly interest you—topics that take your mind off yourself.

4. *Talk about subjects with which you're familiar.* Confidence born of knowledge increases your perceived credibility and helps you control your nervousness. Knowing something about the subject may be part of the answer: subject mastery is closely related to self-mastery.

5. *Analyze both the situation and the audience.* The more you know about the audience and what is expected of you, the less there is to fear. In the speech classroom, students are usually less nervous during their third speech than during their first. They're more comfortable with the audience and more aware of the demands of the situation. Careful analysis of any audience and its expectations goes a long way toward reducing a natural fear of the unknown.

6. *Speak in public as often as you can.* Sheer repetition of the public-speaking experience will not eliminate anxiety, but will give you greater confidence in managing your apprehension. Speaking a number of times in front of the same group can help reduce your fright. Speaking up in class discussions, engaging in conversations with friends and others, and contributing ideas or thoughts in meetings of organizations to which you belong, you will gain more knowledge about the strategies that work for you in reducing nervousness.

think or act in a certain way, you run into many ethical questions. Is it ethical to make explicitly racial references when defining a people? Should you tell both sides of the story when you are giving people information on a new wonder drug? Can you in good conscience suppress certain kinds of information when you're trying to change people's minds? These and hundreds of other ethical questions face you as you prepare and deliver speeches. Whether you want to or not, you make decisions with moral implications many, many times—even when you're building a comparatively simple speech. The principles offered below are not exhaustive, but they will give you a sense of what is at stake.

Being a Principled Speaker _____

1. *Honesty is the best policy.* An old aphorism, tainted by the practices of legions of speakers seeking to bend the truth or not provide it at all, this still holds true as a starting point for deciding what to say or not to say in a public setting.

2. *Maximize audience responsibility for decision making.* Public speaking in a democratic society demands openness with respect to information. Whether you are informing or persuading, respect your audience enough to allow them to make a decision based on all that you have to offer in the way of information and support.

3. *Maximize help while minimizing harm to others.* Your reasons for speaking out should result in actions that would help rather than harm other individuals. Inciting others to believe or act in a manner that produces physical or emotional harm to other persons is a misuse of the power of communication.

4. *Place your ego at the service of others, not simply of yourself.* While self-interest and a sense of self-esteem go a long way toward making you a successful speaker, the purpose is not to simply display your ability but rather to put it at the service of the community.

5. *Follow both the letter and the spirit of the law.* Your language should be within legal bounds; the question of libelous or harassing language should never arise in the speaking situation.

6. *When in doubt, apply the "parent" test.* When you are faced with an ethical dilemma, ask yourself: "What would I do if I were talking to [insert "Mom," "Dad"]? Given the principles with which you were raised, an answer should pop up rather quickly.[17] ∎

No one can presume to tell you precisely what ethical codes you ought to adhere to when giving a speech. Given a textbook's educational mission, however, we'll regularly raise ethical questions and urge you to deal with them. Throughout the book, you'll encounter "Ethical Moments." These features are designed to confront you with a problem; working through ethical dilemmas will make you a more thoughtful speaker.

ℰHAPTER SUMMARY

We live in an Age of Diversity, characterized by a fragmented population and subgroups within society separated from each other even while needing a sense of the whole to live together. Speaking skills are important to society because we collectively use speeches for self-definition, information giving, debate about questions of fact, value, and policy, and individual and social change. A useful model of public speaking incorporates six elements and their variable aspects:

- The message: content, structure, style
- The speaker: speaker's purpose, knowledge, attitudes, and credibility
- The listeners: listeners' purposes knowledge, listening skills, and attitudes
- The channels: verbal, visual, pictorial, and aural
- The situation: physical setting, social context; and
- The cultural context: social and communication rules

Because public speaking is a complex *transaction,* you need certain skills and competencies to be successful: *integrity, knowledge, rhetorical sensitivity,* and *oral skills.*

$\mathscr{K}$EY TERMS

audience analysis (p. 16)
aural channel (p. 17)
communication competence (p. 20)
communication rules (p. 18)
content (p. 13)
credibility (p. 13)
cultural diversity (pp. 6, 8)
culture (p. 19)
ethos (p. 13)
feedback (p. 16)

paralinguistic channel (p. 17)
pictorial channel (p. 17)
rhetorical sensitivity (p. 22)
self-image (p. 12)
social context (p. 17)
state apprehension (p. 23)
trait apprehension (p. 23)
verbal channel (p. 16)
visual channel (p. 16)

$\mathscr{A}$SSESSMENT ACTIVITIES

1. To learn to assess your own speeches and other's speeches, watch a speech on videotape; pause each time something strikes your attention—jot down notes as you watch and listen. After viewing the speech several times, answer the following questions:
    a. Does the speech seek to define community, share information, take a position in a debate, or call for social change? Does it have more than one of these general purposes? Which predominates? Why do you think so?
    b. How does the choice of channel influence the speaker's approach to this audience? Is this the most appropriate channel to use in conveying the speaker's message? Why or why not?
    c. Does the speaker appear to be rhetorically sensitive to the situation and the audience? Given the content, structure, and style of the speech, what is the image the speaker appears to have of the audience? Does the speaker view listeners as passive consumers or active, intelligent critics of the message?
    d. What attitudes might the audience bring to this speech? Why would they be listening to the speaker?

   e. How would you rate the speaker's skills and competencies? Does the speaker seem knowledgeable, self-assured, trustworthy? Does the speaker's use of verbal and nonverbal communication result in a message that is clear, forceful, and compelling? Why or why not?

   f. List at least three ways the speaker could improve on this particular speech. Refer to the model discussed in this chapter as you formulate your answer.

2. Explore a recent public event in which the ethics or credibility of a person was called into question. Prepare a three-to-four-minute presentation in which you briefly summarize the ethical issue, and then add your own views as to whether the person was fairly accused, and if so, what you think of the choice the person apparently made.

ℛEFERENCES

1. For other examples, see Rebecca Nordyke, "Celebrating Cultural Diversity in the Communication Classroom," in *Public Speaking: A Repertoire of Resources,* ed. Susan Schultz Huxman (New York: McGraw-Hill, 1992), 23–28.

2. Frederick Douglass, "Speech at the National Convention of Colored Men (1883)," reprinted in *The American Reader: Words That Moved a Nation,* ed. Diane Ravitch (New York: HarperCollins, 1990), 172.

3. Elizabeth Cady Stanton, "Speech at the Seneca Falls Convention, 1848," reprinted in *Man Cannot Speak for Her,* vol. 2, *Key Texts of the Early Feminists,* ed. Karlyn Kohrs Campbell (New York: Praeger, 1989), 42.

4. Henri Mann Morton, "Strength Through Cultural Diversity," in *Native American Reader,* ed. J. Blanche (Juneau, AL: Denali Press, 1990), 196–197.

5. Barbara Jordan, keynote speech to the 1992 National Democratic Party Convention, July 13, 1992, New York City, telecast on the C-SPAN television network; personal transcription.

6. For additional information on the controversy over political correctness on the college campus, see Paul Berman, ed., *Debating P.C.* (New York: Dell, 1992).

7. See Rhea A. Nagle, "The Ideal Job Candidate of the 21st Century," *Journal of Career Planning and Employment* (1987): 40; G. Wakefield and L. P. Cottone, "Knowledge and Skills Required by Public Relations Employers," *Public Relations Review* 13 (1987): 24–32; "Leadership Depends on Communicating," *Nation's Business* 70 (1982): 17; James C. Bennett and Robert J. Olney, "Executive Priorities for Effective Communication in an Information Society," *Journal of Business Communication* 23 (1986): 13–23. These reports all indicate that graduates in the working world find communication skills to be essential for both hiring and promotion. See also the Communication Research Dateline in this chapter.

8. The word *transaction* is being used to indicate that public speaking is not a one-way mode of communication. Just as the speaker offers a message, so the listeners in return offer messages in the form of feedback. Speakers and audiences have mutual obligations to be forthright and honest in their appraisal and treatment of each other. Each thus plays complementary roles during public speeches, and hence the word *transaction* clearly applies to this sort of communication exchange. For a more complete discussion of this concept, read the classic essay on it: Dean C. Barnlund, "A Transactional Model of Communication," in *Language Behavior: A Book of Readings,* ed. Johnny Akins et al. (The Hague: Mouton, 1970), 53–71.

9. On the interrelationships between self-concept and communication, see Joseph DeVito, *Messages: Building Interpersonal Communication Skills,* 3rd ed. (New York: HarperCollins, 1996), ch. 2, "The Self," 26–55.

10. Still the most complete summary of research on credibility is Stephen W. Littlejohn, "A Bibliography of Studies Related to Variables of Source Credibility," *Bibliographic Annual in Speech Communication: 1971,* ed. Ned A. Shearer (Annandale, VA: Speech Communication Association, 1971), 1–40. For a more recent overview, see James B. Stiff, *Persuasive Communication* (New York: Guilford Press, 1994), ch. 5, "Source Characteristics in Persuasive Communication," 89–106.

11. For more information on such matters, see James B. Stiff, *Persuasive Communication* (New York: Guilford Press, 1994), ch. 7, "Receiver Characteristics," 132–152.

12. For a fuller discussion of physical and social context, see Sarah Trenholm, *Persuasion and Social Influence* (Englewood Cliffs, NJ: Prentice-Hall, 1989), ch. 8, "The Persuasive Environment." A good overview on social context is provided in Joseph DeVito, *Messages: Building Interpersonal Communication Skills,* 3rd ed. (New York: HarperCollins, 1996), ch. 6, "Nonverbal Messages," 108–139. The best review of research on communication rules is found in Susan B. Shimanoff, *Communication Rules: Theory and Research,* Sage Library of Social Research (Beverly Hills, CA: Sage, 1980).

13. See Roderick P. Hart and Don M. Burks, "Rhetorical Sensitivity and Social Interaction," *Speech [Communication] Monographs* 47 (1980): 1–22. Some similar points are made in Wayne Brockriede, "Arguers as Lovers," *Philosophy and Rhetoric* 5 (1972): 1–11.

14. For a philosophical analysis of the need for continuing public conversation about political and social choices, see Richard Rorty, *Contingency, Irony, and Solidarity* (Cambridge, England: Cambridge University Press, 1989).

15. James McCroskey, "Oral Communication Apprehension: A Summary of Current Theory and Research," *Human Communication Research* 4 (1977): 78–96.

16. John A. Daly and James C. McCroskey, eds., *Avoiding Communication: Shyness, Reticence, and Communication Apprehension* (Beverly Hills, CA: Sage, 1984); Philip Zimbardo, *Shyness: What It Is, What to Do About It,* rev. ed. (Reading, MA: Addison-Wesley, 1990.)

17. For a more complete discussion of these and other principles, see James Benjamin and Raymie E. McKerrow, *Business and Professional Communication: Concepts and Practices* (New York: HarperCollins, 1994).

CHAPTER
2
PUBLIC SPEAKING AND CRITICAL LISTENING

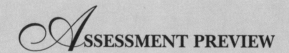

ASSESSMENT PREVIEW

After reading Chapter 2, the student with basic communication competencies will be able to

- distinguish between hearing and listening.
- comprehend the central idea or claim of a speech and its development.
- take notes recording the basic outline of a speech.
- offer a general substantive and formal critique of a speech.

The student with average communication competencies will also be able to

- assess the speaker's purposes from clues offered in the speech.
- identify the primary grounds upon which listeners are asked to think or act by a speaker.
- take notes recording key portions of the supporting materials.
- evaluate a speech, assessing the speaker, message, channel use, and adaptation to the audience.

The student with superior communication competencies will also be able to

- listen in five different ways.
- identify and critique a speaker's purposes and the grounds upon which the speaker is asking an audience to think or act.
- assess the strengths and weaknesses of the supporting material of the speech.
- take notes that include personal reactions to the ideas presented.
- evaluate a speech, making significant suggestions for improvement.

George called his neighbor Frank, who ran a trucking business. "I want to ship three sows and seven sheep to market tomorrow," George said. "Fine, I'll be there at 6 A.M, replied Frank." At 5:50 A.M., George looked out his kitchen window to see a fleet of semis. Frank climbed out of the front cab, came to the door, and said, "We're ready." "Ready?" said George. "Why all those trucks?" "Well," replied Frank, "I figured that if you had 3,007 sheep to ship, I'd need every truck I have."

In your daily life, you spend more time listening than do you do reading, writing, or speaking. While you may assume that you're a good listener from all that practice, you usually don't know about problems you might have until you miss something important. The fact is, you've probably never had any training in listening, especially for situations such as class lectures where you're expected to acquire technical or abstract materials aurally. Just ask Frank and George about the problems that can result from mishearing numbers!

Listening accounts for over 40 percent of your communication time. Through conversations, classroom lectures, group meetings, electronia media, and other forms of aural communication, you amass an amazing amount of information. You also learn to anticipate the actions of others and to gauge their feelings and moods through listening.

Listening is one of the two fundamental activities in the communication process. As a speaker, you reach out to your audience; and, in turn, as a listener, you respond. Both speaker and listener are active participants in communication events. Listeners provide two kinds of feedback: immediate and delayed. **Immediate feedback** consists of verbal or nonverbal responses during an interaction. Some immediate feedback is *direct*—for example, when questions are asked—while some is *indirect*, as when speakers look for frowns, smiles, nodding heads, and other nonverbal cues to reactions. **Delayed feedback** consists of oral, auditory, or visual signals received after the message has been transmitted—for example, voice votes on matters a speaker has recommended, the sound of applause or boos, or written evaluations from an instructor.

After more fully introducing the idea of listening, this chapter will focus on practical listening techniques you can use in almost any situation in which someone else is doing most of the talking. We'll finish by suggesting how you can put new listening skills to work in your classes.

HEARING AND LISTENING

Hearing is the first step in the listening process. To listen to a message, you first must hear it. **Hearing** is the physiological process of receiving sound waves. Sound waves travel through the air and set up vibrations on the eardrum; these vibrations are transmitted to the brain. Hearing is affected by the laws of physics and the neurophysiology of the body. Any number of factors can interfere with hearing—distracting noises in the environment, sounds

FIGURE 2.1   The Types of Feedback

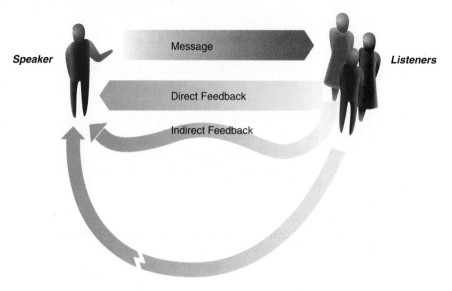

too loud or too soft for the aural mechanisms, or impediments such as illness or hearing loss. Generally, the hearing process is beyond the speaker's control, except for the ability to change speaking volume, seating arrangements, or conditions in the room before talking.

Listening, on the other hand, is the cognitive process whereby people attach meanings to aural signals. After sound waves are translated into nerve impulses by the middle ear and the auditory nerve, they're sent to the brain for interpretation. The processes of interpretation—registering impulses, assigning them to meaningful contexts, and evaluating them—constitute listening.

$\mathscr{B}$ARRIERS TO GOOD LISTENING

Listening is easy to define but hard to practice. You've probably developed some barriers to good listening. You'll have to remove those barriers from your mental habits if you're going to improve. Each of us has idiosyncratic listening habits, but many people share four problems:

1. *Passive listening.* Many of us are just plain lazy listeners, hoping that the speaker will be exceptionally clear. As a result, we can forget more of speeches and conversations than we remember.
2. *Drifting thoughts.* You can comprehend many more words per minute than someone can utter; you probably can process about 400 words per minute, while most speakers produce only about 125 to 175 words per minute. A time lag is created in your mind that you likely fill with other thoughts. You may enter your **internal perceptual field:** the

world of your own thoughts (about a friend, upcoming event, or to-morrow's term paper). Or you may be distracted by elements in your **external perceptual field:** things in your physical environment such as a loud truck, the sun's glare off your teacher's bald head, or the smell of sulfur from the lab in the classroom next door. Listeners tend to drop in and out of speeches, taking time out to play in their internal and external perceptual fields.[1]

3. *Intrusion of the past.* We often bring our past—our feelings, values, and attitudes—into the speech setting. Memories of past events can be trig-gered by a mere word or a reference to a place. Many people spend time mentally debating with speakers, thereby remaining stuck on one idea in the past while the speaker moves ahead to others. Past feelings you remember from previous encounters with a speaker also can color the way you understand the person today.

4. *Self-fulfilling prophesy.* Preset ideas can get in the way of good listening. You may have heard that Professor Holstein is a dull lecturer, so you enter the class expecting to be bored.

There's nothing wrong with having beliefs and attitudes about topics and people when you're in an audience. But, if you let your feelings, musings, and

FIGURE 2.2 Personal and Environmental Constraints on Listening

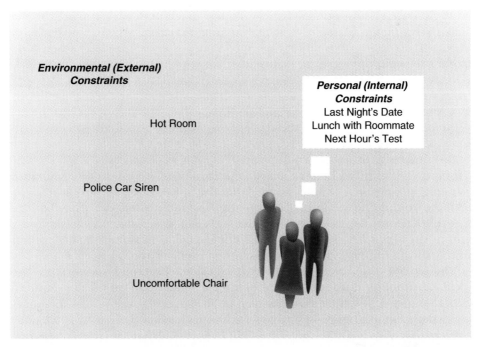

Competing demands on your attention usually allow you to hear and symbolically process only part of a spoken message. Listening with full discrimination rarely occurs.

guesses get in the way of careful listening, you're likely to miss the important parts of speeches. You've got to become and remain an active, engaged listener.

*P*RACTICAL LISTENING TECHNIQUES

While hearing is a more or less natural physiological process for most people, listening is another matter. You've got to work hard to listen well. There's no alternative to brainwork if you're going to keep out of trouble when receiving oral messages. The good news, though, is that you can train yourself to listen better. You can attack the problems of listening well in four ways: (1) know your purposes when trying to listen; (2) develop techniques that help you comprehend speeches; (3) design questions that help you evaluate or assess speeches on criteria that matter to you; and (4) sharpen your note-taking techniques.

Know Your Purposes

This may sound foolish, but the first thing good listeners do is figure out why they're listening. That's not really as silly as it sounds, because if you think about it, you know that you listen for different reasons on different occasions. On any given day, you may listen intently to your instructors in order to learn new concepts and facts, you may listen to your favorite music to relax, and you may listen to sales personnel in a stereo shop to make sure that the person isn't skipping over some essential feature of the machine's performance or the dealer's guarantee. After reviewing listening research, Wolvin and Coakley identified five kinds of listening that reflect purposes you may have when communicating with others: appreciative, discriminative, therapeutic, comprehension, and critical.[2]

Appreciative listening focuses on something other than the primary message. Some listeners enjoy seeing a famous speaker. Others appreciate the art of good public speaking. On these occasions, you listen primarily to entertain yourself.

Discriminative listening requires listeners to draw conclusions from the way a message is presented rather than directly from what is said. In discriminative listening, people seek to understand what the speaker really thinks, believes, or feels. You're engaging in discriminative listening when you draw conclusions about how angry your parents are with you, based not on what they say but on how they say it. An important dimension of listening depends upon your ability to draw relatively sophisticated inferences from messages.

Therapeutic listening is intended to provide emotional support for the speaker. Although it is more typical of interpersonal than public communication, therapeutic listening does occur in public speaking situations—for example, when a sports figure apologizes for unprofessional behavior, a religious convert describes a soul-saving experience, or a classmate reviews a personal problem and thanks friends for their help in solving it.

Listening for comprehension occurs when you want to gain additional information or insights from the speaker. This is probably the form of listening with which you're most familiar. When you listen to radio or TV news, to a classroom lecture on the ethnic-religious factions involved in Yugoslavian-Bosnian fighting, or to a counselor explaining computerized registration procedures, you're listening to understand—to comprehend information, ideas, and processes.

Critical listening demands that you both interpret and evaluate the message. It is the most sophisticated and difficult kind of listening. It demands that you go beyond understanding the message to interpreting it, judging its strengths and weaknesses, and assigning it some value. You'll practice this sort of listening in class. A careful consumer also uses critical listening techniques to evaluate sales pitches, campaign speeches, advice from financial advisers, or arguments offered by controversial talk show guests. When you're listening critically, you decide whether to accept or reject ideas and whether to act on someone's advice.

Evaluating messages through critical listening requires you to identify mentally the key ideas and phrases. You might need to rephrase or reorganize those ideas and note the signposts and other clues to rational structure offered by the speaker. Summarize the message periodically. Ask yourself these crucial questions about the information provided:

To prepare for a communication transaction, you must determine your purpose for listening. Even in informal exchanges between friends, knowing your purpose can aid you in responding appropriately.

- Do I understand the ideas?
- What's the main thrust of the speech?
- Does the speaker's message coincide with other things I know to be true?
- Does the speaker provide supporting material and acceptable explanations?
- Do these explanations support the speaker's conclusions?

So, think about key questions to ask yourself: What's my purpose in listening to this speech? Do I expect to gain information and insight in order to make a decision? Or am I listening to enjoy myself, to understand the feelings of another human being, to assess someone's state of mind, or to test some ideas? Knowing why you're listening will help you listen more efficiently and effectively.

Comprehend the Message

Listening for comprehension is the kind of listening you usually do and, in a sense, is the key to all of the other types. Fully comprehending what's being said requires that you understand the three essential aspects of speech content: *ideas, structure,* and *supporting materials.* You've got to understand clearly what ideas you're being asked to accept, how they're related to each other, and what sorts of facts and opinions underlie them. Asking three questions will help you to comprehend the message:

1. *What are the main ideas of the speech?* Determine the central idea of the speech and look for the statements that help the speaker to develop it. These main ideas should serve as the foundation upon which the speaker builds the speech. The next time you listen to a soap commercial, listen for the main ideas: are you encouraged to buy it because of its cleaning ability, smell, sex appeal, or gentleness to your skin? Before you decide to change brands, you ought to know something about those characteristics and which of them are important to you. Transfer that same listening behavior to a speech: always know what ideas you're being sold.
2. *How are the main ideas arranged?* Once you've identified the main ideas, you should figure out and assess the relationships between them. If the speaker is recounting some of the history of the Vietnam war but rearranges some of North Vietnam's initiatives and leaves out references to such events as the Mai'Lai massacre, you know you'd better be on your guard. (Always be on the lookout for speakers who leave out key events to make the story sound better.) Are causes and effects reasonably related to each other? (Let your experience in the world guide you here, but keep an open mind.) In other words, identify what the structure of ideas is, and then probe the speaker's use of that form.
3. *What kinds of material support the main ideas?* Consider the timeliness, quality, and content of the supporting materials. Are facts and opin-

COMMUNICATION RESEARCH DATELINE
LISTENING AND YOUR CAREER

One approach to listening research has focused on "the relationship between listening skills and individual performance." In their study, Michael Papa and Ethel C. Glenn hypothesized that a listening training program would improve employees' ability to adapt to a new computer system. They concluded that there was "strong evidence that listening ability impacts on employee productivity levels with new technology" and that "the provision of listening training programs improves employee's ability to perform with new technology."

Beverly Sypher, Robert Bostrom, and Joy Hart Seibert examined the relationship between listening and factors associated with one's communication ability, job level, and upward mobility. As in the case of Papa and Glenn, they used the Kentucky Comprehensive Listening Test to evaluate the relationships. They also distinguished between several types of listening behavior. Their conclusions regarding "short term listening" (STL) and "lecture listening" (LL) included the following observations: (1) Persons with persuasive ability and sensitivity to social contexts have higher levels of skill in both STL and LL. (2) There is some evidence that a person's listening skill has a positive impact on job level; the better the skill, the higher the job. (3) There also is some evidence to support the notion that better listeners are more upwardly mobile within an organization.

M. H. Lewis and N. L. Reinsch, Jr., examined behaviors contributing to effective and ineffective listening. In a study of listening behavior in a bank and a hospital, they found that the work setting did not influence the kinds of behaviors that people appreciated or disliked. Effective behaviors included maintaining eye contact when listening to others, generally appearing attentive to the person talking, and following directions to demonstrate that you did listen. Ineffective behaviors included not following directions, not reacting verbally or nonverbally to the message, talking to others while someone is speaking, and not recalling prior messages (perhaps indicating a pattern of not listening).

Further Reading

Michael J. Beatty and Steven K. Payne, "Listening Comprehension as a Function of Cognitive Complexity: A Research Note," *Communication Monographs* 51 (1984): 85–89.

Michael J. Papa and Ethel C. Glenn, "Listening Ability and Performance with New Technology: A Case Study," *Journal of Business Communication* 25 (Fall 1988): 6–15.

Beverly Davenport Sypher, Robert N. Bostrom, and Joy Hart Seibert, "Listening, Communication Abilities, and Success at Work," *Journal of Business Communication* 26 (Fall 1989): 293–303.

Robert N. Bostrom, *Listening Behavior: Measurement and Application* (New York: Guilford Press, 1990).

Marilyn Lewis and N. L. Reinsch, Jr., "Listening in Organizational Environments," *Journal of Business Communication* 25 (1988): 49–67.

ions derived from sources too old to be relevant to today's problems? Is the speaker quoting the best experts? Ask yourself whether the materials clarify, amplify, and strengthen the main ideas of the speech. For example, if someone tells you to protest next year's 3.5 percent tuition increase, consider the following: If your school charges $15,000 or more per year, the protest may well be justified, but if it charges $25 per credit hour, protesting a $10–$15 increase would not be worth the effort and ill will. Examine the fact's ability to support the conclusion. Also, be sensitive to *types* of supporting materials: Are you getting facts and figures or only some vague endorsements from self-interested parties?

In other words, to comprehend the content, make sure you've got it straight so that you know what ideas, relationships, and evidence you're being asked to accept. Be an active listener.

Assess the Speech

Once you've figured out why you're listening, how the ideas are arranged, and what supporting materials are being presented to you, you're in a position to form some opinions. You, after all, are the reason the speech is being given, so you're the one who must make the judgments: good/bad, beautiful/ugly, just/unjust, fair/unfair, true/false. Making such assessments is the only way to keep yourself protected from inflated claims, dated information, and no-good cheats. Completely assessing a speech could include asking yourself all of the following questions:

THE SITUATION

1. *How is the situation affecting this speech and my understanding of it?* Is this the featured speaker or a warm-up act? Is the speaker expected to deal with particular themes or subjects? Am I in tune with this speech occasion? Speeches in churches, basketball games, and Rotary lunches are very different from each other, and you must adjust your judgment-making criteria accordingly.

2. *How is the physical environment affecting the speaking and my listening?* Is it too hot or too cold? Is the room too big or too small? Are other distractions affecting either of us? The physical environment can have an important impact on your listening. You might have to compensate: lean forward, move up, or listen more closely.

THE SPEAKER

3. *What do I know about the speaker?* The reputation of this person *will* influence you whether you want it to or not, so think about it: Are you being unduly deferential or hypercritical of the speaker just because of

$\mathcal{H}$ow to
Be an Active Listener

- *Review* what the speaker has said. Mentally summarize key ideas each time the speaker initiates a new topic.
- *Relate* the message to what you already know. As you bring more ideas to bear on what you're hearing, your ability to listen effectively will increase.
- *Anticipate* what the speaker might say next. Use this anticipation to focus on the content of the message. If your expectations are accurate, you know you're tuned in.

Using the **RRA Technique**—review, relate, and anticipate—you can keep your attention centered on the message.

his or her reputation? Don't let such reactions get in the way of critical listening.

4. *How believable do I find the speaker?* Are there things about the person's actions, demeanor, and words that make you accepting or suspicious? Try to figure out why you're reacting positively or negatively and then

Listeners' interest and attention in a communication transaction depend on how well the speaker adapts the message to the audience.

ask yourself whether it's reasonable for you to believe this person or not.

5. *Is the speaker adequately prepared?* Imprecise remarks, repetitions, back-tracking, vague or missing numbers, and the lack of solid testimony are all signs of a poorly prepared speaker. For example, a talk about how audiences influence TV programming decisions should discuss, among other things, the networks' use of focus groups. If the speaker doesn't discuss this, you'll know that he or she hasn't gotten very far into the topic. Similarly, if the speaker can't clearly explain the difference between Arbitron and Nielsen rating systems, you should question the reliability of other information in the speech.

6. *What's the speaker's attitude toward the audience?* How is the audience being treated: cordially or condescendingly, as individuals or as a general group, as inferiors or as equals? Answering these questions will help you not only to understand your own experience but also to form some questions for the speaker after the speech.

THE MESSAGE

7. *How solid are the ideas being presented?* We've been hammering on this point throughout the chapter because it's crucial for you to assess the ideas in terms your own knowledge and experience. Just one warning:

you could be mistaken yourself, so don't automatically dismiss new ideas. That's how you stagnate intellectually. But do listen all the more carefully when ideas seem strange, making sure that you understand them and that they're well supported.

8. *Are the ideas well structured?* Are important ones missing? For example, anyone who talks about managing computer programs without mentioning Windows 95 either has sold his or her soul to the Apple Corporation or else hasn't kept up with the news. Are logical links visible? Listen for the signposts "therefore," "hence," "because." Your comparisons must also be fair; comparing Apple computers' managing systems with pre-Windows 95 versions of DOS-based windows systems loads the comparison in favor of Mac users. Structural relationships between ideas are what give them their solidity and coherence as a package.

9. *Is sufficient evidence offered?* You can skip ahead to Chapter 14, if you want, to see some of the tests of evidence and reasoning that you should make when faced with crucial decisions based on a speech you're hearing. The world is filled with slipshod reasoning and flawed evidence. Bad reasoning and a refusal to test the available evidence, after all, are what led the American high command to believe that Pearl Harbor was an absolutely safe port in 1941. Listen for evidence; write down the key parts so that you can mull it over, asking yourself if it's good enough to use as a basis for changing your mind. Adopt a "show me" attitude.

You certainly won't ask all nine of these questions every time you hear a speech. Remember that your listening purposes vary considerably from occasion to occasion. You'll need all nine questions only when doing critical listening at times of significant decision: which presidential candidate to vote for, what lifestyle to follow, which side to support when land developers fight over where to put an expensive municipal stadium. Tailor your listening practices to your purpose for attending a speech.

Take Good Notes

What we said earlier bears repeating: you're going to have to *practice* your listening skills to *improve* them. Period. You've got to train yourself, and one of the easiest ways to do that while in college is to work on note taking. As you become a better note taker, you'll also become a better listener. Here are some tips for improving your note-taking skills.

Get organized. Develop your own note-taking system and refine it. Some people like loose-leaf notebooks so that they can add, rearrange, or remove notes; others like the tidiness of spiral or glue-bound notebooks. Whichever you choose, use separate notebooks for different courses and life experiences to avoid confusion. And learn to file.

Set aside a few minutes each day to review the syllabi for your classes, to scan your readings, and to review the previous class session's notes. This will prepare you to ask

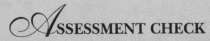

ASSESSMENT CHECK

The next time you listen to a speech, ask yourself the following questions to help you become a more active, involved, and critical listener.

- Which particular aspects of the speech situation are most critical in affecting how I perceive the speaker and the message?
- Does the speaker's reputation, attitude, or preparedness seem important in how I respond to the speech? Why or why not?
- Am I able to process the message easily? Are the ideas solid? Is the evidence sufficient? Is the information structured to guide me through the speech?
- If I had the opportunity to listen to the same speech again, how could I adjust my listening behavior in order to participate more fully in the communication transaction?

questions while the lecture or readings are still fresh in your mind and will help you to keep oriented to the class. Being oriented to what's going on helps you take notes on the most important materials.

Leave two- to three-inch margins when taking notes. When reviewing notes later, that marginal area will provide space for making additional comments. A great way to review and study is to write critical comments about what you agree or disagree with, what you don't understand, what you think is significant, and what you've found to be confirmed or contradicted by another source. Such critical commentary is an important stage in merging the material in the notes with your own thoughts.

Develop a note-taking scheme that works for you. Consider the possibilities:

a. *Outline form.* Making a conscious effort to outline a speech or lecture as you hear it will help you to isolate the important ideas, structure, and supporting evidence.

b. *Abbreviations.* Some abbreviations you'll want to use are obvious: the ampersand (&) for *and,* and *w/o* for *without.* Some go with particular subject matters, as when business majors write *mgt* and *acctg* for *management* and *accounting* and when biology majors use the ♂ and ♀ symbols for male and female. Others will be your own. Just make sure that you can remember the ones you invent!

c. *Textual space.* Leave enough space throughout your notes so that later you can add facts, clarification, and other alterations after comparing your notes with other students' or after doing related reading.

d. *Multicolors.* You'll probably profit as well from color-coding—say, black or blue for the main notes, red for questions or disagreements, green for additional content. Highlight pens also are big sellers at college bookstores.

By taking these actions, you're no longer a couch or desk potato, a passive listener. You're an engaged, active listener who's demonstrating how public

Speech Evaluation Form

ASSESSING SPEECHES: Use this form as a checklist in evaluating your own speeches and those of others; the competent speaker will fulfill most of these (few speeches are entirely error-free) most of the time.

The Speaker

☐ poised?
☐ positive self-image?
☐ apparently sincere?
☐ apparently concerned about the topic?
☐ apparently concerned about the audience?
☐ apparently well prepared?

The Message

☐ suitable topic for audience, occasion?
☐ topic narrowed to fit time available?
☐ clear general purpose?
☐ sharply focused specific purpose?
☐ well-phrased central idea or claim?
☐ clear preview of main points?
☐ attention gained at the beginning?
☐ adequate information to create understanding?
☐ clear explanation of ideas, events?
☐ claim adequately supported (enough, varied, trustworthy sources)?
☐ supporting materials tailored to the audience?
☐ attention held well throughout?
☐ transitions between main points clear?
☐ major subdivisions clear, balanced?
☐ concluded effectively?

Transmission

☐ voice varied for emphasis?
☐ voice conversational?
☐ delivery speed controlled?
☐ body alert and nondistracting?
☐ gestures used effectively?
☐ face expressive?
☐ language clear (unambiguous, concrete)?
☐ language forcible (vivid, intense)?
☐ notes and lectern handled well?

The Audience

☐ all listeners addressed?
☐ their presence recognized and complimented?
☐ their attitudes toward subject, speaker, and occasion taken into account?

The Speech as a Whole

Speaker appears knowledgeable, honest, trustworthy?

_____
_____
_____
_____

Audience's expectations met?

_____
_____
_____
_____

Short-range effects of the speech?

_____
_____
_____
_____

Long-range effects?

_____
_____
_____
_____

Possible improvements?

_____
_____
_____

speaking ought to work as a two-way channel. And the more you practice, the more effectively the channel will carry two-way traffic.

$\mathcal{D}$EVELOPING CRITICAL LISTENING SKILLS IN THE CLASSSROOM

As noted in Chapter 1, your speech classroom is set up to teach you multiple listening skills that will be of great use to you the rest of your life. Listening is one of those skills you'll need to have to survive in the worlds of work, politics, and social life. You'll have to listen to understand work instructions, to make reasonable decisions between political candidates who envision for you a better life, and to follow a neighbor's instructions as she tells you how to rewire a light fixture. The ability to listen makes you money and friends, helps you to be an active citizen, and keeps you from frying your fingers on a 110-volt circuit.

Your classrooms are excellent settings for practicing new listening skills and refining old ones. Use the Speech Evaluation Form on page 43 as a checklist when listening to speeches. It will sharpen your skills, forcing you to consider a full range of speechmaking dimensions. During this term, improve your listening skills in the following ways:

1. *Practice critiquing the speeches of other students.* Practice outlining techniques; take part in postspeech discussions; ask questions of the speaker. You can learn as much from listening well as from speaking yourself.
2. *Listen critically to discussions, lectures, and student-teacher interactions in your other classes.* You're surrounded with public communication worth analyzing when you're in school. You can easily spot effective and ineffective speech techniques in those classes.
3. *Listen critically to speakers outside of class.* Attend public lectures, city council meetings, or political or religious rallies. Watch replays of presidential or congressional speeches on C-SPAN. You'll be amazed by the range of talent, techniques, and styles exhibited in your community every week.
4. *Examine the supporting materials, arguments, and language used in newspapers and magazines.* Refine your critical listening skills by practicing critical reading. Together, they represent the skills of critical thinking you need to survive in this world. **Critical thinking** is the process of consciously examining the content and logic of messages to determine their bases in the world of ideas and to assess their rationality. Critical thinking is the backbone of evaluation. It's what happens when you listen and when you read the messages of others with your brain fully engaged. Don't leave home with it.

Overall, then, listening makes public speaking a reciprocal activity. Listeners seek to meet their diverse needs, ranging from personal enjoyment to critical decision making, through specialized listening skills designed for each listening purpose. When both speakers and listeners work at making the speech transaction succeed, public speaking reaches its full potential as a medium of human integration and social identity.

CHAPTER SUMMARY

Practicing and refining your listening skills in your speech class and in other classes will help you to acquire improved tools for success in the worlds of college, business, politics, and social life. *Listening* is a psychological process by which people seek to comprehend and evaluate aural-visual signals, unlike *hearing,* a physiological process. To improve your listening ability, practice these skills:

- Know why you're listening. Your purpose may be appreciative, discriminative, therapeutic, comprehension, or critical.
- Sort out the essential aspects of the speech content: ideas, structure, and supporting materials.
- Use the RRA technique when listening: review, relate, anticipate.
- Work on note-taking techniques: get yourself organized with a particular system; take time to review course materials so you'll know what to listen for; leave margins in which you can later write commentary; and develop note-taking techniques that work for you.

To improve your speech evaluation skills, practice assessing the *situation,* the *speaker,* and the *message.*

KEY TERMS

appreciative listening (p. 34)
critical listening (p. 35)
critical thinking (p. 44)
delayed feedback (p. 31)
discriminative listening (p. 34)
external perceptual field (p. 33)
hearing (p. 31)

immediate feedback (p. 31)
internal perceptual field (p. 32)
listening (p. 32)
listening for comprehension (p. 35)
RRA technique (p. 39)
therapeutic listening (p. 34)

ASSESSMENT ACTIVITIES

1. Keep a listening log. For two days, record your oral communication interactions, noting (a) to whom you were speaking, (b) what your listening purposes were, and (c) how effectively you listened, given your purposes. Include talks with roommates, class meetings, coffee shop or lunchroom conversations, and evening activities. After completing the log, do a self-assessment: What are your strengths and weaknesses as a listener? What changes do you need to make to become a better listener?

2. Make a line drawing of an irregular geometric figure, then describe it verbally to an audience. Ask each listener to draw the figure when you're done. Your instructor will collect the drawings and lead a discussion on relationships between the encoding and decoding of oral messages.

REFERENCES

1. Adapted from Wayne C. Minnick, *The Art of Persuasion* (New York: Houghten Mifflin Co., 1957).
2. Andrew Wolvin and Carolyn Coakley, *Listening* (Dubuque, IA: William C. Brown, 1982), 3–11.

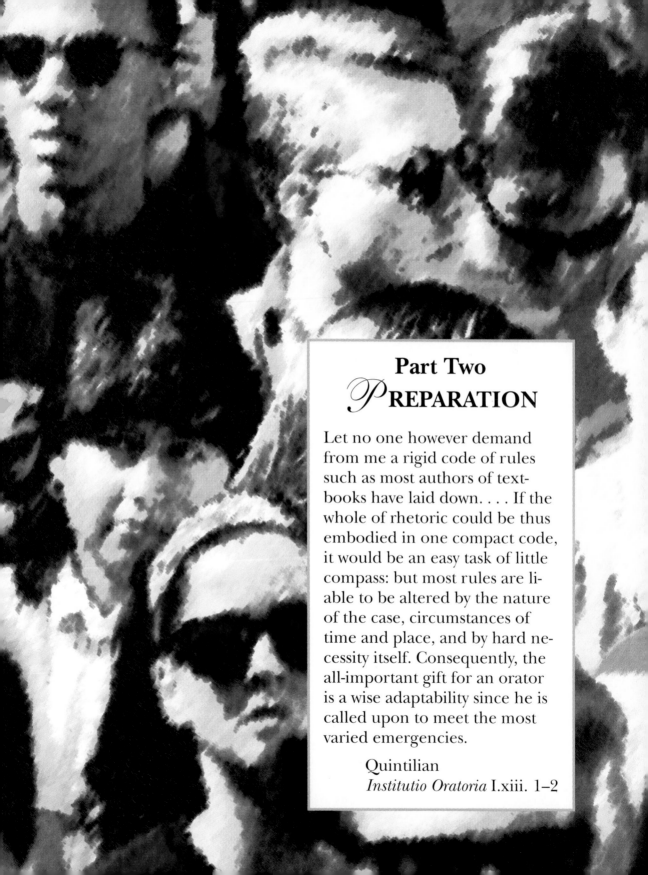

Part Two
PREPARATION

Let no one however demand
from me a rigid code of rules
such as most authors of textbooks have laid down. . . . If the
whole of rhetoric could be thus
embodied in one compact code,
it would be an easy task of little
compass: but most rules are li-
able to be altered by the nature
of the case, circumstances of
time and place, and by hard necessity itself. Consequently, the
all-important gift for an orator
is a wise adaptability since he is
called upon to meet the most
varied emergencies.

Quintilian
Institutio Oratoria I.xiii. 1–2

3

ℊETTING STARTED:
PLANNING THE SPEECH

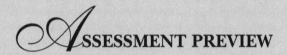

𝒜SSESSMENT PREVIEW

After reading Chapter 3, the student with basic communication competencies will be able to

- demonstrate a basic understanding of the essential steps in speech preparation.
- prepare a speech using an appropriate method of presentation.
- identify and use at least two of the factors of attention.
- manage anxiety in communicating ideas.

The student with average communication competencies will also be able to

- select and prepare a speech on a topic that is of interest to the audience and meets the demands of the occasion.
- identify which factors of attention are appropriate to the speech situation, and use them.
- establish a comfortable atmosphere for communicating ideas with confidence.

The student with superior communication competencies will also be able to

- maximize audience interest and involvement in the speech through mastery of the essential steps of preparation and creative use of the factors of attention.
- evaluate presentations by self or others with respect to the essential steps, and suggest improvements to each step.
- suggest creative methods to gain and hold the audience's attention.
- evaluate the ability of self and others to communicate with confidence, and suggest ways to manage anxiety.

*T*he first two chapters provided an overview of public speaking as a *process:* the essential elements involved in communicating ideas from their creation to their reception. Now we'll turn our attention to an overview of speaking as a *practice:* planning what to say and how to say it. All speech teachers have heard students say, "Well, yeah, I knew what I wanted to do. I just lost it!" When their teachers probe a little—did you find and carefully arrange supporting arguments? did you phrase your key ideas ahead of time?—the answer is usually "No, I just thought it would all happen as I planned it in my head."

If you've had a similar experience, you now know that public speaking takes preparation. Although this chapter won't cover all that you can learn about the intricacies and shortcuts of speech preparation and speechmaking, it will provide you with sufficient information so that you can think and act in more rhetorically sound ways. Having a **rhetorical frame of mind** means thinking your way strategically through the decisions you have to make as you prepare for any speech: (1) selecting the subject; (2) narrowing the subject; (3) determining your purposes, including central ideas and claims; (4) considering the audience and occasion; (5) gathering the speech material; (6) making an outline; and (7) practicing aloud in preparation for standing in front of an audience and presenting your ideas. Working through each of these steps in a systematic manner will keep you from wandering aimlessly through the library or waiting endlessly at your desk for inspiration. This chapter will review each of these steps to provide a basic foundation for planning your presentation.

*T*HE ESSENTIAL STEPS IN SPEECH PREPARATION

There's no magical formula for getting ready to speak. However, if you pay close attention to the series of seven steps—either in the order presented here or in another that works for you—you'll be ahead of the game and ready for an audience. We'll supplement the seven steps with four additional subjects that will help you develop your first speech: how to decide on an appropriate method of presentation; how to gain and hold your listeners' attention; how to project self-confidence; and how to evaluate your own and others' presentations.

Selecting the Subject

Oddly, one of the most difficult jobs many speakers in classrooms face is choosing a subject. When you are confronted with a speech assignment, the following guidelines will help you select a subject that's appropriate to the rhetorical situation.

Select a subject about which you already know something and can find out more. Begin with an inventory of what you already know. This will help you focus your ideas and distinguish between strong and weak choices (less familiar topics are weaker choices). If you need to update statistical data or locate additional examples to flesh out your basic knowledge, consider whether the needed information is readily accessible. Research is easier if you know something about the subject because you will have a better idea about potential sources of information. Selecting a topic familiar to you also increases your self-confidence as you rise to speak.

Select a subject that interests you and will interest your audience. First, resist the temptation to speak on an issue that is more interesting to the audience than it is to you. This can be a disastrous choice, for gathering information will be unexciting, and your presentation will reflect your lack of enthusiasm. If you have a personal interest in an issue, your commitment will come across to the audience. You'll find that researching the issue is more interesting and that preparing the speech becomes easier.

Talking without regard to your audience, however, may leave you with a subject that interests an audience of one—you. You need to balance your interest with the needs and interests of the audience. Resist the temptation to force a topic on listeners because you think "it's good for them to hear this." It may be, but will they listen? A topic may interest listeners for one or more of the following reasons:

- *It concerns their health, happiness, or security.* For instance, you might talk to senior citizens about changes in Medicare regulations or to college students about recent employment trends.
- *It offers a solution to a recognized problem.* You may suggest ways your group could raise funds in order to participate in a national competition, or ways college students might protest increases in tuition.
- *It is surrounded by controversy or conflict of opinion.* You might speak on the proposed relocation of a town dump to a site near your campus or on proposed strategies to implement recycling in the community.
- *It provides information on a misunderstood or little understood issue.* You might speak to a local business group about the community service contributions of college students or to the class about the services provided by the campus writing and math centers.

FIGURE 3.1 The Essential Steps in Speech Preparation

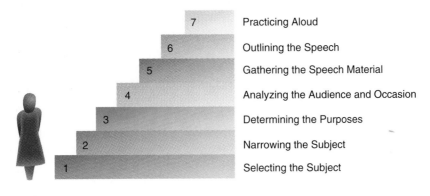

7	Practicing Aloud
6	Outlining the Speech
5	Gathering the Speech Material
4	Analyzing the Audience and Occasion
3	Determining the Purposes
2	Narrowing the Subject
1	Selecting the Subject

Select a topic appropriate to the occasion. Several factors may limit your degree of freedom in selecting an appropriate subject. Often, the freedom to choose an appropriate subject will be virtually unlimited. An in-class speech assignment often asks that you seek to inform or persuade but gives you freedom to select a subject. Consider whether the occasion is the right setting for what you want to accomplish: a demonstration speech on body-building might go over very well in your speech classroom, but bringing a dog to class to demonstrate training commands may not work equally well. The speech on body-building may not be appropriate at the dedication of a new senior citizens' center, but a speech describing the need for exercise at all ages and the new center's exercise room would be fitting. If an invitation to speak at a breakfast meeting of a local service organization is generally phrased, you may have greater latitude in selecting a subject. For example, if you were asked to address an issue of concern to students, you could focus on a local noise ordinance's impact on student lifestyles, on recent increases in student costs, from tuition to books, or on student-landlord relations. In each instance, your choice would be affected as much by your personal interests as by the needs of the audience. At other times, your speech topic will be determined, at least in part, by the group to whom you will speak. Usually, you are invited to speak because you have specific expertise or knowledge to share with the group. As part of the invitation, you'll be asked to address a particular issue, policy, or question that relates to your work, community involvement, or special skills. In the classroom setting, the instructor may limit choices by requiring you to consider only certain issues or subject areas, or may place certain topics "off-limits."

In sum, whether the topic is a free choice or is assigned, it's advantageous to approach it in ways that play off your strengths. Any speech must reflect interests that you and your audience share and must be appropriate to the speaking occasion. Playing off your strengths means talking about a subject you can handle. Playing off your audience's interests means finding an approach to that subject that engages them.

Narrowing the Subject

A general subject is of little value until it's narrowed down to a manageable size. Narrowing a subject to a more precise speech topic involves three primary considerations:

Narrow your subject so that you can discuss it adequately in the time allotted for the speech. If you are responding to an in-class speech assignment that will last 5 to 7 or 8 to 10 minutes, you cannot begin to do justice to "The Growth of the Winter and Summer Olympics Since Early Times." Instead, you might give an overview of the newest sports recognized for winter or summer Olympic competition, or you might discuss the impact of pro players on the Olympic amateurism ideal, using the "Dream Team" as your prime example. Fit the topic's breadth to the time you have to speak.

Narrow your subject to meet the specific expectations of your audience. Listeners expecting to hear an informative presentation on clear-cutting rain forests may be upset if you request their financial support for an environmental group formed to counter the devastation. The announced purpose of the meeting, the demands of the particular context, and the traditions of the group can influence an audience's expectations of what it is to hear. Violate audience expectations only when you feel it's absolutely essential; be prepared for and willing to accept the consequences if you break with those expectations.

Gauge your subject to the comprehension level of the audience. If, for example, you want to talk about laser technology or the existence of "black holes" to students in your speech class, focus your attention on basic principles. If the audience were a group of senior physics majors, the nature and complexity of the material you present would necessarily change.

$\mathcal{H}$OW TO

NARROW A TOPIC: AN ILLUSTRATION

1. Identify a broad subject you know and care about—for example, science fiction.
2. Identify subtopics of the broad subject area that also interest you. For example, subtopics of science fiction might include the following:
   - The differences between science fiction and fantasy
   - The nature of "hard science" in science fiction novels
   - Major writers of science fiction: Heinlein, LeGuin, Asimov, Clarke
3. Ask five questions about each subtopic:
   - Which of these possible subtopics is of most interest to me?
   - Is the audience likely to be interested in the topic?
   - Is it appropriate to the occasion?
   - Can I cover it in the time available?
   - Will the audience comprehend it?
4. Narrow each subtopic until you can answer "yes" to all the questions above.

Time constraints might limit the first general topic to "*two or three* major differences between science fiction and fantasy" and the third to "*a single* major writer or a writer's *major series.*" Since you really aren't that excited about the differences between fantasy and fiction, it would be difficult to seem enthusiastic when speaking; hence that topic would be dropped. The audience's lack of background knowledge might cause you to discard the hard science topic if you have only 8–10 minutes to present your speech.

The process of narrowing may lead to a subject that is "best" for a particular occasion, or as the science fiction illustration indicates, it may leave you with several possibilities. If that is the case, you need to decide which subject, given your time limit, will best fit your interests as well as those of the audience. Which topic can you make the most interesting—which will be the most engaging for you and your audience?

Determining the Purposes

Once you know what you want to talk about, the next task is to consider a series of "why's" already implicit in much that's been discussed: Why do *you* wish to discuss this subject? Why might an *audience* want to listen to *you?* Why is this topic appropriate to *this occasion?* These questions can be answered easily by considering the following four points in sequence: (1) think about the *general purposes* that people have in mind when they speak in public; (2) consider your own *specific purposes;* (3) focus on the *central idea* or *claim* that expresses the principal message you wish to communicate; and (4) create a *title* for the presentation that captures your goals and tells the audience what your central idea or claim will focus on. Finally, we will examine strategic considerations relevant to selecting purposes.

General Purpose.   What is the state you wish your listeners to be in when you complete the speech? For example, are you trying to tell them something they do not—but should—know? Are you seeking to alter the way they feel about a social, economic, or political issue? Are you interested in having them do something as a result of your speech? Do you want them to laugh and learn at the same time? Answering "yes" to one of these questions will help focus your general purpose.

The **general purposes** for speaking reflect the "end states" you wish to create in your audience. More precisely, what is the general purpose of your speech? To *inform?* To *persuade?* To *activate?* To *entertain?* While these "end states" are not mutually exclusive (you may make a moral point through humor, for example), they are sufficiently discrete to treat them as individual purposes. We'll consider the types of speeches that accompany each of these general purposes later in the book, with a major emphasis on the processes of informing and persuading. In this section we will consider the major *goals* of informative, persuasive, actuative, and entertaining speeches.

To Inform.   The general purpose of a **speech to inform** is to help listeners understand an idea, concept, or process, or to widen their range of knowledge. This is a primary goal of elected officials when they seek to explain their actions to their constituents, of college professors when they teach chemistry, speech, philosophy, art, or any other subject, and of supervisors when they explain how to use new equipment to plant workers. Conveying new information changes the level or quality of knowledge your listeners possess. By providing examples, statistics, illustrations, and other materials containing data and ideas, you seek to expand or to alter their concrete knowledge about an idea, policy, process, concept, or event. The message must be comprehensive, accurate, and timely in order to accomplish your informative goal. For example, an informative speech on how to build your own weather station or how to conduct a successful science experiment must include the necessary information, must present it in a factually accurate manner, and must be perceived as useful to the audience to whom it is directed. Successfully conveying information in these instances depends not only on learning *what* to do, but also on *when* and *why.*

Several types of speeches are considered informative: speeches of definition, demonstrations, oral instructions, reports from committees or task forces, lectures, and so forth. In each instance, *sharing information* is the primary thrust of the presentation.

To Persuade or to Actuate. The purpose of a **speech to persuade** or **to actuate** is to influence listeners' minds or actions. Because both have similar goals, we'll consider them together. While it may be argued that all speeches are persuasive to some degree, there are many situations in which speakers have outright persuasion or action as their primary purpose.[1] For example, promoters and publicists try to make you believe in the superiority of certain products, persons, or institutions. Social action group leaders exhort tenants to believe in the need for city codes to protect their rights. Politicians debate campaign issues and strive to convince voters that they will best represent their interests in state legislatures, Congress, or the White House.

Beyond speaking to influence your listeners' beliefs and attitudes, you also may go a step further and try to move them to specific action: buy my product, join the protest, vote for the preferred candidate. Or, you may want listeners to participate in a walkathon, contribute money, sign a petition, or join your organization. The distinguishing feature of an actuative speech is that instead of stopping with an appeal to beliefs or attitudes, you ask your listeners to alter their behavior in a specified way.

To influence or alter your listeners' beliefs and actions, you need to present well-ordered arguments that are supported by facts, figures, examples, and the opinions of experts. You also need to do more than simply state the facts. To

FIGURE 3.2 The General Purposes of Speech

To Inform	Clear Understanding
To Persuade	Acceptance of Ideas
To Actuate	Action
To Entertain	Enjoyment and Comprehension

Martin Luther King, Jr., presented his "I Have a Dream" speech at the 1963 March on Washington.

change minds and move people to action, you must be sensitive to both the rational and the motivational aspects of audience psychology, topics that will be discussed at length in later chapters. For the present, keep in mind the principle that facts alone, even if "airtight" as far as the case for change is concerned, are often insufficient to move people to change their behavior. Consider all of the information connecting cigarette, cigar, and pipe smoking to various forms of cancer, as well as to the issue of secondary smoke effects. If facts alone were sufficient, wouldn't people stop smoking? What motivational appeal will lead a listener to take action in such an instance? Thus persuasion and actuation involve far more complex tasks than simply telling people what you think.

To Entertain.   To entertain, amuse, or provide other enjoyment for listeners is frequently the general purpose of an after-dinner speech, but talks of other kinds also may have enjoyment as their principal aim. A travel lecture, for example, contains information, but it may also entertain an audience through exciting, amusing tales of adventure or misadventure. Club meetings, class reunions, and similar gatherings of friends may provide the opportunity for a "roast" of one or more of the people present. In these situations, the effective use of humor is a key ingredient in being judged funny as opposed to tasteless by the audience.

A **speech to entertain** is *not* just a comic monologue. The humor in speeches to entertain is purposeful. Even the humor at a roast is intended to convey affection and genuine appreciation for the talents of the person being honored by friends and colleagues. Humor can have a social role: humorist Will Rogers used his radio talks and commentaries on political realities during the Depression to help create a sense of American unity and common effort. More recently, Whoopi Goldberg, Sinbad, Paula Poundstone, and others use humor to call attention to social issues. In short, a speech to entertain is humorous yet serious. Forms of public-speaking humor, such as parodies and satires, are subtle and often difficult to master; we will discuss them later in this book.

As you have learned, to inform, to persuade, to actuate, and to entertain are the general purposes that guide your reason for speaking. Just as subjects are narrowed to subtopics, and often further, your general purpose needs to be narrowed to more specific ones in order to focus your audience's attention on the content of your presentation.

Specific Purposes.   Given your topic, specifically what do you want the audience to know, value, or do? Within the context of a general purpose, a **specific purpose** focuses your attention on the particular, *substantive* goal of the presentation. Once you determine your specific purpose, you'll be in a position to describe the exact response you want from your listeners: "I want my audience to understand the classification scheme for levels of professional baseball." In this instance, you want to inform your audience (general purpose), but, more specifically, you want to teach them about the different levels of expertise they're likely to encounter at the different levels of professional baseball.

You may have more than one specific purpose for a speech; some may be clearly expressed, others held privately. For example, you tell your listeners precisely what you want them to understand or do as a consequence of listening to your presentation. You also hope to make a good impression on the audience or receive a high grade for the presentation, but you are not likely to make these purposes explicit.

Specific purposes can be short-term or long-term. If you are speaking to members of your class on the value of eating fat-free foods, your short-term purpose may be to get a decent grade; your long-term objective might be to induce them to change their eating habits.

Theoretically, you may have any number of public and private, short-term and long-term specific purposes when you speak. Practically, however, you will want to reduce your list of goals to a *dominant* one: *the response you wish to elicit from the audience.* Formulated into a clear, concise statement, this specific purpose delineates exactly what you want the audience to understand, enjoy, feel, believe, or do.

Stating Specific Purposes: An Illustration ━━━━━━━━━

You've just decided on your topic for a speech that you'll give in one of your classes: the impact of MTV on recent presidential election campaigns. While your classmates may have seen some of the events, they probably do not have the "whole picture" with respect to MTV's participation. Hence your overall objective may be to expand the audience's knowledge of MTV's role. More precisely, your specific purposes would include:

1. In terms of the subject, you want to provide background on MTV's actions in the 1988 campaign, and contrast that with the 1992 and 1996 presidential campaigns. You also want to highlight the specific events that took place, including interviews with the candidates. Finally, you want to cover the actual impact MTV's role had in terms of voter participation by young adults.

2. In terms of yourself, a private goal may be the hope that, if they understand the role MTV plays, they will also see the value in greater participation in political campaigns and in voting. Undoubtedly, you want to convey to the class, and to the instructor, a sense that you understand what it means to plan and prepare an informative speech. You want to show the students and instructor that you are knowledgeable and competent to speak on the issue. The first specific purpose addresses a long-term goal of creating understanding and expanding knowledge. The personal goals are private rather than public. All of these specific goals can be summarized, however, in a statement of *the* dominant specific purpose: "to expand the audience's knowledge of MTV's role." ∎

Determining the Central Idea or Claim.   For most speakers, this step flows directly from the preceding one. Can you state your message in a single sentence? If you are seeking to explain an idea or inform an audience about a process or event, that sentence is the **central idea.** It is a declarative statement that summarizes your speech: "The reemergence of the Northern Lights League in 1992 reshaped the structure of professional baseball." On the other hand, a **claim,** expresses the intent of your argument: "The re-emergence of the Northern Lights League in 1992 improved professional baseball in three important ways." Thus, *central ideas are characteristic of informative speeches, while claims form the core of persuasive and actuative speeches.* Speeches to entertain also have a controlling thought—either as a central idea aiming to convey information, or as a claim aiming to make a moral point or exhort the audience to action.

Both central ideas and claims share the same function: They identify the primary thrust of your message. Precise phrasing of your central idea or claim is crucial because it focuses the audience's attention on *your* reasons for speaking, rather than on *their* reasons for listening.

Phrasing Central Ideas.   Assume that you're giving an informative speech on the use of science fiction to present political messages. Each of the following central ideas suggests a different emphasis for the speech:

1. Science fiction novels are as much about the present as they are about the future.

2. Ursula LeGuin's novel *Always Coming Home* carries an implicit political message about how we should live our lives in the present.
3. The political worlds created in science fiction must remain believable.

A speech on central idea 1 would be developed differently than one on either idea 2 or 3; each would utilize different kinds of material for support or illustration. The first version would stress the idea that science fiction, although ostensibly set in the future, actually tells us something about our everyday lives. The second version would use the same theme but develop it through a close analysis of one work by a major writer. The third version would state that authors' political views influence their writing and would cite examples from novels that would reflect those views.

Phrasing a Claim. Phrasing your claim can be an even more crucial preparatory step than casting the central idea, because the wording colors the emotional tone of the message and its line of development; it also suggests the relationship between you and your audience. Note how you can vary the audience's perception of your intensity:

1. Clear-cutting in the world's rain forests is *unwise.*
2. Clear-cutting in the world's rain forests is *a despicable act.*
3. Clear-cutting in the world's rain forests is *a moral outrage.*

Precise phrasing of your central idea or claim is important, because your wording captures the essence of your subject matter and purpose, focusing audience attention on your reasons for speaking.

As you move from version one to three, feelings are phrased with greater intensity; each successive version expresses your attitude in harsher, more graphic language. In the next examples note how you can vary the reasons for taking some course of action:

1. Make use of the Writing Lab because it will help you in your English courses.
2. Make use of the Writing Lab because you will get higher grades in all courses in which writing is expected.
3. Make use of the Writing Lab because better writing will lead to better jobs on graduation.

As these examples illustrate, your listeners may choose to act for a variety of reasons; phrase your claim in a way that captures what you think will be the most compelling ones for *this particular audience.*

You can also vary the evaluative criteria for judging something:

1. The city's landfill is an *eyesore.* (aesthetic judgment)
2. The city's landfill is a *health hazard.* (personal-safety judgment)
3. While the city's landfill is *cheaper* than other solid-waste removal options, we should still explore other means of handling garbage. (political value judgment)

Each of these claims condemns a community facility. The first version judges the landfill's lack of beauty, the second considers its safety and health costs, while the third acknowledges it is a cheaper alternative but implies the community should value safety above economic cost. In each case, selecting particular criteria will control the main features of the speech's ultimate development: (1) to focus on the values of judging aesthetics in relation to community development; (2) to emphasize the facts related to health and safety; and (3) to seek an accommodation based on economic considerations.

When you've decided the general and specific purposes of your speech and considered ways to phrase central ideas and claims, you can start developing your speech outline. These points will focus your research efforts, because they will indicate the type and quantity of information needed to accomplish your goals. More importantly, succinctly phrased central ideas and claims will enable you to *preview the main points* of your speech. As you flesh out the central idea or claim, it will be apparent that two or three main points will be necessary to cover the subject. For example, if you are talking about MTV, you could easily indicate to the audience how the speech would develop by leading into the main points in this manner: "In explaining the role played by MTV in the recent election, I will focus on three key points: prior activities by MTV, the specific events it was involved with in the recent election, and the impact its role had on voter participation among young viewers of voting age."

Integrating General and Specific Purposes with Central Ideas and Claims

The following examples illustrate the outline process:

INFORMATIVE SPEECH

Subject: Science fiction
General Purpose: To inform
Specific Purposes: Indicates dominant purpose, recast as central idea
  To show how science fiction conveys a political message
  To explain LeGuin's use of political themes
  To convey confidence in handling the subject
Central idea: LeGuin's novel *Always Coming Home* contains a political message.

ACTUATIVE SPEECH

Subject: Housing conditions of migrant farm workers
General Purpose: To actuate
Specific Purposes: Indicates dominant purpose, recast as claim
  To illustrate, with specific cases, the substandard housing provided for migrant laborers
  To force farmers hiring migrant laborers to provide adequate housing
  To be perceived favorably by the audience.
  To overcome opposition from farmers to this proposal
Claim: Farmers/owners hiring migrant laborers must provide adequate housing. ■

Central ideas and claims make different demands on the audience. Where central ideas explain and clarify information, claims give audiences reasons to believe or act in a certain way. The speech to entertain encompasses both possibilities, since its goal may include either informing or persuading an audience.

Wording the Title. To complete your initial thinking about purposes, you often will want to decide on **wording the title.** Although it may seem odd or even unnecessary to consider a title during the preliminary stages of speech preparation, there are several concrete advantages of doing so. First, a title highlights the key concept or idea that the speech content will reflect. Second, speakers often are required to announce titles ahead of time, in order to allow for publicizing the event. Just as a title helps the speaker focus on content, it assists those who might attend in deciding whether the speaker's subject is of interest. The following guidelines will assist you in selecting and phrasing a title:

A title should be relevant to you, the audience, and the occasion. If you were to give a speech on business and political ethics, you might consider a title such as

FIGURE 3.3 Central Ideas and Claims

General Purpose	**Inform**	**Persuade/Actuate**	**Entertain**
Specific Purpose	**Central Idea (preview main points)**	**Claim (preview main points)**	**Central Idea or Claim (preview main points)**

"The Eleventh Commandment," as did the speaker who claimed that the commandment "Thou shalt not steal" has been supplanted in some business and political circles by another: "Thou shalt not get caught."

A title should be provocative. Linda G. Stuntz, the acting deputy secretary of energy for the Bush administration, delivered a speech entitled "The Environmentally Ugly American," at MIT's Center for Energy and Environmental Policy Research. The title reflected the image of the inconsiderate American and focused attention on her primary claim "that while the United States, of course, has challenges . . . we are hardly the evil empire of environmental deregulation that some would have you believe."[2] The title was worded in such a way that audience members would not know for certain which side of the issue she would defend.

A title should be productive. Titles should convey to the audience the central idea or claim, or at the very least, give them a reason to attend to the message. Provocative titles (as in the case above: "Environmentally Speaking, we are THE Ugly Americans,") become unproductive when they turn off significant portions of the audience, hence lessening a speaker's chance of a fair hearing.

The title should be brief. Imagine the effect of announcing your title as "The Effects upon High-Track, Mean-Track, and Low-Track High School Juniors of Pretesting for Senior Year Competency Testings." Besides not being terribly clear, the title is far too long and doesn't do much to stimulate curiosity in your audience. A better choice might be "Tracking Juniors: A Means to Successful Testing as Seniors?" or "A Pretest in Time Saves Nine—or More." These two may lack some precision, but they are decidedly more provocative than the first choice.

When committing to a title for advance publicity, select a general phrase. If you have to commit to a title well in advance, you want to preserve flexibility in how you develop the speech itself. The title "Science Fiction as Political Statement" is sufficiently precise to give the audience an idea of your general topic area while allowing you to alter the development of the subject as you plan the speech.

Strategic Considerations. The preceding discussion has focused on the general and specific purposes in terms of the *desired response* you wish to obtain

---

A̶SSESSMENT CHECK

Attend a speech or lecture on campus with a small group of classmates. As you listen to the presentation, each of you should take notes on the following: general purpose, specific purpose, and statement of central idea or claim. When you compare your notes after the presentation, how much agreement is there about these factors? What accounts for any discrepancies in agreement? In addition, how well does the speaker meet your needs as an audience member? How is this done, or not done? Discuss your reactions with the group during a class session.

---

from your audience. What remains is to examine some of the reasons you may elect to (or have been asked to) inform, persuade, or entertain your audience. Some of the factors that will determine your actual decisions include an assessment of risks taken, the listeners' authority to act, their preexisting attitudes, the nature of the speech occasion, and the time available to speak.

Taking Risks.   There are times when we must ask ourselves how much we are willing to risk personally in front of others. For example, suppose you work for a firm that you're convinced is patently sexist in its promotion policies. The past record clearly suggests that it seldom promotes women to upper-level managerial positions. You find that you are given a chance to talk about promotions at an open meeting of the firm. How far do you go? What do you say? Your **private aim** may be one of getting your frustrations heard, regardless of the consequences. Your **ultimate aim** is to get some women, including yourself, into higher managerial positions. How you balance these purposes, and the degree to which you put your own job at risk, becomes a real rather than theoretical issue.

Listeners' Authority or Capacity to Act.   For a speaker to demand of students that they should "abolish all required courses" is futile; any decision concerning course requirements is in the hands of the faculty. In this case, the listener's **authority to act** is nonexistent. As a speaker, limit your specific purposes and claims to behaviors that are clearly within the domain of the audience's authority or power.

Listeners' Preexisting Attitudes.   If your listeners' **preexisting attitudes** are hostile to your message, you might, in a single speech, be able to convince them that there's merit in your side of the issue. You'll be hoping for too much if you expect the audience to disavow their current beliefs and embrace yours, or to take positive action on the basis of your request. Thus you must adjust your specific purpose to what you can reasonably obtain from the audience, given its past history, experiences, and present attitudes.

The Nature of the Speech Occasion. Under most conditions, you will automatically seek to speak in a way that is in tune with what audiences will expect on the occasion. Violating their expectations can have negative consequences; hence, you should willingly go "against the grain" only when your principles dictate a need to "say what needs saying" regardless of the audience's attitude toward the occasion. Be willing to accept the audience's anger should you disappoint them. Otherwise, adapt your specific purpose to the mood and spirit of the occasion on which you are to speak.

Time Limits. The person assigning the speech, those inviting you to speak, or the occasion itself may dictate **time limits**—the amount of time you will have available. You will need to adjust what you hope to accomplish to fit the time constraints in the rhetorical situation. For example, you may be able to induce a hostile audience to postpone a decision without talking very long; however, if your goal is to change their feelings and convictions so they endorse your proposal, you'll need more than a few minutes. Similarly, if your subject is complex, a 15-minute speech may be able to achieve listener comprehension but not convince the audience to act. Don't try to secure a response that an audience cannot give in the time available. Knowing more about the audience and occasion will assist you in making sound strategic choices.

Analyzing the Audience and Occasion

A good speech is one that reflects your interests while being seen as responsive to the interests, preferences, and values of the audience to whom it is presented. You must regularly ask yourself: "How would I feel about this topic if I were in their place?" "How can I adapt this material to their interests and habits, especially at points where their experiences and understanding differ from mine?" To answer such questions, you need to analyze the people that compose your audience—their age range, gender, social-political-economic status, culture, backgrounds, prejudices, and fears. While you cannot interview everyone, of course, you need to get some sense of how they'll react to your central idea or claim.

In a public speaking class, you can estimate these factors by listening to comments made during class discussions and by asking some class members what they think. In other circumstances, gathering this information is more difficult, requiring you to become more creative in assessing the audience. Among the kinds of information you may wish to gather, consider the following:

The audience's knowledge of and attitude toward you. What does the audience already know about you, and what information would be useful to convey your own expertise? Have they had a chance to form an opinion about you as a speaker?

The audience's knowledge of and attitude toward the topic. What they know and how they feel about the topic is critical; you may bore them if you simply duplicate their existing knowledge, and you may anger them if you ignore their own attitudes. Regardless of how it's done, **audience analysis** is a primary determinant of success. You also need to consider the setting and circumstances in which you're speaking:

Are there specific rules or customs that you need to know and follow? You need to be aware of anything that will affect the audience's reception of you or your message. When Ross Perot spoke to an African-American audience during his 1992 run at the presidency, his continued use of "you people" was an affront to those present, as it widened the gulf between the races.

How long will you have to speak? Will you precede or follow other speakers who could influence your reception? If you overtalk your time limit, it may be the same as "overstaying your welcome." When others will speak, knowing your "place" in the line-up will help you adapt to an audience who has heard too many speeches already.

What impact will events before or after your speech have on topic selection, phrasing of your central idea or claim, or supporting materials? As we will note later, timing is a critical variable. The words of President Clinton in the aftermath of the bombing of the federal building in Oklahoma City sought to call attention to an atrocity. From the perspective of those involved in militant groups, his words were a self-fulfilling prophecy—confirming their worst fears of government suppression. If you are speaking in the aftermath of a major catastrophe, your ideas may be easier for the audience to accept, or may brand you as an insensitive person.

Will the physical circumstances support your speaking style? If not, can you alter them? Speaking to an audience when some people are positioned behind pillars, as in a residence hall dining room, can make for anxious moments. You may have to move further from a lectern than normal so that parts of the audience see you more easily, at least part of the time. Examining such issues in advance is the key here. You want to be as forewarned and as comfortable as you can be in the circumstances you face when it's your time to speak.

Gathering the Speech Material

Once you've analyzed the audience and context of the speech, you're ready to assemble some ideas and information to support your central idea or claim. You need to (1) assess what information you think is needed in order to accomplish your objectives, (2) reflect on what you already know, (3) figure out how much of it is relevant to your central idea or claim, (4) investigate where additional information can be found if it is needed, and (5) obtain the additional information. In almost every speech situation, you will have to gather additional information to develop, expand, or reinforce what you already know and believe.

You may wish to talk to others, such as friends or local experts, to check out your perceptions. Critical listening is important here. You undoubtedly will want to gather other materials from newspapers, magazines, books, government documents, or radio and television programs. You'll soon learn some traditionally solid sources: the "News of the Week in Review" section of the *New*

*E*THICAL MOMENTS
ETHICS AND PUBLIC SPEAKING

Occasionally, in this book, we'll include a boxed area devoted to "ethical moments"—ethical decisions public speakers must make in preparing and delivering their talks. Some of these moments will fit you and your circumstances, and some will not. In either case, we hope that you'll take a moment to think about the problems presented and their solutions. Some of these problems might be discussed in class. Here are some typical ethical questions that you might face in the speeches you'll give this term:

1. When is it fair to borrow other people's ideas and words, and when is it not?
2. You recognize that a major portion of a speaker's informative speech came from an article that you read last week. The speaker does not cite the source.

During the critique session, should you blow the whistle on the speaker?
3. An article says exactly what you intended to say about the use of pesticides on garden vegetables. Then you find a more recent article claiming that new research contradicts the first article. Should you ignore the new evidence?

You will face ethical moments such as these regularly, both in your speech classroom and throughout the rest of your life. Taking a few moments to consider such situations, and even to articulate your position in discussion, can save you many embarrassing times later. Know what your moral stands are and know why you take them *before* you face ethical dilemmas on the platform.

York Times; articles in *Time, Newsweek, U.S. News and World Report;* journal articles surveyed in *Readers' Guide to Periodical Literature* and more specialized indexes; and all of the annuals, yearbooks, almanacs, and so on that fill the reference area of your library. Computerized index searches also will be helpful to you as you seek new information or supporting material for your ideas. We will review these and other resources in Chapter 6.

Outlining the Speech

Once you've compiled your materials, you have to sort them. Developing a preliminary outline of main ideas will help. An outline lets you see how your various materials relate to your central idea or claim, shows you where you have plenty of (or too little) material, and makes the structure of your speech clear to you. You'll probably jockey back and forth between your materials and your outline, looking for just the right fit between what you *know* and what you can *justify* publicly to a critical audience.

We will examine outlining in more detail later. For now, follow these rules: Arrange your main ideas in a clear and systematic order; arrange the subpoints under each main idea in a manner that clearly illustrates their connection to the main point; and preserve the unity of your speech by making sure that each point, whether main point or subpoint, is directly related to your specific purpose and central idea or claim.

Practicing Aloud

With your outline completed, you're ready for the most terrifying task of preparation: practicing your speech. This is not easy! You can feel like a fool talking aloud in your room; the sound of your voice rings hollow and you find that some of the materials you wrote out come off as simplistic, clichéd, stiff, or silly. Nevertheless, practicing aloud is essential if you're to improve some of the decisions you've already made and work on your delivery skills.

Give practice a chance. It can, quite literally, save your communicative life. Talk through your outline aloud, in a confident, conversational (not a mumbling) tone that will help you get used to the sound. Repeatedly read through the outline until you've made all the changes that seem useful and until you can express each idea clearly and smoothly. Practice until the ideas flow easily, all the time talking in a conversational voice. Finally, if you dare, get a friend to listen to your speech, give you direct feedback, and help you practice making eye contact with a real person.

The steps—from selecting and narrowing a subject through practicing aloud—take you to the brink of public speaking with real audiences. Good work on preparation pays off in effective performance.

$\mathcal{D}$ELIVERING YOUR FIRST SPEECHES

For most beginners, delivering their first speeches is very difficult. Many feel anxious and nervous: "I'm too nervous to stand up there." "What do I do with my hands?" "Will people think I'm a jerk?" Self-doubts, from actual fright to a more general lack of self-confidence, creep into every speaker's mind; the trick is to learn to control them. In the remaining part of this chapter, we'll examine three strategies for self-control: (1) selecting the right method of presentation, (2) focusing not on yourself but on capturing and holding the attention of your listeners, and (3) communicating self-confidence.

Selecting the Method of Presentation

Which method should you use to present your speech? Your choice should be based on several criteria, including any restrictions imposed by an instructor:

type of speaking occasion, the seriousness and purpose of your speech, your audience analysis, and your own strengths and weaknesses as a speaker. Attention to these considerations will help you decide whether your method of presentation should be impromptu, memorized, read from a manuscript, or extemporaneous.

The Impromptu Speech.   As the name suggests, the **impromptu speech** is delivered on the spur of the moment with little preparation. The speaker relies entirely on previous knowledge and skill. When an instructor in a meteorology class calls on you for an explanation of the jet stream's course through the atmosphere, you don't have time to prepare more than a quick list of three or four words to remind you of points you want to make. Impromptu speeches are given in rhetorical emergencies—at public meetings, in classes, in conventions. When using this method, try to focus on a single idea, carefully relating all significant details to it. In this way, you'll avoid the rambling, incoherent remarks that the method too often produces.

The Memorized Speech.   The **memorized speech** is written out word for word and committed to memory. Although a few speakers are able to do this well, it presents problems for most of us. Instead of sounding conversational, a memorized speech often results in a stilted presentation; speakers tend to pause too often while trying to remember the words, or rush past ideas so as not to forget the words. In either case, meaning is at the expense of memory. This form is well-suited to drama, as in the speeches in a Shakespearean play, or for intercollegiate competition in original oratory. But for general purposes, it is not a recommended method of presentation.

The Read Speech.   Like the memorized speech, the **read speech** is written out, but in this method the speaker reads from a manuscript. If extremely careful wording is required—as in the president's annual message to Congress, in which a slip could undermine domestic or foreign policies—the read speech is appropriate. It also is used in the presentations of scholarly papers, where exact, concise, often technical exposition is required. Reading a speech while retaining a conversational style is more difficult than it sounds. No matter how experienced you are, when you read your message, you'll inevitably sacrifice some of the freshness and spontaneity necessary for effective speechmaking. You'll also have trouble reacting to feedback and may be tempted to use more formal, written language. If you do use this method, talk through the speech over and over to ensure an effective oral style.

The Extemporaneous Speech.   Representing a middle course between the memorized or read speech and the impromptu speech, the **extemporaneous speech** requires careful planning and a good outline. This whole chapter has been aiming at preparing you to present an extemporaneous speech. Working from your outline, practice the speech aloud, expressing the ideas somewhat differently each time through it. Use the outline to fix the order of ideas in your mind, and try out various wordings to develop accuracy, conciseness, and flexibility of expression. Through such preparation, you'll be able to deliver the actual speech from a few notes.

If the extemporaneous method is used carelessly, the result will resemble a bad impromptu speech, a fact that sometimes leads to a confusion of these two terms. When used well, however, the method will produce a speech that is nearly as polished as a memorized one but more relaxed, flexible, and spontaneous, hence more like natural conversation than the other methods. The best lecturers at your college or university undoubtedly are extemporaneous speakers. Most of the advice in this textbook assumes the use of the extemporaneous method.

CAPTURING AND HOLDING ATTENTION: NINE FACTORS

Listeners' behaviors vary considerably, thanks to the thoughts and sensations in their internal and external environments. Essentially, your listeners need reasons for *wanting* to listen. Even when you have their attention, it tends to ebb and flow. So, you must constantly watch for lapses. James Albert Winans, a twentieth-century pioneer in public-speaking instruction, expressed the problem succinctly: *Attention determines response.* If you cannot gain it or hold it once gained, audience attention will wander and you will be hard-pressed to achieve your objective. If you can attain and hold your listeners' attention, you have a chance to drive home your points.

What is **attention?** For our purposes, it can be thought of as a *focus* on one element in a given environment, with the result that other elements fade from the conscious perception.[3] For example, in 1968, Martin Luther King, Jr., went to Memphis, Tennessee, to support striking African-American sanitation workers in their demands for improved wages. The evening of April 3 he spoke in a hot, crowded church about the history of civil rights, about his joy to be living "just a few years in the second half of the twentieth century,"[4] about the tense times in his life, about his upcoming Poor People's Campaign that was planning a March on Washington, and about Christian injunctions to social action. Videotapes of the speech show an audience interacting with King, moving and jostling, laughing and talking. But the audience became quiet and transfixed as he moved through the conclusion of the speech[5]:

> We've got some difficult days ahead. But it really doesn't matter with me now because I've been to the mountaintop. And I don't mind. Like anybody I would like to live a long life. Longevity has its place, but I'm not concerned about that now. I just want to do God's will, and He's allowed me to go up to the mountain, and I've looked over and I've seen the Promised Land. I may not get there with you, but I want you to know tonight that we as a people will get to the Promised Land. So I'm happy tonight, I'm not worried about anything. I'm not fearing any man. Mine eyes have seen the glory of the coming of the Lord.

FIGURE 3.4 The Factors of Attention

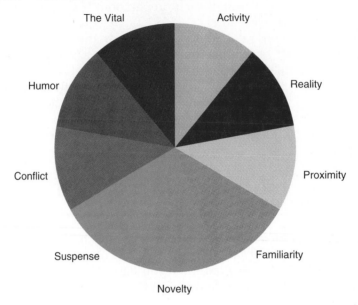

That crowd had talked and shouted through the speech, then was quieted as it focused intently on King's prophetic concluding words. As King finished, they exploded in joy and appreciation as his concluding religious image broke through their focus and returned them to the church, Memphis, the strike, and the interracial problems of America in 1968.

Few of us will ever rivet onto ourselves the undivided focus of an audience in the way King did just before his assassination. Yet, we all can work to gain and hold attention. A *vigorous and varied delivery* will help. Likewise, your reputation as a trustworthy and honest person (positive *ethos*) can command respect—and attention. *Lively and picturesque language* shows audiences word-pictures and makes it easier for them to stay with you. Fundamentally, however, you'll capture and hold attention through the types of ideas you present. Some types of ideas or images have greater attention value than others.

Ideas can be presented in a variety of ways often called the **factors of attention.**

Activity

Suppose you have two TV sets side by side. One shows Janet Jackson performing motionless behind a microphone; the other carries one of her music videos—a fully choreographed production number. Which one will you look at? Nothing is so boring as talk that seems to stand still, providing far too much detail on a minor point. Instructions and demonstrations, in particular, demand orderly, systematic progress. Keep it moving!

Reality

The earliest words you learned were names for tangible objects—"Mama," "milk," "dog." While the ability to abstract or generalize is one of the marks of human intelligence, there still persists in all of us an interest in concrete reality, the here-and-now of sense data. A few paragraphs ago, we might have written: "Consider, for example, a preacher who is reviewing his church history and present circumstances." Such a depersonalized anecdote about "a preacher" doesn't carry the punch, human interest, and memorableness of one about a specific person.

Proximity

Consider the following: "Do you realize how much fast food is consumed on this campus? Within four blocks of this classroom are nine restaurants, including a McDonald's, a Wendy's, and a Pizza Hut. Two are local submarine houses. Even the student union runs a fast-food bar. A key question we face is this: What are our lunch habits doing to our nutrition—to our body and mind?" Such an introduction brings the topic close to home.

Familiarity

Especially in the face of new or strange ideas, references to the familiar will sustain attention. One way to use familiarity to advantage is to employ *analogies:* noting that the London postal or zip codes are arranged like directions on a compass (the initial letters indicate directions and the next set of numbers representing degrees or positions) uses something familiar to explain something unfamiliar. Another positive use of familiarity is to begin a speech with allusions to former or current major addresses: Lincoln's Gettysburg Address, Susan B. Anthony's "Is It a Crime for a U.S. Citizen to Vote?" speech; Malcolm X's "Ballot or Bullet" speech, Martin Luther King's "I Have a Dream" speech or Hillary Clinton's "Remarks for the United Nations Fourth World Conference on Women" at the 1995 international women's conference in Beijing, China. You might also refer to well-known past or present international leaders, such as Nelson Mandela, Margaret Thatcher, Indira Gandhi, or Boris Yeltsin; cite a piece of conventional wisdom; or refer to an experience that most everyone has had.

Novelty

As the old adage has it, when a dog bites a man, it's an accident; when a man bites a dog, it's news. Two special types of novelty are *size* and *contrast*. In a speech on the high cost of national defense, a speaker caught the attention of his audience with this sentence: "Considering that it costs more than $5000 to equip an average soldier for combat, it is disquieting to learn that in a year his equipment will be 60 percent obsolete."[6] In a speech entitled "Common

Ground and Common Sense," Jesse Jackson employed the following historical contrast[7]:

> Twenty-four years ago, the late Fanny Lou Hamer and Aaron Henry—who sits here tonight from Mississippi—were locked out on the streets of Atlantic City, the head of the Mississippi Freedom Democratic Party. But tonight, a black and white delegation from Mississippi is headed by Ed Cole, a black man, from Mississippi, 24 years later.

In using novel materials, be careful not to inject elements that are so different or unusual as to be unfamiliar. Listeners must at least know what you're talking about.

Suspense

Much of the interest in mystery and detective stories arises from uncertainty about their outcome. Films such as *Pulp Fiction* have so many twists that they leave viewers spellbound. When giving a speech, you can create uncertainty by pointing to puzzling relationships or unpredictable forces.

Introduce suspense into the stories you use to illustrate your ideas, building up to a surprising climax. For example, you might begin a speech on retardation with the scenario of a developmentally disabled child; then, after describing the causes of and care for those who are developmentally disabled, reveal that you've been talking about your brother.

Conflict

Controversy compels attention; consider the ratings of prime-time TV soap operas that emphasize extremely strong interpersonal conflicts in their plots. Over 30 years ago, Malcolm X gave voice to the frustration of African Americans in that generation with his now classic words: "if you never see me another time in your life, if I die in the morning, I'll die saying one thing: the ballot or the bullet, the ballot or the bullet."[8] The contrast was vivid, and the implication of conflict equally vivid.

Humor

Listeners usually pay attention to a speech when they're enjoying themselves. Humor provides a chance for listeners to participate more actively in the transaction by sharing their laughter. When using humor to capture or hold attention, follow two guidelines:

Be relevant. Beware of wandering from the point. Don't tell a joke just for the sake of telling a joke. If the humor doesn't reinforce an important idea, leave it out.

Use good taste. Consider the occasion. You don't want to tell a knee-slapper during a funeral, and you should avoid off-color stories as they will offend most if not all audience members.

*A*SSESSMENT CHECK:

After you have completed the preparation of your first speech, ask yourself these questions:

- Have I selected a topic that will be well-received by the audience and that fits the occasion?
- Have I narrowed the topic to fit the situation?
- Will my purpose be clear to the audience, or do I need to revise the phrasing of my central idea or claim?
- Do I have sufficient materials to support or clarify my ideas?
- How complete should my outline be: What needs to be written out? Can I work from key ideas or phrases?
- Have I used all of the factors of attention that would help make this speech a success?
- Am I personally confident that I have done everything I need to do to make this speech a success?

The Vital

Finally, people nearly always pay attention to matters that affect their own well-being. When you hear "Students who take an internship while in college find jobs after graduation three times as fast as those who don't," you're likely to pay attention. Appealing to the vital, therefore, is a matter of *personalizing* your speech, making it unavoidably relevant, not just to the group, but to specific individuals in your audience.

Each of these nine attention getters and holders should be at your beck and call in developing the speech. They enliven your speech, focusing audience attention directly on you and your message.

*C*OMMUNICATING SELF-CONFIDENCE

The third matter you need to think about when speaking in front of a real audience is yourself. In Chapter 1 we discussed speech anxiety and some ways to overcome it. Now you need to consider how you can convey an air of dynamism and self-assuredness to your listeners. Many students ready to give their first speech ask, "How should I deliver my speech? How can I communicate a sense of self-confidence to an audience?" The following guidelines are a start to answering those questions.

   1. *Be yourself.* Act as if you were having an animated conversation with a friend. Avoid an excessively rigid posture, but don't become so comfortable in front of the group that you sprawl all over the lectern.

ℋow to
Get Your Audience's Attention

- Keep it moving! Ideas that "move" tend to attract attention; like ideas, the speech should march or press forward (activity).
- Keep refocusing on the here and now. Refer to specific events, persons, and places. Audiences can hang abstract ideas on specific details (reality).
- Bring the topic close to home. A direct reference to something nearby in time and space often orients an audience who may be wondering what you're talking about (proximity).
- Show how the unfamiliar is like the familiar. People are generally more comfortable when you refer to familiar ideas (familiarity).
- Introduce novelty. New and unusual developments attract wide notice. Just be careful that your audience can relate what you're saying to things they know about (novelty).
- Add suspense. Create uncertainty by pointing to puzzling relationships or unpredictable forces. Use suspense in stories you use to illustrate your ideas, building up to a surprising climax (suspense).
- Note conflicts or controversies. Controversy compels attention. Like suspense, con-

When you speak, you want your listeners to focus on your ideas rather than their form of presentation.

2. *Look at your listeners.* Watch their faces for reactions. Without this feedback, you can't gauge the effectiveness of your speech or make adjustments as you speak. Also, people tend to mistrust anyone who doesn't look directly at them. They also may get the impression you don't care about them and aren't interested in their reactions. *In speaking, the eyes have it!*

3. *Communicate with your body as well as your voice.* Realize that as a speaker you're being seen as well as heard. Bodily movements and changes in facial expression can help clarify and reinforce your ideas. Keep your hands at your sides so that when you feel an impulse to gesture, you can do so easily. If there is no lectern, and you're working from an outline, use a hard backing to hold the papers firm. (This also makes your nervousness less visible!) If you are using notecards, hold them up so you can see them clearly rather than hiding them. Your speech will

troversy suggests uncertainty; like activity, controversy is dynamic (conflict).

- Share humor. Listeners pay attention when they're enjoying themselves. Humor allows listeners to participate actively, diffuses tension, and revives a tired audience (humor).

- Personalize your speech. People pay attention to matters affecting their health, reputation, property, or employment. Make your speech unavoidably relevant (the vital).

flow more smoothly if your outline or notecard is easy to read from. As you speak, don't become so relaxed you curl your papers or fold your cards. Let your body move as it responds to your feelings and message. If you hear a tremor in your voice or see one in your hand, remember that neither is as noticeable to listeners as it is to you. Overall, if you're being yourself, appropriate bodily responses will flow from the act of communicating.

*L*EARNING TO EVALUATE SPEECHES

The classroom serves as a laboratory for studying and evaluating speech materials and delivery. The evaluation form on page 43 is designed to help sharpen your critical listening skills as well as your sensitivity to the fundamentals of the speechmaking process. You can use it to evaluate speeches in classrooms, settings around your campus or community, and televised presentations on C-SPAN and other networks. Depending on the assignment, the audience, and the demands of the occasion, some checkpoints on the form will be more significant and applicable than others. For now, use the form as a general guide; later, concentrate upon those parts of it that are relevant to specific assignments.

What makes a "good speech?" While the answer to this question will vary among listeners, a positive "yes" to the following questions serves to highlight some of the key issues involved.

First, does the speaker appear sincerely interested in the consequences of his or her speechmaking? That is, is the speaker willing to assume responsibility for what happens as a result of presenting ideas?

Second, does the speaker take time at the beginning to indicate interest in, and appreciation for, divergent points of view? Does the speaker appear willing to consider opinions or perspectives other than those he or she is advancing?

Third, is the information comprehensive and accurate, insofar as it is possible to obtain credible information on the topic being addressed?

Fourth, if central ideas or claims are advanced, are they supported with up-to-date and credible testimony, statistics, examples, and other supporting materials?

Fifth, is the presentation understandable? That is, can you fathom what the speaker is talking about? Is the organization clear? Is the language appropriate? Is the delivery easy to listen to?

As you participate regularly in speech evaluations, even of early classroom assignments, use these broad questions, and others that seem appropriate to raise, in providing direct feedback to your classmates. Constructive criticism is both positive and negative—but it is always personally supportive. Telling someone both what worked as well as what you think should be changed provides beginning speakers with much-needed feedback, and it forces you, the listener, to formulate your thoughts and to come to grips with your own standards and expectations. In this way, both you and the speaker gain. As another strategy in this class, read the sample speeches in this book, analyzing them systematically to isolate the communication cues that facilitate listener comprehension and acceptance.

ASSESSING A SAMPLE SPEECH

The following speech by Andy Wood of Berry College (Georgia) is well adapted to a student audience and a persuasive speech assignment.[9] Paragraph 1 orients the listener to the principal issue. Paragraph 2 provides a clear preview of the main ideas and the order in which they will be discussed. Paragraphs 3–5 detail the dangers of superbugs; paragraphs 5–8 outline the reasons current control methods are not working and paragraphs 9–12 outline new measures that could be taken. The final paragraph summarizes the major issues and issues the plea for action on the part of the audience. The speech offers detailed support for each of the main points.

$\mathcal{S}$UPERBUGS: SCOURGE OF THE POST-ANTIBIOTIC ERA

Andy Wood

It always happens when you're the busiest. Your body gives out on you. Like any forensicator, you don't have time to get sick. So you see a doctor, grab an antibiotic and feel better. Problem solved . . . or created. You see, every year 15,000 people die of pneumonia caused by a form of strep throat. Nineteen thousand die of hospital acquired infections. And so far, a deadly form of tuberculosis has killed 22,000 people. Now you may be thinking, "wait a minute, I take one antibiotic and all these people die? What's the connection?" The connection is that the more we use antibiotics, the stronger these diseases become. They're called superbugs and they're growing out of control. In *Newsweek,* March 7, 1994, Dr. Mitchell Cohen of the Centers for Disease Control warned: superbugs threaten us all. He said: "many of the diseases we once had under control are coming back." /1

Now is the time for us to adopt a new strategy in this biological war. First, we must examine the emergence and the dangers of superbugs. Then we'll explore why our defenses fail against them. Finally, we'll outline a new offensive strategy that works. /2

Three of the deadliest superbugs are tuberculosis, streptococcus and staphylococcus. The critical connection is that these infections have developed resistance to antibiotics. Thus, our only resistance to them is luck. Consider TB. At the turn of the century, tuberculosis killed over a third of all U.S. adults between age 20 and 45. With antibiotics, we discovered what appeared to be a magic bullet to fight this menace. However, according to *Science News,* February 6, 1993, 36 states have reported cases of TB that are resistant to antibiotics. In fact, *Medical World News,* January, 1993 reports 30,000 cases of drug-resistant TB nationwide. Of those cases, 22,000 people have died. /3

But TB isn't the only threat. Resistant streptococcus pneumonia is so dangerous, any delay in treatment is fatal. That's why on May 16, 1990, in one of the world's most advanced hospitals, a team of doctors could do nothing to save the life of a man with what appeared to be a simple infection, but was actually a deadly form of strep. Dose after dose of antibiotic failed. His name was Jim Henson. And his tragedy is not uncommon. According to *The Atlanta Constitution,* May 18, 1993, resistant streptococcus causes 500,000 cases of pneumonia a year. Of those cases, 15,000 people die. /4

But, perhaps the most dangerous resistant strain is staphylococcus aureus: one superbug that's almost impossible to kill. According to the journal, *Antimicrobial Agents,* March, 1993 staph can attack and grow on any surface and can carry resistance to other bacteria. Ironically, its favorite breeding ground is the hospital. During the 50's, methicillin and vancomycin put the bug on the defensive. But according to *Science Magazine,* July 16, 1993, 95 percent of all staph infections are resistant to methicillin. If reports of vancomycin resistant staph are accurate, we face a real-life andromeda strain that can't be stopped. These three examples prove we're fighting superbugs on a postantibiotic battleground in which our big guns no longer work. /5

There are three reasons why limited national surveillance, faulty hospital infection control and dangerous public perceptions are problems. Dr. Steven Joseph writes in *The American Journal of Public Health,* May, 1993 that with the apparent success of antibiotics, America practically dismantled its infectious disease surveillance system. As a result, superbugs usually go undetected until they reach a hospital. Even then, it's often too late. In a June 24, 1993, Personal Interview, Dr. Robert Gaynes, Director of the CDC, said "we track resistant bacteria in only 160 out of 5,000 hospitals. There could be a strain of vancomycin-resistant staph out there and we wouldn't know it." /6

Surprisingly, much of this threat comes from hospitals themselves. Their indiscriminate use and abuse of antibiotics lead to a selective killing of weak bacteria, allowing the strong to thrive. Without natural enemies, these bugs are free to concentrate on developing resistance. In fact, the *Buffalo New York News,* January 25, 1993, quotes a CDC report stating: of the 35 million Americans admitted to hospitals every year, two million catch something new after they check in. And in 60 percent of the cases, those infections are resistant to one or more drugs. These infections kill 19,000 people directly and contribute to another 58,000 fatalities a year. Of course, this problem isn't confined to hospitals. Any doctor who overprescribes antibiotics, helps bacteria develop resistance. /7

At this point, one may assume that reckless doctors or unscrupulous drug companies are behind all of this. (There are plenty of both.) But in truth, we are all part of the cause when we demand antibiotics for all that ails us. Dr. Richard Platt writes in *Harvard Health Letter,* April, 1993 that doctors often prescribe antibiotics even for viral infections (when they'd be ineffective) because patients "have a strong expectation that when they see a doctor, they should come away with a drug prescription." As a result, *The Journal of the American Medical Association,* April 14, 1994, reports that of the 220 million prescriptions written for oral antibiotic every year, one half are unnecessary. Certainly doctors are the ones writing these prescriptions. But all too often they are reacting to our assumptions about what antibiotics can do. As we've seen, these assumptions expose us to bacteria that can kill us. But can't be killed. /8

Refortifying our antibiotic defense against superbugs requires three steps: redesign of our national surveillance system, disciplined response by the medical community and increased vigilance on all our parts. /9

The Public Health Service Act of 1993 increased funding to the National Institutes of Health, as well as the Centers for Disease Control—two essential watchtowers that protect us from superbugs. However, if you read the *Congressional Quarterly,* July 24, 1993, you'll find no increased funding for research on antibiotic resistance in either the NIH or CDC. While it would be easy to just ask for more money this year, there is a better solution in the private sector. It's called the Alliance for the Prudent Use of Antibiotics. The *APUA Newsletter,* Spring, 1993, explains this group is a network of physicians, microbiologists and public health workers sharing information on emerging superbugs in 95 countries. Hospitals, testing labs, even medical schools should build on this skeleton, creating an effective surveillance body. Such a network would focus on surveillance, putting the NIH and CDC in better positions to attack superbugs that threaten us. /10

The second step involves hospitals, doctors and their use of antibiotics. Last September, the CDC released the first new guidelines on hospital-borne infections in over a decade. Obviously, the medical community should implement these standards without waiting for another outbreak of resistance like staph or TB. That's not enough. This next step requires that hospitals and doctors discipline their use of antibiotics. According to *The Annals of Internal Medicine,* April 1, 1993, the Infectious Disease Society of America is establishing guidelines on antimicrobial drug use. These guidelines limit the prescribed length of antibiotic treatment in non–life-threatening cases. *The Lancet,* February 27, 1993, illustrates this concept, noting that Meningococcal Meningitis—a recent killer of college students—can itself be killed by a single dose of long-acting penicillin as opposed to the commonly used seven-day treatment cycle. Limiting the use of antibiotics in this manner, limits the opportunity for bacteria to develop resistance. /11

But, if all this talk about national surveillance and hospital infections seems a bit remote, remember: our use of antibiotics is our front lime of defense against superbugs. That's why there are two things you should do. First, if your doctor prescribes an antibiotic, ask why and whether there are alternatives like vaccines. Because they are harder to resist, vaccines are successful against diseases like strep and according to *Nature Magazine,* July 1, 1993, research is underway for a TB vaccine. Second, if we must use an antibiotic, stick to the prescribed treatment. After all, when we use antibiotics as "home remedies" or share them with friends like they're cough drops, we increase the risk of resistance. By serving as individual gatekeepers of antibiotic use, we can fight superbugs without tearing down our best line of defense. /12

In the past few minutes, we've examined how superbugs threaten our health, why we've lowered our defenses and how America can answer this call to battle. In doing so, we've learned about the dangerous relationship between antibiotics and superbugs. It's ironic, isn't it? Our most powerful medical tool is used against us by a simple lifeform. Clearly, victory in this war demands more than brute force. It requires vision and foresight. And not just from doctors and scientists—but from all of us. After all, in the battle against resistant bacteria there are no volunteers. In this war, we are all enlisted. /13

CHAPTER SUMMARY

In preparing a speech, the competent speaker must follow seven essential steps: selecting the subject; narrowing the subject; determining the central idea or claim; analyzing the audience and occasion; gathering the speech material; making an outline; and practicing aloud. Going through these steps prepares you to deliver speeches to audiences. In preparing an initial speech, the competent speaker will be able to

- select an appropriate method of presentation (impromptu, memorized, read, extemporaneous);
- capture and hold attention by using one or more of the nine factors of attention (activity, reality, proximity, familiarity, novelty, suspense, conflict, humor, the vital);
- communicate confidence; and
- use the evaluative questions and form as a check on the adequacy of your presentation.

KEY TERMS

attention (p. 69)
audience analysis (p. 65)
authority to act (p. 63)
central idea (p. 58)
claim (p. 58)
extemporaneous speech (p. 68)
factors of attention (p. 70)
general purposes (p. 54)
impromptu speech (p. 68)
memorized speech (p. 68)
preexisting attitude (p. 63)

private aim (p. 63)
read speech (p. 68)
rhetorical frame of mind (p. 50)
specific purpose (p. 57)
speech to actuate (p. 55)
speech to entertain (p. 56)
speech to inform (p. 54)
speech to persuade (p. 55)
time limits (p. 64)
ultimate aim (p. 63)
wording the title (p. 61)

ASSESSMENT ACTIVITIES

1. Listed below are two groups of three statements about a single topic. Read all three statements in each group and write what you believe to be the claim of the group's message. Compare your phrasing of the claims with those of members of your class.

I. **a.** Many prison facilities are inadequate.
    b. Low rates of pay result in frequent job turnovers in prisons.
    c. Prison employees need on-the-job training.

   II. a. There is a serious maldistribution of medical personnel and service.
      b. The present system of delivering medical service is excellent.
      c. Rural areas have a shortage of doctors.

2. Rewrite the following statements, making each one into a clear and concise central idea for a speech:

   a. Today I would like to try to get you to see the way in which the body can communicate a whole lot of information.

   b. The topic for my speech has to do with the high amount of taxes people have to pay.

   c. A college education might be a really important thing for some people, so my talk is on a college education.

     Now rewrite statements (b) and (c) as claims. Be ready to present your versions in a class discussion.

3. Following the principles and guidelines presented in this chapter, prepare a three-to-four-minute speech to inform. Narrow the subject carefully so that you can do justice to it in the allotted time. Concentrate on developing ways to gain and hold the audience's attention. Hand in an outline along with a brief analysis of the audience and the occasion when you present the speech. In your analysis, indicate why you think your approach to attention will work in this situation.

4. Working in small groups, prepare an "Issues Survey." Each group member will come to class prepared with five suitably narrowed subjects for an informative speech and five for a persuasive speech (there may be some overlap). Discuss your lists with your group, sorting out overlapping ideas in order to develop one list (there may be more than five topics listed for informative and for persuasive speeches). Have one person collate the list in readable form and bring it to the next class, with copies for everyone in the class. Using a simple three-point scale (1—very interesting; 2—interesting; 3—very uninteresting), have class members respond to the subject lists of the various groups. The instructor and one or two students will collate responses and prepare a master copy for everyone in class. Select one informative or persuasive topic that scores among the lowest (most uninteresting) on this final list, and develop a speech that has arousing audience interest as a specific purpose.

$\mathcal{R}$EFERENCES

1. It can be argued that all speeches are persuasive. *Any* change in a person's stock of knowledge, beliefs, attitudes, or ways of acting represents the kind of adjustment in mental and emotional state that can be attributed to persuasion, as long as symbols were employed to induce the change. From a psychological perspective, it may be argued that it's impossible to separate "informative" and "persuasive" messages. We're taking a *rhetorical* perspective, in which the symbols used to evoke a certain kind of response, as well as the strategies

employed in that process, provide an *orientation* that's overtly one of informing, persuading, actuating, or entertaining an audience. Hence you'll find separate discussions of these later in this book. For a cogent discussion of persuasion, see Deirdre D. Johnston, *The Art and Science of Persuasion* (Dubuque, IA:
Brown and Benchmark, 1994), ch. 1; Gary C. Woodward and Robert E. Den-
ton, Jr., *Persuasion and Influence in American Life* (Prospect Heights, IL: Waveland, 1988), ch. 1.

2. Linda G. Stuntz, "The Environmentally Ugly American," *Vital Speeches*, 58
(June 15, 1992): 527.

3. Psychologist Philip G. Zimbardo has likened attention to "a spotlight that illu-
minates certain portions of our surroundings. When we focus our attention on
something and thus become conscious of it, we can begin to process it cogni-
tively—converting sensory information into perceptions and memories or developing ideas through analysis, judgment, reasoning, and imagination. When
the spotlight shifts to something else, conscious processing of the earlier material ceases and processing of the new content begins." In *Psychology and Life*,
12th ed. (Glenview, IL: Scott, Foresman, 1988), 225.

4. Martin Luther King, Jr., "I've Been to the Mountaintop," in *Contemporary American Voices: Significant Speeches in American History, 1945–Present*, ed. James R.
Andrews and David Zarefsky (New York: Longman, 1992), 115.

5. King, 120.

6. Neal Luker, "Our Defense Policy," a speech presented in a course in advanced
public speaking at the University of Iowa.

7. Jesse Jackson, "Common Ground and Common Sense," *Diversity in Public Communication: A Reader*, eds. Christine Kelly, E. Anne Laffoon, and Raymie E.
McKerrow (Dubuque, IA: Kendall-Hunt, 1994), 140.

8. Malcolm X, "The Ballot or the Bullet," in *Diversity in Public Communication: A
Reader*, eds. Christine Kelly, E. Anne Laffoon, and Raymie E. McKerrow
(Dubuque, IA: Kendall-Hunt, 1994), 138.

9. Andy Wood, "Superbugs: Scourge of the Post-Antibiotic Era," in *Winning Orations 1994*. Reprinted by permission of Larry Schnoor, Executive Secretary, Interstate Oratorical Association, Mankato State University, MN.

CHAPTER
4
ANALYZING THE AUDIENCE AND OCCASION

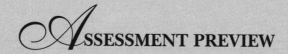

ASSESSMENT PREVIEW

After reading Chapter 4, the student with basic communication competencies will be able to

- identify at least two demographic characteristics of an audience that should influence speech preparation in specific ways.
- identify a belief or attitude that may affect the audience's understanding and evaluation of the speech.
- identify the major segments of the audience.

The student with average communication competencies will also be able to

- identify a set of beliefs, attitudes, and values that may affect the audience's understanding and evaluation of the speech in specific ways.
- identify a set of factors of a particular speaking occasion that should affect speech preparation in specific ways.
- identify the major segments of the audience, specifying at least one targeting strategy for each segment.

The student with superior communication competencies will also be able to

- identify a set of beliefs, attitudes, and values that may affect an audience's understanding and evaluation of the speech, sketching out a rhetorical vision as well as the specific adaptations that should be made to account for them.
- identify a set of situational factors that should affect speech preparation, and specify at least four adaptations to those factors.
- identify the major segments of the audience, and indicate a strategy for unifying all segments.

*P*ublic speaking is **audience** and **occasion centered.** You always speak so as to affect the informational repertoire, psychological state, or behavior of others, and you always speak somewhere: someplace where people (usually) have spoken before and where audience members expect particular kinds or ranges of speeches. The audience and the occasion act as guides to and constraints on speechmaking. In the words of Donald C. Bryant, since ancient Greece the essence of public rhetoric has been that of "adjusting ideas to people and people to ideas."[1]

Obviously, you can't address your speech to each person in your audience. But you can identify some common features among your listeners. Think of your audience as an onion. You peel away one layer and find others. The most effective way to understand your audience may be to peel away as many layers as possible. Once you know how each layer is composed, you can begin to adapt your ideas to them.

A primary theme will be stressed throughout this chapter: *The goal of audience analysis is to discover which facets of listeners' demographic and psychological characteristics are relevant to your speech.* When you understand who your listeners are and which of their characteristics need to be taken into account when you talk on a particular topic, you can adapt your ideas to those characteristics. You also need to be sensitive to the demands that the occasion places on your choice of themes and language. *An "occasion" includes a time and place set aside for particular events and activities; speakers must learn what people expect on those occasions and meet those expectations as fully as possible.* So, in this chapter, we will first discuss the demographic and psychological features of listeners; we will then take apart the rules governing speech occasions and indicate some of the specific moves you should be making while constructing your speeches to maximize your chances for rhetorical success.

*A*NALYZING AUDIENCES DEMOGRAPHICALLY

A **demographic analysis** is a study of the social and physical traits people hold in common. Many of these analyses are available publicly (e.g., public opinion polls distinguishing between men's and women's attitudes toward a set of presidential candidates), and many others can be located through research (e.g., government studies of the comparative costs of health care by age). Because you can directly observe many demographic characteristics of an audience just by looking at them, it's a good idea to begin an audience analysis with demographic factors. For most audiences, you can identify certain traits, at least generally: age, gender, education, some group memberships, and cultural and ethnic background.

Interrogating Demographic Categories

The competent speaker learns to ask questions about the demographic characteristics of audiences to see which, if any, are relevant to the speech he or she is delivering. Consider the following questions:

- *Age:* Will the expected listeners be primarily young, middle-aged, or elderly, or will the group more likely be of mixed ages? Is there a special relationship between age groups, such as parent/child or teacher/student? Is your speech likely to be more familiar and interesting to one age group than another?
- *Gender:* Will the listeners be primarily male or female, or will the group be split? Is this a topic likely to divide the audience along gender lines?
- *Education and experience:* How much will the listeners already know about the subject? Do their educational or experiential backgrounds allow them to grasp easily the essential ideas you want to convey?
- *Group membership:* Do these people belong to groups that represent specific experiences, attitudes, or identifiable values? Think how varied your answer to that question would be if you were talking to the Future Farmers of America, a Rotary International chapter in downtown Chicago, a League of Women Voters political platform meeting, or a social hour sponsored by the American Association of Retired Persons.
- *Cultural and ethnic background:* Do audience members predominantly belong to specific cultural or ethnic groups? Are those group identifications likely to be raised by your speech? A speech on California Proposition 187 (denying social and educational services to undocumented citizens of other countries) will make cultural-ethnic background relevant; a speech on where to find wild flowers for a fall bouquet will not.

Using Demographic Information

The importance of demographic analysis for you as a speaker doesn't lie in simply answering these questions. Rather, *the key is to decide if any of these demographic factors will affect your listeners' ability or willingness to understand and accept what you want to say.* That is, does a particular group affiliation, age, or gender factor have any *relevance* in the situation you face? Does it influence the rhetorical choices you make in selecting a subject and developing a central idea or claim?

For example, if you're addressing a group of citizens gathered to hear proposals for new low-income housing, you should consider all of the above questions. Your adaptation to this group of citizens might well assume that most of them will be young to middle-aged, many will be family members, and some will bring children to the meeting. Others in the audience will be elderly living on fixed incomes who are unable to afford more expensive housing. You also may assume, if you know something about the neighborhood, that they belong to one or more specific ethnic groups and that you'll have to relate to them in terms of their cultural backgrounds. You might also assume that some will be on Aid to Families with Dependent Children, others will be employed in low-paying jobs, some will be unemployed, and others will be in job training programs. With these demographic characteristics in mind, you will probably adapt to your listeners by using these strategies:

- avoid technical jargon;
- considering that children may be present, limit your remarks to the essential items;
- give examples demonstrating that you understand that the audience members are looking for low-income housing by necessity, not choice; and
- convey an attitude that shows you're genuinely interested in moving the project forward in order to improve their living conditions.

Demographic analysis can help you select and phrase your key ideas. It sensitizes you to crucial factors that may influence your choice of themes, examples, and other supporting material. If your analysis is cursory or incomplete, you decrease your chances of being understood and agreed with. Even when you're aware of the demographic characteristics, you may still create problems with your choice of language. Speaking to a group of African Americans, for example, and referring to them as "you people" and "your people" will demonstrate your lack of sensitivity or judgment (as Ross Perot discovered to his dismay when he addressed such an audience during the opening weeks of his 1992 presidential campaign). Appropriate use of demographic information can help you avoid such problems and convey a sensitive and caring attitude toward your listeners.

$\mathscr{A}$NALYZING AUDIENCES PSYCHOLOGICALLY

Dividing audience members into **psychological profiles** on the basis of their beliefs, attitudes, and values also helps you adapt to their needs and interests. This is especially important if you intend to influence your listeners' thinking on issues. You need to know what ideas they already accept before you try to alter their thoughts and actions. Sometimes careful demographic analysis will create such groupings naturally and provide clues about what your audience members are thinking. For example, you certainly expect that members of a songbird preservation club will favor state set-aside laws that give farmers who maintain uncut grass lands a tax break. Those club members can be expected to support the loss in tax revenue because of their commitment to actions that can increase the bird populations of their state. They likely oppose, on the national level, the selling off or leasing of federal lands to timber interests for the same reasons; Audubon Society members in fact fought congressional efforts in 1995 to do just that. At other times, when information is limited, you'll have to rely less upon demographic information and more upon direct data from psychological profiles. You'll have to explore beliefs, attitudes, values, and rhetorical visions in other ways.

Beliefs

The first task of psychological profiling is understanding an audience's beliefs. **Beliefs** are convictions about what is true or false. They arise from firsthand experiences, public opinion, supporting evidence, and authorities, or even from blind faith. For example, you might believe that "Quantitative methods is a difficult course," based on your own experience. At the same time, you may believe that quantitative methods is important to you because it's required for a bachelor's degree in business administration, which you want to pursue as a major. So although each of these beliefs is held for different reasons, both are considered true.

Beliefs that can be demonstrated are called **facts.** Others are personal opinions. Facts are generally supported by strong external evidence. When you say, "Research has proven that infant blue whales gain an average of ten pounds per day," you're very sure of that belief. While you may not know much about baby blue whales, you have confidence in the researchers who do. You hold facts with certainty because you have hard evidence to support them.

Opinions, however, are another matter. An opinion is a personal belief that may not be supported by strong external evidence. You may think that all cats are nasty animals because you have been scratched by cats or because you are allergic to them. However, your experience is limited. Many people like cats. Normally, you signal to your listeners when your beliefs are opinions. You might say, "It's my opinion that cats are worthless creatures," or "In my opinion, cats are vicious." In this way, you are telling your listeners that your evidence to support your claims is limited. Thus an opinion is a personal belief supported with less compelling external evidence than a fact.[2]

Since both facts and opinions are matters of belief, sometimes the difference between them is blurred. In colonial America, for instance, many people knew "for a fact" that regular bathing caused disease, just as their ancestors knew that the earth was flat and located at the center of the universe. If many people harbor similar opinions, those opinions may be taken for facts. It's important to recognize that opinions and facts are psychological constructs.

Once you have investigated your audience's beliefs, how can you use this information? You need to determine which beliefs will help you and which are obstacles to be overcome. Suppose that you oppose granting rights to gay personnel in the military. You want to convince your classmates to accept your point of view. Immediately you recognize the swirling controversy centering on this subject, about which people hold many different facts and opinions. First, consider what your listeners believe to be true. If they accept that gays already serve in the military and have served with distinction, then you may have to convince them that the presence of gays is disruptive. If, on the other hand, they think that the number of gays in the armed forces is negligible or that gay personnel do not make good soldiers, your job is much easier. Thus determining your audience's beliefs will help you to focus your ideas.

Some beliefs are variable, or relatively open to change, while others are fixed. **Fixed beliefs** are those that are highly resistant to change. They have been reinforced throughout a lifetime, making them central to one's thinking. Many early childhood beliefs, such as "Bad behavior will be punished" and "If you work hard, you'll succeed," are fixed. Some beliefs may harden in your mind and become resistant to change as you mature. For example, as you grow older, you may tend to vote for candidates from one political party and to purchase the same make of vehicles. The demographic variable of age may indicate to you that a more mature audience possesses fixed beliefs.

Some fixed beliefs can even be called **stereotypes**—the perception that all individuals in a group are the same. For example, one might believe "All police officers are honest" or "Rich people cheat on their taxes" or "Never trust a politician." The problem with stereotypes is that not all police officers are honest, rich people may pay the taxes they owe, and many politicians are trustworthy. Stereotypes ignore individual differences and exceptions to rules.

In contrast, **variable beliefs** are less well-anchored in your mind and experiences. You might enter college thinking you want to be a dental hygenist; however, after an instructor praises your abilities in a composition class, you may consider becoming a writer. Then you take a marketing class and find out you're good at planning advertising campaigns. This sort of self-discovery goes on as you take additional classes. Your beliefs about your talents change with your personal experiences. The same is true, of course, for members of your audience. One of your jobs in assessing beliefs is figuring out which of your listeners' beliefs relevant to your speech are variable: which of their beliefs can you change to get them to go along with your central idea or claim?

So, before you lay out your speeches, decide what beliefs are fixed (difficult to change) and which are variable (more easily altered). Use that kind of assessment to help you frame your speech and select particular arguments for it. Consider trying to convince your classmates that education is a waste of time. Most likely, their belief that education is valuable is so deeply fixed that you'd waste everyone's time trying to change it. Yet, you might have some luck getting them to change majors, take a class outside their majors, or even consider

FIGURE 4.1 The Varieties of Belief

	Beliefs of Fact	Beliefs of Opinion
Fixed Beliefs	Vegetarians live longer, healthier lives.	Broccoli tastes good.
Variable Beliefs	The quality of life I live depends on eating no meat.	It might be fun to learn to cook vegetarian meals.

changing colleges or universities to pursue their hopes in a more specialized atmosphere. In all these areas, you're likely to find vulnerable, variable beliefs.

Attitudes

The second task of psychological profiling is to identify audience attitudes. **Attitudes** are tendencies to respond positively or negatively to people, objects, or ideas. Attitudes are emotionally weighted. They express individual preferences and feelings such as, "I like my public speaking class," "Classical music is better than rap music," and "Cleveland is a beautiful city."

Attitudes often influence our behavior. One dramatic example of the strength of attitudes occurred when the Coca-Cola Corporation introduced new Coke, a refigured formula, with disastrous results. Although extensive blind taste tests indicated that people preferred new Coke's flavor, consumers reacted negatively because of their loyalty to the classic formula. Their attitudes controlled their purchasing behavior, and the corporation wisely "reintroduced" Coca-Cola Classic.[3]

As a speaker, you should consider the dominant attitudes of your listeners. Audiences may have attitudes toward you, your speech subject, and your speech purpose. Your listeners may think you know a lot about your topic, and they may be interested in learning more. This is an ideal situation. However, if they think you're not very credible and they resist learning more, you must deal with their attitudes. For example, if a speaker tells you that you can earn extra money in your spare time by selling computer communication programs, you may have several reactions. The thought of extra income from a part-time job is enticing. At the same time, you suspect that it might be a scam because so many programs are easily available at bookstores and because you don't know the speaker well. Relationships among your attitudes toward the speech topic, purpose, and speaker can be complex, and how you trace out those relationships in your own mind will influence your final decision about selling computer disks door-to-door.

Values

The third component of psychological profiling is understanding audience values. **Values** are relatively enduring conceptions of ultimate goods and evils in human relationships as well as the best and worse ways of pursuing those goods and evils. According to Milton Rokeach, such a definition recognizes that human beings have both **terminal values** and **instrumental values**—that is, values toward which they aspire as well as values about the best ways of living out those aspirations.[4] So, you and a friend might agree that "prosperity" is a value worth pursuing, yet disagree about how to best go after it. You might hold "efficiency" as an instrumental value, and hence look for ways to gain wealth quickly and with the least effort, while your friend might hold "caution" as an important instrumental value, and hence pursue wealth carefully, in a step-by-step fashion. Both of you can cite popular wisdom guiding your action—you, "A stitch in time saves nine," your friend, "Haste makes waste"—so it's not as though one of you is legitimated by society and the other is not. Rather, the two of you hold conflicting instrumental values even while pursuing the same terminal value.

Values are more foundational than beliefs and attitudes because they represent the broad conceptual categories that help attitudes and beliefs cohere. Values serve as the foundations for the beliefs and attitudes that cluster around them. For example, a person may hold a value such as "Life is sacred." That value can be expressed in multiple attitudes, including: "Abortion is wrong" or "Hunting is immoral." That value also may be expressed in beliefs such as "A fetus is a living human being with human rights," "Most Americans are opposed to abortion rights legislation," or "Religious authority ought to be respected on questions of morality."

Values, then, underlie an individual's particular attitudes and beliefs. Former president Ronald Reagan, regarded by many as "The Great Communicator," frequently appealed to values in his public speeches. He often combined values in a single sentence. In his 1980 acceptance speech, Reagan declared that people from all walks of life, regardless of political party, were bound together "in the community of shared values of family, work, neighborhood, peace, and freedom."[5] Family values, the importance of work to one's dignity, the neighborhood as a place where strangers learn to live together harmoniously, the hope for peace, and the celebration of freedom—the collection of values referenced in Reagan's simple statements demonstrates how easily we assemble multiple values into a single frame.

Because values exist in broad mixtures for most of us, as for Reagan, they're often thought about collectively as **value orientations** or **ideologies.** Value orientations are aggregations of values shared by large numbers of people. Over the last decade, Americans have discussed neoconservatism, welfarism, the new world order, Perot conservativism (and liberalism), Rainbow politics, me-ism, and a multitude of other value orientations or ideologies. They organize a great range of attitudes and serve as what Kenneth Burke called "terministic screens"—that is, as sieves that let some ideas through while filtering out others.[6] Being able to refer to value orientations held by audience members is a great advantage for speakers.

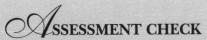

ASSESSMENT CHECK

When preparing your next speech, ask yourself:

- Have I taken into account the relevant audience factors—age, gender, education and experience, group memberships, cultural and ethnic background—when thinking about my purpose, central idea or claim, supporting materials, and mode of delivery?
- Have I attempted to find out which of my listeners' beliefs, attitudes, and values are likely to impact the ways they understand and evaluate my speech?

FIGURE 4.2   Belief, Attitude, and Value Clusters

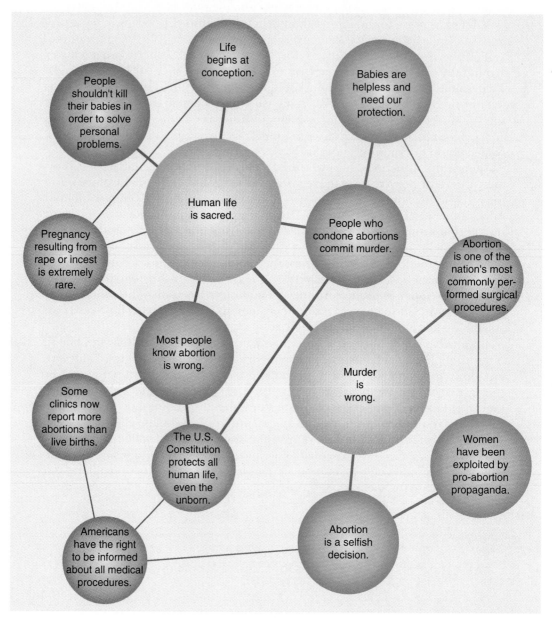

Rhetorical Visions

Closely related to value orientations are rhetorical visions. Ernest Bormann has been writing for a quarter of a century about the ways in which groups of people construct together a past, a present, and a future for themselves, what he calls a "dramatizing message" that creates a sense of group identity and self identity within those groups. That sense of identity comes from what he terms **symbolic convergence,** which is an interpretation of "events in terms of human action [that] allows us to assign responsibility, to praise or blame, to arouse and propitiate guilt, to hate and to love." The primary linguistic mechanism for achieving that convergence of ideas is the rhetorical vision.[7]

A **rhetorical vision** is "the unified putting-together of the various scripts which give the participants a broader view of things."[8] That putting-together may take place around a master analogy, such as Franklin Roosevelt's "New Deal" or Bill Clinton's "New Covenant." Even more potent, perhaps, is the narrative center of such visions: the story of the New Israel that the Puritan pioneers used to envision the society that they were building in seventeenth-century America, the story of the proletarian revolution and upheaval of the social world that lay at the base of Marxism, the vision of a new society created in love, creative suffering, and soul force that Martin Luther King, Jr., regularly described for his audiences. When all of an audience's existence is captured in such depictions, Bormann calls them "life-style rhetorical visions."[9]

Rhetorical visions of society and of listeners' lives within that society are regularly built by powerful speakers to renew or redirect an audience's political energies, to justify traditional courses of action, and to articulate new motivations for moving down new paths. They become the lenses through which members of a group are asked to view the world and to act within it. For example, notice the use of a rhetorical vision in this quotation from Henri Mann Morton, a Native American woman addressing the Colville and Okanogan National Forest conference on cultural diversity:

> I share your 1995 vision of a racially, culturally, gender-based, and humanistically representative workforce in which attitudes of respect, acceptance, and understanding are all pervasive.
>
> The vision I see is dedicated to a love of life, to a love of people, and love of the environment, particularly the land—the earth, she who is our grandmother, who must be revered and protected; she upon whom we walk and live; she who supports our feet and gives us life; she who nurtures us, her children. We all share this bond and as culturally diverse people we can draw strength from our rich cultural diversity.
>
> I would like to share with you this Cheyenne philosophical belief: "A nation is not conquered until the hearts of its women are on the ground. Then it is done, no matter how brave its warriors nor how strong its weapons."
>
> This shows the acceptance of, and respect for, the power of women. As equal partners of men, who too, have their own power, we then can see why the most powerful of all pairs in the universe are men and women working together.[10]

Notice how she intertwines a general vision of cultural diversity with a specific depiction, through quotation, of male-female union. The source of social life is seen in a feminine image of the grandmother and then is elaborated in the

Cheyenne aphorism. This allowed Morton's rhetorical vision to have breadth yet a unitary focus—on grandmother earth as the center of her dream.

Rhetorical visions are grand pieces of talk; they're not appropriate in every speech. Yet, knowing how to construct them, especially in actuative speeches where you're calling upon listeners to undertake major efforts, is an important skill you'll want to develop.

Using a Psychological Profile

After you've developed a profile of your audience's beliefs, attitudes, values, and rhetorical visions, how can you use this information? Three ways are obvious:

1. *Understanding your audience's beliefs, attitudes, values, and visions will help you to frame your ideas.* For example, if an audience generally believes that childhood is crucial to human development, you might be able to persuade them to volunteer for a day-care cooperative. If they espouse family values, your job should be even easier. On the other hand, if you have no indication that they're particularly interested in child development, then you'll have to establish the crucial nature of youth and its development before you can ask for volunteers.

2. *Understanding your audience's beliefs, attitudes, values, and rhetorical visions will help you select your supporting materials.* Statistics generally work well with highly educated audiences, less well with people who have had little education. People who are attitudinally and valuatively involved with a topic are much more likely to scrutinize the evidence you use than people who are not.[11] Churchgoers are likely to understand and appreciate a rhetorical vision in which divine intervention in human life is described.

3. *Understanding your audience's beliefs, attitudes, values, and rhetorical visions allows you to set realistic expectations as you plan your speech.* Not all audiences are equally amenable to change. You must always look for signs of resistance—deeply anchored beliefs, attitudes, and values—when designing a speech. It's not likely that you'll convert a Christian to Islam or a Muslim to Judaism in one shot. But, in a group of college sophomores, you are likely to find several people looking for a new major, in which case a speech on the usefulness and value of majoring in communication studies might prove most provocative.

ANALYZING THE SPEECH OCCASION

Sometimes analyzing the speech occasion is simple: You know you're attending a Speech Communication Association Speech Club meeting, you've been there often, and you know what's expected from you when asked to present a five- to ten-minute report on sports information internship possibilities in your city. At other times, the occasions are complex, with rules and traditions governing what can be said, who can talk, how and when people can talk, and in what manner you must treat other people. While you may not have thought much about it, "an occasion" can control how you behave when talking to others.

An "occasion" is a set of activities that occurs in a predetermined time and place to fulfill collective purposes for and by people who have been taught the special meanings of those activities.

As we've suggested, an **occasion** is a set of activities that occurs in a time and place set aside expressly to fulfill the collective goals of people who have been taught the special meanings of those activities. Let us unpack that definition: *In a time and place* . . . Regular occasions, such as religious services, usually occur at special times (Fridays, Saturdays, Sundays) in special places (mosques, synagogues, churches). Special events, such as political conventions, happen at specific times in halls designed to accommodate the large number of people present and decorated to capture the value orientation and rhetorical vision of the party. These times and places take on special meanings of their own. Sunday morning in the United States is such a special time that few activities other than churchgoing are scheduled then. The places where justice is handed down—courtrooms—are specially designed to emphasize permanence (made of marble), spaciousness (high ceilings in oversized rooms), elevation (the bench raised above all other chairs so the judge looks down on everyone else), and impartiality (a black robe to hide the individualized features of the judge). As such, courtrooms have come to be known as quiet, decorous places where respect is shown to all parties.

Fulfilling collective goals . . . Most important, perhaps, people design occasions to meet the particular needs of particular groups. For example, worship (church), justice (courts), passage to adulthood (bar mitzvahs, confirmations, debutante balls, and commencement ceremonies), remembrance of basic values or heroes (monument dedications and holidays such as Memorial Day), and recognition of leadership and power (inaugurals and coronations). These are all activities in which individuals tend to participate as part of a group; a one-person ceremony or dedication doesn't mean much. A group ceremony does because it recognizes the importance of those belonging to the group, its claims upon its membership, and the group's power to confirm status upon people.

Special meanings . . . You do not enter the world knowing how to pray, to cheer, to dedicate, to mourn with others, or to inaugurate. Those are all *social* activities you must learn, either through instruction or through imitation.[12] Knowing and understanding what is expected of you and others are signs of belonging to a particular group. Outsiders do not possess this knowledge; insiders do.

The purposes, complexity, and even formality of occasions vary widely. A presentation to your public relations club may be an informal yet important occasion; other occasions, such as funerals and political conventions, are much more formal. No matter what their formality, however, all occasions are governed by *rules* (do's and don'ts), by *roles* (duties or functions that different people perform), and judgments of *competency* (assessments about how well people play their parts). Occasions normally carry with them rather precise expectations of what will happen, to whom it will happen, who will participate, and how they will take part.[13]

A speech occasion is thus every bit as demanding as any other social or political event. Like other occasions, speech occasions are characterized by rules, expected roles, and judgments of competency—in other words, by audience expectations. Those expectations take two forms: general audience and specific audience. **General audience expectations** are those associated with any public speaker working in a particular society. In the United States this includes such rules as speakers shouldn't mumble; the larger the room, the larger your gestures should be; trusted speakers look audience members right in the eyes; an excessive number or randomness of gestures detracts from your message. Not all of these rules would hold in every society; they're the products of this society. **Specific audience expectations** arise from habitual speaking practices in particular settings. Coaches are expected to be intense at halftime; preachers are expected to break eye contact with congregations when praying or talking directly to God; insurance sales people are trained to ask questions of their listeners in the middle of their presentations ("How does this sound to you?" "Are these problems you face?" "Doesn't this make sense, given how young your children are?"). In some situations, you're expected to be an informer (orientation meeting); in others, a comic (an after-dinner speech honoring a close friend); in others, a persuader (a real estate office).

As you face such audience expectations, you have three choices:

1. *Ignore the rules.* Sometimes, a free spirit—a David Letterman or a Howard Stern—can ignore the usual rules for public speech and get away with it. Most of us, however, aren't nearly as interesting as they are. If you break too many rules, you yourself could be broken—by your audience who thinks you don't know or care about their traditions.
2. *Cave in.* Equally dangerous is just to accept all the rules, even if they go against your beliefs and backgrounds. If you visit a family with an overbearing father, no one ever crosses him, and if you feel insulted by something he says about you, do you cave in and say nothing? If so, the rules for speaking have stifled you.
3. *Adapt to the rules.* There are good ways, of course, for disagreeing with the man. You can verbally recognize his place in the family but then also note the injury his remark has done to you, defending yourself from an unfair attack. You can work within his aura of family position even while making your point if you're very, very careful.

Audience expectations, in other words, should be seen as opportunities for you to find ways into people's minds, not as barriers that will stop communication. For that to happen, you must learn to read occasions—to interpret their impact upon your speaking.

USING AUDIENCE ANALYSIS IN SPEECH PREPARATION

Neither demographic analysis nor psychological profiling is an end in itself, nor will merely thinking about the speech occasion produce foolproof speech

HOW TO
ANALYZE THE SPEECH OCCASION

- *What is the nature and purpose of the occasion?* Make sure the subject and purpose of your speech relate to the purpose of the meeting. If your speech is part of a series or will follow others' speeches, find out the other speakers' approaches and decide how you will distinguish yours. If you are facing a **captive audience** (a group that is forced to attend), make an extra effort to show the significance of your subject to them.

- *What are the prevailing rules or customs?* Find out what customs are accepted in the speech situation: Is there a fixed program into which your speech must fit? Will listeners expect a formal speaking manner? An expression of respect for a tradition or concept? Also, find out whether there are more specific rules: for example, the audience at the Friars Club in New York expects the speaker to mercilessly "roast" (verbally abuse) the object of the speech, but in a good-natured way.

- *What are the physical conditions?* Will you speak outdoors or indoors? Will the audience sit or stand? How large will the room be? Will you need to bring your own audiovisual equipment? If the conditions will negatively affect your presentation, consider moving your audience closer together or helping them change locations to avoid excessive heat or moisture. If outside noise interferes, speak more loudly and distinctly than you usually would.

- *What events precede and follow your speech?* If you will speak right after a meal or at the end of a long program, acknowledge your listeners' reduced interest and potential drowsiness: give them time to stretch and otherwise get comfortable. If you are the "warm-up" speaker, be careful to follow the customs and rules of the occasion. Consider the character of any other items on the program to get a sense of how the group functions, perhaps even getting clues about its basic values.

preparation strategies. Rather, you carry out these twin analyses to discover what might affect the reception of you and your message. You're searching for relevant factors that can affect the audience's attitudes toward you, your subject, and your purpose. These factors, in turn, should guide your rhetorical choices with respect to subject matter, themes covered, language used, and the appropriateness of visual aids in the speech setting. What you learn about your listeners and their expectations through systematic investigation has the potential to affect every aspect of your speech—right down to the way you deliver your thoughts.

Audience Targeting: Setting Realistic Goals

There are few occasions in which the choice of general speech purpose—to inform, to persuade or actuate, to entertain—is problematic. Once you have passed beyond this step, you need to determine what you can hope to accomplish with a particular audience in the time available. As you think about **audience targeting,** five considerations are relevant: your specific purpose, the audience's areas of interest, their capacity to act, their willingness to act, and the degree of change you can expect. While what appears to be a reasonable or realistic aim may fall short of your actual goal, working within these parameters will make it far easier for you to obtain audience support for your ideas. Moving too far beyond what is realistic will, in general terms, increase the risk that your listeners won't follow you, even if they're in sympathy with the thrust of your remarks.

Your Specific Purpose. Suppose you have a part-time job with your college's Cooperative Education Office. You're familiar with its general goals and the programs, and you have sufficient personal interest to speak about these to other campus groups. What you have discovered about different audiences should help you determine appropriate specific purposes for each. If you were to talk to a group of incoming first-year students at new student orientation, for example, you would know these things beforehand:

- They probably know little or nothing about the functions of a cooperative education office (they have few, if any, fixed beliefs about the office).
- They probably are predisposed to look favorably on cooperative education once they know how it functions (given their own career aspirations).
- They probably are, at their stage of life and educational level, more concerned with practical issues such as selecting their courses, seeing an advisor, registering, and learning about basic degree requirements (whether a foreign language is required for English majors; whether a calculus course is required for business majors). While they want to be well-positioned to make the most of their junior or senior year, learning specifics about what they can do "if and when" is not a high priority at this time. Hence, they may require external motivation (provided by your arguments and illustrations) to develop interest in the subject.

- They are likely to see you as an authoritative speaker, especially if you're introduced (or introduce yourself) as a staff member from Cooperative Education, and are willing to listen to what you have to say.

Given these audience considerations, you probably should keep your presentation fairly general; explain the principal functions of Cooperative Education and review the prerequisites that must be met in order to be qualified (for example, having selected a major and completed a set number of courses). Stress the ways that a cooperative education experience can give them an early start on a possible career or serve to introduce them to new career possibilities, all while earning academic credit. You might phrase your specific purpose as follows: "To brief incoming first-year students on the range of service offered by the Cooperative Education Office." That orientation would include a basic description of each service and a general appeal to use the services to make some curricular decisions.

Were you instead to talk about this subject to a group of college juniors, you would address the audience differently. You would know these things beforehand:

- They are more likely to be aware of the general goals and programs of the Cooperative Education Office, but they may be misinformed or uninformed about details.
- They have generally positive feelings about the advantages of cooperative education, but some may be unsure of whether it's well suited to their major or career interest, or aren't sure they meet the prerequisite conditions for enrollment.
- They tend to value education pragmatically—that is, for how it's prepared them to earn a "decent living."
- They may view your qualifications with somewhat more skepticism since you're one of their peers.

Given these factors, you should be much more specific in some areas. You should describe your own recent experience as a "co-op" student or, if you have yet to enroll in a co-op program, those of students who have completed the experience. First-person stories will help convince the audience that a wide variety of students can avail themselves of this opportunity and that all they need do is check with the office to see if they can qualify. In addition to fleshing out particulars about the "what" of cooperative education (for example, can you enroll if the placement site is two hours away in your hometown, and you plan to enroll during summer session?), you will need to spend time on the "how": What steps should students take if they're interested in enrolling? Should they pursue employers on their own? If they know an employer, can he or she be involved? By presenting a variety of narratives demonstrating the breadth of the experience, you also erase any doubts about your expertise. You might phrase your dominant specific purpose in this way: "To inform juniors about the benefits gained by enrolling in Midstate University's Cooperative

Education Program." Your subordinate purposes might include "Demonstrating the ease with which students can enroll in the program" and "Illustrating that almost every student may be served."

Areas of Audience Interest.   You can use both demographic analysis and psychological profiling to help you decide what ideas will interest your listeners. This is critical in narrowing your topic choice and choosing specific ideas to develop. Suppose you know something about communicating with people from diverse cultures. An audience of new management trainees for an international firm would be very interested in hearing about how communication may differ as one moves from a Japanese to a Latin American market; an audience of mid-level managers for the same company could want to know more, if only to assess for themselves whether a new training program should be put on-line; an audience of vice-presidents and regional managers would want to know how insensitivity to communication across cultures may affect employee morale and company productivity and profits.

Sometimes, however, you will want to create a new set of interests in an audience. For example, you might want to inform a group of eastern college students about the exciting new directions taken by southwestern artists. Some audience members may already have more than a passing interest in art, while others are relatively uninformed and uninterested. For those already interested, you can draw connections to the kinds of painting and sculpture that is invigorating art in southwestern states. For those without interest, you may work from the general value they place on broadening their horizons. You also might underscore your interest by being energetic in presenting the ideas and by using two or three prints that will enable the audience to see what you're talking about. For this speech, you might phrase your central idea as "Knowing more about southwestern art will expand your interests in positive ways." Phrasing the central idea in this way ties the subject to a more general interest in expanding one's experiences and knowledge.

The Audience's Capacity to Act.   As noted in the section on narrowing speech subjects, limit your request to an action that lies within your listeners' range of authority. Don't ask them to accomplish the impossible. To demand of a group of college students that they take direct action to stop the killing of innocent dolphins is unrealistic, especially if you're in the corn belt of the United States. However, you can ask them to boycott tuna and other products associated with tuna harvesting that are not marked "dolphin safe." You can also urge them to write their local congressional representatives to implore their support for more stringent fishing regulations protecting dolphins.

Sometimes, an audience analysis reveals that different segments of your audience have varying capacities to undertake actions. In that case, you'll want to address those segments separately in the action step of your speech. For example, in addressing an open meeting of the city council on why the city should sponsor a major fund-raising road race, you'll want to target different subgroups with different calls to action:

Speakers must determine what they can expect to accomplish with a particular audience in the time they have available.

- *Council members:* "Pass a special appropriation to the recreation services budget that funds a part-time race director and publicity chair."
- *Potential race sponsors:* "Support the race by contributing money, food, and prizes for the various race categories."
- *Runners:* "Use your contacts at other marathons, 10K and 5K races, and charity walks to bring out-of-towners into this event."

By using this method, each call for action is suited to the range of authority and talents possessed by each subgroup among the listeners.

The Audience's Willingness to Act.   Not only must you be concerned with audience authority, but also with audience will. You'll need to assess the degree to which listeners are willing to put themselves on the line on behalf of your ideas or proposals. For example, a speech soliciting blood donors has a better chance of success when given at a fraternity or sorority meeting about service projects than it does in your speech classroom. People attending the meeting are committed to the idea of public service or they wouldn't have come to listen. On the other hand, people in your classroom are strongly aware that you're "practicing" public address; hence, they're usually more distanced from you, more attuned to the quality of your appeals and style of speaking and less caught up in the spirit of advice-following. They are difficult listeners to reach because they hear so many appeals from fellow students during the term.

Your assessment of an audience's will or desire may influence the wording of your claim. Addressing a fraternity or sorority or a panhellenic council comprising both groups, you might phrase a claim in this fashion: "Running a campuswide blood drive is the best service project our organization can undertake this semester." Dealing with the same subject in your speech classroom would suggest a different claim: "You should give blood as a matter of personal commitment to human beings in need." The first version acknowledges the purpose of the meeting (identifying a service project) and acknowledges the willingness of the listeners to act on some project. The second version plays down or ignores the occasion (classroom speech), because that occasion doesn't encourage listeners to take your advice. Instead, the wording personalizes the subject, allowing the speaker to tug on at least a few heart strings. Thus, willingness to act is usually related to listeners' expectations in a situation and should be taken into account when you phrase your goals or purposes.

Degrees of Change.   Finally, as suggested earlier, you must be realistic in targeting the degree of change you can reasonably hope for. In an informative context, there is a natural limit on how much information you can present about the topic, due to the time limits and the complexity of the subject. For instance, it would take more than a five-minute speech to do justice to the controversy surrounding the changes in saltwater fishing stock. Demographic factors such as age, work experience, and educational development will influence how much change you can effect. Also, deciding whether the information is new or is already known will influence how much material you can cover in a single speech. Talking to lobster fishermen off the coast of Maine is one thing; addressing a group of Iowa farmers is quite another when you're deciding what is known and understood about saltwater fishing.

How intensely can you motivate your listeners to react positively to your ideas or proposals for action? If your listeners are strongly opposed to downtown renovation, a single speech, no matter how eloquent, probably won't reverse their opinions. One attempt may only neutralize some of their objections; to aim at some rather than all objections is a more realistic goal. If your prespeech analysis indicates that your listeners vehemently oppose locating a work-release prison facility in your community, you can probably persuade many of them to contribute funds to the defeat of the proposal, to work long hours as volunteers at a variety of activities, such as picketing, lobbying, and telephone marathons; however, if they're only moderately opposed to the facility, you might ask for a small monetary donation and no actual time commitment.

In other words, audience analysis should help you determine how to phrase your specific purpose, central ideas, and claims for maximum effectiveness. The understanding you gain about your audience in this manner also gives you a more realistic expectation of the degree of change possible in behavior, beliefs, attitudes, values, and commitments to action.

Audience Segmentation: Selecting Dominant Ideas and Appeals

The preceding demographic analysis and psychological profiling of relevant beliefs, attitudes, and values focus on targeting your audience as a group. Keep in mind, however, that no matter how people are crowded together, arranged in rows, or reached electronically, they're still individuals. Although influenced by culture and society, each person holds unique beliefs, attitudes, and values. Each is a unique product of experience and thought. You also function as a unique individual when approaching the audience as a speaker.

Ideally, it would be most effective if you could approach each listener one-on-one. Sometimes you can, but such communication is time consuming and inefficient in matters of broad public concern. Imagine for a minute the president of this country talking to each one of us individually. If you assume 160 million adults and five minutes per person, it would take 300 million minutes or over 570 years of nonstop talking! Rather than take that approach, it's no wonder politicians have resorted to television to broadcast their messages simultaneously to millions of viewers. Candidates have found that they can simulate the atmosphere of personal conversation through their delivery and choice of language. In so doing, they can begin to think of listeners as individuals hearing the message in the privacy of their homes.

They and their advisors have adopted a technique long familiar to advertisers: audience segmentation. **Audience segmentation** is a matter of dividing a mass audience into subgroups, or "target populations," that hold common attitudes, beliefs, values, or demographic characteristics. The earlier illustration of addressing council members, sponsors, and runners in terms of their different capacities to act is an instance of such segmentation. A typical college-student audience might be segmented by academic standing (freshmen through seniors), academic majors (art through zoology), classroom performance (A through F), and even extracurricular activities (officer training programs, varsity sports, recreational clubs, political groups).

Accurately Identifying Subgroups/Segments. Identifying subgroups must be accurate and relevant to the speech purpose and occasion. This will not only allow you to better phrase your appeals, but it will help you avoid irritating your listeners unnecessarily. A speaker who began, "Because all you girls are interested in efficient cooking, today I want to talk about four ways a food processor will save you time in the kitchen," would probably alienate two subgroups in the audience. The females probably would be irritated by being called "girls," and by the assertion that all females are interested in cooking; the males who cook also would be offended by having been excluded. The appeal would be better phrased "Because everyone who cooks is interested in efficiency. . . ." This appeal aims at the proper audience segment—those who like to cook.

In finding ways to talk about controversial issues, be sure to avoid stereotyped references to people and to groups and avoid blanket condemnation of groups of people. When possible, work around controversial issues; when that is not possible, know the risks ahead of time and decide to what extent you wish to or must confront specific subgroups that will be present in your audience.

Selecting Relevant Psychological Statements. Audience segmentation should also help you identify statements of belief, attitudes, and values to include in your speech. If you can accurately identify the relevant subgroups, you can include psychological appeals for each in your speech, thereby greatly increasing the personal appeal and potential effectiveness of your message.

Suppose that you are to give a speech to a local Rotary Club about the desirability of their funding a scholarship program for local students. Because Rotary Clubs International generally are made up of the professional and business men and women of a community, you should be able to segment the audience and to give each value-based reasons for supporting the program. Your claim ("This Rotary Club should support a community-based scholarship fund.") can be followed by statements based on audience segmentation:

- *For medical professionals:* "Well-educated people take better care of themselves, are in better positions to have insurance, and are more likely to seek early treatment for serious health problems than less well-educated people."
- *For community business people:* "Well-educated citizens contribute more to the financial resources of the community as investors, property owners, and skilled employees."
- *For educators:* "Scholarships provide great motivation and a high level of hope for students who don't automatically think of going on to college after high school."
- *For social services personnel:* "A community-based scholarship program is a sign of community health and vitality—a mechanism for bringing some healing self-esteem into the lives of children with talent, even if they're from troubled homes."

While this segmentation has not used every conceivable value term, the procedure should be clear: (1) Think through possible reasons people might accept your claim because of values they hold, and (2) use a value-sensitive vocabulary to phrase your actual appeals for acceptance. There is an implicit reference to medical ethics based on serving humankind, to business commitments, to financial responsibility and success, and to the social service profession's commitment to growth. Thus, audience analyses, in combination with audience segmentation, are valuable tools for selecting your main lines of appeal and argument.

Choosing Among Valuative Appeals. Finally, as you might guess, audience segmentation will help you select a valuative vocabulary for your speeches. Even informative speeches, as we will discuss more fully later, need to contain appeals to audience interests. You can use a **valuative vocabulary** to motivate different segments of the audience to listen to and accept your information. For a class demonstration speech, you might introduce your speech in this way:

> Today I want to teach you three basic techniques of Oriental cooking—cutting meats and vegetables, using spices, and quick-cooking your food in a wok. If you learn these techniques, you'll expand your range of expertise in the kitchen [*personal value*], you'll save money on your food and energy bills [*economic value*], you'll prepare more-than-satisfying meals for your friends [*social value*], and you'll prepare more nutritious, healthful meals for everyone [*pragmatic value*].

With that statement, you give your audience four different reasons for listening and will have a good chance of appealing to every listener. If you want, you also can tell them that the meals will be beautiful, thereby adding an *aesthetic value* to your set of appeals.

Creating a Unifying Rhetorical Vision

An audience still is an audience, and ultimately must act together. Therefore, even though you can individualize appeals to particular segments, ideally you should find a vision—a big picture—that brings all the segments back into a whole. One of two approaches is traditionally used. When addressing the 1988 Democratic National Convention, Jesse Jackson used the *additive method,* reassembling the segments but allowing each sub-audience to keep it own identity. After describing how his grandmother in Greenville, South Carolina, sewed together old, mismatched pieces of cloth to make blankets, he admonished his audience to do likewise:

> Now, Democrats, we must build such a quilt. Farmers, you seek fair prices and you are right, but you cannot stand alone. Your patch is not big enough. Workers, you fight for fair wages. You are right. But your patch, labor, is not big enough. Women, you seek comparable worth and pay equity. You are right. But your patch is not big enough. Women, mothers, you seek Head Start and day care and prenatal care on the front side of life, you're right, but your patch is not big enough.
>
> Students, you seek scholarships. You are right. But your patch is not big enough. Blacks and Hispanics, when we fight for civil rights, we are right, but our patch is not big enough. Gays and lesbians, when you fight against discrimination and for a cure for AIDS, you are right, but your patch is not big enough. Conservatives and progressives, when you fight for what you believe, right-wing, left-wing, hawk, dove—you are right, from your point of view, but your point of view is not enough.
>
> But don't despair. Be as wise as grandmama. Pool the patches and the pieces together, bound by a common thread. When we form a great quilt of

unity and common ground, we'll have the power to bring about health care and housing and jobs and education and hope to our nation. We the people can win.[14]

Jesse Jackson thus added the segments of his audience together, sewing their patches into a large, Democratic quilt. Using the additive method, he enabled each segment to retain its identity in the rhetorical vision.

The *integrative method* for constructing a rhetorical vision strips the individual segments of their identities, attempting to make everyone feel like everyone else. When using such a technique, the speaker hopes to make the audience members feel as one. This was the tactic used by Louis Farrakhan at the "Million Man March" to Washington in the fall of 1995. He built his final appeal around a pledge, asking the audience to forget about their former activities and to become new men, committed to each other and to their society. The pledge was long. Here is the opening:

> Now, brothers, I want you to take this pledge. When I say I, I want you to say I, and then say your name. I know that there's so many names, but I want you to shout your name out so that the ancestors can hear it.
>
> Take this pledge with me. Say with me please, I, say your name, pledge that from this day forward I will strive to love my brother as I love myself. I, say your name, from this day forward will strive to improve myself spiritually, morally, mentally, socially, politically, and economically for the benefit of myself, my family, and my people. I, say your name, pledge that I will strive to build businesses, build houses, build hospitals, build factories, and then to enter international trade for the good of myself, my family, and my people. I, say your name, pledge that from this day forward I will never raise my hand with a knife or a gun to beat, cut, or shoot any member of my family or any human being, except in self-defense.
>
> I, say your name, pledge from this day forward I will never abuse my wife by striking her, disrespecting her for she is the mother of my children and the producer of my future. I, say your name, pledge that from this day forward I will never engage in the abuse of children, little boys, or little girls for sexual gratification. But I will let them grow in peace to be strong men and women for the future of our people.[15]

When rhetorical visions are well crafted, they surround an audience, helping it feel like an integrated group. When listeners are caught up in the same vision, they can be forged into a working unit.

Sample Audience Analysis

In this chapter we have surveyed various factors that you will consider as you analyze your audience and occasion. If you work systematically, these choices

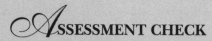

ASSESSMENT CHECK

When preparing your next speech, ask yourself:

- Have I thought carefully about the nature and purpose of the speech occasion? What customs and conditions are likely to impact on how the audience understands and reacts to my speech?
- Have I figured out ways to target specific appeals to each significant segment of the audience?
- Can I create a rhetorical vision that will encompass both my purpose and my listeners' understandings of the world?

will become clearer. Suppose you were invited by a community group to increase their understanding of AIDS (acquired immunodeficiency syndrome). You might prepare the following comprehensive analysis of your audience as you prepare your speech:

UNDERSTANDING AIDS

I. General description of speech

   A. *General purpose:* To persuade.

   B. *Specific purpose:* To prove to members of a local political action caucus that AIDS poses a health threat even to this community.

II. *General description of the audience:* The political action caucus is a community group whose function is to promote political consciousness and action in the community. It consists of varied membership, including local homemakers, business owners, the mayor, the chair of the state Republican Committee, and approximately one dozen interested listeners. A synopsis of the monthly meeting is broadcast over local radio stations and included on the editorial page of the local newspaper (reaching a large secondary audience).

III. Audience analysis

   A. Demographic analysis
      1. *Age:* Most of the individuals attending the meeting are between 30 and 65. Except when I urge the audience to attend future events, age is probably not an important factor. I am significantly younger than members of my audience (21), and I will need to enhance my credibility as a speaker to compensate for my relative youth and inexperience.

2. *Gender:* The caucus is a mixed group with slightly more women than men. Given the topic, the audience may initially have the attitude that AIDS only affects people who engage in high-risk sexual behaviors.

3. *Education:* Approximately one-third of the listeners have completed B.A. degrees in various fields including political science, pharmacy, nursing, home economics, and accounting. All but four of the remaining members have finished high school; several have taken college courses. While several health professionals in the audience are familiar with disease history and control, most listeners are acquainted with the topic only through media coverage.

4. *Group membership:* All listeners are politically active and registered voters. Although they do not necessarily share party affiliation, they all value participation in the democratic process.

5. *Cultural and ethnic background:* Ethnic background is primarily European. Most consider AIDS to be a problem associated with minorities, including homosexual males, hemophiliacs, and intravenous drug users. All members of the caucus were either born or raised in this small, midwestern community whose small-business economy is agriculturally based.

B. Psychological profile

1. *Factual beliefs:* Anyone who contracts AIDS likely will die of it; there is no cure. The disease is confined primarily to the East and West coasts. The only local resident to die from AIDS had visited New York—it is assumed that he contracted the disease during his visit.

2. *Opinions:* Homosexual behavior is morally wrong and should not be condoned.

3. *Attitudes:* Members of the caucus probably consider me naive and idealistic. While they were surprised by the recent news of the AIDS death of a community resident, they are probably not very concerned about the spread of the disease because they don't consider themselves likely targets of it.

IV. *Values:* They are committed to the democratic process and take pride in community political involvement at the state and national levels. They see themselves as common people—"the heart of America"—fulfilling the American dream. Caucus members often point to community progress in civil rights issues, general educational reforms, and high voter turnout during elections.

With this prespeech audience analysis completed, the next steps in preparing the speech are clearer. The audience analysis points to the kinds of supporting materials needed. For instance, you need to supply accurate facts about the disease, especially its impact on those who are not considered to be at risk. You need to explain how AIDS can disrupt employees' lives, corporate health policies, and the community health care system. You can also heighten your listeners' understanding of the disease through examples of individuals who have contracted AIDS. To locate this information, you should do the following:

1. Use the library's computerized database to investigate the history of AIDS in the United States.
2. Find out projected levels of AIDS infection for the future.
3. Identify the populations that are currently infected by AIDS: men, women, and children.
4. Read local newspaper articles concerning the community resident who died of AIDS.
5. If possible, interview community residents who knew the local AIDS victim.
6. Search out examples of people who tested HIV-positive, including schoolchildren and heterosexual residents of midwestern towns.
7. Develop a "typical" disease profile, detailing what occurs in the body and how the body copes with the disease.
8. Interview local medical authorities to discover the kinds of treatment currently used and the chances of AIDS infection occurring in the community.
9. Prepare a list of other midwestern communities that have held community discussions or adopted measures regarding AIDS.
10. Anticipate and list potential questions and objections to the topic.

While this list seems extensive, it is likely to yield useful information because it is a *specific* rather than a *general* search for facts on AIDS. With the demographic and psychological profile of the audience completed and research compiled, you can adapt your ideas and appeals to your audience. You might include the following main ideas in your speech:

1. Stress the listeners' commitment to the welfare of the community and nation, their belief in the democratic process, and their belief in the rights of citizens in minority groups. Encourage their feelings of pride in previous civic accomplishments and challenge them to face the AIDS crisis. In other words, show them that it is in their best interests to confront and discuss unpopular issues for the well-being of the entire community.
2. Make it clear that this is not simply a moral issue. While recognizing the importance of traditional national values, also stress the practical importance of treating disease, regardless of moral issues. Use projections of future infection rates to emphasize that everyone's health may be affected if the disease is allowed, through ignorance or neglect, to spread unchecked.
3. Point out that other midwestern communities have debated the issues involved as they were faced with enrolling infected children in local schools and treating AIDS patients in local hospitals. Emphasize predictions of future infection affecting broader populations. Overcome audience apathy and hostility by encouraging members to discuss the disease further.

4. Push for an open forum for continued discussion on the issue rather than demanding immediate commitments or political action.

5. Recognize the group's excellent efforts at political reform in local projects. Remember that listeners have taken the time to attend, and their commitment should be recognized. Stress the farsightedness of the group on difficult issues such as this one. Point out that, in a democracy, fair play requires that each side be given equal time and consideration before anyone reaches a final decision. Aim the bulk of the speech at gaining approval for open-minded discussions. ■

*C*HAPTER SUMMARY

Public speaking is *audience* and *occasion centered*. The primary goal of audience analysis is to discover the aspects of listeners' demographic and psychological backgrounds that are relevant to your speech purposes:

- *Demographic analysis:* the age, gender, education, group membership, cultural and ethnic background of the audience
- *Psychological analysis:* the beliefs, attitudes, values, and rhetorical visions of the audience.

Once you can profile your listeners, you can adapt your speech purposes and ideas to them.

Analysis of the occasion complements that of the audience. An occasion is a set of activities that occurs in a time and place set aside for the express purpose of fulfilling collective goals for and by people who have been taught the special meanings of those activities. You should attempt to analyze your speech occasion's rules for speaking, habitual roles played by both speaker and audience, and the standards of competency that will be applied to your speech.

The analysis of both audience and occasion will help you with *audience targeting:* deciding on realistic specific purposes, areas of audience interest, the audience's capacity and willingness to act, and the degree of change you can expect. Your analysis will also aid you in *audience segmentation:* creating basic appeals that accurately identify subgroups, applying psychological statements that are relevant to their lives, and using appropriate valuative appeals.

The ability to adapt your speech to the needs of a particular audience and occasion is the mark of a competent public speaker.

*K*EY TERMS

attitudes (p. 90)

audience centered (p. 85)

audience segmentation (p. 104)

audience targeting (p. 99)

beliefs (p. 87)

captive audience (p. 98)

demographic analysis (p. 85)

facts (p. 88)

*A*SSESSMENT ACTIVITIES

1. Using the Sample Audience Analysis near the end of this chapter, as a checklist, respond to each item for your next speech and turn it in two class periods before you're due to speak. Your instructor will examine and comment upon it before you speak to be sure that you've maximized your chances to succeed.

2. Study the occasion of presenting a speech in your classroom. Working either in groups or alone (depending upon your instructor's instructions), answer the following questions: (a) What are the prevailing rules and customs you must follow in this classroom? (b) What physical conditions affect the way you speak? (c) How do speech days work? (What will precede and follow your speech? Are there any special challenges presented in the ways speech days are run in this class?)

    After you've answered the questions, write three things you will do to adapt to this situation.

3. Secure a copy of Minister Louis Farrakhan's speech, either from the Information Arcade at the University of Iowa Libraries or from CNN U.S. News. (Both are on the Internet.) (a) Identify beliefs, attitudes, values, and visions that you think are hostile to those of the white viewers of that day. (b) Note how, if at all, Minister Farrakhan narrows the gaps between his beliefs, attitudes, and values and those of his white audience. (c) Name or label the tactics he used, discussing briefly in what kinds of situations you can use them.

*R*EFERENCES

1. Donald C. Bryant, *Rhetorical Dimensions in Criticism* (Baton Rouge: Louisiana State University Press, 1973), 19.

2. See Henry Z. Scheele, "Ronald Reagan's 1980 Acceptance Address: A Focus on American Values," *Western Journal of Speech Communication* 48 (1984): 51–61.

3. The relationships between beliefs and attitudes and between attitudes and behaviors are complex because while attitudes often are defined in terms of beliefs, there are no guarantees that they are consistently associated with each other, especially in the ways we act. So, attitudes often are defined as the evaluative dimension of beliefs, as in "In 1984 Ronald Reagan tried to convince

Germany to accept Pershing II missiles as a defensive weapon [belief statement], and that was a morally bad policy [attitudinal statement]." Yet, you know in your everyday life that beliefs and attitudes can float apart. You might know that each year the number of abortions in the U.S. is increasing, yet your attitude can vary depending upon whether you think about that fact in terms of women having the right to control their own bodies or in terms of overly casual thoughts about sex and death. Even worse, you might have a set of relatively clear attitudes, say about lying, and yet your own behavior might not reflect them all of the time; you might actually lie sometimes in spite of your attitude toward lying as immoral. Do not, in other words, think of attitudes' relationships with either beliefs or behaviors as direct or clear. For further discussion of definitions and relationships, see James B. Stiff, *Persuasive Communication* (New York: Guilford Press, 1994), 10–22.

4. Milton Rokeach, *The Nature of Human Values* (New York: Free Press, 1973).

5. See the analysis of Reagan's multiple values in Henry Z. Scheele, "Ronald Reagan's 1980 Acceptance Address: A Focus on American Values," *Western Journal of Speech Communication* 48 (1984): 51–61.

6. See Kenneth Burke's ideas on terministic screens in his *Lanaguage as Symbolic Action: Essays on Life, Literature, and Method* (Berkeley: University of California Press, 1966). For a clear discussion of value orientations, see Malcolm O. Sillars, *Messages, Meanings, and Culture: Approaches to Communication Criticism* (New York: HarperCollins, 1991), ch. 7, "Value Analysis: Understanding Culture in Value Systems."

7. The idea of the rhetorical vision was introduced in Ernest G. Bormann, "Fantasy and Rhetorical Vision: The Rhetorical Criticism of Social Reality," *Quarterly Journal of Speech* 58 (1972): 396–407; the notion of symbolic convergence was first developed in his "The Symbolic Convergence Theory of Communication and the Creation, Raising, and Sustaining of Public Consciousness," in *The Jensen Lectures: Contemporary Communication Studies* ed, J. I. Sisco (Tampa: University of South Florida Press, 1983), 71–90. All of Bormann's ideas as well as his analysis of the history of public speechmaking in America are found in his book, *The Force of Fantasy: Restoring the American Dream* (Carbondale: Southern Illinois University Press, 1985).

8. Bormann 1985: 8.

9. Bormann 1985: 8; see also Bruce E. Gronbeck, "Rhetorical Visions from the Margins, 1963–1988," in *Retoriska Frågor: Texter om tal och talare från Quintilianus till Clinton tillägnade Kurt Johannesson,* ed. Christer Åsberg (Stockholm: Nordstedts Förlag, 1995), 267–281.

10. Morton's speech, "Strength Through Cultural Diversity," is reprinted in Bruce E. Gronbeck et al., *Principles and Types of Speech Communication,* 12th ed. (New York: HarperCollins, 1994), 319–327; the quoted paragraphs are from pp. 326–327.

11. Topic involvement and rational message analysis are discussed by R. E. Petty and J. T. Cacioppo, *Communication and Persuasion: Central and Peripheral Routes to Attitude Change* (New York: Springer-Verlag, 1986).

12. In his classic examination of communication and culture, Edward Hall argues that you learn about culture and social expectations in three ways: formally

(when someone tells you what to do), informally (when you learn by imitating others), and, when you are older, technically (when you learn *why* members of a sociey do certain things and not others). See Hall, *The Silent Language* (Greenwich, CT: Fawcett, 1959), ch. 4, "The Major Triad," 63–91.

13. For a broader discussion of occasion, see Elihu Katz and Daniel Dayan, *Media Events: The Live Broadcasting of History* (Cambridge: Harvard University Press, 1992).

14. Jesse Jackson, "Common Ground and Common Sense," *Vital Speeches of the Day* (15 August 1988), 54 (21): 651.

15. Louis Farrakhan, "Transcript from Minister Louis Farrakhan's Remarks at the Million Man March, October 17, 1995," orig. from CNN U.S. News, copyright © 1995 Cable News Network, Inc., and distributed on the World Wide Web by the Information Arcade, University of Iowa Libraries, 1995 (www.arcade.uiowa.edu).

5

OBTAINING FAVORABLE AUDIENCE RESPONSE: DETERMINING THE BASIC APPEALS

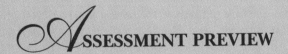

ASSESSMENT PREVIEW

After reading Chapter 5, the student with basic communication competencies will be able to

- distinguish appeals in Maslow's hierarchy of needs.
- articulate a basic definition of McClelland's motive types.
- identify at least four appeals within each of the motive types.

The student with average comunication competencies will also be able to

- identify appeals that illustrate each of the motive types.
- create appeals that illustrate each of the motive types.
- create at least four appeals that can be used in a specific speech to influence audience belief or action.

The student with superior communication competencies will also be able to

- identify those appeals that will be influential in moving people to action.
- distinguish between effective and ineffective appeals.
- assess the ethics of using appeals to influence belief or action.

Chapter 4 emphasized the importance of audience analysis—knowing who people are, what experiences they've had, what they believe, and what they think is appropriate to say on various occasions. Such appeals to audience beliefs, attitudes, and values allow speakers to obtain a favorable response. This chapter will consider another dimension of audience analysis: determining the basic **motives**—basic biological, physical, social, and emotional needs, wants, and desires—which, singly or in concert, can be tapped in moving audiences to see your ideas in a favorable light.

If you've ever gone to a professional or college football game, you may have noticed that you were surrounded by appeals for you to act: to *buy* a product advertised on billboards or the trailing signs pulled by airplanes overhead, to *cheer* loyally for the home or visiting team, to *join* the alumni or athletic support group, to *eat* a hot dog or *wear* a souvenir cap. To buy, cheer, join, eat, or wear—all these are appeals for you to act in a way desired by a communicator. Often, such appeals are expanded to include reasons for acting:

"Buy a Geo and save!"
"Show your support. The team needs *you!*"
"Join the alumni association; it's pay-back time!"
"What's a baseball game without a hot dog?"

The first section of this chapter will focus on motivational studies of individual behavior, including a discussion of the various clusters of motivational appeals. Beyond determining these basic appeals, we will focus on guidelines for using them effectively. As the rhetorical critic Kenneth Burke has suggested, your ability to gain acceptance for your ideas or plans is based on how well you appeal to the basic interests, needs, and wants of your audience.[1]

MOTIVATION AND MOTIVES: THE ANALYSIS OF HUMAN BEHAVIOR

For our purposes, human behavior will be divided into two categories: activity that is the result of *biological* needs, drives, or stimuli, and activity that is the result of *social* motives, desires, and deliberate intent.[2] The motive to eat when you are hungry or to sleep when tired is the result of biologically determined needs or drives. External stimuli such as a stuffy room can also affect your physiological state; attending classes between noon and 1 P.M. affects students' concentration because they're used to eating then. Satisfying a **biological need,** then, is a matter of giving in to or meeting a physiological urge.

Social motives are individual goals, desires, or behaviors that are the result of acting in accordance with your understanding of what others expect or value. Your desires to achieve success on a speech, to feel wanted or needed by others, and to be the kind of person others admire are all examples of social motives. Some social motives are related to how you want to see yourself (as a nice or good person), and others to what you want from the world: higher pay, approval from teachers and friends, awards. "Buy a Geo and save" appeals to a social motive: saving money is seen by most as a positive act. While it isn't the only reason to buy the car, it appeals to your sense of how you want to behave, and to be seen by others as acting.

Appeals can tap both biological and social motives. "What's a baseball game without a hot dog?" has the potential to appeal to hunger—you rushed to get to the game and haven't eaten yet—and to tradition: eating a hot dog just goes with the game. As this example attests, most biological and social motives are relatively enduring.

Over time, however, some interests and needs will change; hence, the social motives that might appeal to you, or others, will also change. For example, a serious car accident may motivate you to "buckle up" and to request that others do so as well. Or, social motives will change from situation to situation; you may be open and honest with your feelings among close friends but put on a different "face" in showing respect to your boss (whom you fervently dislike). Your motive in one situation is to be seen as honest and worthy as a friend, while in the other your motive is to keep your job. Social motives also change over time; your need to belong to a business group, a religious group, or any other social organization will change several times over the years. From your perspective as a speaker, then, engaging audience motives must be seen as a dynamic, ever-changing process. Nonetheless, never underestimate the power of speech in tapping human desires and thus altering beliefs, attitudes, and values.

CLASSIFYING MOTIVES: HIERARCHY OF NEEDS AND CLUSTERS

To enable you to tap into those desires, we'll first introduce two classification systems that can help you group or cluster together individual motives. Then, we'll define "motivational appeal" and illustrate ways of expressing individual motives within speeches.

Maslow's Hierarchy of Needs

A now-classic approach to the study of motives was proposed by Abraham Maslow. Maslow's hierarchy of needs has had a major impact on consumer-oriented studies of marketing and sales and in the field of communication studies. Maslow presents the following categories of needs and desires that drive people to think, act, and respond:

- *Physiological:* The needs for food, drink, air, sleep, and sex—the basic bodily "tissue" requirements;
- *Safety:* The needs for security, stability, protection from harm or injury, structure, orderliness, predictability, freedom from fear and chaos;

FIGURE 5.1   Maslow's Hierarchy

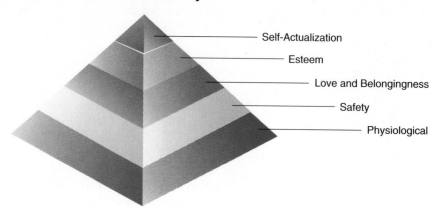

- *Love and belongingness:* The needs for devotion and warm affection with lovers, spouses, children, parents, and close friends; for feeling a part of social groups; for acceptance and approval;
- *Esteem:* The needs for self-esteem based on achievements, mastery, competence, confidence, freedom, and independence; for recognition by others expressed in reputation, prestige, recognition, and status;
- *Self-actualization:* The need for self-fulfillment, for realizing individual potential and actualizing capabilities, for being true to the essential self and satisfying an aesthetic sensibility.[3]

These needs and desires interrelate biological and social motives. In Maslow's theory, lower-level needs usually must be satisfied in whole or in part before higher-order desires become operative. Maslow labels this interrelationship as the **hierarchy of prepotency,** best exemplified by considering the plight of the homeless: They have little time and energy to worry much about esteem or self-actualization, so appeals to such needs would fall on deaf ears in the soup kitchens of American cities. At the other end of the socioeconomic scale, it's often difficult to get the rich and famous to understand the importance of the welfare system as a safety net for the homeless because they have no physiological and few safety needs unmet in their own lives. To Maslow, needs or motivational appeals must be aimed at that level in the hierarchy where individuals' lives are centered. Maslow's hierarchy is crucial to audience analysis and determining which needs are salient: are physiological or achievement needs most important to your audience at this moment? Using Maslow's strategy centers your message on the most critical level of the hierarchy—where your audience will receive the greatest impact of the appeal being made.

McClelland's Motive Types

Generally, there are three primary cluster motives: affiliation, achievement, and power or social influence. **Affiliation motives** focus on the desire to belong to a group, to be well liked and accepted. **Achievement motives** are related to both the intrinsic and extrinsic desire for success, adventure, creativity, and personal enjoyment. **Power motives** involve activities in which influence over others is the primary objective.[4] These broad clusters are critical in considering your overall purpose in speaking. For example, consider the distinction between *affiliation* and *power:* Are you going to appeal to your listeners' sense of belongingness or to their sense of dominance? It's important as well to think of the relationships between *power* and *achievement* motives: Do you approach audience members with a focus on their desires to control others or their hopes for personal development and self-satisfaction? McClelland's motive types help you target your exploration of the specific appeal that might be most useful in addressing your audience.

Comparing Maslow and McClelland

Motive Appeal	Maslow	McClelland
Prestige	Esteem	Achievement
Loyalty	Belongingness	Affiliation
Authority	Self-Actualization	Power

𝒰SING MOTIVATIONAL APPEALS

Thus far, we've treated motives as general concepts. Translating any of these into specific appeals is the focus of this section. We now are ready to move from Maslow's hierarchy or McClelland's clusters to actually employing these appeals in speeches.

In specific terms, a **motivational appeal** is an attempt to code or translate a biological or social motive into language. Consider using the social motive *prestige:* "If you're elected president of this organization, people will look up to you" is an attempt to work an appeal to prestige into the language of a speech. You have two choices when attempting to encode motives into the language of speech: (1) you can use the **visualization process** to project a scene or setting in which people are enjoying the advantages of accepting your ideas or (2) you can use the **attribution process** in claiming that someone is acting on the basis of specific motives.

Using Visualization and Attribution in Expressing Motives

Suppose you wanted your classmates to join in a demonstration against a proposed tuition hike when the Board of Regents is in town next month. While most students would, of course, like to see the school hold the line on tuition, many would be reluctant to protest publicly. Your best bet to engage them might well be to *visualize* various motives:

Just think of what we can accomplish. If we all (*affiliation*) gather in front of the Administration Building, we can show the regents that this is a serious matter. We can show the regents that we're as much a part of the decision-making process as they are (*authority*) and that our voice (*independence*) deserves to be heard as much as theirs. When we present our petition to the President of the Board, even after he's tried to ignore us (*perseverance*), he'll see that we're serious and will have to admit we've got a right to be heard (*success/display*). There's no need to be afraid (*fear*) when you're among friends (*companionship*) in a cause that's right (*pride*). On that day, we'll demonstrate our solidarity (*loyalty*) and force the Board (*aggression*) to listen to our side of the story!

You can also relate motivational concepts directly to other concepts through what is technically called "a process of attribution."[5] Suppose you've shunned going to church because you've always thought of religions as conformist, authoritarian, dominating, repulsive, and destructive. One night, however, go to a religious meeting where people seem to accept you for who you are and where the minister talks about the adventure of worship within a community where companionship and loyalty to others are valued. Upon reflection you decide you may have misconstrued the church's motivation and even misanalyzed yourself. What happened? You changed the former attributions of "churchness" in your mind, which caused your previous behavior, to new ones that will guide your personal behavior. You replaced the old association between "going to church" and the attributes of conformity, authority, and dominance with a new association between church and the attributes of adventure, companionship, and loyalty. This sort of realignment of some object, idea, or person and attributed motives occurs often in persuasive speeches. ∎

Motivational appeals, therefore, are verbal attempts to make a series of motives salient and relevant to an audience. Motivational appeals work through visualization (*verbal depiction*)[6] or attribution (*verbal association*) in order to produce a change in thought or deed in an audience. As we examine individual motivational appeals, always remember to consider your ethical responsibilities in various situations: motivational appeals ought to be appropriate to the moral standards of your community (see "Ethical Moments," on p. 129).

Present in all of us is a near infinite number of needs and desires to which others might direct their appeals. Listing them could be an endless process. Nevertheless, we need some starting point; see the prepared list of appeals in the table on page 121. These motivational appeals have been used by successful speakers, product advertisers, and political persuaders to tap the motives for action in their audiences. By understanding the general thrust of each **motive cluster** and its specific appeals, you'll be in a good position to (1) choose among appeals we've identified here when preparing your speeches, and (2) come up with others we don't deal with. In selecting specific appeals, be guided by one principle: *motivational appeals work only when they are relevant to* *audience members and when they have features that listeners can visualize or can relate to attributes on which they want to act.*

The Affiliation Cluster

Affiliation motives are dominated by a desire for acceptance or approval. They're more focused on the social or interpersonal bonds between people than with personal success or power over others.[7] All motives falling into this cluster, therefore, depend upon whether a sense of belonging to a group or collectivity is important to your listeners. Here are some examples of such motives and appeals to them.

Companionship. *"Birds of a feather flock together."* The human being is one of the weakest of all animals and is ill-equipped to survive alone. We all need others—their presence, recognition, touch, help. Maslow saw belongingness as the most important human need once basic physiological needs are satisfied. Thus appeals to companionship fill sermons, political testaments, and ads for a majority of consumer products. Such appeals can be phrased explicitly, as in "We care about you," "Join our group and find the fellowship of kindred souls," or the ever-present TV appeal, "Thousands of people like you have found. . . ." The appeal may also be more indirect; whenever people recite a creed or credo in church, they affirm not only their common beliefs but also their membership in a group.

Conformity. *"To get along, you need to go along."* Appeals to be like others, to adopt their behavior and even attitudes or values, ask that you not stand out. Comparing your behavior to those around you and then adopting their actions is an example of conforming to social norms or expectations. Extensive social scientific research on the power of social *comparison* and conformity pressures amply documents the power of this appeal.[8]

TABLE 5.1 Motive Clusters

Affiliation	Achievement	Power
Companionship	Acquisition/saving	Aggression
Conformity	Success/display	Authority/dominance
Deference/dependence	Pride	Defense
Sympathy/generosity	Prestige	Fear
Loyalty	Adventure/change	Autonomy/independence
Tradition	Perseverance	
Reverence/worship	Creativity	
Sexual attraction	Curiosity	
	Personal enjoyment	

Deference/Dependence. *"Nine out of ten doctors recommend. . . ."* We live in an age of specialized knowledge and, hence, great expertise. This is why testimony is such an important kind of supporting material—if experts acknowledge the worth of the idea, product, or activity, their judgment can influence your audience to accept your proposal.

Sympathy/Generosity. *"For only one dollar a day, you could be the parent this child has never known."* Appeals such as this one appear in numerous magazine ads asking you to support efforts to save children around the world through financial foster-parenting. All appeals to giving, to support for others, and to self-sacrifice in the name of the common good are based on the assumption that your *social self* (the part of you that is bonded to others) will overcome your *private self* (the inward-directed part of you). "Give that others might live": this and similar appeals remind you of your obligations, not to yourself, but to the society of which you're a part.

Loyalty. *"The camaraderie becomes something that you carry the rest of your life with those individuals. Sometimes you never get a chance to see those individuals again, but in your heart you know you'd do anything for them because they did that for you in a situation which could have gotten them killed."*[9] In these words Vietnam veteran Ron Mitscher tried to describe the loyalty he felt to his fellow soldiers. Periodically, these vets celebrate their membership in "the Brotherhood," as they call their group, and renew their commitments to each other. Speakers often ask listeners to be loyal to friends, family, organizations, states, geographical regions, or country. Such appeals rarely appear in change-oriented speeches but tend to dominate appeals to those who already share the speaker's beliefs and values. They're typical of *reinforcement speeches.*

Tradition. *"Always for them: duty, honor, country. Always their blood, and sweat and tears, as they saw the way and the light."*[10] When General Douglas MacArthur wanted to unite the West Point cadets he was addressing with those who had preceded them, he appealed to tradition—the values that mark the entrance arch to the academy. The past is stationary, stable; it has great rhetorical power when used to connect our lives with those who came before. Even those pushing for new ideas often try to ground them in past principles: "This new health insurance plan is simply a modernization and extension of our continuing tradition of concern for the welfare of our workers."

Reverence/Worship. *"As God gives us the light to see the right, so will we act."* Going beyond deference and tradition, the appeal to reverence or worship leads to submission or dependence. Such reverent submission can take three forms: (1) *hero worship,* (2) *reverence for institutions,* and (3) *divine worship.* As in the appeals to conformity and tradition, this motive appeal elicits audience support for that which is already accepted. Where audiences revere specific individuals, institutions, or spiritual entities, evoking these can strengthen your message.

Sexual Attraction. *"Nothing gets between me and my Calvin's."* With that campaign, Calvin Klein used the same sexual appeal that has sold deodorant, hair rinse and spray, beer and liquor, automobiles—and blue jeans. This particular campaign depended upon the stock technique of *double entendre,* wherein two appeals are being sent in one phrase. While sex sells, the selling may be objectionable. As a recent Klein ad showing teens in their underwear illustrates, the appeal can be considered in bad taste. (Klein pulled the ads off buses after strong objections were aired through the media.) The potency of sex-based appeals lies, for the most part, in an appeal to people's desire to look their best, to be seen as attractive to others. Most of us respond positively to messages that promote an enhancement of our personal attractiveness to others. In most ads these days, the verbal appeal to sexual attraction is approached indirectly ("When you want to look your best. . . "). Using this appeal requires that you be sensitive to the values of your audience—you want their support without being perceived as insensitive or sexist.

The Achievement Cluster

Achievement motives are focused on individual urges, desires, and goals—a concern for self and for excellence, prestige, and success. The fourth and fifth levels of Maslow's hierarchy generally fit here; once your basic physiological and social needs are satisfied, you become centered on personal accomplishment. These motivational appeals are aimed at individual members of the audience.

Acquisition/Saving. *"Earn good money now in our new Checking-Plus accounts!"* We live in an era of investment clubs, Supplemental Retirement Accounts (SRAs), and more investment counselors than bankers. The appeal to acquire possessions and money is a potent one in our society. *Reward* is the name of the game: "Play the lottery and win!" These appeals target the individual rather than the group; hence they fit into the achievement cluster and are used in speeches calling for personal action.

Success/Display. *"Successful executives carry the Connerton electronic organizer."* Appeals to success or to display depend upon an interest in making a mark, or, in Maslow's terms, achieving self-actualization. These appeals can be used when your goal is to get listeners not only to be successful but also to display that success to others; thus, they can tie in with appeals to conformity and pride ("Join us and wear your membership pin with pride") or with appeals to stand out from the crowd ("Be the envy of your neighborhood").

Pride. *"Lose weight through our diet plan and feel great about your body."* These and similar fitness appeals prey on a sense of pride in being attractive to others. Pride can also work in conjunction with appeals to patriotism and display: "Show your pride in America: Display the flag on the Fourth of July." In both cases, the appeal calls for extra effort on our part: engage in activity designed

Advertisers use motivational appeals to influence the buying behavior of carefully segmented audiences.

to become proud, or take the time to put up the flag. If you are delivering an actuative speech that contains a call for extra effort, an appeal to pride may be a potent means of gaining a positive response.

Prestige. *"L'Oréal—Because you're worth it!"* As with pride, this appeal is to an individual's sense of worth and place in a community or within a power structure. Ads for luxury cars, fine clothes, and expensive personal grooming products use the appeal to prestige; ownership conveys status.

Whether the audience wishes to be enticed by a status-related appeal or affiliate with those so enticed becomes the central issue: Do listeners value driving a Mercedes Benz because they will be seen as members of an elite group, or would they be turned off by such a pitch?

Adventure/Change. *"Come to Marlboro Country!"* Cigarette commercials as well as beer commercials such as "Come to the High Country" regularly appeal to adventure. The human soul yearns for escape and release; and seeks risk as a way to validate personal worth. In release and risk, however, are potentials for danger, and not every listener is willing to be put into danger. Appeals to adventure are seldom used as a speaker's primary thrust; they tend to work only when individuals are ready for change but still need a nudge to move them to action.

Perseverance. *"If at first you don't succeed, try, try again."* Conventional wisdom such as this saying recognizes that change does not come easily. Many motivational appeals tap into the way that people persist, even when change seems impossible. Especially potent are appeals to the future: "We shall overcome" (civil rights song), "Let the word go forth from this time and place . . . that a new generation. . . " (John Kennedy's inaugural address). Visualizing what the future will be like if listeners work hard can be an effective appeal in persuasive speeches, especially those that promote new ideas.

Creativity. *"Dare to be different: design your own major!"* As Maslow noted, the height of self-actualization is a sense of individualized abilities and talents, and such requests appeal to that need. For most listeners, however, this appeal rarely can stand alone. Creativity may be at odds with the desire to conform; after all, most college students select a major rather than design their own. How different one wishes to be in this kind of situation will determine the effectiveness of the appeal. What rewards, what success, what sense of adventure is tapped in engaging in creative pursuits? Addressing these as well may strengthen the appeal to creativity.

Curiosity. *"Curiosity killed the cat; satisfaction brought him back."* This old aphorism alludes to the sense of exploration and experimentation linked to curiosity (and to the belief that cats have nine lives). Children take apart alarm clocks to find out where the tick is, and adults crowd sidewalks on a cold day to watch a celebrity filming a movie. Appeals to curiosity, as you might imagine, won't work well with people worried about more basic needs, but, especially with college-aged people or others looking for changes in their lives, it helps a speaker to gain and sustain attention. A speech asking that people trek into the unknown would do well to stress appeals to curiosity.

Advertisers change motivational appeals when aiming at different segments.

Personal Enjoyment. *"Let the good times roll!"* Perhaps the most totally self-centered appeal is the appeal to pleasure. Maximizing one's pleasure, as Freud told us at the beginning of this century, is one of the two driving forces (along with avoiding pain) of the individual. As an ad for Keds shoes suggests, "For the first time, pounding the pavement felt like jumping on an unmade bed," associating pleasure with finding a job seems to make the task a little less onerous. In most persuasive speeches there can be appeals to enjoyment, recreation, rest, relief from home and work pressures, aesthetic pleasure, or just plain fun.

The Power Cluster

All appeals in the power cluster focus on influence or control over others or the environment. All motives in this group feature appeals to one's place in the social hierarchy, a dominant place. Although people with power motives seek to manipulate or control others, not all uses of power are negative. With power comes social responsibility—the demand that power be used in socially approved ways to benefit the group, community, and society. Actually, it is the relationship between power and affiliation, in McClelland's terms, that determines how constructively power is wielded; one of your ethical challenges is to reconcile appeals to power and affiliation. You'll want to consider that relationship when framing motivational appeals to power.

Aggression. *"We have not raised armies with ambitious designs of separating from Great Britain and establishing independent States. We fight not for glory or for conquest. We exhibit to mankind the remarkable spectacle of a people attacked by unprovoked enemies, without any imputation or even suspicion of offense."*[11] With these words, John Dickinson, the "Pennsylvania Farmer" as he called himself in pamphlets, urged the colonists to fight back against the British in the spring of 1775. Because human groups tend to be very hierarchical, the biological urge to fight for rights and territory is translated into appeals to personal and social competition. Ad after ad tells you how to "get ahead of the crowd" or "beat the competition to the punch." You must be careful with this appeal, especially when you identify an "enemy." Blatant negative appeals to aggressive action must always be examined for their fairness. If you're too aggressive, the appeal may *boomerang*—generating sympathy for rather than anger against the enemy.[12]

Authority/Dominance. *"However, until . . . national action can be taken there are a few steps we can take in our own lives. First and foremost, stop buying generic drugs. To be completely safe, buy only name brand drugs.*[13] When Richard C. Delancey drew that conclusion in a speech on the dangers associated with taking generic drugs, he was appealing to the human desire to control the future. Often used in actuative speeches, it helps motivate the audience to take the kind of action necessary to remain in control, rather than allow events to control them.

Defense. *"I want the public to at least see the charges and see my responses."*[14] In speaking these words following an unprecedented Senate Ethics Committee recommendation that he be expelled from the Senate for "sexual and official misconduct," Senator Robert Packwood gave expression to a defensive appeal. This is an instance in which an appeal to fairness failed to accomplish what the speaker intended. (Packwood indicated he would resign from the Senate the following day.) Nonetheless, it illustrates how a speaker might at least attempt to elicit a favorable response from an audience. It is usually acceptable to protect one's own interests or "to save the lives of our children and our children's children." Such appeals tap our basic safety needs. The appeal is linked to power in terms of listeners' ability to control their own environment, to exert authority over their collective needs through the defense of vital interests.

Fear. *"Friends don't let friends drive drunk."* This slogan of an extended MADD (Mothers Against Drunk Driving) campaign makes double use of the fear appeal: It appeals to your fear of not being a true friend as well as to your fear of accidents involving drunk drivers. While fear appeals can be productive, they also can be negative, as when "hate speech" produces socially unacceptable expressions and behaviors toward others. The power of fear makes its way into many advertising campaigns: "Speed kills," "Ring around the collar!" "American Express: don't leave home without it." In using fear appeals, stay within the range of acceptable taste; hyper-strong appeals are much less effective than medium-range appeals.[15]

Autonomy/Independence. *"Just do it."* In a series of highly successful ads, Nike appealed to the sense of independent spirit that animates personal achievement. You've heard similar expressions appealing to your sense of autonomy: "Be your own person; don't follow the crowd." Appeals to "know yourself" and "be yourself" are like appeals to adventure—both draw their force from our struggles for independent achievement. H. Ross Perot drew on this appeal in asking voters to elect him president during the 1992 campaign.

A Final Comment

You may have noticed that some appeals in the three clusters seem to contradict each other. Fear appeals may be antithetical to adventure; generosity seems opposite to aggression. Of course, human beings are bundles of contradictory impulses, balancing urges and making decisions between personal gratification and public good. McClelland's analysis of motive types is based on just such observations of human behavior. Your *ethos*—your ethical standing in a community—is related directly to your choice of motivational appeals. You cannot avoid that fact.

As a result, this discussion of individual motivational appeals is not designed to present the human psyche as if it were orderly and consistent. Rather, we're trying to give you a basic understanding of human motivation and of various kinds of appeals you can use to enhance your rhetorical effectiveness. Even in

𝒜SSESSMENT CHECK:

As you consider the appeals you might use in your next speech, ask yourself how you have responded to appeals when listening to a speaker. Answer the following questions, and then consider each in your own speech presentation to help you assess your use of appeals.

- Did the speaker appeal to your personal needs, as in the need to belong to a group?
- Did the speaker remind you of the power she or he has to reward or punish you?
- Did the speaker appeal to your sense of adventure or pride in achieving a goal?
- Were the appeals used legitimate? Were they ethically appropriate for the situation?
- In my own speech, have I used affiliation, achievement, or power appeals in an appropriate and ethical manner?

all of their confusing aspects, humans nonetheless usually act in a motivated way. Hence we turn next to questions concerning the use of these appeals in speech development.

𝒰SING MOTIVATIONAL APPEALS IN SPEECH PREPARATION

The material we've discussed thus far raises an extremely important question: *How do you decide which motivational appeals to use in your speech?* While precise choices depend on the specific group of listeners you face, the occasion, and even your own preferences and motives for speaking, three factors should guide your thinking about motivational appeals: (1) the type of speech you are to give, (2) the demographic characteristics of your audience, and (3) your personal predilections.

Throughout the discussion of motivational appeals we've suggested that thinking about the *type of speech* you're delivering helps you select appeals. For example, appeals to individuality often appear in persuasive and actuative speeches, the goals of which are to free people from previous modes of thinking.

Motivational Appeals: Developing an Integrated Set ───────

General Purpose: Persuade/Actuate
Specific Purpose: Having classmates pursue a flexible Bachelor of General
Studies degree.

Claim: For many students, the B.G.S. is the best available college degree.

1. *[appeal to creativity]* Without a major and with few requirements, the B.G.S. allows you to build a program suited to your individual desires.
2. *[appeal to adventure]* Break away from the crowd and do something unique in structuring your life here.
3. *[appeal to curiosity]* Explore subjects as deeply as you wish.
4. *[appeal to success]* Get a feeling of achievement from designing and completing your own program. ∎

In contrast, speeches can tap into collective motives—tradition, companionship, defense, deference, conformity, and loyalty. Exploring the *demographic characteristics* of your audience members—their age, educational level, and so on—will also help you sort through possible motivational appeals. As noted,

---

ℰTHICAL MOMENTS
YOUR ETHICAL BOUNDARIES

What are your ethical limits? What are the appeals *you* wouldn't make? Consider the following examples:

1. [*Honesty in relation to appropriateness of authority appeal*] Afraid that your listeners will not take your concerns about inadequate protections against theft seriously, you embellish statistical data obtained from campus security on thefts. Some incidents happened; you just made them appear more frequent, and more serious than the statistics suggest.
2. [*Appropriateness of fear appeal*] Would you show third graders pictures of mouth sores and completely decayed teeth as a way of getting them to brush and floss better?
3. [*Appropriateness of fear appeal*] Would you bring pictures of fe-tuses to class to show the audience what happens to the unborn in an abortion?
4. [*Honesty/openness—in relation to success appeal*] Would you tell your classmates that they can earn up to five thousand dollars a month selling encyclopedias, even though commissions average only three hundred dollars a month?

Your reputation, credibility, or *ethos* is created largely by what you say and by what others think about what you say. Know the limits of the audience, and, more importantly, know your own limits. In that way, you won't be surprised when listeners question the motive appeals you have employed. In the process, anything you do to promote the common good and the basic humanity of others will earn you many points in life.

for example, people who have less need to be concerned about survival or safety needs are more likely to respond to appeals to creativity, independence, personal enjoyment, and generosity. As Maslow's hierarchy of prepotency suggests, a speech on urban renewal presented to inner city tenement dwellers should feature discussions of food, shelter, and safety rather than achievement and self-actualization. Appeals to ethnic traditions and a sense of belonging work well with homogeneous audiences gathered to celebrate such occasions as Hispanic Heritage Week (*Cinco de Mayo*) or Norwegian Independence Day (*Syttende Mai*). Consider, too, McClelland's analysis of motive types, particularly the relationship between affiliation and power motives.

Illustrating the Integration of Motivational Appeals ——————

General Purpose: Persuasive/Actuative
Specific Purpose: Convince the nonprofessional employees at your school that they need a labor union.

On joining the union for reasons of affiliation:

1. [*conformity*]: All your friends are joining.
2. [*dependence*]: The union has leaders with the strength to stand up for your rights.
3. [*sympathy*]: Unions better understand the way you live and what you need than university professors do.

On joining the union for reasons of power:

1. [*aggression*]: If you don't fight for your rights, who will?
2. [*dominance*]: With the union, you can take charge of your workplace and run it properly.
3. [*fear*]: Without a union, you can be dismissed from your job at any time and for any reason.

General Purpose: Persuasive/Actuative
Specific Purpose: Convince listeners to take a summer trip to Europe.
ACHIEVEMENT [acquisition and savings] 1. The tour is being offered for a low price of $2000 for three weeks.
POWER [independence] 2. There'll be a minimum of supervision and regimentation.
AFFILIATION [companionship] 3. You'll be traveling with friends and fellow students.   ■

The two examples above give you a clear sense of how to integrate affiliation and power, and add achievement to the mix in planning a speech. Never will it be the case, of course, that the audience is all achievement-oriented or affiliation-oriented or power-oriented; life is not that simple. But assessing tendencies will help you select the appeals you want to feature.

Always look to your *personal predilections*—your own beliefs, attitudes, and values—when framing motivational appeals. Ask yourself questions like these: "Am I willing to ask people to act out of fear, or am I committed instead to higher motives such as sympathy and generosity?" "Do I actually believe in the importance of loyalty and reverence as they relate to this situation?" Use the appeals that you think are important and that you can defend to yourself and others.

$\mathscr{A}$SSESSING A SAMPLE SPEECH: MOTIVATIONAL APPEALS

Maria Ciach, a student at West Chester University, develops a clear set of motive appeals in the following speech.[16] She works primarily from the "Power Cluster" of motives, with a strong emphasis on fear appeal—warning college students that they have more to worry about from hepatitis B than they might think. From the beginning paragraph forward, Ciach makes a special effort to create a sense of "you should worry about this disease" in her audience. As her forecast of the main ideas indicates (paragraph 4), the strategy employed is one of making the audience feel vulnerable, and then illustrating a clear solution to the problem identified. Paragraphs 2–9 identify the problem: this is where the fear appeal is most evident. Paragraphs 10–12 illustrate why the problem remains, and paragraph 13 provides a clear transition to the discussion of the solution. Interspersed throughout the speech are appeals to authority, as Ciach draws on respected sources for specific factual information on the disease. As she closes the speech, she also draws on an appeal to success in imploring audience members to take the initiative in obtaining the vaccine, and thereby preventing the onset of serious problems caused by hepatitis B.

$\mathscr{H}$EPATITIS B—WHAT EVERY COLLEGE STUDENT DOESN'T KNOW

Maria E. Ciach

Early in November, 24-year-old Wendy Marx visited her doctor with some slight nausea, low grade fever and the chills. Her doctor diagnosed her with a case of the flu, and sent her home to drink lots of liquids and get plenty of rest. Three weeks later, Wendy's liver was raging with infection and she lapsed into a coma. It wasn't until then that her doctor diagnosed that Wendy was suffering from Hepatitis B. Without an emergency liver transplant, Wendy would only have 24 hours to live. /1

$\mathscr{H}$OW TO
SELECT MOTIVATIONAL APPEALS

1. *Be tactful.* Don't insult your audience's intelligence by making blatant or over-aggressive appeals.

2. *Organize your appeals effectively.* If listeners need to be jolted out of lethargy or indifference, find a strong opening appeal. If listeners are ready to act, save your big appeal for the end of the speech, to channel their energy in the desired direction.

3. *Use appeals judiciously.* How many appeals to use will depend on how much time you have to speak, and how much the audience will approve or disapprove of your ideas. In a short speech, develop just two or three lines of motivation fully. If your listeners are hostile, target different appeals to different segments of the audience. If they are predisposed to your view, concentrate on appeals that will spur listeners to action.

4. *Use appeals ethically.* Carefully consider the moral or ethical boundaries your listeners draw to avoid risking social censure for overzealous appeals. What will your audience accept? What are you willing to risk for the positions you take and the ways you advocate them?

As shocking as it sounds, cases like Wendy's are not unique. *The Journal of the American Medical Association* of March 16, 1994, reports that over 300,000 people between the ages of 18–39 will contract life-threatening cases of Hepatitis B each year. Even more frightening, the *American College Health Association* of May 28, 1993, reveals that Hepatitis B has now reached near epidemic proportions in colleges and universities across the country. /2

Every college student in America is in the highest risk group in the nation and thousands of us will die each year. These deaths are slow and painful, much like those of AIDS, but different, in that Hepatitis B is completely preventable. Even though a safe and highly effective vaccine has been available for over the past ten years, the *Centers for Disease Control* reported on February 4, 1994, that cases of acute Hepatitis B have actually increased since the vaccine was first introduced. /3

In order to learn how the spread of Hepatitis B can be stopped we will; first, expose the extent of the dangers posed by Hepatitis B; second, determine why Hepatitis B continues to spread; and finally, show how the Hepatitis B vaccine provides a very simple solution to a very deadly problem. /4

When the Hepatitis B vaccine was first introduced in 1982, the medical community assumed that reports of the disease would decrease dramatically. However, the September 24, 1993, *Mortality and Morbidity Weekly Report* states that the number of chronic infectious carriers has already crested 1.5 million people and continues to grow. Of those infected, approximately 30,000 people will actually develop the acute form of the disease and, without immediate medical attention, they will die. What's worse, the *American Family Physician* of April, 1992, reports that in the past ten years, our chances of contracting Hepatitis B have increased by over 37%. And according to *Mortality and Morbidity Weekly Report* of February 4, 1994, every four weeks about 400 students are infected throughout the country. /5

However, the statistics don't reveal the pain and suffering experienced by the victims. *Nursing* of March, 1992, states that once a person contracts Hepatitis B, the prognosis is grim. Initial symptoms usually include vomiting, fatigue, muscle ache, bone pain and some right upper quadrant discomfort. Over 1/3 of the acutely stricken victims will develop into hepatocellular carcinoma, a form of incurable liver cancer fatal four to six months after its onset, if not sooner. /6

However, the most dangerous aspect of Hepatitis B is how easily the disease can be spread. *The Wall Street Journal* of February 2, 1993, reports that Hepatitis B is spread through homosexual and heterosexual activity, through the sharing of IV drug paraphernalia and from mother to child. But that's not all. The virus can last for up to a week outside of the human body, predominantly on the surfaces of counter tops in doctor's offices, restaurants and also on the desktops of college classrooms. /7

Right now, take a look at your hands. You may be examining the hangnail you've been picking at all morning or maybe the paper cut you received from your schematics. That's all the opening you need in order to contract this life-threatening virus. Thus, it is no coincidence that the *FDA Consumer* of May, 1993, reports that over 30% of the people who contract Hepatitis B lead low risk lifestyles and have no idea how they contracted the disease. /8

Hepatitis B kills more people in their college years than any other sexually transmitted disease; and yet, students everywhere are not getting the vaccine that could potentially save their life. Why? Simply, it is due to the lack of effort by the government, the medical community, as well as patient ignorance. /9

When we arrived at college, we all made certain that our Tuberculosis Tine test and Measles vaccinations were up to date, and if they weren't, we received our shots at our college health clinic. That's the law. However, Hepatitis B vaccinations are not mandated by the government, but merely "urged" by the American College Health Association one year ago. It took over ten years of increasing rates of Hepatitis B on college campuses just to get the government to "urge" students to take a responsibility that the government refused to shoulder. Three organizations, the Immunization Practices Advisory Committee, the U.S. Public Health Service and the American Academy of Pediatrics concocted a plan on May 28, 1993, that only recommended certain groups of people, including college students, to get the vaccine. The government left the matter up to the individual. /10

The medical community has been additionally non-committal, with squabbles over which fields of doctors should be held responsible for giving out the vaccine. *The New York Times* of March 3, 1993, stated that many pediatricians don't want to give out the vaccine, thinking that it would be best for the children to get the vaccine in their teen years. However, many family doctors feel it is the duty of the pediatrician to give out the vaccine, along with other childhood vaccinations. Because no doctors feel responsible for giving out the vaccine, none of their patients are receiving it. /11

Moreover, we suffer from ignorance concerning how to protect ourselves. According to Marjorie Haas, the Director of Health Services at the University of Delaware, in a telephone interview on December 3, 1993, most college students don't even know about Hepatitis B. Few colleges and universities have programs designed to educate students about Hepatitis B, leaving many students to suffer needlessly later on. /12

What we must now do is make our college campuses safe against Hepatitis B. Well, our colleges are always doing things to make our surroundings safe, but this undiscriminating killer will not be deterred by a security light, a safety desk or a self-defense course. And no 911 number can stop it. /13

First, our federal government must make the Hepatitis B vaccine mandatory at either childhood vaccination or as part of a mandatory prematriculation vaccination. The U.S. Public Health Service must be appointed to regulate the vaccine program to make certain the plan is implemented, just as it regulates and enforces other vaccinations. /14

Second, health officials must enforce what the government implements, following the lead of the University of Delaware. In a telephone interview on December 3, 1993, the Director of Health Services stated that within five years the Hepatitis B vaccine will become mandatory for all students. /15

Unfortunately, the National government and medical community are slow to reform; however, there is a step we can all take to protect ourselves. /16

It's simple: get the vaccine. Dr. David Estock of St. Francis Hospital stated in a personal interview on August 13, 1993, that the vaccine is 95% effective and reported cases of side effects have been minimal. The vaccine is cheap, highly effective and is available throughout the country at our family physicians, area hospitals and even some college health clinics. Ask your university health center or family physician about the Hepatitis B vaccine because it can save your life. /17

After examining the extent of the dangers posed by Hepatitis B, determining why Hepatitis B continues to spread and showing that the vaccine provides such a simple solution, it's clear that cases like Wendy's are unnecessary. /18

Wendy required two liver transplants and thousands of dollars before she eventually left the hospital and is now a permanent infectious carrier of Hepatitis B. Stated Wendy in the *Los Angeles Times* of June 2, 1992, "It's a tragedy that anyone should get this. I only wish I had known about the disease." It's time to get smart, be safe and get vaccinated. Because Hepatitis B is not an incurable illness, just an illness we're failing to cure. /19

ℭHAPTER SUMMARY

We can think of motives as *springs*—needs or desires tightly coiled and waiting for the right appeal or verbal depiction to set them off. Worked by a skillful speaker, these motives can convert the individuals in an audience into a cohesive group ready to think and act in ways consistent with a specific purpose. The motives, phrased in language appealing to biological needs or social motives, include three categories:

- *Affiliation motives:* the desire for acceptance and approval by others
- *Achievement motives:* individual urges, desires, and goals
- *Power motives:* the desire to influence or control others or the environment

The competent speaker will be able to draw on these motives, singly or in combination, in meeting the speech purpose in an ethically sound manner. In doing so, the speaker will avoid the obvious, select appeals appropriately for the subject and occasion, and organize them effectively.

𝒦EY TERMS

achievement motives (p. 119)
affiliation motives (p. 118)
attribution process (p. 119)

biological need (p. 116)
hierarchy of prepotency (p. 118)
motivational appeal (p. 119)

motives (p. 116)
motive cluster (p. 120)
power motives (p. 119)

social motives (p. 116)
visualization process (p. 119)

$\mathscr{A}$SSESSMENT ACTIVITIES

1. View a videotaped speech or listen to a speech presented by a classmate. Assess how successful the speech is in appealing to the motives of the audience and to your own individual motives by asking these questions:
   a. Has the speaker chosen motivational appeals appropriate to the type of speech? Why or why not?
   b. Do the speaker's appeals seem to be geared to the demographics of the specific audience? How can you tell?
   c. Are the appeals organized effectively? Why or why not?
   d. Do the appeals seem ethical to you? Why or why not?
   e. Are the majority of the appeals to biological needs or to social motives (affiliation, power, or achievement)? Which is the most effective of the appeals used? Which is the least effective?
2. What relevant motivational appeals might you use in addressing each of the following audiences? Be ready to discuss your choices in class.
   a. A group of students protesting federal reductions in financial aid programs
   b. A meeting of prebusiness majors concerned about jobs
   c. Women at a seminar on nontraditional employment opportunities
   d. A meeting of local elementary and secondary classroom teachers seeking smaller classes
   e. A group gathered for an old-fashioned Fourth of July picnic
3. Working in groups of three to four persons present a two-to-three-minute speech in which, through the combined use of three related motivational appeals, you attempt to persuade your audience to accept a particular belief or engage in a specific action. (For example, combine appeals to adventure, companionship, and personal enjoyment to persuade listeners to go on a group tour of Europe, or combine sympathy and pride to elicit contributions to a charity drive being conducted by a campus group.) As you speak, the other members of your group will be isolating the appeals used (following the chart on page 121). Once all members have spoken, engage in a discussion about the adequacy and effectiveness of the various appeals used—which appeals worked and which did not as each of you spoke?

$\mathscr{R}$EFERENCES

1. Kenneth Burke, *A Rhetoric of Motives* (Berkeley, CA: University of California Press, 1950/1984).

2. Katherine Blick Hoyenga and Kermit T. Hoyenga, *Motivational Explanations of Behavior: Evolutionary, Physiological, and Cognitive Ideas* (Monterey, CA: Brooks/Cole, 1984), ch. 1. Psychologists are divided over several important issues. For example, some argue that all motives are innate (Maslow's theory assumes motives are instinctual), while others (e.g., McClelland) argue that at least some are learned (see citations below). Likewise, psychologists differ on the issue of conscious awareness of motives: Are we aware of the drive, and if not, how do we control it? We won't get into such controversies but take the position that, whether innate or learned, conscious or not, motives are the *foundations for motivational appeals* and, hence, are reasons for action; it's this characteristic that makes motives important to the student of public speaking.

3. Abraham Maslow, *Motivation and Personality*, 2nd ed. (New York: Harper and Row, 1970). In the 1970 revision, Maslow identifies two additional desires—to know and understand and an aesthetic desire—as higher states. These frequently operate as part of the satisfaction of self-actualization, and hence we've included them in that category.

4. Hoyenga and Hoyenga; Donald R. Brown and Joseph Verloff, eds. *Frontiers of Motivational Psychology: Essays in Honor of John W. Atkinson* (New York: Springer-Verlag, 1986); Abigail J. Stewart, ed., *Motivation and Society: A Volume in Honor of David C. McClelland* (San Francisco: Jossey-Bass, 1982); Janet T. Spence, ed., *Achievement and Achievement Motives* (San Francisco: W. H. Freeman, 1983).

5. For a discussion of motivation and attribution, see Hoyenga and Hoyenga. To review attribution theory and communication studies more generally, see Alan L. Sillars, "Attribution and Communication: Are People 'Naive Scientists' or Just Naive?" in *Social Cognition and Communication* eds. Michael E. Roloff and Charles R. Berger (Beverly Hills: Sage Publishing, 1982), 73–106.

6. To understand the power of verbal depiction, read Michael Osborn, "Rhetorical Depiction," in *Form, Genre, and the Study of Political Discourse*, eds. Herbert W. Simons and Aram A. Aghazarian (Charleston: University of South Carolina Press, 1986), 79–107.

7. Hoyenga and Hoyenga, ch. 4. A classic work on affiliation is Stanley Schachter, *The Psychology of Affiliation: Experimental Studies of the Sources of Gregariousness* (Stanford, CA: Stanford University Press, 1959).

8. For discussions of conformity and social comparison theory, see Mary John Smith, *Persuasion and Human Action: A Review and Critique of Social Influence Theories* (Belmont, CA: Wadsworth, 1982), esp. chs. 7 and 11.

9. From an interview with Ron Mitscher, in *Parallels: The Soldiers' Knowledge and the Oral History of Contemporary Warfare*, eds. J. T. Hansen, A. Susan Owen, and Michael Patrick Madden (New York: Aldine de Gruyter, 1992), 137.

10. Douglas MacArthur, "Duty, Honor, Country," in *The Dolphin Book of Speeches*, ed. George W. Hibbitt (New York: Doubleday, 1965).

11. John Dickinson, "The Declaration on Taking Up Arms," speech delivered on July 6, 1775, in *The World's Best Orations,* ed. David J. Brewer (St. Louis: Ferd. P. Kaiser, 1899), 5:1855.

12. For a description of the boomerang effect, see Stephen W. Littlejohn and David M. Jabusch, *Persuasive Transactions* (Glenview, IL: Scott, Foresman, 1987), 79, 92.

13. From Richard C. Delancey, "About the Same Is Not the Same," in *Winning Orations* (Mankato, MN: Interstate Oratorical Association, 1993), 96.
14. As quoted in "Ethics Committee Votes to Expel Oregon Senator," *Athens Messenger* (September 7, 1995), A1.
15. On fear appeals, see Erwin P. Bettinghaus and Michael J. Cody, *Persuasive Communication,* 4th ed. (New York: Holt, Rinehart and Winston, 1987), 158–61; see also Hoyenga and Hoyenga, 154–67.
16. Maria E. Ciach, "Hepatitis B: What Every College Student Doesn't Know," in *Winning Orations 1994.* Reprinted by permission of Larry Schnoor, Executive Secretary, Interstate Oratorical Association, Mankato State University, MN.

6

*D*EVELOPING IDEAS: FINDING AND USING SUPPORTING MATERIALS

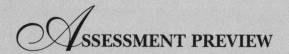

*A*SSESSMENT PREVIEW

After reading Chapter 6, the student with basic communication competencies will be able to

- locate and employ in a speech at least two pieces of supporting materials.
- use a library's card catalog and reference department to locate print and nonprint sources of relevant supporting materials.
- articulate a basic definition of plagiarism.

The student with average communication competencies will also be able to

- locate and employ in a speech at least four different kinds of relevant supporting materials.
- use electronic search resources for in-library searches.
- identify an example of plagiarism.
- use the principles of critical thinking to justify the use of at least half of his or her supporting materials.

The student with superior communication competencies will also be able to

- use the World Wide Web to locate supporting materials.
- identify two relevant sources of information accessible through face-to-face inter-actions or snail-mail inquiries, and employ at least one of them in preparing a speech.
- justify his or her use of every piece of supporting material included in a speech.
- demonstrate knowledge of at least two ways to avoid plagiarism.

Consider the student who wanted to do a speech on the Gulf War of 1990–1991. She went to the electronic card catalog at her university library to do a search. She typed in "Gulf War." Nothing came up. So she typed in "Persian Gulf War 1991." Bingo! Up came a list of 402 items—books only. Needless to say, she was distraught, and knew better than to search the electronic version of the *Readers' Guide,* for of course it would turn up thousands of references from the last five years alone.

This student's experience reflects a paradox that you will surely encounter as a speaker: on the one hand, as you prepare your speeches, you will want to make them substantive and worthwhile for your audience. You need to have materials that are concrete, reasonably connected to claims you are making, and convincing. Yet knowing what you need—some statistics, some testimony from reliable sources, some explanations, and so on—is only half the battle. For as you search for such materials, you will probably find yourself overwhelmed by the volume of information available. The search tools of today—such as the World Wide Web, where you can access libraries and home pages from around the globe—will deluge you with information, enough not for a six-minute speech of explanation, but for dozens of such speeches.

In this chapter we will explore some of the kinds of supporting materials speeches demand; a good speech burns supporting materials as its fuel, and this chapter will discuss the various kinds of energy that fuel speeches. Then we'll tackle the questions of where to find those fuels and how to burn them: we'll discuss electronic, print, face-to-face, and mailed forms of supporting materials, and then we'll look at some strategies for putting them together to achieve maximum power and effectiveness.

Thinking through the kinds of material you need before you actually hit the library or an http:// command on your computer is a habit you must cultivate. Searching for supporting materials *purposively* is the key to success.

WHAT TO LOOK FOR: FORMS OF SUPPORTING MATERIALS

Six types of supporting materials are regularly used by competent speakers: (1) explanations, (2) comparisons and contrasts, (3) illustrations and narratives, (4) specific instances, (5) statistics, and (6) testimony.

Explanations

An **explanation** is a description or expository passage that makes a term, concept, process, or proposal clear or acceptable. Explanations tell what, how, or why; they are useful in showing relationships between a whole and its parts. They also may make it easier to understand concepts that are difficult to grasp. As with other forms of support, explanations have to be presented clearly and attached explicitly to the ideas central to your speech to be useful.

Explanations of how things work, with demonstrations of portions of a total process, can help increase audience attention and interest.

An explanation tells an audience what something is by offering defining and clarifying details. So, when vice-chairman of the board of AT&T Randall Tobias introduced an audience at West Virginia University to fiber optics communication, he first made sure they understood what fiber optics was:

> Fiber optics systems combine lasers as small as grains of sand with glass fibers as thin as strands of hair. Unlike ordinary glass, it's ultra-pure. If oceans were made of this glass, you could see to the bottom.
>
> In fiber optics systems, lasers transmit billions of light pulses each second as bits of data through these glass strands. The bits represent conversations, computer data or images. Currently we transmit about 3.4 billion bits a second, equal to 50,000 simultaneous phone calls on a pair of fibers. But within not-too-distant developments in the technology, we expect to transmit one trillion bits per second, or about 70 million simultaneous conversations on a single pair of wires.[1]

Notice that the explanation begins with a little analogy; Tobias hopes that the references to sand and hair will help the audience visualize fiber optics. Then he launches the explanation with descriptive material. If more than one concept is being explained at once, then the explanation will have to be more extended. Robert Lutz, president of Chrysler Corporation, wanted to explain inconsistencies in U.S. tariff rules and the unfair advantage they gave some foreign auto exports to the United States. Here's the explanation he offered Cal-Berkeley students:

Let me tell you . . . the story of multipurpose vehicles, or "MPV's" for short. An MPV is a vehicle like, say, the Toyota 4-Runner sport utility. A funny thing happens to a 4-Runner when it's imported into this country. Four U.S. regulators all look it over. The fellow from the Environmental Protection Agency inspects and declares that it is "a truck," and will therefore only have to meet the emission standards for U.S. trucks, which are not as strict as those for cars. Behind him is the man from the National Highway Safety Administration, who certifies that it is indeed a truck so it won't have to have the same safety devices as a car. And then comes the inspector from the Department of Transportation, who also agrees that the vehicle is a truck so it won't have to meet the higher fuel economy requirements of a car. But then comes the fourth inspector. He's from the U.S. Customs Service. He looks at the 4-Runner and says, "Nope, this isn't a truck at all; it's a car!" And that means it pays a duty of only two-point-five percent instead of the 25 percent duty on trucks.

Now what's going on here? Well, back in February of 1989, after intense lobbying by Japanese automakers, the U.S. Treasury Department, in a virtually unprecedented decision, overruled its own Customs Service and reclassified Japanese sport utilities and minivans from trucks to cars. It was, as President Clinton himself put it in a press conference last month, a "$300-million-dollar-a-year freebie to the Japanese for no apparent reason."[2]

Notice the way this explanation works. Lutz sets up the four regulators, follows a Japanese MPV through them, offers the explanation, and then brings the audience up to date with a reference to President Clinton. He doesn't waste time with irrelevant details about the inspections, because he wants to keep our attention focused on the switch in definition.

Although explanations are good ways to clarify ideas, they shouldn't be too long or complicated and they shouldn't have to carry the weight of the argument. For example, Lutz's explanation was clear, but by itself it didn't point to a solution to the problem. Explanations clarify but seldom prove anything.

Comparisons and Contrasts

Comparisons and contrasts are useful verbal devices for clarifying ideas—to make them distinctive and focused. Pointing out similarities and differences helps listeners comprehend your ideas and opinions.

Comparisons. **Comparisons** are kinds of analogies that connect something already known or believed with ideas a speaker wishes to have understood or accepted. Comparisons, therefore, stress similarities. During the darkest days of the Civil War, when critics attacked the administration's policies, Lincoln answered them by comparing the plight of the government with that of the famous tightrope walker, Blondin, attempting to cross the Niagara Falls:

Gentlemen, I want you to suppose a case for a moment. Suppose that all the property you were worth was in gold, and you had put it in the hands of Blondin, the famous rope-walker, to carry across the Niagara Falls on a tightrope. Would you shake the rope while he was passing over it, or keep shouting to him, "Blondin, stoop a little more! Go a little faster!"? No, I am sure you would not. You would hold your breath as well as your tongue, and keep your hands off until he was safely over. Now the government is in the same situation. It is carrying an immense weight across a stormy ocean. Untold treasures are in its hands. It is doing the best it can. Don't badger it! Just keep still, and it will get you safely over.

Contrasts.   **Contrasts** help to clarify complex situations and processes by focusing on differences. A speaker explaining arena football would want to contrast it with the more familiar rules governing interscholastic football. To clarify the severity of the 1993 midwestern flood, the news networks contrasted the width and depth of rivers in more normal summers with their status that year. Contrasts can be used not only to clarify unfamiliar or complex problems, but also to strengthen the arguments that you wish to advance. H. Ross Perot testified against the North American Free Trade Agreement (NAFTA) before the Senate Joint Economic Committee in 1993. A series of contrasts helped him made his case:

> Let's contrast the burdens that businesses carry in our country. We're running a business now. You're paying your manufacturers ten times what they make in Mexico. The minimum wage in the United States is, as you know, $4.25. The minimum wage in Mexico is 58 cents. The single most expensive item in making a car in the United States is health care. No problem in Mexico. Our companies also spend a great deal on retirement, worker's compensation, life insurance, and many other benefits not available in Mexico. The recently passed employee leave bill, while a very nice thing, adds to the cost of manufacturing. It's one more reason to head south. . . . Now, if all you want to do is make money, I'll give you some reasons to head south.[3]

Perot's contrasts were startling and, because there were several of them, cumulatively served as clear support for his central idea that the United States should junk NAFTA. Helping an audience reason along with you by visualizing differences is an excellent strategy for getting them to accept your ideas.

Comparisons and Contrasts Used in Combination.   You can use comparisons and contrasts together to double your audience's ability to see. For example, Professor Dudley Herschbach, Baird Professor of Science at Harvard and 1986 Nobel Prize winner in chemistry, gave the 1992 Phi Beta Kappa oration to the Harvard-Radcliffe chapter. To help his listeners understand relationships between human beings and dolphins, he used comparisons and contrasts in tandem:

> The evolutionary gulf between humans and dolphins is immense. We both evolved from land mammals, but the primordial ancestors of the dolphins returned to the sea fifty million years ago. Dolphins resembling those we know today appeared fifteen million years ago. Homo sapiens emerged much

more recently—not more than about a quarter of a million years ago, following the earliest versions of humankind some three million years ago. . . .

In relation to body size, the brain of a bottlenose dolphin is comparable to ours. The cortex, seat of intelligence and language, is more convoluted and contains about 50 percent more cells. It has the same six differentiated layers but is thinner and much different in shape.[4]

Whenever using comparisons and contrasts, try to make sure that one of the items is familiar to listeners. Comparing arena football and interscholastic football will make no sense to listeners from Ireland, who probably don't know anything about either one. You'd have to compare and contrast arena football and European soccer to clarify the arena game for them.

Illustrations and Narratives

A detailed example of an idea you wish to support is either an illustration or a narrative. If the example describes a concept, condition, or circumstance, it's called an **illustration;** if it's in story form, it's called a **narrative.** An illustration or narrative is always, however, a big "for instance"—something concrete that makes abstract or general ideas easier to comprehend. Illustrations share many characteristics with explanations, the difference being that an illustration is always a "for instance" while explanations can take different forms.

Some illustrations and narratives are hypothetical (made up) while others are factual—recitations of events that actually happened or persons, places, and things that actually exist. If you were giving a speech on why students should move out of dormitories and into apartments, you might narrate a "typical" evening in a dorm: loud music, a constant flow of pizza delivery people through the hall, a traveling party, a false fire alarm, nonstop card games, illegal alcohol, and an engagement shower. Although not all of these occurred on the same night, asking listeners to imagine what life would be like if they *did* would help you to convey the intensity of your antidormitory feelings through a made-up narrative.

For many audiences, fact-based illustrations and narratives are more potent. President Ronald Reagan was famous for his reliance on homey little narratives. Hillary Rodham Clinton was equally successful using them in her travels around the country in search of a better health care system. Here's one of them:

Dr. Rob Barrinson, one of the practicing physicians who spent hours and hours working with us while also maintaining his practice, told us recently of an experience that he had as one of many. He admitted an emergency room patient named Jeff. Jeff suffered from cirrhosis of the liver. Dr. Barrinson put him in the hospital and within 24 hours received a call from Jeff's insurance company. The insurance company wanted to know exactly how many days Jeff would be in the hospital and why. Dr. Barrinson replied that he couldn't predict the precise length of stay. A few days later the insurance company called back and questioned whether Jeff would need surgery. Again, Dr. Barrinson said he wasn't yet sure.

And what was Dr. Barrinson's reward for his honesty and his professionalism? He was placed on the insurance company's "special exemptions" list. You know, that's a list of troublesome doctors who make the insurance company wait a few days or a few weeks to determine the bottom line on a particular patient. From that point on, the insurance company called Dr. Barrinson six times in two weeks. Each time, he had to be summoned away from a patient to take the call. Each time, he spoke to a different insurance company representative. Each time, he repeated the same story. Each time, his role as the physician was subverted. And each time, the treatment of the patient was impeded.

Dr. Barrinson and you know that medicine, the art of healing, doesn't work that way. There is no master checklist that can be administered by some faceless bureaucrat that can tell you what you need to do on an hourly basis to take care of your patients; and, frankly, I wouldn't want to be one of your patients if there were.[5]

Mrs. Clinton's narrative met all three of these criteria, especially the third one. She also was very good at drawing lessons or conclusions from her story.

Specific Instances

Specific instances are undeveloped illustrations or examples; usually they are grouped into a list, so that they pile one upon the other to drive the speaker's point home. The Roman orator Cicero was the first advocate of "filling the mind" with examples; he called the technique *accumulatio,* or accumulation, in Book III of his treatise on rhetoric, *De Oratore.*[6] They're undeveloped because their power comes from cumulative effect rather than vivid detail. Sometimes, you can use a single specific instance if all you need is a quick example: "You're all familiar with the windows in this classroom, but you might not have noticed their actual construction. I want to talk about windows like the ones around you—these double-glazed, low emissivity, gas-filled windows—and how the use of such seemingly expensive windows contributes to reduced energy consumption on campus and in your life." More often, though, speakers pile on instances either to clarify their point or to prove it. That is, in informative speeches, specific instances are the means by which ideas are made concrete. University of Iowa President Hunter R. Rawlings III told his faculty they had to better understand the communities of people around them before the faculty could expect the people of Iowa to put more money into the universities:

So if we don't know Iowa, how can we expect Iowa to know us? How can we expect a farming family in Benton County, a tractor dealer in Fort Dodge, a grocer in Oelwein—people who have their own problems to worry about—to put themselves in our shoes? . . . [What we do] is hard work, and not everyone can do it, but that doesn't mean that its value to society is always self-evident.[7]

At other times, speakers use specific instances as a series of items tending, as a whole, to prove a point. In his commencement address to Emory University, Donald Keough, retired president of the Coca-Cola Company, used them in that way when he urged students to keep on dreaming:

> No matter how wise the prognosticators are, deep down they really don't know. They don't know. And usually I've found that they're far too pessimistic. Listen to some of these pearls of wisdom: (1) "Heavier than air flying machines are impossible." Lord Geldon, noted British physicist, 1895. (2) "Everything that can be invented has been invented." Director of the U.S. Patent Office suggesting that his operation close down, in 1899. (3) "The battle to feed all humanity is over. In the 1970s hundreds of millions of people

$\mathcal{H}$OW TO
CHOOSE ILLUSTRATIONS AND NARRATIVES

Three considerations should be kept in mind when selecting illustrations and narratives, whether hypothetical or factual:

1. *Is the illustration or narrative clearly related to the idea it's intended to support?* If the connection is difficult to show, it won't accomplish its goal. If your hypothetical story about a typical night in a dorm is more attractive than repelling for some listeners, you're in trouble!

2. *Is it a fair example?* An audience can be quick to notice unusual circumstances in an illustration or story; exceptional cases are seldom convincing. Having parachutists landing on the dorm roof in your story, for example, would stretch the credibility of your listeners.

3. *Is it vivid and impressive in detail?* Be sure your extended examples

are pointed, fair, and visually appealing. Visual depiction is a powerful device for speakers.[8]

FIGURE 6.1 **The Forms of Supporting Materials**

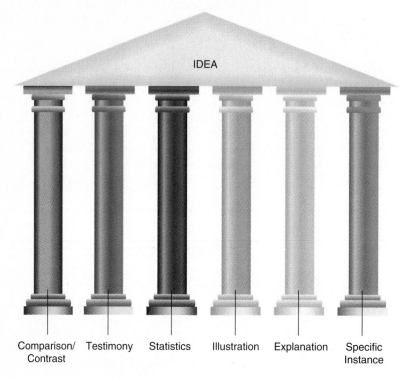

all over the world are going to starve." Paul Ehrlich, noted Stanford biologist and demographer, 1960.

Occasionally, of course, these prognosticators have erred on the side of excessive optimism. *Business Week* in 1979 said, "With over 50 foreign cars on sale here the Japanese auto industry isn't going to carve out a big slice of the U.S. market." [Secretary of the Navy] Frank Knox, December 4, 1941: "No matter what happens, the U.S. Navy is not going to be caught napping."[9]

With these accumulated instances, Keough demonstrated to his listeners that even new graduates ought to dream—to "seize the day," as he said. Those specific instances could bring a smile to the seniors' faces and—more important—a positive thought to their brains.

Statistics

Statistics are numbers that show relationships between or among phenomena—relationships that can emphasize size or magnitude, describe subclasses or parts (segments), or establish trends. By reducing large masses of information into generalized categories, statistics clarify situations, substantiate potentially disputable central ideas, and make complex aspects of the world clear to listeners.

Magnitudes. We often use statistics to describe a situation or to sketch its scope or seriousness—that is, its size or **magnitude.** Especially if one statistical description of the size of a problem is piled up on others, the effect upon listeners can be strong. Notice how the former U.S. Surgeon General Antonia Novello used multiple statistical descriptions of magnitude while urging citizens to think of violence as a community health problem:

> Violence is a legitimate public health concern. It is your challenge—and mine. My friends, it is no small problem that: homicidal violence is now the leading cause of death among our youth; and that, in fact, every 14 hours a child younger than 5 is murdered. Firearms are now involved in one in every four deaths among 15- to 24-year-olds. And it is no small problem that domestic violence—along with child abuse and the abuse of the elderly—is found in every community and one-fourth of all American families; and up to six of ten married couples. Domestic violence today is the second most common cause of injury to women overall, and the leading cause of injuries to women ages 15 to 44. It is more common than automobile accidents, muggings, and rapes combined.[10]

Not all uses of magnitudes, of course, need such piling up of instances. Simple, hard-hitting magnitudes sometimes work even better. For example, Brenda Theriault of the University of Maine, arguing that there is "very little nutritional value in a hamburger, chocolate shake, and fries," simply noted that "of the 1,123 calories in this meal, there are 15 calories of carbohydrates, 35 calories of protein, and 1,073 calories of fat."[11] These were all the numbers the listeners needed in order to understand the nutrition in a typical fast-food meal.

Segments. Statistics also are used to isolate the parts of a problem or to show aspects of a problem caused by separate factors; parts or aspects can be treated as statistical **segments.** In discussing the sources of income for a college or university, for example, you'd probably segment the income by percentages coming from tuition and fees, state and federal money, gifts and contributions, special fees such as tickets, and miscellaneous sources. Then you'd be in a position to talk reasonably about next year's proposed tuition hike. Student speaker Eddie Hunter used poll results in this fashion to show that incumbent politicians are not always unwanted by their electors:

> Nobody forces people to vote for incumbents. Last October the *New York Times* reported a New York Times-CBS Survey, which found 44 percent of those surveyed believed their representative deserves re-election, while 40 percent say they want someone new. However, these percentages swing dramatically when people are asked about Congress as a whole. Only 20 percent then say most lawmakers deserve re-election, while 67 percent would give new people a chance. Apparently people perceive everyone else's legislator as the bad guy.[12]

As Hunter's example illustrates, the value of statistics lies less in the numbers themselves and more in how they're interpreted and used—prepared for audience use. In using statistical data, always ask and answer the question, "What do these numbers mean or demonstrate to *this* audience?" In Hunter's case, when the separate polls are compared, there's support for his argument that "If they're in, vote 'em out" doesn't apply across the board.

Trends.   Statistics often are used to point out **trends,** or indicators that tell us where we were, where we are now, and where we may be heading. The comparison of statistical representations across time allows you to say that a particular phenomenon is increasing or decreasing (see Table 6.1). Consider the use of a statistical trend made by Paul Carlin, chairman of the board of Business Mail Express, addressing an audience of experts: private and public mail-related corporations. He wanted to demonstrate that all of the new technologies still left the postal service with a hefty bill for personnel. To set up his argument that personnel costs were the culprit in the mail business, he used a statistical trend:

> And in order to make [the postal system] work, it is imperative that the Postal Service get control of its employee-related costs that continuously drive postage prices upward.
>
> In 1968, the commission whose studies led to the creation of the Postal Service—the Kappel Commission—reported that the net fixed asset investment per postal employee then averaged $1,145.
>
> Twenty-five years later—in fiscal 1993—this net average had increased to $16,810 per postal employee.
>
> Thus, over the past quarter-century the capital asset investment per postal employee had increased fifteenfold.
>
> In 1968, the ratio of employee-related costs to the total postal budget was 80.3 percent.
>
> In other words, 80 cents of every postal dollar was used to offset employee-related costs.
>
> So, what has happened to that ratio over the ensuing years?
>
> It has remained virtually unchanged!
>
> Despite the billions of dollars spent on automation to process the mail, extended-life vehicles to transport it and other asset investments that today are 15 times greater, the ratio of employee costs to total costs is 80.8 percent.[13]

Notice the mode of address Carlin used. He was talking with mail professionals, people for whom the dollars-and-cents bottom line was a most important criterion. For this audience, he not only gave them the numbers demonstrating that costly technology has not reduced personnel costs but he couched his speech in business language—in terms of costs, fixed assets, investment, and so on. The statistical trend he found was a solid argument for him, and his language reflected the perspective he was taking on the mail system.

Using Statistics.   When you use statistics to indicate magnitude, to divide phenomena into segments, or to describe trends, help your listeners by making the numbers more user-friendly:

1. *Translate difficult-to-comprehend numbers into more immediately understandable terms.* In a speech on the mounting problem of solid waste, Carl Hall illustrated the immensity of 130 million tons of garbage by explaining that trucks loaded with that amount would extend from coast to coast three abreast.[14]

2. *Don't be afraid to round off complicated numbers.* "Nearly 300,000" is easier for listeners to comprehend than "296,454." "Just over 33 percent" or, better yet, "about a third" is preferable to "33.5 percent."

3. *Use visual aids to clarify complicated statistical trends or summaries whenever possible.* Hand out a photocopied sheet of numbers; draw graphs on the chalkboard; prepare a pie chart on an overhead transparency. Such aids will allow you to concentrate your words on explaining the significance of the numbers rather than on making sure the audience understands and remembers them.

A speaker can use statistics to describe a situation or to sketch its scope or magnitude. By reducing large masses of information into general categories, statistics can clarify and substantiate a claim.

TABLE 6.1   Types of Statistics

In a speech to inform, a speaker might use three types of statistics to describe students at Central University. What other forms of supporting material could complement these numbers?

Magnitudes	Segments	Trends
"Three fourths of all Central University students come from the state."	"Sixty percent of all Central University students major in business; 25 percent are humanities majors; the remaining 15 percent are in fine arts."	"Since 1975, enrollment at Central University has increased by 20 percent every five years."

4. *Use statistics fairly.* As the "Ethical Moments" box in this chapter suggests, it's easy to mislead with statistics even if you don't exactly lie. Arguing that professional women's salaries increased 8.3 percent last year may sound impressive to listeners until they ask how much professional men's salaries increased and until they realize that women are still paid more than a quarter less than men on comparative jobs. Provide fair contexts for your data.[15]

Testimony

When you cite the opinions or conclusions of others, you're using **testimony.** Sometimes testimony merely adds weight or impressiveness to an idea, as when you quote Mahatma Gandhi or a clever turn of a phrase by Dorothy Parker. At other times, it lends credibility to an assertion, especially when it comes from expert witnesses. When Daniel Lashof of the Natural Resources Defense Council wanted to emphasize the point that serious steps toward control of toxic emissions must be taken now, he used testimony from one international conference and then indicated that other conferences had come to the same conclusion:

> The Toronto Conference on the Changing Atmosphere, in June 1988, warned that "humanity is conducting an unintended, uncontrolled, globally pervasive experiment whose ultimate consequences could be second only to a global nuclear war," and called on the world to cut CO_2 emissions from fossil fuel combustion 20 percent by 2005. In the last two years the declaration of this ad hoc group of scientists, environmentalists, and policy makers has been strongly reinforced by the Intergovernmental Panel on Climate Change (IPCC), the Second World Climate Conference, and the Stockholm Environment Institute.[16]

All testimony should meet the twin tests of pertinence and audience acceptability. When used to strengthen a statement rather than merely to amplify or illustrate an idea, testimony also should satisfy four more specific criteria:

1. The person quoted should be qualified, by training and experience, to speak on the topic being discussed. Athletes are more credible talking about sports equipment or exercise programs than they are endorsing breakfast food or local furniture stores.

2. Whenever possible, the authority's statement should be based on first-hand knowledge. An Iowa farmer is not an authority on a South Carolina drought unless or he or she has personally observed the conditions.

ETHICAL MOMENTS
THE NUMBERS GAME

The rise of science in this century has been accompanied by the rise of numerical data—and its public exhibition. By now you've been told by one poll that the public favors a liberalization of abortion laws two-to-one but by another poll that the public favors tightening abortion laws by an equal percentage. You know that four out of five dentists surveyed recommend a particular brand of toothpaste. You've heard that a brand of cigarettes has the lowest level of tar and nicotine—from more than one manufacturer. As both listener and speaker, you have to make some ethical calls when encountering such data:

1. Contradictory polls such as the ones on abortion usually result when questions are asked in slanted ways. "Do parents have to right to know when their underaged kids seek a dangerous abortion?" tends to encourage a positive answer, while "Ought women have the right to control their own bodies without external interference from others?" also encourages a positive answer—but one in favor of a very different public policy than the first. Questions can be loaded in favor of opposing public policies. You're wise to report the actual questions when quoting poll results.

2. Who were those "four out of five dentists surveyed?" Is it ethical to cite statistics without reviewing how they were gathered and calculated?

3. If your favorite brand of cigarettes is one of five brands that all have the same low tar and nicotine content, technically, of course, yours has the lowest—and so do the other four brands. Is it ethical, however, to claim your brand is "the lowest" or must you say that it is "one of the lowest"?

It's easy to fiddle with numbers: to round up or down, to compare only parts rather than wholes, to ignore key details that would properly contextualize information for listeners. It's easy, but if you play fast and loose with numbers, you might get caught. Learn to play the numbers game honestly so as to protect your reputation.

✐SSESSMENT CHECK

Before giving your next speech, ask yourself these questions about your use of supporting materials:

- Have I clearly connected any explanations, illustrations, narratives, or specific instances to the main thrust of the speech? Will they help make my ideas more concrete for these particular listeners?
- Have I supported my use of testimony by giving the qualifications of the person I'm citing? Will my audience accept this person as an impartial, expert authority?
- Have I used statistics fairly? Have I found a way to present the statistics so they will clearly point to the scope of the problem, trends in the data, or particular aspects of the issue for this particular audience?

---

3. The judgment expressed shouldn't be unduly influenced by personal interest. Asking a political opponent to comment on the current president's performance will likely yield a self-interested answer.
4. The listeners should perceive the person quoted to be an actual authority. An archbishop may be accepted as an authority by a Roman Catholic audience but perhaps not by Protestant or Hindu listeners.

When citing testimony, don't use big names simply because they're well known. The best testimony comes from subject-matter experts whose qualifications your listeners recognize.

Finally, always acknowledge the source of an idea or particular phrasing. Avoid *plagiarism*—claiming someone else's ideas, information, or phraseology as your own. Plagiarism is stealing. Give your source credit for the material, and give yourself credit for having taken the time to do the research (see "Using Source Material Ethically" below).

✐HERE TO LOOK: SOURCES OF SUPPORTING MATERIALS

So, you may know what kinds of materials you want for your speech—some solid numbers, a nice list of specific instances, a well-developed illustration or story, testimony from credible people, a hard-nosed explanation along with some clarifying comparisons and contrasts. But where do you find such materials? You'll find those materials exactly where you find all ideas in this world: in electronic networks and storage technologies, in print, in interaction with others, and in information-gathering instruments you yourself construct.

TABLE 6.2 Checklist for Supporting Materials

You should evaluate your supporting materials when you plan your speeches. Answer the questions on this checklist as you plan your supporting materials.

General Considerations

_____1. Have I included sufficient supporting material?
_____2. Are my supporting materials distributed throughout my speech?
_____3. Do I provide extra support for confusing or controversial ideas?
_____4. Are my supporting materials interesting and clear?
_____5. Do I adequately credit the sources of my supporting materials?

Explanations

_____1. Are my explanations short and direct?
_____2. Do I provide other forms of support in addition to explanations?

Comparisons and Contrasts

_____1. Is at least one of the items in a comparison or contrast familiar to my listeners?
_____2. Is the basis of the comparison clear?
_____3. Is the contrast distinct enough?

Illustrations and Narratives

_____1. Is the illustration or narrative clearly related to the idea it's intended to support?
_____2. Is the illustration or narrative typical?
_____3. Is the illustration or narrative vivid and adequately detailed?

Specific Instances

_____1. Have I provided enough specific instances?
_____2. Can listeners easily recognize or understand the instances I mention?

Statistics

_____1. Are my statistics easy to understand?
_____2. Have I rounded off complicated numbers?
_____3. Am I using statistics fairly?
_____4. Should I use visual materials to clarify complicated numbers?
_____5. Have I adequately interpreted the statistics I've cited for my listeners?

Testimony

_____1. Is the authority qualified to speak on the topic being discussed?
_____2. Is the authority's statement based on first-hand knowledge?
_____3. Is the authority's opinion subject to personal influence or bias?
_____4. Do my listeners know the authority's qualifications?
_____5. Will my listeners accept this person as an authority?

The Electronic World

You've seen the ads: AT&T promising you access to information from everywhere, the Aptiva computer bringing you sounds and images from every imaginable society, and your own college or university promising to link you internationally with other institutions of learning and ideas. Working your way through government, commercial, and educational networks takes a few skills, though probably not as many as the nonplayer might think. At most schools in the country and through an increasing number of inexpensive commercial services, you can surf the Internet, upload information from CD-ROMs of data in your libraries, and search your own library electronically with relative ease.

The Electronic Card Catalog.   Most college and university libraries either have or will soon install a computerized search system for their holdings and for journals or magazines generally. If you have access to such a system, it should be your first stop. For example, the University of Iowa uses the Oasis system, popular among larger research libraries. It allows you to search Iowa's card catalog, that of a consortium of libraries, the Humanities and Social Science Indexes (see below), and a couple of versions of Psychological Abstracts.

Suppose you want to do a speech on the organic production of foods via a subject search of Iowa's card catalog. In early 1996, searching with the word "gardening" turned up 208 books—far too many to use. If you added the word "organic" to the search (subject = "organic gardening"), then you reduced the list to thirteen items, two of which were bibliographies. Shifting the search to "organic farming" gave you forty-two books, five of which were bibliographies. One way to control electronic searches, therefore, is to use additional words to increase your precision.

Other controls are possible. If you want to do that speech on the 1991 Gulf War mentioned at the beginning of this chapter, you'll have to look for ways to whittle down those 402 entries. You can limit your thinking to, say, what you saw in the newspapers and on television. Specifying a subtopic (done with hyphens in the Oasis system) "Persian Gulf War 1991--Press Coverage" yields eleven books: six on press coverage in general, three dealing specifically with U.S. coverage, one on coverage in Great Britain, and another on the war and public opinion. Here are more manageable materials.

Learning to narrow through precise specification of topic or through subcategorization will make your searches less frustrating. Also knowing authors, titles, and the like will help even more. Take time to look at the pamphlet or online help menu to make sure you use your local electronic card catalog with maximum efficiency.

One last point: Find out what databases you have access to through your library system. ERIC (Educational Resources Information Center) will help you locate scholarly papers in the humanities; MEDLINE will get you into psychosocial and physiological studies of disease and associated medical problems; LEXUS-NEXUS will give you access to a staggering number of public and commercial information sources.

CD-ROM Searches. We're living through a great explosion in the use of the **CD-ROM**—a technological device that uses the CD as a storage vehicle for computer data. CDs hold much more information than comptuer disks and so are used to store and to retrieve data from multiple volumes' worth of materials. Check to see what your local libraries have: perhaps *The New York Times Index, The Oxford English Dictionary on CD-ROM, The Modern Language Association Indexes,* perhaps the *Table of Contents to Communication Journals* (which will include as databases all articles published in Speech Communication Association journals since 1990). As more and more databases become available on CD-ROM, you'll be able to link electronically with the actual articles you want.

The World Wide Web. The **Information Superhighway** was the great metaphor of the 1980s and early 1990s—a system allowing everyone to access information electronically from around the globe. Today, you can use a variety of search tools to access unlimited information sources yielding truckloads of data. You can also link pages of data together, and with a mere click of a mouse or a tap of an "enter" key, enter the **World Wide Web.** The Highway is transportation; the Web is a way of reading many assembled sources at once. The Web is an access protocol that allows you to enter the maze of computerized language, pictures, and sounds from any point in that maze, and then to move from site to site simply by clicking on a word or symbol.

We do not have the space here to teach you how to surf the 'Net. You may wish to work from books such as *The Internet for Dummies* or *The Internet Navigator.*[17] Better yet, sign up for a short course at your school or local library. And, if you join one of the private, for-profit services—America Online, Prodigy, CompuServe, or more localized services—you'll find many helps online—that is, available on your computer screen. If your college or university does not subscribe to accounts that bring in pictures and sound as well as words, you may have to subscribe to a private service for that luxury, or to use the lines coming into your library. However you do it, you'll want to learn to follow the various threads in the World Wide Web, among them:

- Telnet: a command taking you to remote sites
- FTP: a file transfer protocol that lets you retrieve information
- Usenets: interactive accounts that link you to newsgroups—that is, to interactive discussions
- Archie, Gopher, Veronica, WAIS (Wide Area Information Servers): multiple tools for accessing information sites in useful ways

By now, you probably cannot tune into a sports broadcast, a news hour, or even a primetime television show without being told that you can use a "www." command to get to its "home page": ESPNET's sports scores for the day, CNN International's informational background on big stories, *USA Today* online, National Public Radio's discussion group, or propaganda put out by the Republican and Democratic parties. You soon discover you can go to Mississippi State University for the Internet Movie Database, to SCREENsite for links between the Library of Congress and directories on film and television resources, to the Harvard-MIT-Tufts consortium on negotiation and conflict resolution, to the University of Maryland's site full of resources and simulations for high school students, to state and federal government sources through ".gov" locations. Taking time to discover how to draw on such information will make your speech preparation time not only well-spent but even fun.

The Print World

Most speakers, however, still do most of their information-searching the old fashioned way: by trudging to the library to search through the books, newspapers, magazines, and pamphlets that are available in a hands-on way. The trick for making use of the traditional print world competently is to look for the different kinds and qualities of information in different places.

Newspapers.   Newspapers are obviously a useful source of information about events of current interest. Moreover, their feature stories and accounts of unusual happenings provide a storehouse of interesting illustrations and examples. You must be careful, of course, not to accept as true everything printed in a newspaper, since the haste with which news must be gathered sometimes makes complete accuracy difficult. Your school or city library undoubtedly keeps on file copies of one or two highly reliable papers, such as the *New York Times,* the *Observer,* the *Wall Street Journal,* or the *Christian Science Monitor,* as well as the leading newspapers of your state or region. If your library has the *New York Times Index,* you can locate the paper's accounts of people and events from 1913 to the present. Another useful and well-indexed source of information on current happenings is *Facts on File,* issued weekly since 1940.

Magazines.   The average university library subscribes to hundreds of magazines and journals. Some, such as *Time, Newsweek,* and *U.S. News & World Report,* summarize weekly events. *Omni* and *Harper's* are representative of monthly publications that cover a wide range of subjects of both passing and lasting importance. The *Nation, Vital Speeches of the Day, Fortune, Washington Monthly,* and the *New Republic,* among other magazines, contain comment on current political, social, and economic questions. More specialized magazines include *Popular Science, Scientific American, Sports Illustrated, Field and Stream, Ms., Better Homes and Gardens, Byte, Today's Health, National Geographic,* and *The Smithsonian.*

This list is, of course, just the beginning. There are hundreds of periodicals available, covering thousands of subjects. To find specific kinds of information, use the *Readers' Guide to Periodical Literature,* which indexes most of the magazines you'll want to consult in preparing a speech. Or, if you'd like more sophisticated material, consult the *Social Sciences Index* and the *Humanities Index,* now computerized in most libraries. Similar indexes are available for publications from technical fields and professional societies; a reference librarian can show you how to use them.

Yearbooks and Encyclopedias.   The most reliable source of comprehensive data is the *Statistical Abstracts of the United States,* an annual publication covering a wide variety of subjects ranging from weather records and birth rates to steel production and election results. Information on Academy Award Winners, world records in various areas, and the "bests" and "worsts" of almost anything can be found in the *World Almanac, The People's Almanac, The Guinness Book of World Records, The Book of Lists,* and *Information Please.* Encyclopedias, such as the *Encyclopaedia Britannica* and *Encyclopedia Americana,* attempt to cover the entire field of human knowledge and are valuable chiefly as initial reference sources or for background reading. Refer to them for important scientific, geographical, literary, or historical facts; for bibliographies of authoritative books on a subject; and for ideas you do not need to develop completely in your speech.

Documents and Reports.   Various government agencies—state, national, and international—as well as many independent organizations publish reports on special subjects. The most frequently consulted governmental publications are the hearings and recommendations of congressional committees in the publications of the United States Department of Health and Human Services or Department of Commerce. Reports on issues related to agriculture, business, government, engineering, and scientific experimentation are published by many state universities. Such endowed groups as the Carnegie, Rockefeller, and Ford Foundations and such special interest groups as the Foreign Policy Association, the Brookings Institution, the League of Women Voters, Common Cause, and the U.S. Chamber of Commerce also publish reports and pamphlets. Though by no means a complete list, *The Vertical File Index* serves as a guide to some of these materials.

Books.   Most subjects suitable for a speech have been written about in books. As a guide to these books, use the subject-matter headings in the card catalog of local libraries. Generally, you will find authoritative books in your school library and more popularized treatments in your public library. You can now access the card catalog via computer in many libraries. This often makes your search more efficient and productive.

Biographical Dictionaries.   The *Dictionary of National Biography,* the *Dictionary of American Biography, Who's Who, Who's Who in America, Current Biography,* and more specialized works organized by field contain biographical sketches especially useful in locating facts about famous people and in documenting the qualifications of authorities whose testimony you may quote.

The Face-to-Face World

As you become a more proficient oral communicator in this course, you should not forget that you can use the skills you're gaining in speech preparation and analysis to help you acquire information. You can prepare and conduct interviews with people who can supply you with facts, opinions, background information, and leads to other sources.

Conducting Informational Interviews.   The goal of an **informational interview** is clear: to obtain answers to specific questions. In conducting the interview, you hope to elicit answers that can be woven into your speech. Further, the answers can increase your general understanding of a topic so that you avoid misinforming your audience or drawing incorrect inferences from information obtained through other sources. The interviewee may be a "content expert" or someone who has had personal experience with the issues you wish to discuss. If you are addressing the topic of black holes, who better to help you than a physicist? If you are explaining the construction of a concrete boat, you might contact a local civil engineer for assistance. If, on the other hand, you wish to discuss anorexia nervosa, it may be helpful to interview a person who's suffered through the disorder. Interviews can provide compelling illustrations of human experiences.

You should observe the following general guidelines in planning an informational interview:

- *Decide on your specific purpose.* What precise information do you hope to obtain during the interview? One caution: if you are interviewing a controversial figure, you may not be best served by engaging in an argument or by assuming a belligerent or self-righteous manner. Even if you disagree with the answers being given, your role isn't that of Perry Mason, seeking to win a jury's vote by grilling the witness. This doesn't mean that your purpose cannot encompass tough questions or questions that seek further clarification of answers that seem "not right." You can raise such questions without provoking an argument.
- *Structure the interview in advance.* The beginning of an interview clarifies the purpose and sets limits on what will be covered during the session. You can also use this time to establish rapport with the person being interviewed. The middle of the interview comprises the substantive portion: information being sought is provided. Structure your questions in advance so that you have a rough idea of what to ask when. The interview may not follow your list exactly, but you will have a convenient checkpoint to see whether all the information you need has been presented. Finally, you will find the list useful as you summarize your understanding of the major points. This will help you avoid misinterpreting the meaning given to specific points by the person interviewed. The following format is an example of one you might follow in an informational interview:

I. Opening
  A. Mutual greeting
  B. Discussion of purposes
    1. Reason information is needed
    2. Kind of information wanted
II. Informational Portion
  A. Question #1, with clarifying questions as needed
  B. Question #2, with clarifying questions as needed
  C. [and so on]

III. Closing
    A. Summary of main points
    B. Final courtesies

- *Remember that interviews are interactive processes.* There is a definite pattern of "turn-taking" in interviews that allows both parties to concentrate on one issue at a time and assists in making the interview work for the benefit of both parties. The interactive pattern requires that both parties be careful listeners, for one person's comments will affect the next comment of the other. You'll need to remain free to deviate from your interview plan as you listen to the answers to your questions. You'll have to listen to what is said and almost simultaneously think ahead to the next item on your list of questions. Should you forge ahead or ask intervening questions to clarify or elaborate on a previous response? Constantly ask yourself that question.

Communicative Skills for Successful Interviewers. It should by now be clear that adept interviewers must have certain communicative skills.

- *A good interviewer is a good listener.* Unless you take care to understand what someone is saying and to interpret the significance of those comments, you may misunderstand. Because questioning and answering are alternated in an interview, there is plenty of opportunity to clarify remarks and opinions. You can achieve clarification only if you are a good listener (see Chapter 2 on listening for comprehension).
- *A good interviewer is open.* Many of us are extremely wary of interviewers. We are cynical enough to believe that they have a hidden agenda—unstated motives or purposes—that they are trying to pursue. Too often interviewers have said they "only want a little information" when actually they were selling magazine subscriptions or a religious ideal. If, as an interviewer, you're "caught" being less than honest, your chances for success are vastly diminished. Frankness and openness should govern all aspects of your interview communication.
- *A good interviewer builds a sense of mutual respect and trust.* Feelings of trust and respect are created by revealing your own motivation, by getting the person to talk, and by expressing sympathy and understanding. Sometimes, of course, your assumptions of integrity and goodwill can be proved wrong. To start with suspicion and distrust, however, is to condemn the relationship without giving it a fair chance.

The Snail-Mail World

Even as you acquire e-mail and other computer-based electronic communication skills, you should not neglect "snail-mail"—the mail that travels in semis, little white Jeeps, and the leather bags that postal carriers bring to your front door daily. You may get enough junk mail to realize that there's still profit to

To generate new information, a speaker can conduct an informational interview with an expert or someone who has had personal experience with the issue under discussion.

be made in writing people the old fashioned way, through letters of inquiry and questionnaires.

Letters of Inquiry.   Sometimes a simple letter requesting information from an institutional source is all you need in order gain some useful material. You might want to write to your college president, asking for a copy of her fall convocation speech; to the Volkswagen—American Division, for the World Wide

Web address of their home page so that you can get texts to their TV ads; to the U.S. Government Printing Office, for their latest catalog on consumer-protection pamphlets. When writing such a letter, follow a few simple rules:

1. *Keep it short.* Explain why you're writing and what you want, as specifically as you can. Three to four short paragraphs—certainly less than two-thirds of a page—are enough. Don't say "where can I find out about your ads?" but rather "where can I locate the text for the first Neon ad that was broadcast during the 1994 Super Bowl?"
2. *Keep it easy.* If you need only minimal information—say, an address— leave room at the bottom of your letter where your correspondent can reply and then return the same letter to you.
3. *Include a stamped, self-addressed envelope.* Ok, so General Motors could afford to put a stamp on a letter. But, if you save them typing an envelope and make them feel a little guilty by even stamping it, it will be harder for them to simply toss it.

Let's now look at an example of a short letter of inquiry.

A LETTER OF INQUIRY

Customer Service Representative
ABC Beverage Distributing Company
Local Address
    Re: Posters for Current Advertising Campaign

Dear Customer Service Representative:

    I am a student at Middle College, taking a course in public communication. As part of a class assignment, I have decided to give a speech analyzing the current imaginative advertising campaign for Drink-a-billy Root Beer. I would like to include as visual aids for my speech some posters that have been prepared for this campaign. I have seen them locally and find them even more effective than the TV ads.

    Could you please send me one or two of the posters that have been distributed to local grocery stores? I will be needing them by November 16 in order to show them during my speech. If there's any cost associated with sending the posters, let me know and I'll be happy to reimburse you.

    If you cannot send the posters, please indicate so on the enclosed postcard. Thank you for your help in this matter.

                                      Sincerely yours,
                                      Holly Hamilton

    In this letter, Holly has explained what she needs and has used positive language so that the distributer does not think that she's going to attack the product; she has also specified the date she needs it, so that the process doesn't drag on forever, and has sent along a card so that she won't be expecting something that's not going to come. (If the ABC representative wants to tell Holly that she has to write somewhere else for the posters, that can also be written on the card and mailed to her with minimal effort.)

Questionnaires. On other occasions, you may wish to discover what a group of people knows or thinks about a subject. If, for example, you wanted to give a speech on a proposed halfway house for the mentally ill, you might survey residents in the vicinity. You could send a questionnaire to people chosen randomly from the phone book or to all residents within a three-block radius from the proposed home. If you're seeking information on a new college drinking policy, you could survey dormitory residents or members of several classes. With the results, you could construct your own statistical summaries for presentation as part of your speech.

When developing a questionnaire, keep these guidelines in mind:

- Be sure the form explains the exact purpose of the questionnaire and the procedures to follow in responding to the questions.
- Keep the form short and to the specific points you wish to have responses on.
- For ease of summarizing, use closed questions (for example, ask for "yes/no" responses where appropriate and use such categories as "strongly agree/agree/disagree/strongly disagree" if you want ranges of opinion).
- Phrase questions in clear, neutral language. Do not use loaded terms (for example, "Do you wish to see mentally unbalanced, unpredictable people living next to your children?").
- Pilot-test the form with a few people to see whether the instructions are clear and to determine if any questions need to be rephrased.
- If mailing the questionnaire, include a stamped, self-addressed envelope to encourage returns.

Recording Information in Usable Forms

When you find the information you have been looking for, either photocopy it or take notes. Whether you use four-by-six-inch notecards or a notebook, it is helpful to have an accurate, legible record of the materials you wish to consider for your speech. An incomplete source citation makes it difficult to find the information again if you need to recheck it; hurried scribbles, too, are hard to decipher later.

Many people find that notecards are easier to use than a notebook because they can be shuffled by topic area or type of support. If you use a notebook, however, try recording each item on half a page. Since most of your information will not fill a page, this will save paper; cutting the sheets in half will make it easier to sort your data or to adopt a classification scheme and relate information to particular themes or subpoints of your speech. When preparing notecards, place the subject headings at the top of the card and the complete source citation at the bottom, as in the sample presented here. This way, the card can be classified by general subject (top right heading) and by specific information presented (top left heading).

You need not, of course, always follow these directions exactly. You will find, however, that you will need a classification system so you can put your hands on specific pieces of information as you construct your speeches.

*U*SING SOURCE MATERIAL ETHICALLY

Now that we've discussed locating and generating material for your speeches, we come to a major ethical issue—plagiarism. **Plagiarism** is defined as "the unacknowledged inclusion of someone else's words, ideas, or data as one's own."[18] One of the saddest things an instructor has to do is cite a student for plagiarism. In speech classes, students occasionally take material from a source they've read and present it as their own. Many speech teachers and members of audiences habitually scan the library periodicals section. Even if listeners have not read the article, it soon becomes apparent that something is wrong: the wording differs from the way the person usually talks, the style is more typical of written than spoken English, or the speech is a patchwork of eloquent and awkward phrasing. In addition, the organizational pattern of the speech may lack a well-formulated introduction or conclusion or be one not normally used by speakers. Often, too, the person who plagiarizes an article reads it aloud badly—another sign that something is wrong.

Plagiarism is not, however, simply undocumented verbatim quotation. It also includes (1) undocumented paraphrases of others' ideas and (2) undocumented use of others' main ideas. For example, if you paraphrase a movie review from *Newsweek* without acknowledging that staff critic David Ansen had

FIGURE 6.2 A Sample Notecard

Specific Information	Dropping the A-Bomb Saved Lives in World War II	Dropping the A-Bomb in World War II	General Subject

"And if the majority opinion of the Japanese leaders interrogated immediately after the war had turned out to be right—that the war would have lasted into 1946—the carnage doubles, or triples. Marquis Kido claimed to have saved twenty million Japanese lives by engineering an August (1945) surrender. Togo Shigenori also places the anticipated slaughter sans atom in the millions...The atom saved many lives in the Pacific War. It also saved may lives in unfought future wars."

Source — Robert P. Newman, *Truman and the Hiroshima Cult* (East Lansing: Michigan State University Press, 1995), 188

those insights, or if you use economic predictions without giving credit to *Businessweek,* you are guilty of plagiarism.

Suppose you ran across the following idea while reading Neil Postman's *Amusing Ourselves to Death: Public Discourse in the Age of Show Business:*

> The television commercial is not at all about the character of products to be consumed. It is about the character of the consumers of products. Images of movie stars and famous athletes, of serene lakes and macho fishing trips, of elegant dinners and romantic interludes, of happy families packing their station wagons for a picnic in the country—these tell nothing about the products being sold. But they tell everything about the fears, fancies and dreams of those who might buy them. What the advertiser needs to know is not what is right about the product but what is wrong about the buyer. And so, the balance of business expenditures shifts from product research to market research. The television commercial has oriented business away from making products of value and toward making consumers feel valuable, which means that the business of business has now become pseudo-therapy. The consumer is a patient assured by psycho-dramas.[19]

Imagine that you wanted to make this point in a speech on the changing role of electronic advertising. Of course, you want to avoid plagiarism. Here are some ways you could use the ideas ethically:

1. *Verbatim quotation of a passage.* Simply read the passage aloud word for word. To avoid plagiarism, say, "Neil Postman, in his 1985 book *Amusing Ourselves to Death: Public Discourse in the Age of Show Business,* said this about the nature of television advertisements." You can then quote the paragraph.
2. *Paraphrasing of the main ideas:* Summarize the author's ideas in your own words: "We've all grown up with television advertising, and most of the time we endure it without giving it much thought. In his book *Amusing Ourselves to Death: Public Discourse in the Age of Show Business,* Neil Postman makes the point that instead of selling us on the virtues of a product, advertisers sell us our own fears and dreams. Advertisements are more about us than about the products being sold."
3. *Partial quotation of phrases:* Quote a brief passage and summarize the rest of the author's ideas in your own words: "Postman suggests that the shift from product research to market research indicates a shift in emphasis away from the product being sold and to the consumer. He says that business now focuses on making the consumer feel better through 'pseudo-therapy. The consumer is a patient assured by psycho-dramas.'" Be sure to pause and say "quote" to indicate when you are quoting the author's words.

Plagiarism is easy to avoid if you take reasonable care. Moreover, by citing such authorities as Postman, who are well educated and experienced, you add their credibility to yours. Avoid plagiarism to keep from being expelled from the class or even from your school. Avoid it for positive reasons as well: to improve your *ethos* by associating your thinking with that of experts.

USING SUPPORTING MATERIALS STRATEGICALLY: CRITICAL THINKING

It's one thing to consider the range of materials appropriate to your purpose, then to gather the relevant information; it's quite another to use the information effectively. The effective use of supporting materials is an exercise in **critical thinking**—assessing the rational requirements for clarifying thoughts and proving something to someone else. As was suggested earlier, when you illustrate a central idea or a claim, you have to ask yourself two important questions: "What information is reasonable as support for my ideas?" and "What do the listeners need to know in order to accept my ideas?" Thinking critically about these two questions involves the following subissues:

- The rational requirements your claims put on you
- The range of supporting materials available
- The demands a particular audience might make of someone defending such a claim
- The generally perceived power-to-justify of particular forms of support

Suppose you want to defend the claim that "All public restaurants should be smoke-free environments." Thinking about the claim, you might come to the following conclusions:

1. *Rational requirements of the claim.* This claim demands that you demonstrate the relationship between smoking and health and between passive smoke and health. The first is relatively easy to support, given the Surgeon General's warning and the plethora of studies on the harmful effects of smoking. The second is somewhat more difficult, because one could argue that proper ventilation and separation of smoking and nonsmoking areas will effectively minimize any danger from passive smoke. Complicating the issue is the observation that a smoker's civil rights are being violated by acceptance of your claim. What sort of supporting materials will help you make your case? Providing statistical evidence to support the relationships as well as authoritative or expert opinion on the dangers of passive smoke will be helpful. Using personal narratives that detail the consequences of inadvertently inhaling smoke will make the issue more vivid and compelling. Locating appropriate legal precedents on the constitutionality of smoke-free regulations addresses the civil rights issue head-on.

2. *Range of available supporting materials.* Can you find all the materials you need? Do you have access to medical information and expert testimony on the effects of smoking and smoke inhalation? Do you have access to appropriate legal sources? In other words, it's one thing to contemplate what would make for excellent support but quite another to find it. You may have to settle for thinner evidence than you would like, simply due to your lack of access to certain kinds of material.

3. *Audience demands.* The need to address some issues will depend in large part on who is in the audience. The civil rights issue may be less critical if the audience is the local chapter of the American Cancer Society, but more criticism if it's from the American Civil Liberties Union. Consider the kinds of questions your audience is likely to ask and then attempt to address each one. As a nonsmoker, do I really have to be wary of how close to the smoking section I sit at a restaurant? Am I really in that much danger from inhaling the smoke in a room, when I'm not actually smoking? Do I have the right to a smoke-free environment? What are the appropriate limits to that right and is eating in a smoke-free restaurant within the limits?

4. *Power-to-justify.* You may use any of the forms of support to clarify, to amplify, or to strengthen a central idea or claim. However, some forms tend to accomplish these goals more effectively than others and are more effective with particular audiences. Explanation, comparison, specific instance, and segment statistics are especially helpful in clarifying an idea. These methods allow the speaker to present information that simplifies an idea for the audience. They also are useful when listeners have little background or knowledge about the topic or when the subject matter is complex. Explanations, comparison, illustration, and statistics of magnitude and trend can help the speaker amplify an idea, expanding on it so the audience can better examine the concept. These forms of support may be especially useful when the audience has only a slight knowledge of the concept. To strengthen or lend credibility to a point, try factual illustrations, specific instances, statistics, and testimony from respected sources. These forms strengthen the idea by making it vivid and believable.

Once you've thought through these issues and selected your materials, ask yourself one more question: *When my speech is completed, what reasonable questions will still remain in the minds of the smartest listeners?* You'll not address all issues and answer every question in a single speech, but you ought always to look ahead, anticipate what can be questioned, and then be ready to handle questions probing those issues after the speech. If you build the speech as solidly as you can and then anticipate what needs to be done next, you'll go a long way toward accomplishing every speaker's goal: obtaining acceptance of your ideas.

CHAPTER SUMMARY

Competent speakers use six primary forms of supporting materials to clarify, amplify, and strengthen their presentations:

- *Explanations,* which answer the questions "what," "how," or "why"
- *Comparisons and contrasts,* which explain the similarities and differences between ideas and processes familiar and unfamiliar to listeners
- *Illustrations and narratives,* which provide detailed examples or stories
- *Specific instances,* which group a number of undeveloped illustrations or examples
- *Statistics,* which show the numerical relationships between or among phenomena
- *Testimony,* which cites the opinions or conclusions of qualified experts.

These materials can be assembled from the *electronic world* (electronic card catalog, CD-ROM indexes, World Wide Web searches), the *print world* (newspapers, magazines, yearbooks and reports, books, biographical dictionaries), the *face-to-face world* (informational interviews), and the *snail-mail world* (letters of inquiry, questionnaires). Record information from any source fully and accurately, either on notecards or notebook pages. Avoid *plagiarism.* As you speak, know enough to not only adequate support your ideas and argument, but also to anticipate questions and issues you didn't address. The competent speaker knows both what's been said and done, and what additional work remains.

KEY TERMS

CD-ROM (p. 157)	*narrative (p. 145)*
comparison (p. 143)	*plagiarism (p. 165)*
contrast (p. 144)	*segments (p. 149)*
critical thinking (p. 167)	*specific instances (p. 146)*
explanation (p. 141)	*statistics (p. 148)*
illustration (p. 145)	*testimony (p. 152)*
Information Superhighway (p. 157)	*trends (p. 150)*
informational interview (p. 160)	*World Wide Web (p. 157)*
magnitude (p. 149)	

ASSESSMENT ACTIVITIES

1. Read one of the speeches in this textbook and identify its forms of supporting material. Down the lefthand side of the page, record the idea or assertion being made. Across from it, on the righthand side, indicate the type(s) of supporting materials used to clarify, amplify, or strengthen it. Then, with the help of advice given in the "Critical Thinking" section of this chapter, as-

sess the speaker's use of supporting materials: Were good choices made (or not)? That is, was the material adequate to clarify, amplify, and strengthen ideas? What could have been done better? How?

2. Work in groups of two to four students, trying to make sure at least one member of the group has access to the Internet (though all of this information can be found in a good library). Work in pairs, with each pair assigned four items to find—one student working in print resources, the other, electronically if possible. (If that's not possible, work together in the print resources.) One person should work on even-numbered items, the other, on odd-numbered items. When the pairs turn in their reports, they should include a careful citation of where they found the information.

1. Weekly or daily summary of current national news
2. Daily summary of stock market action
3. Text of Bill Clinton's address during the Million Man March of October 1995
4. Text of Newt Gingrich's first speech as House Majority Leader in January 1995
5. Origin of the word "rhetoric"
6. At least three different meanings for the word "wit" and dates when those meanings came into use
7. Current status of national legislation on education reform
8. Description of a recent traffic accident, locally or nationally reported
9. Brief analysis of the accomplishments of Ted Turner
10. Brief sketch of the hits of Tina Turner

ℛEFERENCES

1. Randall L. Tobias, "In Today Walks Tomorrow," in *Representative American Speeches, 1992–1993*, ed. Owen Peterson, Vol. 65, No. 6 (New York: H. W. Wilson, 1993), 105.
2. Robert Lutz, "Managed Trade: Spring of Hope or Nuclear War?" *Vital Speeches of the Day* 59 (July 1, 1993): 554.
3. H. Ross Perot, "Testimony Before Senate Banking, Housing, and Urban Affairs Committee," April 22, 1993. *The Impact of the North American Free Trade Agreemaent on US Jobs and Wages,* Senate Hearing, 103rd Congress (Washington: U.S. Government Printing Office, 1993), 10.
4. Dudley Herschbach, "1992 Harvard-Radcliffe Phi Beta Kappa Oration," *Harvard Magazine* 93, no. 3 (January–February 1993): 57–58.
5. Hillary Rodham Clinton, "Health Care—We Can Make a Difference," *Vital Speeches of the Day* 59 (July 15, 1993): 600.
6. For a study of Cicero's own use of the technique, see Donovan J. Ochs, "Rhetorical Detailing in Cicero's Verrine Orations," *Communication Studies* 23 (Spring 1982): 310–318.

7. Hunter R. Rawlings III, "The University and the Public," in *Representative American Speeches, 1992–1993*, 84.

8. For an excellent study of depiction, see Michael Osborn, "Rhetorical Depiction," in *Form, Genre, and the Study of Political Discourse,* ed. Herbert W. Simons and Aram A. Aghazarian (Columbia, SC: University of South Carolina Press, 1986), 79–108. To think more broadly yet about the role of the visual in contemporary communication, see sample essays in Chris Jenks, ed., *Visual Culture* (New York: Routledge, 1995).

9. Donald Keough, "The Courage to Dream—Seize the Day," *Vital Speeches of the Day* 59 (July 15, 1993): 600.

10. Antonia Novello, "Your Parents, Your Community—Without Caring There is No Hope," *Vital Speeches of the Day* 59 (July 15, 1993): 591.

11. Brenda Theriault, "Fast Foods," speech given at the University of Maine, Spring 1992.

12. Eddie Paul Hunter, "Term Limits: A Solution Worse than the Problem," *Winning Orations, 1991:* 90.

13. Paul N. Carlin, "Privatizing the U.S. Postal Service," *Vital Speeches of the Day* 61 (November 15, 1994): 77.

14. Carl Hall, "A Heap of Trouble," *Winning Orations,* 1977.

15. Still entertaining and insightful is Darrell Huff, *How to Lie with Statistics* (New York: W. W. Norton, 1954).

16. Daniel Lashof, "Testimony Before House Subcommittee on Energy and Power," March 3, 1992. *Global Warming,* House of Representatives Hearing, 102nd Congress (Washington: U.S. Government Printing Office, 1992), 1.

17. John R. Levine and Carol Baroudi, *The Internet for Dummies* (San Mateo, CA: IDG Books Worldwide, Inc., 1993); Paul Gilster, *The Internet Navigator,* 2nd ed. (New York: Wiley, 1994). No matter what you buy, always check the copyright date, what with changes occurring almost monthly. By now, *The Internet for Dummies* has been updated at least once.

18. Louisiana State University, "Academic Honesty and Dishonesty," adapted from LSU's Code of Student Conduct, 1981.

19. Neil Postman, *Amusing Ourselves to Death: Public Discourse in the Age of Show Business* (New York: Viking Penguin, 1985), 128.

ADAPTING THE SPEECH STRUCTURE TO AUDIECES: THE MOTIVATED SEQUENCE AND PATTERNS OF INTERNAL ORGANIZATION

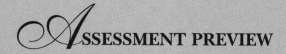

ASSESSMENT PREVIEW

After reading Chapter 7, the student with basic communication competencies will be able to

- name the five steps in the motivated sequence.
- use the five steps in a speech to actuate.
- name and use at least three of the internal patterns of organization in a speech to inform.

The student with average communication competencies will also be able to

- understand when each of the steps is most applicable in speaking to inform, persuade, actuate or entertain.
- identify different patterns of internal organization.
- use at least one of the internal patterns in a speech.
- correctly organize main points with subpoints

The student with superior communication competencies will also be able to

- distinguish between effective and ineffective use of the motivated sequence.
- apply the motivated sequence steps in the most effective manner.
- use more than one of the internal patterns of organization in a speech.

*F*or his first major classroom speech, Tom decided to talk about a subject he was interested in—doing research at the Library of Congress. Since he had just been there, he wouldn't need to do any more work in preparing the speech; he could just tell the audience how much he learned while there. When his turn came, he walked confidently to the lectern and simply began telling his story. Midway through the speech, he thought he sensed disinterest on the part of the audience. "What could be wrong with them?" went through his mind as he moved on to the most exciting part of the speech—looking up sources on the computerized catalog. When he finished, the instructor asked for any comments from his listeners. The first question shocked him: "What was the reason for that speech?"

Tom's experience is not far off the mark when one speaks without thinking about the audience. Tom had assumed that since students wrote research papers, they would automatically find his descriptions worthwhile. He had given no thought to the audience's interests or needs; hence he didn't even bother to think about using specific motivational appeals. He also hadn't given much time to structuring his speech so as to keep the flow of events clear in the audience's mind. If he forgot to mention something, he just circled back and filled in the missing information. ("When I talked about bringing your laptop into the building, I forgot to tell you . . ."; right, most students would need that information as they normally take their laptops when they travel to the Library!) Considering the audience's interests, choosing motivational appeals to channel everyone's interest in your direction, and selecting supporting materials that are appropriate are essential tasks—and as Tom's experience suggests, tasks that are best considered before the presentation. Even if Tom had given some thought to these issues, the fact that he also gave little time to structuring his message would still have doomed his presentation. Unless presented in a strategically sound structure, the motivational appeals of Chapter 5 and the supporting materials of Chapter 6 would fall scattered among the listeners. Structuring ideas provides direction for the audience; it lets them follow the development of your message so that, by the time you conclude, they know the central idea or claim, and how it has been explained or supported. In this chapter, we'll explore organizational patterns that will assist you in arranging your materials in the most effective manner.

There are many ways to organize speech materials. Depending on the topic, your purpose, and audience needs, some approaches will work better than others. Before looking at those differences, however, we will first look at the nature of structure as a general concept and study one general-purpose organizational pattern known as the motivated sequence. Then we'll examine other patterns for organizing speeches.

*O*RGANIZATION FROM THE LISTENER'S PERSPECTIVE

People actively seek organization in their environment, imposing it if they cannot find it naturally. Watch young children: They learn early that one set of furniture goes in a bedroom, another set in a kitchen, a third in a living room.

By elementary school, they can determine what is *foreground* in a picture and what is *background* or supporting detail. Such processes of differentiation lend coherence to their perceptions of objects and events. They can also complete or fill in missing elements in fields. For example, if someone says to you, "One, two, three, four," you almost automatically continue with "five, six, seven, eight." If a cartoonist draws a few pen lines of a well-known person you can probably identify the individual. Or, if you see an unclosed circle, you'll likely perceive it as a circle because of its resemblance to complete ones you've seen.[1] Generally speaking, the principles of **differentiation** and **closure**—of sorting items into groups and of psychologically completing pictures or experiences—are central to our understanding of verbal organization or order as well.

The key idea underlying verbal organization is this: *People use their language to structure—that is, to make sense out of—their world.* Think of some of the language strategies you use to organize parts of your life:

- *Numerical order:* "In the first place. . . ." Such language use establishes sequence.
- *Physical space:* "In the middle"; "to the west, east, and, south." Establishing spatial relationships allows you to "see" a kind of physical order through language.
- *Topics or types:* "Executive, legislative, and judicial branches of government"; "animal, vegetable, and mineral"; "past, present, and future." Dividing a subject into manageable and memorable topics helps to clarify relationships.
- *Narrative order:* "Once upon a time"; "I heard a story the other day"; "I awoke with a start that morning." Turning a series of events into a story—with a beginning, a middle, and an end, even a "moral" or message—is a way of making disorganized experiences coherent and of giving them a point or application.
- *Logical inference:* "Because of this . . . , therefore . . . "; "As evidence for this assertion"; "I believe that because." These phrases show connections between ideas, indicating what follows from what.
- *Hierarchies:* "Higher, lower"; "inside, outside"; "under class, middle class, upper class"; "important, unimportant"; "main points, secondary points." We often build hierarchies out of social or intellectual judgments to help us understand or argue for what's more or less central to our lives.

These are just some of the language devices used in organizing or ordering life experiences. The phrases show relationships among ideas, events, objects; as we convey our perceptions to others, these phrases become indispensable aids in making ideas clear. As listeners, we depend on a speaker's use of these phrases to make sense of the ideas. Listeners look for the same sense of order in a speech, as the speaker moves from central idea to explanatory points, from claim to supporting reasons. This chapter introduces a general method for thinking about speech organization from the listener's perspective. Since 1935, when the first edition of this textbook was published by Alan H. Monroe

[1903–1975], that structure has been called **Monroe's Motivated Sequence.** The rest of this chapter will be devoted to this holistic structure for organizing messages.

THE FIVE BASIC STEPS OF THE MOTIVATED SEQUENCE

The steps of the motivated sequence conform to a listener's desire for coherence and order. As a holistic way of organizing speeches, it is responsive to the thought processes listeners often follow when receiving new information or trying to solve problems. When you find yourself listening to a classroom speech, you probably experience a predictable series of reactions: "Why should I listen?" "Ok, what do you mean? Why is that true?" "How does this affect me?" "So, what do you want from me as a result of this speech?" These and other questions are typical of the kinds of responses audience members have as they listen to an informative or persuasive presentation.

The motivated sequence provides a template of sorts, arranged in five basic steps, for this natural progression of audience queries. As a starting place, you must get people to *attend* to a problem or to feel strongly enough to be willing to hear more about the deficiency you want them to help correct. Then, you can address more specific needs or desires, in relation to an individual's personal sense of *need*. Once these have been established, you can attempt to *satisfy* them by showing what can be done to solve the problem or alleviate its impact on their lives. Simply describing a course of action may be insufficient to move an audience to act; hence, you can move to *visualizing* what the situation would be like if the action were carried out or, conversely, what it would be like if the action were not taken. With these motivational tasks completed, you can appeal to the audience members to *act*—to put into practice the proposed solution to the problem.

As you think through the order of these steps, recall Maslow's concept of a hierarchy of needs and desires that build naturally upon one another. In a similar fashion, speeches proceed from one step to the next; omitting the attention step, for instance, may result in listeners not hearing the rest of your ideas. On the other hand, the audience may be so intent on the issues that you already have their attention—hence this step would be a waste of valuable time. Thus the sequential patterning of the steps is not a hard and fast rule; you will need to adapt it to the rhetorical situation you face. Nevertheless, as a rule, adhering to its general order increases the likelihood of success. As a holistic organizational tool, the motivated sequence can be used to structure many different sorts of speeches on many different topics. As your purpose shifts from informational to persuasive or actuative, the specific form each step takes likewise shifts.

Using the Motivated Sequence to Organize Speeches

As an overall pattern of development, the most obvious use of the motivated sequence is in persuasive or actuative situations. For example, it can structure

FIGURE 7.1 The Motivated Sequence

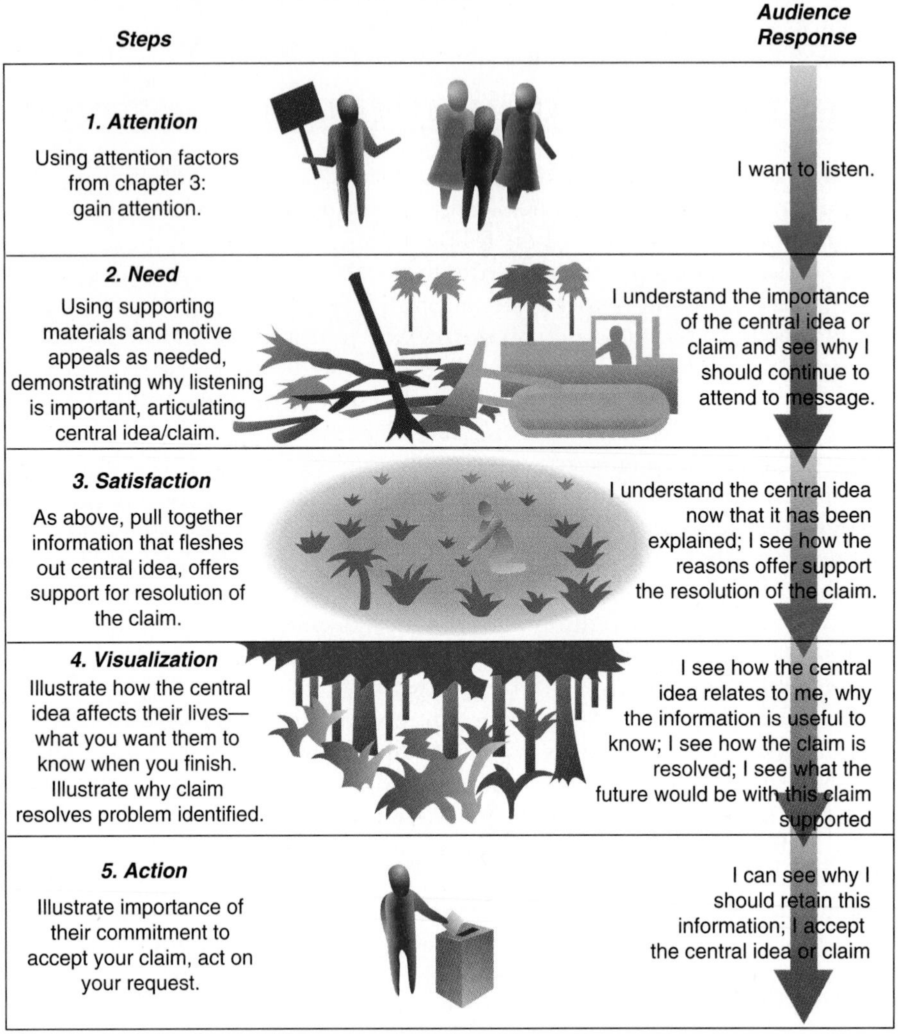

Steps

Audience Response

1. Attention

Using attention factors from chapter 3: gain attention.

I want to listen.

2. Need

Using supporting materials and motive appeals as needed, demonstrating why listening is important, articulating central idea/claim.

I understand the importance of the central idea or claim and see why I should continue to attend to message.

3. Satisfaction

As above, pull together information that fleshes out central idea, offers support for resolution of the claim.

I understand the central idea now that it has been explained; I see how the reasons offer support the resolution of the claim.

4. Visualization

Illustrate how the central idea affects their lives— what you want them to know when you finish. Illustrate why claim resolves problem identified.

I see how the central idea relates to me, why the information is useful to know; I see how the claim is resolved; I see what the future would be with this claim supported

5. Action

Illustrate importance of their commitment to accept your claim, act on your request.

I can see why I should retain this information; I accept the central idea or claim

the major points of a speech urging classmates to join a blood donors' group being formed on campus:

> *Attention:* "If you had needed an emergency transfusion for a rare blood type in Choteau County on December 23, 1996 you might not have received it."
>
> *Need:* "Blood drives seldom collect sufficient quantities of blood to meet emergency needs in an area such as this one."
>
> *Satisfaction:* "A blood donors' association guarantees a predictable, steady supply of needed blood to the medical community."

Visualization: "Without a steady supply of blood, our community will face needless deaths; with it, emergencies like yours can be met with prompt treatment."

Action: "You can help by filling out the blood donors' cards I am handing out."

You also can use the motivated sequence to convey information:

Attention: "Does the prospect of getting AIDS frighten you?"

Need: "If we are to be less frightened by this insidious disease, we all need to be better informed about the ways we can be infected and about the myths concerning how it can be acquired."

Satisfaction: "AIDS can be acquired through specific sexual practices by both males and females and through sharing needles used for drug intake; it cannot be acquired from kissing, from toilet seats, or from sitting across from a person with AIDS."

Visualization: "With this information, I hope to have allayed any irrational fears you may have by being very specific about when you are and when you are not at risk."

Action: "This information can be useful as you consider the meaning of 'safe sex,' as well as when you encounter people who are HIV positive."

ASSESSING A SAMPLE SPEECH

The following speech was prepared by Maria Lucia R. Anton of the University of Guam, a participant in the 1994 Interstate Oratorical Association contest.[2] As you read the speech, note that the attention step (paragraphs 1–4) creates initial curiosity as to the general purpose of the speech and then goes on to identify the source and meaning of the statement in relation to sexual assault policies. In paragraph 5, Maria introduces the need (that not all campuses have such policies in place). In a series of paragraphs (6–9) Maria satisfies the need as presented, and then moves to visualizing what a solution (a policy) would bring (paragraphs 10–18). The action step is introduced in the final two paragraphs of her speech.

SEXUAL ASSAULT POLICY A MUST

Maria Lucia R. Anton

Attention

"If you want to take her blouse off, you have to ask. If you want to touch her breast, you have to ask. If you want to move your hand down to her genitals, you have to ask. If you want to put your finger inside her, you have to ask." /1

What I've just quoted is part of the freshman orientation at Antioch College in Ohio. In the sexual offense policy of this college, emphasis is given to three major points: (1) If you have a sexually transmitted disease, you must disclose it to a potential partner, (2) To knowingly take advantage of someone who is under the influence of alcohol, drugs and/or prescribed medication is not acceptable behavior in the Antioch community, (3) Obtaining consent is an on-going process in any sexual interaction. The request for consent must be specific to each act. /2

The policy is designed to create a "safe" campus environment according to Antioch President Alan Guskin. For those who engage in sex, the goal is 100% consensual sex. It isn't enough to ask someone if they would like to have sex, you have to get verbal consent every step of the way. /3

This policy has been highly publicized and you may have heard it before. The policy addresses sexual offenses such as rape, which involves penetration, and sexual assault, which does not. In both instances, the respondent coerced or forced the primary witness to engage in nonconsensual sexual conduct with the respondent or another. /4

Need

Sexual assault has become a major problem in U.S. campuses today. However, in spite of increased sexual assaults on campuses, many still go without a policy to protect their students. The University of Guam, where I am a senior, is one example. /5

Sexual Assault has become a reality in many campuses across the nation. Carleton College in Northfield, Minnesota, was sued for $800,000 in damages by four university women. The women charged that Carleton was negligent in protecting them against a known rapist. From the June 3, 1991, issue of *Time Magazine:*

> Amy had been on campus for just five weeks when she joined some friends to watch a video in the room of a senior. One by one the other students went away, leaving her alone with a student whose name she didn't even know. "It ended up with his hands around my throat," she recalls. In a lawsuit she has filed against the college, she charges that he locked the door and raped her again and again for the next four hours. "I didn't want him to kill me, I just kept trying not to cry." Only afterwards did he tell her, almost defiantly, his name. It was on top of the "castration list" posted on women's bathroom walls around campus to warn other students

about college rapists." Amy's attacker was found guilty of sexual assault but was only suspended.

Julie started dating a fellow cast member in a Carleton play. They had never slept together, she charges in a civil suit, until he came to her dorm room one night, uninvited, and raped her. She struggled to hold her life and education together, but finally could manage no longer and left school. Only later did Julie learn that her assailant was the same man who had attacked Amy. /6

Ladies and gentlemen, the court held that the college knew this man was a rapist. The administration may have been able to prevent this from happening if they had expelled the attacker, but they didn't. My campus has no reports of sexual assault. Is the administration waiting for someone to be assaulted before they formulate a sexual assault policy? This mistake has been made elsewhere, we don't have to prove it again. /7

Perhaps some statistics will help you understand the magnitude of the problem. According to *New Statesman & Society*, June 21, 1991, issue:

A 1985 survey of sampled campuses by *Ms. Magazine* and the National Institute of Mental Health found that 1 in every 4 college women were victims of sexual assault, 74 percent knew their attackers. Even worse, between 30 to 40 percent of male students indicated that they might force a woman to have sex if they knew they would escape punishment.

In just one year from 1988–1989, reports of student rape at the University of California increased from 2 to 80. /8

These numbers are indeed disturbing. But more disturbing are the effects of sexual assault. A victim feeling the shock of why something this terrible was allowed to happen. Having intense fears that behind every dark corner could be an attacker ready to grab her, push her to the ground and sexually assault her. Many waking moments of anxiety and impaired concentration as she remembers the attack. Countless nights of reliving the traumatic incident in her sleep. Mood swings and depression as she tries to deal internally with the physical hurt and the emotional turmoil that this attack has caused. /9

Satisfaction

Many campuses are open invitations for sexual assault. The absence of a policy is a grand invitation. I have never been sexually assaulted so why do I care so much about a policy? You know why, because I could be assaulted. I won't sit and wait to be among 1 out of every 4 women on my campus to be assaulted. The first step to keep myself out of the statistics is to push for a sexual assault policy on my campus. One way to do this is through a petition to the university. /10

Although the Antioch policy sounds a little far-fetched and has been the target of criticism in comedy routines such as "Saturday Night Live," although students feel this is unnatural, many campuses are taking heed and revisiting their own policies. Campuses like mine don't have a sexual policy to revisit. Does yours? /11

By far the most controversial policy today is that of Antioch. I'm not saying that we need one as specific as theirs, but every university has a responsibility to provide a safe environment for its students. Universities have an obligation to provide a sexual assault policy to protect its students. /12

The following points are fundamental to the safety of the students and need to be addressed by universities:

1. Every campus should have a sexual assault policy that is developed with input from the students, faculty, staff and administration. The policy then needs to be publicized in the student handbook. The school newspaper should print and campus radio broadcast the policy periodically to heighten awareness.
2. Campuses must institute programs to educate students and other campus personnel. Examples of these include discussing the sexual assault policy during mandatory student orientation and conduct special workshops for faculty and other staff.
3. Outline a step-by-step written procedure to guarantee that sexual assault victims are assisted by the university. It is pertinent that they are not without support at this very critical time. /13

Visualization

My vision is a campus where there is no place for any sexual assault. I want to leave my classroom at night knowing that my trip from the building to the car will not be one of fear for my personal safety. /14

You may be saying to yourself that there are laws to handle crimes like these. From *The Chronicle of Higher Education,* May 15, 1991 issue, Jane McDonnell, a Senior Lecturer in Women's Studies at Carleton, says colleges cannot turn their backs on women. "We'd be abandoning victims if we merely sent them to the police," she says. "The wheels of justice tend to grind slowly and rape has one of the lowest conviction rates of any crime." /15

Without a policy, most institutions lack specific penalties for sexual assault and choose to prosecute offenders under the general student-conduct code. In cases such as Carleton College, Amy's attacker was allowed back on campus after his suspension and consequently he raped again. /16

Although the policy may not stop the actual assault, would be offenders will think twice before committing sexual assault if they knew they would be punished. In addition, it guarantees justice for victims of sexual assault. We need to make it loud and clear that sexual assault will not be tolerated. /17

Yes, universities have a big task in the struggle to prevent sexual assault. /18

Action

You and I can actively assist in this task and can make a giant contribution to move it forward. On my campus students have not only voiced their concerns but we have also started a petition demanding that the university formulate a sexual assault policy. /19

The bottom line is, we need to prevent sexual assault on campus. The key to prevention is a sexual assault policy. If you don't have a policy, then you need to petition your administration to have one. I know I won't stop my advocacy until I see a policy on my campus. /20

STRUCTURE AND DEVELOPMENT OF THE STEPS IN THE MOTIVATED SEQUENCE

Now that we've illustrated the motivated sequence in its entirety, we need to examine more closely the individual steps, noting in particular their internal structuring, the methods for developing them, and the kinds of materials that can be used effectively in each.

The Attention Step

As a speaker, your first task is to gain attention. The attributes of attention and the major devices for obtaining it were covered in Chapter 3. As you plan this step in your speech, review these devices and determine which ones might best stimulate audience interest in your topic. If the audience is lethargic or tired, you need to begin with something more innovative than "And so, today I'd like to. . . ." Thus, the nine factors of attention discussed in Chapter 3 (activity, reality, proximity, familiarity, novelty, suspense, conflict, humor, and the vital) take on special relevance in the opening moments of your presentation.

Your manner of delivery also affects the attentiveness of your audience; the vigor and variety of your gestures and bodily movements and the flexibility and animation of your voice are important determinants of audience enthusiasm and interest in your subject. Your credibility, or *ethos,* as it is judged by your listeners, also assists you in securing their attention. If they already have high regard for you, they're more likely to be attentive as you begin your presentation. The color and impressiveness of your language and style also affect the audience's willingness to attend to your message. A lackadaisical delivery, coupled with a colorless and uninteresting style, is counterproductive. Fundamentally, however, you capture and hold attention through the *types of ideas* you present to your listeners. Your ideas must tap their interests and personal motivations before they will feel compelled to listen. Although gaining attention is an initial step in bringing your ideas to an audience, remember that *keeping* their attention also is vitally important. Keep the same attention devices in mind as you develop the remaining steps in the motivated sequence; in particular, they can be used to heighten attention during the need and visualization steps.

The Need Step

Assuming the audience is attending to you and your message, you must set forth reasons for their being concerned about the issue you're discussing: Why is the information or viewpoint vital to their interests? Why should they think the problem is urgent? To provide answers to such questions, the need step can be set up effectively like this:

1. *Statement.* Offer a clear statement of the need. State the central idea or claim, and even offer it phrased in more than one way to make the point clearly.

   Among people of color, there is a growing need for social and political activism on the part young adults—activism that makes a difference.[3]
2. *Illustration.* Present one or more illustrations or specific instances to give listeners an initial idea of the problem's seriousness and scope— its importance or significance.

   Mary Kay Penn, 32, is president of the Institute of African American Folk Culture in Harlem; she recently raised $50,000 for the Institute and convinced an Hispanic organization to donate a photo processing lab.

The New Progressive Party in Wisconsin, largely African American and Latino, has elected 22 officials from its ranks.

The Black Student Leadership Network, a college based arm of the Children's Defense Fund, aided more than 2,000 children this past summer; its southern region coordinator is only 23.

3. *Ramification.* Using the types of supporting materials discussed in Chapter 6, clarify your statement of need and justify the concern you're expressing. Add more examples, additional statistics, testimony from experts, and other forms of support to drive your analysis forward with force.

Nationally, there are four reasons why such activism must continue: First, proposed cuts in student aid may affect as many as 1.5 million students; people of color will be among those affected. Second, historically black colleges and universities, such as Howard University, which depends on federal subsidies for 55 percent of its budget, will be adversely affected by reductions in federal aid to education. Third, court-ordered changes in voting districts may adversely affect communities of color, thereby changing, literally, the complexion of Congress. Fourth, the transition to block grants to states, with state caps on spending for programs like Aid to Families with Dependent Children, will mean lessened flexibility in meeting needs. To the extent people of color are recipients, they, along with others, will find it more difficult to receive needed assistance.

In order to capture and hold attention, a speaker must show listeners the issue's scope and ramifications.

4. *Pointing.* Impress upon your listeners the issue's seriousness, scope, and significance to them. Tie it to their health, happiness, security, or other interests.

Given the national deficit, it is clear that some cuts, especially in the social areas just noted, will be coming. What can you do? Lamont Harris, 27 year old founder of a center devoted to giving people survival skills, Reality Plus One, says this in response: "It's gonna make people fight back. Maybe this time we won't stop short like we did in the 70s." Are you ready to fight back—to organize on your own and provide services where shortages and the absence of assistance will occur?

In the need step, you have two primary goals: to make your subject clear and to relate it to the concerns and interests of your audience. While you may not need to use all four tactics every time you discuss some need, you at least should think about them. When arguing for the end of an armed conflict in Eastern Europe, for example, you wouldn't need to do much with illustration and ramifications; on the other hand, the statement of the need and pointing—how does the problem affect listeners in Two Dot, Montana, or Corea, Maine—are of critical importance. Adjust the development of the need step to your topic, the audience's knowledge base, and their concerns.

The Satisfaction Step

The purpose of this step is to help your listeners understand the information you're presenting or to obtain their assent to the action you're proposing. The structure of this step varies, depending on whether your purpose is primarily informative, entertaining, or persuasive. Consider this step for each type of speech.

The Satisfaction Step in a Speech to Inform. Giving your listeners a clear understanding of a topic is the key to meeting this step. Consider a speech on the need for social and political activism. If this is cast as an informative speech, it doesn't include a well-developed plan for how to respond to the proliferation, as would a speech to persuade or actuate, but you certainly would want your listeners to know that activism is alive and well in communities of color.

1. *Initial summary.* Briefly state the main ideas you'll cover.
   Responding to the challenge will not be easy; it will take personal commitment and hard work. But, as the following examples suggest, it can be done. . . .
2. *Detailed information.* Discuss the facts and explanations pertaining to each of the main ideas. For our speech on activism among people of color, give further examples of the social service work being done and of the political organizing that is going on in communities of color.

3. *Final summary.* Restate the main ideas you've presented, together with any important conclusions you want to leave with your listeners. If your purpose in the speech on social activism is informative rather than persuasive, this step would fall short of actually asking them to act on their own.

> *In this speech, I've given you a number of examples of social service and political activity currently being carried out by young people of color. As students, we need to be concerned about the effects of funding cuts on our and others' lives; we can learn from the examples set by our sisters and brothers.*

The Satisfaction Step in a Speech to Persuade or to Actuate. In these types of speeches, the satisfaction step is developed as a major subdivision of the speech. The following elements are usually included:

1. *Statement.* Briefly state the attitude, belief, or action you wish the audience to adopt.
2. *Explanation.* Make sure your statement is understood by the audience. Diagrams or charts may be useful in explaining a complex proposal or plan.
3. *Theoretical demonstration.* Show how this belief or action logically meets the problem illustrated in the need step.
4. *Workability.* If appropriate, present examples showing that this solution has worked effectively in the past or that this belief has been supported by experience. Use facts, figures, and expert testimony to support your claim about the workability of your proposal or idea.
5. *Meeting objections.* Forestall opposition by answering possible objections that might be raised.

These five elements may not be needed in every speech to persuade or to actuate; they also may not appear in this order. For instance, if workability is the key to the success of your proposal and the audience already is well informed about it, you can shorten the preceding steps and spend most of your time persuading the audience that the idea can work.

Conversely, if workability is not the central issue, but an explanation of how the "plan meets the need" is in order, you may spend a great deal more time on this facet. In any case, the elements, in sequence, offer a useful framework for the presentation of a solution to a problem: (a) briefly state what you propose to do, (b) explain it clearly, (c) show how it remedies the problem, (d) demonstrate its workability, and (e) answer objections.

The Satisfaction Step in a Speech to Entertain. When your purpose is to entertain—to present a useful thought or sentiment in a lighthearted, humorous manner—the satisfaction step can constitute the major part of your

In the satisfaction step of a speech to actuate, a speaker can explain the new action, belief, or attitude that will remedy the problem.

speech. Your goal is to satisfy the audience that the speech is, in fact, entertaining and that it has conveyed an idea or sentiment worth their time and attention. In developing the satisfaction step in a speech to entertain, follow these guidelines:

1. *Initial statement of theme.* Briefly indicate the sentiment or idea that you will discuss.
2. *Humorous elaboration.* Develop the theme with particular attention to hypothetical and factual illustrations and specific instances that will convey a lighthearted, yet meaningful, message to the audience.
3. *Final summary.* Restate your main theme by connecting your illustrations to the point you wish to make.

The Visualization Step

This step is most commonly included in speeches to persuade and to actuate. The function of this step is to intensify the audience's desire or willingness to act—to motivate listeners to believe, feel, or act in a certain way. The primary strategy is to project listeners into the future and illustrate vividly the results of accepting or denying the proposed belief or acting or failing to act as the speaker directs. The step may be developed in one of three ways:

Positive Method.   Describe the favorable conditions that will prevail if the audience accepts your beliefs about the future or your proposals. Use specific examples and illustrations to give audience members a clear sense of what they can look forward to by their agreement.

Negative Method.   Describe the adverse conditions that will prevail in the future if the audience does *not* adopt the belief you advocate or carry out the solution you propose. Graphically describe the danger or unpleasantness that will result from their denial or inaction.

Contrast Method.   This approach combines both positive and negative perspectives on the future. Forecast the negative possibilities first, then introduce the positive attributes that can be expected if the audience members embrace your ideas or act upon your proposal. By means of such contrast, the bad and good effects—the disadvantages and advantages—are more striking than if they were presented in isolation from one another.

Whichever method you use, realize that the visualization step must always stand the test of reality; the conditions you picture must appear believable and probable. In addition, you must make every effort to put your listeners into the picture; use vivid imagery to create mental images that allow the audience members to see, hear, feel, taste, or smell the advantages or disadvantages you describe. The more real you make the projected situation, the greater are your chances of getting a significant, positive response from your audience.

HOW TO USE THE VISUALIZATION STEP THROUGH CONTRASTIVE EFFECTS: AN ILLUSTRATION

Suppose you enter the university, as nearly 40 percent of our students do, as an "undecided"—either with few interests and even less sense of your educational goals or with many interests that are ill defined or poorly focused. How will you select courses? You might approach the problem in one of two ways: either you "go with the flow," or you seek early advice and plan systematically to ensure graduation after four years./1

If you use the first approach, you begin by taking only courses that meet specific requirements (for example, English, speech, math, and science courses). In your second year, you start experimenting with some electives—courses that will not meet specific requirements. You find yourself listening to and accepting your friends' recommendations—"Take Speech 124 because it's easy," "Take Photography 102 because it's cool," or "Take Art 103 because you get to draw what you want." Now comes your junior year. You're nowhere near a major and you're getting close to the three-quarter mark in your education. Your advisor, your parents, and your friends all nag you. You even get down on yourself. In your senior year, you sample some social work courses, finally discovering something you really like. Only then do you realize it will take three or four more semesters—if you're lucky—to complete a B.S.W. degree./2

In contrast, suppose you're one of the other half of the "undecided"—those who seek career and personal advisement early. You enroll for the no-credit "Careers and Vocational Choices" seminar in your first semester. While meeting your liberal arts requirements, you take classes in several different departments to test your interests. During your sophomore year, you work within three or four areas of possible interest; you take more advanced courses in these areas to ascertain your interest and ability. Near the end of your sophomore year, you talk with people in Career Planning and meet frequently with your advisor. By your junior year, you get departmental advisors in two majors, find out you don't like one subject as much as you thought, and consult only the second advisor after midyear. You go on to complete the major, taking a summer course between your junior and senior year to catch up because you are a little behind, and obtain your degree "on time."/3

Carefully planning, experimenting with possible interests, reasoning thoughtfully about your reaction to different areas of study, and rigorously analyzing your own talents are actions that separate the completers from the complainers four years later, so . . . [*move into the action step at this point*]./4

The Action Step

Only the speech to actuate *always* requires an action step. With other speech purposes, such as to inform or to entertain, you may use something resembling an action step: urging further study of the topic dealt with in an informative speech, using humor to engage the audience's interest in further exploration of a subject, or seeking to strengthen a belief or attitude in meeting a persuasive purpose.

The action step should be relatively brief. Two adages apply: "Stand up, speak up, shut up" and "Tell 'em what you're going to tell 'em, tell 'em, and then tell 'em what you told 'em." In the case of the social activism speech discussed earlier, an action step might be phrased as follows:

In this speech, I've claimed that young sisters and brothers need to act on behalf of our own communities. I've presented four reasons why we must continue, as cuts in student aid, education aid, changes in representativeness in Congress, and reductions in social service support will adversely affect communities of color. We can either bury our heads in the sand and hope this crisis will pass, that it won't hurt too much, that our brothers and sisters will not suffer too much, or we can take matters into our own hands, and act. Whether your own interests lead you into social service or political organizing, Tammy Johnson, a member of the New Progressive Party, says it best: "There are those of us who have been doing community work for a while, and we decided that we could establish ourselves through our closeness to the community. If you really want to do the democracy thing, you have to do it block by block."

The primary strategy of visualization is to project listeners into the future by vividly illustrating the results of their action or inaction.

𝒜PPLYING THE MOTIVATED SEQUENCE

We've seen the steps or stages of the motivated sequence and their roles in the structure and development of speeches. Now, let's examine some brief outlines of speeches representing each of the main types you're likely to experience as part of a classroom assignment or at some later point in your career or community involvement. (See Chapters 13 and 14 for more detailed information on the use of the motivated sequence.)

Using the Motivated Sequence in a Speech to Inform

Generally, informative speeches concentrate on the first three steps of the motivated sequence. Of course, you need to elicit listeners' initial attention and then sustain it throughout the rest of the speech. You must also motivate them to listen, approaching the need step in this way: Why should anyone want to know the information you're about to present? Then, to satisfy this need (step 3), you actually supply the material that's the subject matter of your speech. Sometimes, an action step is added in response to the "so what?" question: What should your listeners do with this information? You don't emphasize the action step in an informative speech, but it can provide a nice conclusion. Four steps of the motivated sequence are applied in the following outline of an informative speech.

Using the Motivated Sequence in an Informative Speech

Sleep Apnea

Attention Step	**I.** Do you snore, or do you know someone who does?
	II. If you snore, do you find yourself falling asleep at odd times during the day, even though you're not tired?
Need Step	**I.** For most of us, snoring is simply a laughing matter.
	II. For one out of ten snorers, it may not be.
	A. These snorers suffer from sleep apnea.
	B. This disease causes the person to stop breathing for short periods of time.
Satisfaction Step	**I.** Snoring, when severe enough to cause apnea, produces negative effects on one's health.
	A. Apneic snorers suffer from short moments of oxygen deprivation accompanied by higher than normal levels of carbon monoxide, which affect the heart, the brain, and other vital organs.
	B. Apneic snorers develop hypertension (chronic high blood pressure) at a much faster rate than nonsnorers.
	C. Apneic snorers have a much higher incidence of depression and headaches than nonsnorers.
	D. Apneic snorers experience social problems, such as job instability, marital difficulties, inability to con-

centrate, irritability, and even aggressive behavior at a higher rate than nonsnorers.

II. You can assess the possibility of sleep apnea through a number of methods.

    A. Monitor your own snoring with a tape recorder; listen for pauses that last between ten seconds and one or two minutes.

    B. Have a sleep partner monitor your snoring pattern; time actual breathing lapses characteristic of snoring behavior.

    C. Daytime sleepiness is a major clue to the existence of apnea.

Action Step   **I.** The next time your rest is interrupted by someone's snoring, remember that, for that person, it may not be a laughing matter.[5]

Using the Motivated Sequence in a Speech to Persuade

The following speech outline urges listeners to reconsider the policies governing state lotteries. It is not a complete outline, but its detail shows how supporting material is integrated into the various stages and how the overall speech is developed.

Integrating Supporting Material into the Motivated Sequence

The Cost of Lotteries

Specific Purpose: To convince listeners that we need to reconsider the policies governing state lotteries.

Attention Step   **I.** Yesterday, thousands of men and women in our state stepped up to the cashier at their local convenience stores and purchased lottery tickets. Many of these men and women went home with a chance on a dream instead of the basic necessities of life. It's time we reconsidered this form of institutionalized gambling—our state lottery.

Need Step   **I.** The state lottery has two hidden costs.

    A. It encourages gambling.

    B. It is a regressive tax on the poor.

Satisfaction Step   **I.** We can offset these costs in three ways.

    A. We should fund a program to help compulsive gamblers.

    B. We should limit advertising for lottery tickets.

    C. We should limit the number of tickets any one person can purchase.

Visualization Step   **I.** We would realize specific benefits if these steps are adopted.
    A. We would help more compulsive gamblers than currently.
    B. Reducing advertising would reduce the media mania surrounding the event.
    C. The chance that some would spend beyond their means would be curtailed.
    D. If these three are adopted, we would not affect the current revenue associated with state lotteries.

Action Step   **I.** We need to understand the true, hidden costs of state lotteries.
    A. We need to pay attention to the needs of those most affected: compulsive gamblers and the poor.
    B. We need to urge the adoption of the proposals I've presented.

Using the Motivated Sequence in a Speech to Actuate

All five steps of the motivated sequence are used in a speech to actuate; the audience is asked to go beyond a change in belief or awareness of new information, to actually behave in new ways. The following outline illustrates how the previous speech can be altered from one with a persuasive orientation to one with an actuative intent. Because the initial steps would remain the same, only the changes in the action step are shown.

Action Step   **I.** What do I want from you?
    A. I want you to join me in signing this petition to our state legislature, urging acceptance of the proposals I've outlined.
    B. I also want you to join with me in creating a chapter of Gamblers Anonymous in our community.

Using the Motivated Sequence in a Speech to Entertain

The speech to entertain may exist for humor in its own right, but more often it uses an occasion for humor to make a serious point. In instances when you expect the audience only to sit back and enjoy the presentation (for example, at a comic revue), the attention step is the only one required. When you want to both entertain your audience and make a serious point, additional steps are needed. In the following outline, all of the steps of the motivated sequence are appropriate to the "moral" that the speaker draws from the discussion of optimism versus pessimism and the concluding appeal for acting as an optimist.

Using the Motivated Sequence in a Speech

A Case for Optimism

Attention Step

 I. Perhaps you've heard the expression "The optimist sees the doughnut, the pessimist, the hole."

Need Step

 I. To the pessimist, the optimist is a fool: the person who looks at an oyster and expects to find pearls is engaging in wishful thinking.

 II. To the optimist, the pessimist is sour on life: the person who looks at an oyster and expects to get ptomaine poisoning is missing out on the richer possibilities life can offer.

Satisfaction Step

 I. The pessimist responds to every event with an expectation of the worst that could happen.

 II. The optimist, on the other hand, looks for the bright side.

  A. The day after a robbery, a friend asked a store owner about the loss. After acknowledging that he had indeed suffered a loss, the store owner quipped, "But I was lucky; I marked everything down 20 percent the day before—had I not done that, I would have lost even more."

  B. The optimist is one who cleans her glasses before she eats grapefruit.

Visualization Step

 I. When you look on the bright side, you find things to be happy about.

Action Step

 I. Be an optimist: "Keep your eye on the doughnut and not on the hole."[6]

With this overview as a basis for structuring whole speeches, we are now in a position to address more specific organizational problems.

ＤEVELOPING PATTERNS OF INTERNAL ORGANIZATION WITHIN THE STEPS OF THE MOTIVATED SEQUENCE

The motivated sequence gives you a solid overall structure, but it doesn't really help you with some of the complicated problems of structure you'll face—especially in the need, satisfaction, and visualization steps.

 For example, suppose you're building a speech about problems with the American way of electing presidents. You can think of several needs you could develop: get better candidates, provide more and better information on each candidate's stand on the issues, or reduce the influence of political action committees (PACs) on election outcomes. As you think about that range of needs, you also realize that satisfaction—plans for change—are equally complicated: some of the solutions might involve new campaign laws, regulation of

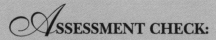

ASSESSMENT CHECK:

Before going further with internal organization of your ideas, consider the following questions:

- Can I identify easily each of the steps in the Motivated Sequence?
- Have I used all of the steps that should be used, given my general purpose in speaking?
- Have I used the steps in an appropriate manner—or is there a better way to utilize one of the steps?

advertising, revitalization of our political parties, or changes in voter attitudes. So, can you organize all of those needs and plans for change in a reasonable way and construct an organizational pattern that will help your listeners comprehend and come to accept your arguments?

The same sort of thing could be said about the visualization step. Usually, it's organized chronologically: "If we don't act today, the situation will be worse tomorrow and, sooner or later, become disastrous." Yet, if your need and satisfaction steps are complicated, visualization will become equally difficult. On the issue of reconstituting the American way of electing presidents, you'll probably want to visualize each area of reform: what things will be like with (a) renewed party participation in the process, (b) a national campaign fairness board, (c) spending limits on all aspects of campaigns, and (d) the elimination of the electoral college. You'd probably want to find a set of topics that covered each aspect of the plan and helped with the visualization process.

Thus, while the attention and action steps usually can be handled pretty easily, the three middle steps often demand a lot of organizational work. Five key criteria for communicating ideas to an audience should be met as you think about speech organization:

1. *The organization of* **main points** *must be easy for the audience to grasp and remember.* Listeners will find it easier to track your ideas if they see relationships among the main points. If the structure is clear, they even *anticipate* your next point through the pattern.
2. *The pattern must allow full, balanced coverage of the material it organizes.* When making three arguments in support of a claim, you usually want to spend roughly the same amount of time on each, because the first point might be important for some listeners, while the second and third points might appeal to others in your audience. Audiences usually can sense *proportion,* and may well wonder if you spend far more (or less) time on one point or another.
3. *The pattern should be appropriate to the occasion.* As we've noted, on some occasions you're expected to observe group traditions. Political fund-raising speeches, for example, are almost always built around a problem-solution format, with a call for contributions as the action step.

ℰTHICAL MOMENTS
HATEFUL AND VIOLENT SPEECH: SHOULD IT BE PROTECTED?

When should speech that is hateful, even incendiary, be protected by the First Amendment? In the wake of campus discussions concerning "regulated speech" (also termed "politically correct speech" by some), this becomes a critical ethical issue. The increased use of the Internet and the World Wide Web has raised questions about the regulation of hate.

Consider, for a moment, the following words spoken by G. Gordon Liddy on a recent radio talk show. In describing how to kill Bureau of Alcohol, Tobacco, and Firearms agents, he said: "Head shots.... Head shots.... Shoot twice to the belly and if that does not work, shoot to the groin area." In the aftermath of the Oklahoma bombing, instructions could be found on the Internet (through *Anarchist's Cookbook*) for similar bombs. At least 50 hate groups are communicating on the Internet, setting forth their specific, and generally negative, views of the United Nations, the federal government, other organizations and races. While one cannot draw a specific causal link between the expression of violence and actual violence, the case of the Oklahoma bombing suggests that probability exists.

The issue of hate speech, specifically that which does violence to the feelings of others, has been a subject of national debate. The "PC" label has been pejoratively applied by some to those who would demand that standards of respect and civility toward others preclude the use of specific phrases or words. College campuses have written codes regulating speech, and in some cases those codes have been subject to judicial review. The courts have decided that personally aggressive speech, especially in situations of uneven power, is unprotected by the First Amendment's free speech clause.

As you interact with others, and as you plan your own public presentations, hateful and violent speech are *not* idle concerns. You will need to make your own ethical choices on these issues, recognizing that others may not accept your decisions. For example, you might claim that another race needs to be protected, through a speech code, from speech that is offensive to that race. Your claim, however well-intentioned, may well be seen by a member of that race as "racist" in the extreme and that to assume the need to protect another race from harmful language diminishes the dignity of that race.

Further Reading

Cass R. Sunstein, "Is Violent Speech a Right?" *The American Prospect* (Summer 1995): 34–37 and Paul Berman, ed., *Debating P.C.* (New York: Dell Publishing, 1992.)

Audiences on this and other occasions expect certain topics, even certain organizational patterns.[7]

4. *The pattern should be adapted to the audience's needs and level of knowledge.* The motivated sequence is based on listeners' fundamental thought processes, while patterns of internal organization depend upon other aspects of audience awareness of an issue or problem. If listeners aren't well informed, say, about problems in the way Americans elect their presidents, you might want to go to a chronological pattern to show them the roots and later evolution of those problems in the need step. If they are knowledgeable, a cause-effect pattern that compacts such an analysis in the need step but then develops a more complicated satisfaction step probably will work better. Start where the audience is and take them where you want to go.

5. *The speech must move forward steadily toward a complete and satisfying end.* Keeping the audience with you is easier if they have a clear idea of where you're heading during the speech. Repeated backtracking to pick up lost points confuses and aggravates your listeners.

These are the primary criteria that should guide you as you assemble the body of your speeches. How can you execute them? Let's now look at the types of organizational patterns that work best for people delivering oral messages.

$\mathscr{P}$ATTERNS OF INTERNAL ORGANIZATION

The four most useful patterns for structuring the bodies of speeches are chronological, spatial, causal, and topical.

Chronological Patterns

The defining characteristic of **chronological patterns** is their temporal structuring of happenings or events. They're useful for orienting listeners who know little about a topic or for providing support for ideas via storytelling. Thus chronological patterns run according to straightforward temporal sequences or to what are called narrative sequences.

Temporal Sequence. To use a **temporal sequence,** you begin at some period or date and move forward (or backward) systematically to provide background information. So, if you wanted to do a speech on why the United States has devoted so much more time and money to manned rather than unmanned space flights, you'd do well to use a temporal sequence, examining the unmanned rocket flights of the 1950s and 1960s, the Kennedy era commitment to manned flights to the moon, and Nixon era commitments to manned space station and shuttle technology, which continued even after the *Challenger* disaster of 1986. Such a *selection* and *sequencing* of events—and both are strategic moves made by a speaker who uses a temporal sequence—allows you to use the past to *explain* the present.

Narrative Sequence.   If you want to do more than explain or provide background for some problem, however, a *narrative* (story) will allow you to draw conclusions about a series of events. For example, Aesop's fables are narratives with morals about human motivations and actions; lawyers, too, tell stories in arguing for their defendant's guilt or innocence. In **narrative sequences,** therefore, stories are the source of supporting material for some claim.[8] Suppose you want to argue that the image of Gypsies in this country does not do justice to their persecution in Eastern Europe. A narrative sequence wherein the story comprises the need step and the lessons-to-be-learned as part of the satisfaction step would work well.

Using Narrative Sequence—An Illustration

The Persecution of Eastern European Roma (Gypsies)

Claim: The Roma of Eastern Europe are a persecuted people.

Attention Step   [Review the romanticized version of Gypsies that is generally given in this country; contrast that with a specific illustration of their actual life conditions in Eastern Europe.]

Need Step   I. [Continue the review of specific illustrations of their life, drawing on the series of Human Rights reports from Helsinki Watch: 1993, *Struggling for Ethnic Identity: The Gypsies of Hungary;* 1992, *Destroying Ethnic Identity: Czechoslovakia's Endangered Gypsies;* end with the question: "How did they come to be treated this way?"]

II. Perhaps the best way is to explain the story of their heritage.

A. The Roma are, as best we know, originally from India—they migrated to Eastern Europe around 800–950 A.D.

1. Their language (Romani) is a derivative of Sanskrit and is close to Hindi.

2. Although not all groups today communicate in some dialect of their original language, the Roma of the southern Balkans use Romani as well as Slavic, Turkish, Albanian, or Greek languages.

3. They were firmly established in Europe in the mid-fourteenth and fifteenth centuries, with reports of Roma in Serbia by 1348, in Germany in 1407, and in Spain by 1425.

B. True to their nomadic culture, they have not established, as have Serbs, Croats, Albanians, etc., a specific homeland.

1. This has caused them to be seen as "outsiders" even though they and their descendants have lived in areas for 500 years.

  2. The absence of a homeland means no one country or nationality speaks for them or defends their interests.

 C. Their persecution is not a recent phenomenon.

  1. They were slaves in two Romanian principalities from the fourteenth to the nineteenth century (slavery was abolished in 1864).

  2. Considered outcasts, they were expelled from other areas, furthering their image as nomads.

  3. When not sold into slavery, there were bounties "for their capture, dead or alive, and repressive measures included confiscation of property and children, forced labor, prison sentences, whipping, branding, and other forms of physical mutilation."

  4. During the Nazi regime, more than 600,000 were exterminated.

 D. Programs of assimilation have been the recent experience of the Roma.

  1. Czechoslovakia banned nomadism in 1958.

  2. Poland banned nomadism in 1964.

  3. In Hungary and in the Balkans, assimilation meant working in the most dangerous, lowest paid jobs.

  4. In Czechoslovakia, a policy of monetary incentive for sterilization of women was disproportionately applied to Roma women (in one city in 1989, half the women sterilized were Roma; Roma women also were often sterilized without their consent).

  5. Education for Roma children often was in what, for them, was a second language, and hence they were considered "retarded and tracked into special classes."

  6. Because they lacked legal status as a minority, they were regarded as "a socially degraded stratum," a "disadvantaged social stratum" or as "other nationalities" in several Eastern European countries without recourse to human rights afforded other peoples.

  7. In Bulgaria, from the early 1970's forward, Roma language, music, musical instruments, and dress were banned.

Satisfaction Step

I. From this story, we can clearly see that the Roma are a persecuted people.

Visualization/ Action Step Combined

I. From this characterization of the Roma, and more could be said about their perceived status as a "socially unacceptable population," I hope to have altered your conception of the life Gypsies experience today in Eastern Europe. A romantic story this is not![9]

Spatial Patterns

Generally, **spatial patterns** arrange ideas or subtopics in terms of their physical proximity or relationship to each other. A specialized form of spatial patterns are **geographical patterns,** which organize materials according to well-known regions or areas; these are especially useful for making comparisons and contrasts between areas or movements across them. So, the evening weather forecast reviews today's high pressure dome over your area, then the low pressure area lying to the west, and the Arctic cool-air mass that seems to be coming in behind that low pressure area from Canada. The notion of geography, however, need not be applied only to landmasses; you can use it to talk about physical spaces—for example, the different services available on the four floors of a university library. In an age when travel is highly popular and comparatively inexpensive, you might well find yourself giving a speech using a geographical pattern, as in the following speech on volcanoes:

Using Spatial Patterning—An Illustration

Ensuring Cultural Survival: Empowering the Lives of Indigenous Peoples	
Central Idea:	Around the globe, projects are being undertaken to ensure that the customs and language of people in remote regions survive.
Attention Step	[Opening story about the Native American experience with respect to a loss of its cultural heritage in the United States; note that the process of assimilation and loss of culture does not stop at our borders.]
Need Step	[Discussion of why loss of culture is an important issue—why should we be concerned with other peoples' loss?]

Satisfaction Step	I. As we move outside our borders, we can travel to specific regions and learn about projects aimed at restoring or maintaining a peoples' identity.
	  A. We can begin by moving just south of our own border, to Mexico, where the San Jtz'ibajom project in the Mayan Chiapas community is working to preserve oral history, as well as to improve literacy in their mother tongue.
	  B. We move further south to the Amazon, where the Amazonian Peoples Resources Initiative is working to improve conditions among Peruvian Amazonians.
	  C. Changing continents, and moving what seems a world away, we travel next to Afghanistan, where the Afghan Refugee Weavers' Project has been undertaken.

Visualization Step	[Visualize what it means to each of these communities as they seek to maintain their local culture.]
Action Step	[Note that the trip they have taken with you has given them some sense of the need for, and activity occurring to ensure, cultural survival.][10]

Giving your audience a sense of physical relationship through spatial ordering will also work with single arguments or ideas. A speech on the effects of nuclear fallout could organize damage assessments from "ground zero," or the point of impact, through areas one mile away, to regions ten, fifty, and a hundred miles out.

The great utility of spatial patterns is their visual component. Helping audiences *see* ideas is a virtue for someone using an oral medium of communication.

Causal Patterns

As the name implies, **causal patterns** of organization move either (1) from a description of present conditions to an analysis of the causes that seem to have produced them or (2) from an analysis of present causes to a consideration of future effects. Because ideas are developed in direct relationship with each other, a sense of coherence is communicated to listeners. When using a *cause-effect pattern,* you might first point to the increasing number of closed courses (i.e., too few places) in your college each semester and then show the result—it takes students longer to graduate. Or, using an *effect-cause pattern,* you could argue that everyone knows how long it's taking students to graduate, then argue that closed classes are the cause, at least in part.

The subject to be discussed may suggest an appropriate organization pattern. Chronological patterns are useful in describing a process or narrating a sequence of events.

Using Cause-Effect and Effect Cause Patterns

Requiring Community Service in High School (Option 1)

Claim: Requiring that high school students engage in community service as a condition of graduation (cause) leads to an erosion of the very volunteer spirit it is designed to promote (effect).

Attention Step	[Draw attention to the importance of the issue.]
Need Step	**I.** Several students have forced the issue by appealing to the courts.

> **A.** Students in Bethlehem, Pennsylvania, already active, refused to report their activities to school authorities.
> > **1.** They lost in court.
> > **2.** The school denied their diplomas.
> **B.** Students in Chapel Hill, North Carolina, filed suit.
> > **1.** As one student, already an Eagle Scout, suggested, requiring what should be a volunteer activity leaves "no heart" for the activity.
> > **2.** The case has not been completed.

Visualization Step	[Indicate what the long-range consequences will be if we ignore the problem.]
Action Step	[Appeal to listeners' self-interest—what is done at the high school level could gravitate to becoming a college requirement—to hold their attention on this issue as something to follow in the future.]

Requiring Community Service (Option 2)

Claim: An enriched understanding of others, and a sense of fulfillment (effects) can result from requiring students to engage in community service (cause).

Need Step	**I.** Students are enriched through their exposure to community service.

> **A.** In Hebbville, Maryland, an elementary teacher regularly incorporates visits to nursing homes.
> > **1.** Students get to practice their reading in the presence of an eager audience.
> > **2.** In the process, they gain a greater understanding of and empathy for the elderly.
> **B.** Young veterans of the Hebbville program are quiet testimony to its success.
> > **1.** One fourth grader who came back to help the younger class prepare for their experience played a garbled tape, and then pointed out that this is how many elderly might hear the students if they are almost deaf.
> > **2.** As another fourth grader noted, it is fun to make people happy.[11]

Both outlines share a common characteristic: each starts with the aspect of the situation *better known* to audience members, and then develops more fully the lesser-known facets of the problem. As a guiding principle, *use a cause-effect sequence when listeners are generally well acquainted with the cause; use an effect-cause sequence when the effect is better known.*

Topical Patterns

Some speeches on familiar topics are best organized in terms of subject-matter divisions that have become standardized. Financial reports are customarily divided into assets and liabilities; discussions of government into legislative, executive, and judicial matters; and comparisons of kinds of telescopes into celestial and terrestrial models. In these instances, the topic suggests its own pattern of development. **Topical patterns** are useful in speeches that enumerate aspects of persons, places, things, or processes. Your coverage of these aspects may be a **complete enumeration** of a subject, as in a four-part sermon on the differences among the gospels, or a **partial enumeration,** as in coverage of the most common types of shots in volleyball.

Using the Topical Pattern of Partial Enumeration

The Basic Shots in Volleyball

Central Idea: Knowing the basic volleyball shots can increase the playing ability even of beginners.

Attention Step	[Elicit interest through the usual devices.]
Need Step	[Point out how the audience can use this information.]
Satisfaction Step	I. There are three basic shots in volleyball.
	A. A "bump" is performed by bringing your shoulders together and clasping your hands under the ball.
	B. A "set" prepares the ball for another player, so you bring your hands above your head and hit the ball near your forehead with your palms open.
	C. A "spike" or "kill" is a quick power shot executed with one hand, driving the ball over the net and down toward your opponent's feet.
Visualization Step	[After encouraging them to hit each shot in warmup, visualize the enjoyment they'll have in their weekend backyard or beach games once they can hit each kind of shot.]
Action Step	[Review the key points you want listeners to take away from your speech, and encourage them to start working on them next weekend.]

Topical patterns are among the most popular and easiest to use in organizing your speech. Given the usual practice of a partial rather than complete enumeration of topics, you may need to justify your limitations by indicating why you're not talking about other facets. If someone asks "Why didn't you talk about the 'diving save' volleyball shot?" they are telling you that they don't think your limitation of the topic was reasonable; you'd better be ready to answer: "Because in friendly weekend games that shot is dangerous; it should be saved for playing organized or league volleyball, when you play with others who know what they're doing." All that's required is that the audience understand why some items were included and others weren't. That understanding can come either from your logical development of the topic ("The Basic Shots in Volleyball") or from an explicit statement about its scope.

INTEGRATING PATTERNS INTO THE MOTIVATED SEQUENCE

Having looked at some internal patterns, you can now consider the relationship between the motivated sequence and the chronological, spatial, causal, and topical patterns:

- *Attention Step—Introduction to Speech:* As introductory devices, you might use chronological or spatial methods in beginning a hypothetical story; overall, organize the introduction to satisfy the functions discussed in Chapter 8.
- *Need Step—Body of Speech:* Use chronological, spatial, causal, or topical patterns to relate the main points to one another. You may even use one pattern for main points and another to organize subpoints (see the next section on organizing main points and subpoints).
- *Satisfaction Step—Body of Speech:* Use any of the patterns to organize this step; you may even use one pattern for main points and another for subpoints. Whatever pattern is used should be tied to needs, for the relationship between the need step and the satisfaction step is key to the body of your speech.
- *Visualization Step—Body or Conclusion of Speech:* You can highlight the positive or negative benefits, or you can contrast these to illustrate why your proposal is worthy of consideration. A chronological pattern running from past to future or a geographical pattern illustrating effects in different regions might also be employed in creating a visual picture for the audience.
- *Action Step—Conclusion of Speech:* A specific pattern is not needed. Conclusions can either call for specific actions or review the main ideas to give listeners a sense of what they could do with the information, ideas, and proposals you've presented.

ORGANIZING MAIN POINTS AND SUBPOINTS

The relationship between the **main points** needs to be clear to the audience. In the example below, spatial ordering connects the two main points of comparison (United States, Germany). Underneath each main point, the ordering of **subpoints** also must follow some kind of ordering pattern. In this case, each point is arranged in a *topical* pattern, with direct contrasts (I. A—II. A . . .) between the subpoints. In addition, the sequence of main points allows the audience to consider the more familiar scene (the United States) before moving to a less familiar one (Germany).

Combining Patterns with Main and Subpoints

Contrasts between United States and German managers

I. The U. S. managers' expectations are as follows:
   A. Communication between colleagues is task centered and impersonal.

How TO
CHOOSE ORGANIZATIONAL PATTERNS

- Does your *subject matter* guide you toward a particular pattern? For example, to explain basic principles of professional flower gardening, a spatial pattern would be a natural choice.
- Does your *specific purpose* suggest which pattern is most serviceable? For example, to explain changing definitions of rape and the social effects of these definitions, a chronological pattern for the main points and cause-effect units for the subpoints would be logical choices.
- Do the needs or expectations of *your audience* call for specific topical patterns? For example, an audience listening to a speech urging the rerouting of three creeks to make room for a new highway might expect you to address particular points: positive impacts of the highway, environmental impact of the rerouting, and costs of the project.

- Does *the occasion* call for specific topical patterns? For example, every presidential inaugural address *must* mention the historicity of the occasion, the binding up of wounds after an ugly political campaign, domestic problems, foreign policy problems, and a call for citizens' help.

      B. The need to be liked by others is a prime motivating factor influencing communicative behavior: more informal address/tone.

      C. Assertiveness, direct confrontation and fair play dominate in the approach to decision-making but there is low level of logical analysis with a usually low level of language sophistication.

  II. The German managers' expectations are as follows:

      A. Communication between colleagues combines socioemotional and task features, hence is not as impersonal.

      B. The need to be seen as credible and to establish one's place in a corporate hierarchy is a prime motivating factor in influencing communicative behavior: more formal address/tone.

      C. Also assertive and directly confrontative, but with a higher level of logical analysis and more sophisticated language.[12]

Causes and effects are often developed in main point/subpoint sets, where the causes appear in the main points, and the effects appear as sub-subpoints.

Using Causal Ordering of Main and Subpoints

Our Disappearing Salmon

  I. Industrial pollution has caused a decline in the U.S. salmon population.

    A. Dam construction has severely affected salmon.

      1. There are fourteen barriers on a major salmon river.

      2. Eleven of the fourteen barriers are hydroelectric facilities.

        a. These facilities produce high water temperatures.

        b. Estimates of fish loss due to excessive temperatures are as high as 16 percent.

    B. Chemical and industrial pollution have also harmed the salmon.

      1. Discharge of chemicals such as PCB has hurt the salmon population.

      2. PCB kills salmon roe (eggs), thus limiting the future population even further.

This lesson is important: *Developing your ideas in parallel forms makes them more coherent and clear, and hence more memorable and powerful.* Controlling the structure of ideas is a key means of getting an audience to see the world as you see it. If they see the way you see, they're more likely to think and act the way you want them to.

CHAPTER SUMMARY

The human need to find or create order in the world is the basis for the need to organize public presentations. Listeners need speakers to provide emphasis via distinctions between foreground and background differentiation and via a sense of completeness that provides *closure* to messages. *Monroe's Motivated Sequence* was introduced early in this century as a means of combining problem- and motivated-centered structures for ideas: It provides an orderly approach to problem solving within a motivational framework. Its five steps—*attention, need, satisfaction, visualization,* and *action*—can be used to structure any type of speech (informative, entertaining, persuasive, actuative).

Building a conceptually clear structure for your major ideas is crucial. Listeners need to see and comprehend a pattern in your ideas if they're to make sense out of them. As long as the pattern you select is sensitive to your topic, your purpose, and the expectations of the audience and occasion, your message should be received as a logically coherent approach to some idea or problem. Five criteria should guide you toward some pattern:

- The organization of the main points must be easy for the audience to grasp and remember.
- The pattern should allow full, balanced coverage.
- The pattern should be appropriate to the occasion.
- The pattern should be adapted to the audience's needs and level of knowledge.
- The speech must move steadily forward.

Four classes of internal organizational patterns include *chronological* (temporal, narrative), *spatial* (as well as geographical), *causal* (effect-cause, cause-effect), and *topical* (complete and partial enumeration) patterns. Different patterns can be combined, especially in ordering main points in one pattern and subpoints in another pattern.

KEY TERMS

action step (p. 203)
attention step (p. 203)
causal patterns (p. 200)
chronological patterns (p. 196)
closure (p. 174)
complete enumeration (p. 202)

contrast method of visualization (p. 187)
differentiation (p. 174)
geographical patterns (p. 199)
main points (p.203)
Monroe's Motivated Sequence (p. 175)
narrative sequence (p. 197)

need step (p. 203)
negative method of visualization (p. 187)
partial enumeration (p. 202)
positive method of visualization (p. 187)
satisfaction step (p. 203)

spatial patterns (p. 199)
subpoints (p. 203)
temporal sequence (p. 196)
topical patterns (p. 202)
visualization step (p. 203)

ASSESSMENT ACTIVITIES

1. Choose a social controversy as a topic for a speech; specify two audiences, one opposing the issue and the other supporting it (for example, a speech on the need for additional day care facilities presented to a liberal audience and a conservative audience). Using the motivated sequence as a pattern, specify how you would develop each step so it is appropriate to each audience. Write a concluding paragraph that explains the differences between the speeches, as they were adapted to the differing positions of the audiences.

2. Develop brief outlines for an informative and a persuasive speech using the samples in this chapter as guides. What are the major differences between the outlines? Which steps are included or left out of the analysis? What do you do differently in each step in orienting your speech toward presenting information or persuading an audience? Following the outlines, write your response to these questions. Hand in your outlines and response for evaluation by your instructor.

3. Prepare a five-to-seven-minute speech on a subject of your choice for presentation in class. Before you present the speech, critically appraise the organization you have used and write a brief paper defending the approach you took in organizing the main points and subpoints. Immediately after presenting the speech, and taking into account comments from the class, write a brief addendum on the experience of presenting the speech. Did it work the way you anticipated? Would you change your approach in any specific area of the speech? Hand in the analysis to your instructor.

4. Working in small groups in class, suggest how the main points can be organized in each of the following topics, assuming the end product is to be a short in-class speech.

   Why many small businesses fail

   Developments in laser technology

   Digging for sapphires, gold, or opals

   Eat wisely and live long

   Problems of the part-time student

   Racquetball for the beginner

   Appreciating impressionist art

   Computer literacy

   Share your results with the rest of the class. How much organizational similarity is there among groups?

REFERENCES

1. The concept of closure is one of the Gestalt principles of perception. The term *gestalt* (meaning "wholeness") is used to refer to a group of psychologists who've researched these aspects of cognitive processes. For a brief review of basic Gestalt principles, see John R. Anderson, *Cognitive Psychology and Its Implications* (New York: W. H. Freeman, 1980), 53–56; Philip G. Zimbardo, *Psychology and Life,* 13th ed. (New York: HarperCollins, 1992), 266–268.

2. Maria Lucia R. Anton, "Sexual Assault Policy a Must," in *Winning Orations 1994.* Reprinted by permission of Larry Schnoor, Executive Secretary, Interstate Oratorical Association, Mankato State University, MN.

3. Information for this speech is derived from Raoul Dennis, "Retroracism," *Young Sisters and Brothers* (September 1995): 80–86.

4. Information for this outline taken from *World Press Review* (September 1995): 47–48. The original source was from an editorial written by Maneka Gandhi in the *Hindustan Times* in New Delhi, January 11, 1995.

5. Information cited in Steve Kaplan, "Snoring," *World and I,* 2 (July 1987): 298–303.

6. Based in part on information from *Friendly Speeches* (Cleveland: National Reference Library). See Chapter 16 for a full text.

7. See the case studies of the presidential inaugural address in Herbert W. Simons and Aram A. Aghazarian, eds., *Form, Genre, and the Study of Political Discourse* (Columbia, SC: University of South Carolina Press, 1986), especially the essays by Karlyn Kohrs Campbell and Kathleen Hall Jamieson, 203–225; Bruce E. Gronbeck, 226–245; and Robert P. Hart, 278–300. See also Roderick P. Hart, *The Sound of Leadership* (Chicago: University of Chicago Press, 1987) and Karlyn Kohrs Campbell and Kathleen Hall Jamieson, *Deeds Done in Words: Presidential Rhetoric and the Genres of Governance* (Chicago: University of Chicago Press, 1990).

8. Walter R. Fisher goes so far as to argue that narrative persuasion is the most powerful kind of speaking. See his *Human Communication as Narration: Toward a Philosophy of Reason, Value, and Action* (Charleston, SC: University of South Carolina Press, 1987). See also Kathleen Hall Jamieson, *Eloquence in an Electronic Age: The Transformation of Political Speechmaking* (New York: Oxford University Press, 1988).

9. Information for this outline taken from Carol Silverman, "Persecution and Politicization: Roma (Gypsies) of Eastern Europe," *Cultural Survival Quarterly* (Summer 1995): 43–49.

10. Information taken from "Special Projects Update," *Cultural Survival Quarterly* (Summer 1995): 8–9.

11. From Suzanne Goldsmith, "The Community Is Their Textbook," *The American Prospect* (Summer 1995): 51–57.

12. From Robert F. Friday, "Contrasts in Discussion Behaviors of German and American Managers," in L. A. Samovar and R. E. Porter, *Intercultural Communication: A Reader,* 7th ed. (Belmont, CA: Wadsworth, 1994), 274–285; originally published in *International Journal of Intercultural Relations* 13 (1989): 429–445.

8

*B*EGINNING AND ENDING
THE SPEECH

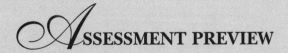

*A*SSESSMENT PREVIEW

After reading Chapter 8, the student with basic communication competencies will be able to

- state a clear central idea or claim that captures the essence of the speech.
- conclude with a summary of the speech and a final statement that signals the end of the speech.

The student with average communication competencies will also be able to

- state a clear central idea or claim and give listeners at least one reason why the speech is relevant to their lives.
- conclude with a summary, an appeal to the audience's interests, and a final statement that signals the end of the speech.

The student with superior communication competencies will also be able to

- state a clear central idea or claim, give listeners one or more reasons for listening, and forecast the development of the speech as a whole.
- conclude with a summary, appeals to listeners' interests, at least one other ending strategy, and a final statement that signals the end of the speech.

*S*o, you stayed up late the night before your speech was due, finding one last statistical trend to help you demonstrate the second point, locating an awfully nice quotation from William Shakespeare to use as a summary of the third point. You worded each argument carefully so that it was clear and forceful. Then you went to bed. . . . A mistake! You forgot to plan out an **introduction** that gets you into the speech—and into your listeners' heads—swiftly and effectively. You forgot to put together a **conclusion** that not only reminds listeners what you've argued but also gives them one last shot before you sit down. You don't just start; you introduce a speech. You don't just quit; you conclude a speech. How you conduct both of these operations is the focus of this chapter.

Think of introducing and concluding your speeches as **framing** activities. When you are building a new house, you first must obtain the financing and order the materials, and then a building contractor will frame the house. Laying out the corners, studs, floor joists, stair openings, door and window frames, rafters, and ridge beams on the subfloor or slab provides the carpenters, heating and cooling personnel, roofers, plumbers, painters, and masons with the spaces within which they'll work. Creating a space where the house can take shape is what framing's all about. Framing also lets you and all of your friends and neighbors see what the house will look like—to be able to judge, finally, the building's utility and beauty.

In this chapter, we'll talk about framing speeches—about the ways you can help your listeners come to grips with the utility and beauty of your ideas and oral expression. First, we'll examine details about framing—about what we'll call **rhetorical orientation**—and then review a series of strategies for introducing and concluding speeches. Finally, we'll show you how introductions and conclusions can be easily integrated into the speech built round the motivated sequence. Introductions fulfill the attention step; conclusions are tied to either the visualization or the action step. We'll also concentrate on making beginnings and endings fit around speeches organized in other ways, for it is in those other cases that genuine rhetorical orientation is occurring.

*F*RAMING THE SPEECH: RHETORICAL ORIENTATION

Rhetorical orientation is a process of effectively positioning listeners in relation to the substance of your speech—to the central idea or claim you are advancing, the arguments you are making, and the supporting materials you have assembled. The new homeowner is likely to say to an admiring visitor, "Here. Stand here, so that you can see the effect we were going for when we designed this house for this lot." Likewise, the effective introduction says, "Look at my central idea in this way. If you do, you'll see that it's interesting and relevant to your life." The successful conclusion says, "Look at the speech in this way. If you do, you'll see that the ideas I've talked about are important, significant for you and your life, and compelling."

Competently built introductions accomplish three goals:

1. The well-framed introduction orients the listeners' *attention.* It gets them to focus on the subject matter at hand and piques their interest. The factors of attention (Chapter 3) we talked about earlier are relevant here, though, as you'll see, you must find ideas that can convince an audience that your speech is important to their lives.

2. The well-framed introduction orients the listeners to the speaker's *qualifications.* The audience must believe that you know what you're talking about (good sense), that you're a straight shooter (good morals), and that you have got their best interests in mind (good will); these are the three grounds—good sense, good morals, good will—that Aristotle identified as central to a speaker's **ethos** or credibility.

3. The well-framed introduction orients the listeners to the *speech's ideas and their development.* An audience must come to understand what you're talking about, why you're talking about it, and how you'll develop those ideas. This aspect of rhetorical orientation usually, at least in part, takes the form of a good **forecast:** "So today, yes, I want to talk to you about the 'people's musical instrument,' the lowly harmonica. First I'll talk about its development through the first half of the nineteenth century in Germany. Then, I'll say something about the coming of Mattias Hohner and his company for manufacturing harmonicas, which set off a craze in harmonica playing in the 1920s. Third, I'll get to the heart of this speech: an explanation of the roles harmonicas have played in the development of country-western, blues, and even rock music in the United States. And finally, if you've paid attention, I'll finish with a little demonstration of why this musical instrument has been called 'the heart's horn.'" Notice that this forecast sets up the three main points of the speech and even promises the audience a little entertainment by the end, if it's been paying attention, as an inducement to stay with the speaker to the end.

In speech introductions, therefore, rhetorical orientation situates listeners to best see the potential of the speech: *why* they should listen, *to whom* they're listening, and *how* they should go about following the speech. Rhetorical orientation has somewhat different roles at the end of the speech. A good conclusion has *focus, flair,* and a sense of *finality.* Even average speakers remind listeners what they've been talking about—the focus of the speech—and why listeners should be interested, the focus of their attention. Better speakers also show a bit of their rhetorical talents in conclusions by wording ideas in compelling ways, by finding just the right quotation or final appeal that captures the tone of the speech, thus reengaging listeners' needs and interests, and by pacing oral delivery in such a way as to capture the sense of an ending.

All speakers must be able to create a sense of **The End,** the feeling that the speech in fact is over, which is to say, that nothing else need be said at this time on this topic by this speaker. You want to end speeches in such a way that listeners say "Amen!"—which means, "Yes, it shall be so." Seeking that sort of affirmation of you and your ideas should become the dominant purpose in your

How to
Frame a Speech

In your introduction:

- Focus on gaining your audience's attention, especially if listeners aren't likely to be interested in your topic.
- Establish your expertise, particularly if the audience isn't aware of your qualifications.
- Satisfy any special demands of the occasion; if you depart from custom, justify your departure.

- Work to create goodwill when the audience isn't sympathetic to you or your ideas.

In your conclusion:

- Signal the audience that the speech is about to end by refocusing them on the message.
- Answer the question "So what?" for your listeners.
- Influence the audience with your own enthusiasm and interest to help keep them involved in the message.

conclusions. The three F's—focus, flair, and finality—represent the three dimensions of your conclusions' orienting work: orienting listeners to your ideas, your talents, and areas of expertise, and The End of their listening experience.

The rhetorical strategies you have available when building both introductions and conclusions are featured in the next two sections of this chapter.

*T*YPES OF SPEECH INTRODUCTIONS

While you can come back to the factors of attention again and again, to gain and hold the audience's focus, you have some special requirements in this regard in those first few seconds of your speech. Your listeners are making a large number of judgments about you and the speech in the first half-minute:

- Interesting or boring?
- Relevant or irrelevant?
- Knowledgeable or dumb?
- Forceful or limp?
- Prepared or just running at the mouth?
- Clear or muddy?
- Confident or unsure?
- Made for me or for someone else?

With all of those questions to answer, listeners actually give you their attention readily—but only for a few seconds. Once most of those questions are answered, they're then ready to tune in, tune out, or graze: the grazers are constantly shifting their focus from you to a person sitting a row ahead to a sound outside to this evening's activities back to you, their minds working like remote control devices, zipping from channel to channel. It's your job to make sure they tune you in.

You need to draw them into your world. As we've said, you need to tie your speech to their needs and interests to hold your listeners' attention, to convince them that you know what you're doing, and to help them comprehend your main ideas and their development. The following techniques aim at one or all of these functions.

Referring to the Subject or Occasion

If your audience already has a vital interest in your subject, you need only to state that subject before presenting your first main point. The speed and directness of this approach signals your eagerness to address your topic. Professor Russell J. Love used this approach when discussing rights for people with severe communication problems: "My talk tonight is concerned with the rights of the handicapped—particularly those people with severe communication disabilities. I will be presenting what I call a bill of rights for the severely communicatively disabled."[1]

Although such brevity and forthrightness may strike exactly the right note on some occasions, you should not begin all speeches this way. To a skeptical audience, a direct beginning may sound immodest or tactless; to an apathetic audience, it may sound dull or uninteresting. When listeners are receptive and

Referring directly to the subject or occasion is a useful introductory strategy when the audience already has a vital interest in hearing the message.

friendly, however, immediate reference to the subject often produces a clear, engaging opening.

Instead of referring to your subject, you may sometimes want to refer to the occasion that has brought you and your audience together. When Pope John Paul II addressed the United Nations General Assembly on its fiftieth anniversary, he certainly was aware of the occasion as historic, and so recognized it:

> *Mr. President, Ladies and Gentlemen.* It is an honour for me to have the opportunity to address this international Assembly and to join the men and women of every country, race, language and culture in celebrating the fiftieth anniversary of the founding of the United Nations Organization. In coming before this distinguished Assembly, I am vividly aware that through you I am in some way addressing *the whole family of peoples living on the face of the earth.* My words are meant as a sign of the interest and esteem of the Apostolic See and of the Catholic Church for this Institution. They echo the voices of all those who see in the United Nations the hope of a better future for human society.[2]

In thus elevating the speaking occasion, the Pope made his speech—and the audiences listening to it—seem more important. Grand occasions demand serious listening.

Using a Personal Reference or Greeting

At times, a warm, personal greeting from a speaker or the remembrance of a previous visit or scene serves as an excellent starting point. Personal references are especially useful when a speaker is well known to the audience. In June 1990, Barbara Bush used a personal reference to a previous visit to Wellesley College as she addressed the senior class. She elaborated on her enthusiasm for the occasion when she added, "I had really looked forward to coming to Wellesley, I thought it was going to be fun; I never dreamt it would be this much fun. So thank you for that."[3]

The way a personal reference introduction can be used to gain the attention of a hostile or skeptical audience is illustrated by a famous speech presented by Anson Mount, manager of public affairs for *Playboy,* to the Christian Life Commission of the Southern Baptist Convention:

> I am sure we are all aware of the seeming incongruity of a representative of *Playboy* magazine speaking to an assemblage of representatives of the Southern Baptist Convention. I was intrigued by the invitation when it came last fall, though I was not surprised. I am grateful for your genuine and warm hospitality, and I am flattered (though again not surprised) by the implication that I would have something to say that could have meaning to you people. Both *Playboy* and the Baptists have indeed been considering many of the same issues and ethical problems; and even if we have not arrived at the same conclusions, I am impressed and gratified by your openness and willingness to listen to our views.[4]

If a personal reference is sincere and appropriate, it will establish goodwill as well as gain attention. Avoid extravagant, emotional statements, however, because listeners are quick to sense a lack of genuineness. At the other extreme, avoid apologizing. Don't say, "I don't know why I was picked to talk when others could have done it so much better" or, "Unaccustomed as I am to public speaking." Apologetic beginnings suggest that your audience needn't waste time listening. Be cordial, sincere, and modest, but establish your authority and maintain control of the situation.

Asking a Question

Another way to open a speech is to ask a question or series of questions to spark thinking about your subject. For example, Nicholas Fynn of Ohio University opened a speech about free-burning of timberland as follows: "How many of you in this room have visited a National Park at one point in your life? Well, the majority of you are in good company."[5] Such a question introduces a topic gently and, with its direct reference to the audience, tends to engage the listeners.

For those who don't really expect an actual audience response, rhetorical questions usually are used to help forecast the development of the speech.

Anne Wilfahrt of Mankato State University, Minnesota, was advocating the re-peal of the 1872 General Mining Law, which grants individuals the mineral rights to their land; she used a rhetorical question as a lead-in to her forecast in this manner: "Does the Mining Law of 1872 affect you and me, and is it in need of repair work? Yes, and such an opinion can be triggered by first briefly clarifying the original intent of the law; secondly, exploring the financial and environmental downfalls of this 1872 law in the 1990s; and finally, exposing proposed legislative measures that address these downfalls."[6]

Making a Startling Statement

On certain occasions, you may choose to open a speech with what is known as the *shock technique,* making a startling statement of fact or opinion. This ap-proach is especially useful when listeners are distracted, apathetic, or smug. It rivets their attention on your topic. For example, the executive director of the American Association for Retired Persons (AARP), after asking some rhetori-cal questions about health care, caught his listeners' attention with several star-tling statements:

> Given what we're spending on health care, we should have the best system in the world.
> But the reality is that we don't.
> Thirty-seven million Americans have no health insurance protection what-soever, and millions more are underinsured.
> We are twentieth—that's right, twentieth—among the nations of the world in infant mortality. The death rate for our black newborn children ri-vals that of Third World countries. And poor children in America, like their brothers and sisters in Third World nations, receive neither immunizations nor basic dental care.
> Those statistics give us a sense of the scope of the problem. What they don't adequately portray is the human factor—the pain and the suffering.
> While terminally ill patients may have their lives extended in intensive care units—at tremendous cost—middle-age minority women die of pre-ventable and treatable cancer, hypertension and diabetes.[7]

Avoid overusing shock techniques. The technique can backfire if your lis-teners become angry when you threaten or disgust them.

Using a Quotation

A quotation may be an excellent means of introducing a speech, because it can prod listeners to think about something important and it often captures an ap-propriate emotional tone. When Agnar Pytte, President of Case Western Re-serve University, spoke to the Cleveland City Club on the topic of political cor-rectness and free speech, he opened his speech with a quotation: "As Benjamin Cardozo said: 'Freedom of expression is the indispensable condition of all our liberties.'"[8] Pytte continued by using Cardozo's statement to investigate the current debate over political correctness on college campuses. The opening quotation provided the groundwork by effectively piquing the interest of the audience and inviting listeners to further consider the impact of political correctness on free speech. Pytte could then proceed into a discussion of current examples of the political correctness debate, confident that his audience was paying attention.

Telling a Humorous Story

You can begin a speech by telling a funny story or relating a humorous experience. When doing so, however, observe the following three rules of communication:

1. Be sure that the story is at least amusing, if not funny; test it out on others before you actually deliver the speech. Be sure that you practice sufficiently so you can present the story naturally. And use the story to make a point instead of making it the center of your remarks. In other words, brevity is crucial.
2. Be sure that the story is relevant to your speech; if its subject matter or punch line is not directly related to you, your topic, or at least your next couple of sentences, the story will appear to be a mere gimmick.
3. Be sure that your story is in good taste; in a public gathering, an off-color or doubtful story violates accepted standards of social behavior and can undermine an audience's respect for you. (In general, you should avoid sexual, racist, antireligious, ageist, homophobic, and sexist humor.)

All three of these rules were observed by Earnest Deavenport, chair and CEO of Eastman Chemical Company, when addressing the American branch of the Société de Chimie Industrielle in late 1995:

$\mathscr{A}$SSESSMENT CHECK

Ask yourself the following questions to ensure that the speech you are working on has a well-framed introduction:

- Have I shown this audience exactly why and how my central idea or claim is relevant to them?
- Have I developed my ethos or credibility adequately by demonstrating my good sense, good morals, and good will?
- Have I given my listeners a sense of how I will develop my central idea or claim, so they will better comprehend the development of the speech?

I want to begin with a story about a tightrope walker who announced that he was going to walk across Niagara Falls. Well, nobody believed that was possible, and the crowd that had gathered tried to talk him out of it. But to everyone's amazement, he made it safely across and everybody cheered. Then he asked, "Who believes I can do it blindfolded?" And everyone cried, "Don't do it, you'll fall!" But again, he made it safely across.

Then he said, "Who believes I can ride a bicycle across?" And they all said, "Don't do it, you'll fall!" But he got on his bicycle and made it safely across.

Then he said, "Who believes I can push a full wheelbarrow across?" Well, by that time, the crowd had seen enough to make real believers of them, and they all shouted, "We do! We do!" At that he said, "Ok . . . Who wants to be the first to get in?"

Well, that's how many investors feel about companies who have adopted the philosophy that balancing the interests of all stakeholders is the true route to maximum value.

They are skeptical at first, then believers after they see some solid results, but are very reluctant to get in that wheelbarrow.[9]

After telling that story and tying it to his topic, he was ready to develop a picture of Eastman Chemical Company's approach to balancing the interests of various groups who watch developments in the industrial world of chemicals.

Using an Illustration

A real-life incident, a passage from a novel or short story, or a hypothetical illustration can also get a speech off to a good start. As with a humorous story, an illustration should be not only interesting to the audience but also relevant to your central idea. Deanna Sellnow, a then-student at North Dakota State University, used this technique to introduce a speech on private credit-reporting bureaus:

John Pontier, of Boise, Idaho, was turned down for insurance because a reporting agency informed the company that he and his wife were addicted to narcotics, and his Taco Bell franchise had been closed down by the health board when dog food had been found mixed in with the tacos. There was only one small problem. The information was made up. His wife was a practicing Mormon who didn't touch a drink, much less drugs, and the restaurant had never been cited for a health violation.[10]

The existence of a problem with private credit-reporting bureaus is clear from this introduction. In addition, when listeners get involved with someone like John Pontier who has encountered the problem, they become more attentive. When this happens, the illustration can have a powerful impact.

Building a Speech Forecast

As we've suggested several times, highly competent speakers are always careful to forecast the development of their speeches. The simplest forecast merely enumerates the sections of a speech, as Whitney Sugarman of Seton Hall University did when beginning her talk on the overuse of cesarean sections at birth: "[The fact that so many cesarean sections are unnecessary] will become evident as we first, understand the process of a cesarean section and the detrimental effects to mother and child; then delve into the nonclinical factors leading to the rise of cesareans in this country; and finally, magnify steps that must be taken to decrease the number of cesareans performed each year in the United States."[11]

With a little more effort, a speaker can use the forecast to suggest the *coherence* of a speech and its development as well. So, in reminding his audience that the day of great oratory is dead but should be recovered, Dean Willich of Wittenberg University offered a simple forecast that succeeded in making his speech feel like a complete unit of thought: "I would like to introduce you to the tradition of oratory, then look at the contemporary state of persuasive speaking; and finally, show you how a synthesis between the two will help us grow to be more effective persuasive speakers."[12] Just by talking about his third point as a synthesis of the first two, Willich was able to leave the impression that his speech would be a unified bundle of ideas; such a forecast undoubtedly helped the audience see and anticipate his developmental strategies.

&NDING YOUR SPEECH

The best conclusions mirror good introductions by returning to the viewpoints articulated early in the speech, by recapturing the tone with which it started, and by reaffirming the speaker's goals for and control over the speech. A good speech often feels like a circle, wherein an audience understands that it's entered a universe of thought and action at some point, taken a trip around that universe, and then returned to the place where it entered, now much wiser and more knowledgeable than when it came in. Creating a sense of having taken an interesting and worthwhile journey through important ideas requires careful attention to various types of speech conclusions.

Issuing a Challenge

You may conclude your speech by focusing directly upon the audience, hoping that you can inspire your listeners to get up and act in constructive ways. Such a conclusion attempts to involve listeners directly, intimately, with your speech. Jerry Junkins, president and CEO of Texas Instruments, used just such a technique when trying to convince fellow business executives to become more active in introducing new technologies to the nation's schools:

> It's up to us . . . to bring the benefits of information technology not only to our companies . . . but also to America's communities and schools . . . so that our infrastructure can become and remain the equal of any in the world.

FIGURE 8.1 Beginning and Ending a Speech

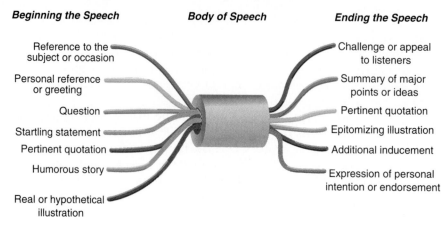

It's up to us . . . to be sensitive and responsive to the social implications of our technology . . . and to be imaginative in our attempts to address those concerns.

It's up to us . . . to do *all* of these things . . . and do them all at once . . . because the future won't wait. The technologies are here. They're already stirring the pot.

Our challenge is not so much to harness those technologies . . . as it is to *unlock their potential.*

It certainly won't be easy. But with the sustained focus of business leaders . . . with the commitment of all of us . . . I believe that we *can* realize the full promise of a networked society: The promise that it will dramatically improve the quality of life for the entire world.

Thank you.[13]

Summarizing the Major Points or Ideas

In an informative speech, a summary allows the audience to pull together the main strands of information and to evaluate the significance of the speech. In a persuasive speech, a summary gives you a final opportunity to present, in brief form, the major points of your argument. For example, a student presented this summary of an informative speech on tornadoes:

> You've seen the swirling funnel clouds on the six o'clock news. They hit sometimes without much warning, leaving in their paths death and destruction. Now you should understand the formation of funnel clouds, the classification of tornadoes on the Fujita scale, and the high cost of tornadoes worldwide in lives and property. Once you understand the savage fury of tornadoes, you can better appreciate them. Tornadoes are one of nature's temper tantrums.

If the student's purpose had been to persuade his listeners to take certain precautions during a tornado alert, the summary of the speech might have sounded like this:

The devastation left in the path of a tornado can be tremendous. To prevent you and your loved ones from becoming statistics on the six o'clock news, remember what I told you this afternoon. Seek shelter in basements, ditches, or other low areas. Stay away from glass and electric lines. And, remember the lesson of the Xenia, Ohio, disaster. Tornadoes often hit in clusters. Be sure the coast is clear before you leave your shelter. Don't be a statistic.

In each case, summarizing the main ideas of the speech gives the speaker another opportunity to reinforce the message. Information can be reiterated in the summary of an informative speech, or the major arguments or actions can be strengthened in the summary of a persuasive speech.

Using a Quotation

You can cite the words of others to capture the spirit of your ideas in the conclusion of your speech. Quotations are often used to end speeches. Poetry may distill the essence of your message in uplifting language. Quoted prose, if the

A speaker can conclude by openly appealing for support or by reminding listeners of their responsibilities in furthering a cause they believe in.

author is credible, may gather additional support for your central idea. Notice how Tim Dolin of West Virginia's Marshall University was able to add the credibility of Senator John Glenn to his plea for public regulation of nuclear weapons waste and disposal:

> After looking at the poor management within the nuclear weapons cycle, its impact on us and how the problem can be solved, it becomes obvious something must be done. As Senator John Glenn said, "The costs of cleaning up these sites will be extraordinarily high, but the costs of doing nothing will be higher. After all, what good does it do to protect ourselves from the Soviets by building nuclear weapons if we poison ourselves in the process?"[14]

Using an Illustration

Illustrations engage your listeners emotionally. If you use a concluding illustration, it can set the tone and direction of your final words. Your illustration should be both inclusive and conclusive—inclusive of the main focus or thrust of your speech and conclusive in tone and impact. Sometimes the same illustration can be used to tie together a whole speech. This is what Michael Twitchell, a student in a speaking contest, did when talking about the causes and effects of depression. Here's his opening:

> Have you ever felt like you were the little Dutch boy who stuck his finger in the leaking dike? You waited and waited but the help never came. The leak became worse and the water rushed around you and swept you away. As you fought the flood, gasping and choking for air, you realized that the flood was inside yourself. You were drowning and dying in your own mind. According to the *American Journal of Psychiatry,* as many as half the people in this room will be carried away by this devastating flood. What is this disaster? Mental depression.

Notice how Twitchell's concluding words reinforce the illustration used in his introduction:

> Let's go back to my illustration of the little Dutch boy. He was wise to take action and put his finger in the dike, preventing the flood. In the case of depression, each one of us must be like the little Dutch boy—willing to get involved and control the harmful effects of depression.[15]

Supplying an Additional Inducement to Belief or Action

Sometimes you may conclude a speech by quickly reviewing the principal ideas presented in the body and then supplying one or more additional reasons for endorsing the belief or taking the proposed action. In his speech, Michael Twitchell spoke at length about the devastating effects of depression. After proposing numerous reasons for people to get involved in the battle, Twitchell offered, in the conclusion to his speech, an additional inducement:

> Why should you really care? Why is it important? The depressed person may be someone you know—it could be you. If you know what is happening, you can always help. I wish I had known what depression was in March of 1978. You see, when I said David Twitchell could be my father, I was making a statement of fact. David is my father. I am his son. My family wasn't saved; perhaps now yours can be.

Stating a Personal Intention

Stating your own intention to adopt the action or attitude you recommend in your speech is particularly effective when your prestige with the audience is high or when you have presented a concrete proposal requiring immediate action. By professing your intention to take immediate action, you and your ideas gain credibility. In the following example, a speaker sets himself up as a model for the actions he wants his listeners to take:

> Today I have illustrated how important healthy blood is to human survival and how blood banks work to ensure the possibility and availability of blood for each of us. It is not a coincidence that I speak on this vital topic on the same day that the local Red Cross Bloodmobile is visiting campus. I want to urge each of you to ensure your future and mine by stopping at the Student Center today or tomorrow to make your donation. The few minutes that it takes may add up to a lifetime for a person in need. To illustrate how firmly I believe in this opportunity to help. I'm going to the Student Center to give my donation as soon as this class is over. I invite any of you who feel this strongly to join me.

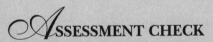

ASSESSMENT CHECK

As you examine the conclusion of the speech you are preparing, answer the following questions to evaluate your conclusion:

- Does my conclusion somehow mirror the introduction in terms of tone, viewpoint, or goals? Will the audience sense the connection between the beginning and ending of the speech?
- Does my conclusion remind the audience what the central idea or claim of the speech is?
- Does my conclusion let the audience know, "This is it—the end"? Do I know what specific language I will use to make sure there is a strong sense of closure?

A speaker can effectively conclude a speech to actuate by indicating her personal intention to take action on a problem.

$\mathscr{S}$ELECTING INTRODUCTIONS AND CONCLUSIONS

So far, we've talked about the functions of introductions and conclusions, about fitting them together so as to provide a solid rhetorical orientation to your speech, and about a variety of strategies you can use to begin and end speeches. At this point, you ought to be able to build a generally serviceable opening and close for a speech. But suppose you want to stretch yourself a bit farther, to move beyond the skills of the average speaker and into the world of highly competent speechmakers of the kind we've been quoting throughout this chapter. What then? How do you become a superior opener and closer?

The answer to that question, as always in this textbook, is that you must learn to assess *yourself, your listeners, the subject matter, and the requirements of the occasion* if you're going to be good at these parts of speechmaking. The answers to four questions should help you construct high-quality introductions and conclusions:

1. *What are your own experiences and abilities?* The best source of powerful illustrations is your own life. Stories of your own experiences usually come across as natural and as involving, especially if your own reactions to those experiences are like those listeners would feel in the same situation. Anecdotes that you've gotten elsewhere, however, have to be practiced and at least put into your own words to make them a part of you. Working from your own experiences also tends to increase listeners' positive reactions to your qualifications. If you don't have first-hand experience, you'll need to show the audience, through explicit statements or the quality of your research materials, that you know what you're talking about. Your abilities as a speaker also may constrain your choices. If you don't tell funny stories in a natural, relaxed manner, attempting a humorous anecdote may not be wise. On the other hand, if you're known as a clown and want to be taken seriously for a change, you need to set forth your qualifications explicitly and, in concluding, create a serious mood for the consideration of your views. Humor may not be your best vehicle under these circumstances.

2. *What is the mood and commitment of the audience?* If you're speaking on a subject already announced and known to be controversial, gaining attention through a startling statement or a humorous anecdote may seem highly inappropriate. If the audience is indifferent or has already heard several presentations on the same subject, a direct reference to the subject may be perceived as dull and unoriginal. A rhetorical question that forces them to think for a moment or a startling statement that creates curiosity may be appropriate. Both induce listeners to participate directly, rather than to listen passively.

3. *What does the audience know about you and your commitment to the subject?* If you're already known as an expert in an area, stating your qualifications would be repetitious and may even convey conceit. If your personal experience and depth of feeling are generally unknown, you'll want to reveal these through personal reference, or, as Michael Twitchell did (see page 222), through an additional inducement at the close of your address. Either approach establishes both your knowledge and your personal involvement in the subject. Allow time to pass before you attempt to bring deeply felt experiences before an audience, however, especially those involving loss of life. If you appear emotionally shaken or teary-eyed, the tension level will increase as the

audience shares your personal discomfort. The effectiveness of your personal revelation will correspondingly decrease. Using a challenge or statement of personal intent also is an effective means of demonstrating your commitment to the subject.

4. *What constraints are imposed by the situation or setting?* A somber occasion, such as a funeral or a dedication of a war memorial, is hardly the place for hilarious stories. On the other hand, some serious occasions, such as commencements, can be enlivened by humor. The student speaker who ended his high-school address by waving a beer bottle and proclaiming "This Bud's for you" quickly discovered that his attempt at humor was received well by only part of his audience. The faculty and parents did not react as pleasantly as did his peers. Not everything goes, even when *you* see nothing wrong with the story or allusion. A reference to the occasion or personal greeting may be an appropriate reminder to the audience that you, as well as they, appreciate the significance of the occasion. Pertinent quotations and epitomizing illustrations, at the beginning or end, also can convey a sense of the event's meaning for everyone present.

This discussion of the use of appropriate introductions and conclusions is not intended to be exhaustive. Rather, it illustrates the general approach to *thinking through* possible audience reactions as you select various means of introducing and concluding your speech. A "thought-through" speech will be perceived as well prepared by your listeners, whether they ultimately agree with you or not.

$\mathscr{S}$AMPLE OUTLINE FOR AN INTRODUCTION AND A CONCLUSION

An introduction and a conclusion for a classroom speech on MADD and SADD, anti–drunk driving organizations, might take the following form. Notice that the speaker uses one of the factors of attention—suspense—together with startling statements to lead the audience into the subject then concludes by combining a final illustration with a statement of personal intention.

Introduction

I. Many of you have seen the "Black Gash"—the Vietnam War Memorial in Washington, DC.
  A. It contains the names of more than 40,000 Americans who gave their lives in Southeast Asia between 1961 and 1973.
  B. We averaged over 3000 war dead a year during that anguishing period.
II. Today, another enemy stalks Americans.
  A. The enemy kills, not 3000 per year, but over 20,000 citizens every twelve months.
  B. The enemy is not hiding in jungles but can be found in every community in the country.

    C. The enemy kills, not with bayonets and bullets, but with bottles and bumpers.

III. Today, I want to talk about organizations that are trying to contain and finally destroy the killer.

    A. Every TV station in this town carries a public service ad that says "Friends Don't Let Friends Drive Drunk."

    B. Those ads are trying to rid our streets of that great killer, the drunk driver.

    C. In response to that menace, two national organizations—Mothers Against Drunk Driving and Students Against Drunk Driving—have been formed and are working even in this community to make the streets safe for you and me.

IV. [*Central Idea*] MADD and SADD are achieving their goals with your help.

  V. To help you understand what these familiar organizations do, first I'll tell you something about the founders of MADD and SADD; then, I'll describe their operations; finally, I'll mention some of the ways community members get involved with them.

[Body]

Conclusion

   I. Today, I've talked briefly about the Lightners and their goals for MADD and SADD, their organizational techniques, and ways you can get involved.

  II. The work of MADD and SADD volunteers—even on our campus, as I'm sure you've seen their posters in the Union—is being carried out to keep you alive.

    A. You may not think you need to be involved, but remember, after midnight one in every five or fewer drivers on the road is probably drunk.

    B. You could be involved whether you want to be or not.

    C. That certainly was the case with Julie Smeiser, a member of our sophomore class, who just last Friday was hit by a drunk driver when going home for the weekend.

III. If people don't take action, we could build a new "Black Gash"—this time for victims of drunks—every two years, and soon fill Washington, DC, with monuments to needless suffering.

    A. Such monuments would be grim reminders of our unwillingness to respond to enemies at home with the same intensity with which we attacked enemies abroad.

    B. Better would be a positive response to such groups as MADD and SADD, which are attacking the enemy on several fronts at once in a war on motorized murder.

IV. If you're interested in learning more about MADD and SADD, stop by Room 324 in the Union tonight at 7:30 to hear the president of the local chapter of SADD talk about this year's activities. I'll be there; please join me.

$\mathscr{C}$HAPTER SUMMARY

Introductions and conclusions provide a rhetorical orientation to your speeches, *framing* them in ways audiences can understand and appreciate. Well-framed introductions orient an audience's *attention,* show them your *qualifications,* and direct them to your *ideas and their development.* Well-framed conclusions demonstrate *focus, flair,* and a sense of *finality* for your talks. Useful ways of beginning a speech include referring to the subject or occasion, using a personal reference or greeting, asking a question, making a startling statement, using a quotation, telling a humorous story, using an illustration, and building a speech forecast. Speeches can be concluded by issuing a challenge, summarizing the major points or ideas, using a quotation, using an illustration, supplying an additional inducement to belief or action, and stating a personal intention. Your decision about which of these strategies you use singly or in combination should depend on you and your experiences, the mood and commitments of the audience, the audience's knowledge of you and your commitments, and constraints imposed by the situation or setting. The most competent speakers carefully think through strategies for moving into and out of their speeches because of the importance of *rhetorical orientation* in making them successful behind the lectern.

$\mathscr{K}$EY TERMS

conclusion *(p. 210)*
ethos *(p. 211)*
forecast *(p. 211)*
framing *(p. 210)*

introduction *(p. 210)*
rhetorical orientation *(p. 210)*
The End *(p. 211)*

$\mathscr{A}$SSESSMENT ACTIVITIES

1. You've been asked to speak on a controversial issue. Assume that the setting for three versions of the speech will include three different occasions: a classroom at your school, where audience members are mixed in their support or rejection of the issue; a favorable ("pro") audience, highly sympathetic to you and your position; and an unfavorable ("con") audience, hostile to you and your position. Write three introductions, one for each setting. Include a brief paragraph explaining your rhetorical orientation to those three audiences. Turn the introductions and rationales into your instructor.

2. Devise one-minute introductions and conclusions for your next informative speech. Deliver them to a small group in class, in round-robin fashion so that everyone gets a crack at the group. Have each member of the group rate your introduction in terms of attention value, perception of your qualifications, and forecast of your speech's development, and your conclusion in

terms of focus, flair, and sense of finality. Collect the ratings from everyone, and use their feedback to refine your opening and closing.

$\mathcal{R}$EFERENCES

1. Russell J. Love, "The Barriers Come Tumbling Down," Harris-Hillman School Commencement, Nashville, May 21, 1981. Reprinted by permission.
2. Pope John Paul II, "Democracy and Christianity," *Vital Speeches of the Day,* 62 (November 1, 1995): 35.
3. Barbara Bush, "Choice and Change," Wellesley College, June 1, 1990, manuscript available from the author.
4. Anson Mount, "The Playboy Philosophy—Pro," in *Contemporary American Speeches,* 5th ed., ed. Wil A. Linkugel et al. (Dubuque, IA: Kendall/Hunt, 1982).
5. Nicholas Fynn, "The Free Burn Fallacy," *Winning Orations 1989.* Reprinted by permission of Larry Schnoor, Executive Secretary, Interstate Oratorical Association, Mankato State University, Mankato, MN.
6. Anne Wilfahrt, "General Mining Law of 1872; Statute 17–90," *Winning Orations 1992.* Reprinted by permission of Larry Schnoor, Executive Secretary, Interstate Oratorical Association, Mankato State University, Mankato, MN.
7. Horace B. Deets, "Health Care for a Caring America: We Must Develop a Better System," *Vital Speeches of the Day,* 55 (August 1, 1989).
8. Agnar Pytte, "Political Correctness and Free Speech: Let the Ideas Come Forth," *Vital Speeches of the Day,* 57 (September 1, 1989).
9. Earnest W. Deavenport, "Walking the High Wire: Balancing Stakeholder Interests," *Vital Speeches of the Day,* 62 (November 1, 1995): 49.
10. Deanna Sellnow, "Have You Checked Lately?" *Winning Orations.* Reprinted by permission of Larry Schnoor, Executive Secretary, Interstate Oratorical Association, Mankato State University, Mankato, MN.
11. Whitney Sugarman, "Cesarean Sections: The Needless Scars of Profit," *Winning Orations 1992.* Reprinted by permission of Larry Schnoor, Executive Secretary, Interstate Oratorical Association, Mankato State University, Mankato, MN.
12. Dean Willich, "Traditional Oratory: Thoroughbred of Persuasive Speaking," *Winning Orations 1992.* Reprinted by permission of Larry Schnoor, Executive Secretary, Interstate Oratorical Association, Mankato State University, Mankato, MN.
13. Jerry R. Junkins, "Realizing the Promise: Our Role as Business Leaders," *Vital Speeches of the Day,* 62 (November 1, 1995): 57.
14. Tim Dolin, "The Hidden Legacy of the Arms Race," *Winning Orations 1989.* Reprinted by permission of Larry Schnoor, Executive Secretary, Interstate Oratorical Association, Mankato State University, Mankato, MN.
15. Michael A. Twitchell, "The Flood Gates of the Mind," *Winning Orations.* Reprinted by permission of Larry Schnoor, Executive Secretary, Interstate Oratorical Association, Mankato State University, Mankato, MN.

CHAPTER
9
DEVELOPING
THE SPEECH OUTLINE

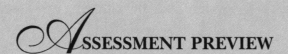

ASSESSMENT PREVIEW

After reading Chapter 9, the student with basic communication competencies will be able to

- understand the requirements of good outline form.
- develop a rough outline.

The student with average communication competencies will also be able to

- develop a full-sentence outline.
- develop a technical plot outline.
- develop a speaking outline to use in presenting a speech.

The student with superior communication competencies will also be able to

- arrange main and subpoints in appropriate order.
- assess deficiencies in an outline and make necessary corrections.
- critically evaluate outlines written by others and make suggestions for improvement.

*W*hy outline a speech? Unless you are able to memorize easily or able to read from a printed text while maintaining the spontaneity of casual conversation, you will need something to guide you as you talk. An outline is that guide; it keeps you on track, makes it possible to concentrate on what needs to be said, and reminds you of points you may otherwise forget to mention. In addition, you can make side notes to remind you when to show a slide, or to pause so that audience members can focus on a graph or other visual aid you have presented. Although your past experiences with outlining may not have been the most pleasant (remember outlining in eighth or ninth grade?), the fact is that outlining is an important tool for the speaker. In addition to *guidance,* an outline helps you *evaluate* the coherence or cohesiveness of your ideas: You can discover what ideas you've overemphasized to the exclusion of other notions, you can see more clearly what should be added, and you can tell at a glance that you've buried your most important point as subpoint 3 under main point 2. Thus, while the outline is written for the speaking situation, it serves as an evaluative tool as well.

Speech outlines come in multiple forms, depending upon the purpose for which they've been constructed. In this chapter, we will review the elements of good outline form (in case you've forgotten those earlier lessons in eighth or ninth grade!). Then, we'll get into the heart of the matter: the process of moving from initial ideas to an outline you can use in presenting a speech.

*R*EQUIREMENTS OF GOOD OUTLINE FORM

There are many "good" outline forms, depending on the way you want to use them. Because the *complete, full outline* is the most comprehensive of the different forms, we will use that to present the five essential rules for developing outlines (and where appropriate, we'll alternate a "wrong" with a "right" illustration to make the application of the rule easier to see).

1. *Each item in the outline should contain one main idea.* When two or more ideas are included in a main point, it is more difficult for an audience to track the development of the point.

   Wrong

   I. Several individuals have been criticized for their participation in the recent Million Man March because it was led by Louis Farrakhan while others have supported participation, arguing that the idea was worthy of merit regardless of who was involved.

   This is a mess. It is hard to discern what the main point of the speech is from this sentence. Is the speaker going to agree with one side or the other, or simply inform people as to the arguments on both sides? The latter seems likely, but it is hard to discern especially if you are only listening rather than reading and rereading the sentence.

By sketching the structure of your speech in advance of presentation, you can determine whether the major sections fit together smoothly.

Right

    I. The 1995 Million Man March on Washington was and remains a controversial event.

        A. On the one hand, people have criticized Reverend Jesse Jackson and others for appearing on the stage with Louis Farrakhan, the controversial leader of the Nation of Islam.

B. On the other hand, Jackson and others have argued that participation should not be equated with support for Farrakhan's controversial views on race relations.

In this case, the main point is restricted to a simple statement about the event, while the subpoints are then developed as contrasting arguments. The idea of the speech as an informative overview of the controversy is much clearer to anyone listening.

2. *Less important ideas in the outline should be subordinate to more important ideas.* You already know this is true; the trick is to actually carry it out so that listeners will understand the rational structure of your arguments.

Wrong

I. The cost of medical care has skyrocketed.
   A. Operating room fees can run to tens of thousands of dollars.
      1. Hospital charges are high.
      2. A private room can cost $1,500 a day.
   B. X-rays and laboratory tests are extra.
   C. Complicated operations may cost over $50,000.
      1. Doctors' charges constantly go up.
         a. Office calls usually cost between $30 and $50.
         b. Surgical procedures costs have increased.
      2. Drugs are expensive.
      3. Most antibiotics cost from $2 to $3 per dose.
   D. The cost of even nonprescription drugs has mounted.

This outline is sloppily arranged. A listener would feel bombarded by numbers and general references to hospitals and doctors, but probably couldn't sort it all out. To help the listener grasp the main ideas, notice what happens when the material is sorted by on the basis of cost in a topical outline:

Right

I. The cost of medical care has skyrocketed.
   A. *Hospital charges* are high.
      1. A private room may cost as much as $1,500 a day.
      2. Operating room fees may be tens of thousands of dollars.
      3. X-rays and laboratory tests are extra.
   B. *Doctors' charges* constantly go up.
      1. Complicated operations may cost over $50,000.
      2. Office calls usually cost between $30 and $50.
   C. *Drugs* are expensive.
      1. Most antibiotics cost from $2 to $3 per dose.
      2. The cost of even nonprescription drugs has mounted.

The second form highlights the three main topics and *subordinates* the examples, which are the supporting materials, to the three main arguments. The key word here is *fit:* what example fits within or under what topic? *Reasons* (A, B, C) fit within or under claims: *supporting materials* (1, 2) fit within or under reasons.

3. *A consistent set of symbols should be used.* Each indention should be designated by the same set of symbols. The most common set looks like this:

   I. Main idea
      A. Major subpoint or topic
         1. Aspect of the subpoint or topic
            a. Perhaps a statistic or quotation
               (1) Perhaps bolstering support

While you can use other sets of symbols (for example, you might use *A., 1., a.* if you only need three levels), the primary concern is to be consistent, so that the rational structure of your thoughts emerges clearly both for evaluative and guidance purposes.

4. *The logical relation of items in an outline should be shown by proper indention.* Why? Because, to put it simply, it makes it easier to see what is subordinate to what. As noted above, reasons and supporting materials should not be on the same level. By indenting, and using a consistent format for the levels used in outlining, the process of evaluating your claim or central idea becomes much easier.

Wrong

   I. Picking edible wild mushrooms is no job for the uninformed.
      A. Many wild species are highly toxic.
         1. The angel cap contains a toxin for which there is no known antidote.
          2. Hallucinogenic mushrooms produce short-lived highs, followed by convulsions, paralysis, and possibly death.
      B. Myths abound regarding ways to choose "safe" mushrooms.
         1. Mushrooms easily peeled still can be poisonous.
          2. Mushrooms eaten by animals are not necessarily safe.
            3. Mushrooms that don't darken a silver coin in a pan of hot water could be toxic.

Right

   I. Picking edible wild mushrooms is no job for the uninformed.
      A. Many wild species are highly toxic.
         1. The angel cap contains a toxin for which there is no known antidote.
         2. Hallucinogenic mushrooms produce short-lived highs, followed by convulsions, paralysis, and possibly death.
      B. Myths abound regarding ways to choose "safe" mushrooms.
         1. Mushrooms easily peeled still can be poisonous.
         2. Mushrooms eaten by animals are not necessarily safe.

3. Mushrooms that don't darken a silver coin in a pan of hot water could be toxic.[1]

5. The first four requirements apply to all outlines. One last rule is made for complete, formal outlines: *All main points and subordinate points in formal outlines should be written as full sentences.* Full sentences maximize the clear expression of your ideas. Using complete sentences forces you to reason your way through points that are fuzzy and incomplete.

COMMUNICATION RESEARCH DATELINE

MEMORY AND ORGANIZATION

If you lost your outline, would you remember the major items? Even with the outline present, could you give your speech without complete reliance upon it, trusting your memory of the points and their sequence? Further, how many points should a speech attempt to cover? These issues are answered in part by research relating organizational processes to human memory. In a classic study, Miller concluded that there is a limit to the number of items a person can easily recall; according to Miller, the "magic number" is seven, plus or minus two. More recent research has suggested that a more manageable number is five, plus or minus two. Using this research as a guideline would suggest using no more than five to seven points in a speech. Your audience will find it easier to recall these main points if, in following the advice contained in this chapter, you *coordinate* concepts of equal emphasis as level *I* and *II* or *A* and *B* under *I*. You can also make recall easier by properly *subordinating* specific items under their respective coordinate points. Thus, in an outline, items *A* and *B* are subordinate when placed under *I* or *II*. This *hierarchical* method of organizing ideas matches the human mind's approach to the recall of items. Thus three to five coordinate points (level *I, II, . . .*) could easily contain additional subpoints under each (*A, B, C, . . .*). Recalling level *I* also brings to mind the relevant subpoints, while recalling level *II* brings into focus the points under that heading.

Further Reading

L. N. Squire, ed., *Memory: Organization and Locus of Change* (New York: Oxford University Press, 1991); R. S. Wyer, *Memory and Cognition in Its Social Context* (Hillsdale, NJ: Lawrence Erlbaum, 1989); G. A. Miller, "The Magic Number Seven, Plus or Minus Two: Some Limits on Our Capacity for Processing Information." *Psychological Review* 63 (1956): 81–97.

It may be painful to write complete sentences, but it's one of the ways you can guarantee good thinking.

DEVELOPING THE SPEECH: STAGES IN THE OUTLINING PROCESS

You should develop your outline, as well as the speech it represents, through a series of stages. Your outlines will become increasingly complex and complete as the ideas of your speech evolve and as you move closer to the final form of your speech. We will examine each of the major stages, beginning with the *rough outline,* and then consider in sequence *the full-sentence outline, technical plot outline,* and *speaking outline.*

Developing a Rough Outline

Suppose your instructor has assigned an informative speech on a subject that interests you. You decide to talk about drunk driving because a close friend was recently injured by an intoxicated driver. Your broad topic area is *drunk driving.*

In the six to eight minutes you have to speak, you obviously can't cover such a broad topic adequately. After considering your audience (see Chapter 4) and your time limit, you decide to focus your presentation on two organizations—Mothers Against Drunk Driving (MADD) and Students Against Drunk Driving (SADD).

As you think about narrowing your topic further, you jot down some possible ideas. You continue to narrow your list until your final ideas include the following:

1. Founders of MADD and SADD
2. Accomplishments of the two organizations
3. Reasons the organizations were deemed necessary
4. Goals of MADD and SADD
5. Action steps taken by MADD and SADD
6. Ways your listeners can help

You can help your listeners follow your ideas more easily by clustering similar ideas. Experiment with several possible clusters before you decide on the best way to arrange your ideas. Your next step is to consider the best pattern of organization for these topics. A chronological pattern will enable you to organize the history of MADD and SADD, but it will not allow you to discuss ways your listeners can help. Either cause-effect or effect-cause would work well if your primary purpose is to persuade. However, this is an informative speech, and you don't want to talk about the organizations solely in terms of their influence on reducing alcohol-related accidents. After examining the alternatives, you finally settle on a topical pattern, which allows you to present three clusters of information:

1. Background of MADD and SADD—information about the founders, why the organizations were founded
2. Description of MADD and SADD—goals, steps in action plans, results
3. Local work of MADD and SADD—how parents work with their teenagers and with local media to accomplish MADD and SADD goals

As you subdivide your three clusters of information, you develop the following general outline:

I. Background of MADD and SADD
   A. Information about the founders
   B. Reasons the organizations were founded
II. Description of the organizations
   A. Their goals
   B. The action steps they take
   C. Their accomplishments so far
III. Applications of their work on a local level
   A. "Project Graduation"
   B. Parent-student contracts
   C. Local public service announcements

A **rough outline** identifies your topic, provides a reasonable number of subtopics, and shows a method for organizing and developing your speech. Notice that you've arranged both the main points and subpoints topically. A word of warning: *As you refine your outline, make sure that the speech doesn't turn into a "string of beads" that fails to differentiate between one topic and the next.*

The next steps in preparing an outline are to phrase your main headings more precisely as full sentences, and then to develop each heading by adding subordinate ideas. As you develop your outline, you'll begin to see what kinds of information and supporting materials you need to find.

$\mathscr{A}$SSESSMENT CHECK

As you move ahead in outlining, evaluate your rough outline in terms of these specific questions:

- Does each item in the outline contain only one main idea?
- Are less important ideas in the outline subordinate to more important ideas?
- Have I used a consistent set of symbols?
- Have I used a consistent indention scheme that shows the logical relation of items?

Developing a Full-Sentence Outline

Consider where you now are in the speech preparation process: You've picked purposes and central ideas or claims, developed your key ideas, dug up some supporting materials, and considered how to use the suggestions for arranging your points. As you work from the rough outline thus constructed and begin to flesh out the main and subordinate points, you'll find yourself going back and forth between the speech materials and the outline. This is where evaluation begins to play a significant role as outlining reveals problems in your proposed presentation. Is everything you need there? Do you have too much or too little material at specific points? Have you made yourself clear, adapted everything you can to the audience, fit the requirements of the occasion? In answering these questions, you may discover that you have four pieces of testimony supporting one idea but none supporting another equally important one. Or, you might have three illustrations for your second point and a not very good one for the third point in setting forth the "need." Outlining the visualization step might reveal that you need another set of statistical trends to develop the argument or that the chronology you're working with has a major gap in it. As your mental map moves onto paper, you'll almost inevitably find problems you need to solve. Whether you use the traditional divisions of the speech (introduction, body, conclusion) or the steps in the motivated sequence (attention, need, satisfaction, visualization, action), your next step is to create the **full-sentence outline,** in full, grammatically correct sentences, following the key elements already discussed. In addition, the sources used in presenting information or support can be placed in parentheses at the end of sentences, perhaps in abbreviated form, with a bibliography attached at the end of the outline. Such an outline creates a clear, comprehensive picture of your speech, with only specific wording and cues to delivery left out.

Once completed, it is possible to speak from the fully developed outline. However, using this format poses some of the same problems as speaking from a typed script. You could end up shuffling through too many sheets of paper, lose your place as you squint to read individual sentences, or drone on once you decide just to read the blasted thing to the audience.

Nevertheless, the full-sentence outline, which represents the factual content of the whole speech in a comprehensive manner, serves a vital, initial preparatory role as you develop your speech. Before you convert your full-sentence outline to a phrase or key-word outline, you will want to develop your material as completely as possible. Once this is done, it is a simple process to write a brief outline incorporating phrases and key words along with supporting material that needs to be presented accurately. Here is an example of a full-sentence outline.

Steps in Preparing a Good Outline

  I. Determine the general purpose of the speech for the subject you have selected.

    A. You will need to limit the subject in two ways.

       1. Limit the subject to fit the available time.

       2. Limit the subject to ensure unity and coherence.

    B. You also will need to phrase the specific purpose in terms of the exact response you seek from your listeners.

II. Develop a rough outline of your speech.

    A. List the main ideas you wish to cover.

    B. Arrange these main ideas according to the methods discussed in Chapter 7.

    C. Arrange subordinate ideas under their appropriate main heads.

    D. Fill in the supporting materials to be used in amplifying or justifying your ideas.

    E. Review your rough draft.

       1. Does it cover your subject adequately?

       2. Does it carry out your specific purpose?

III. Put the outline into final form.

    A. Begin this process by writing out the main ideas as complete sentences or as key phrases.

       1. State the main ideas concisely, vividly, and—insofar as possible—in parallel terms.

       2. State the major heads so that they address directly the needs and interests of your listeners.

    B. Write out the subordinate ideas in complete sentences or in key phrases.

       1. Are they subordinate to the main idea they are intended to develop?

       2. Are they coordinate with other items at the same level (that is, are all A-B-C series roughly equal in importance; are all 1-2-3 series roughly equal in importance)?

    C. You now are ready to fill in the supporting materials.

       1. Are they pertinent?

       2. Are they adequate?

       3. Is there a variety of types of support?

    D. Recheck the completed outline.

       1. Is it written in proper outline form?

       2. Does the speech, as outlined, adequately cover the subject?

       3. Does the speech, as outlined, carry out your general and specific purposes?

Developing a Technical Plot Outline

After completing your full-sentence outline and learning more about your topic through background reading, you're now ready to assemble a technical plot outline. A **technical plot outline** is a diagnostic tool used to determine whether a speech is structurally sound. Use your technical plot outline to discover possible gaps or weaknesses in your speech. Begin by examining your full-sentence outline. Lay the complete sentence outline beside a blank sheet

$\mathscr{C}$OMMUNICATION RESEARCH DATELINE

PERCEPTUAL GROUPING: THE ORGANIZATION OF SUBORDINATE POINTS

What basic principles do we use to organize information into meaningful patterns? Gestalt psychologists, who believe that organization is basic to all mental activity and that it reflects the way the human brain functions, provide some useful clues. As suggested in this chapter, psychologists have argued that people learn by adding new bits of information to old constructs. Although the information that we encounter changes, the constructs remain constant. There are several relatively common constructs that people use to group new bits of information:

1. *Proximity:* We group stimuli that are close together.
2. *Continuity:* We tend to simplify and to find similarities among things rather than differences.
3. *Contiguity:* We connect events that occur close together in time and space.
4. *Closure:* We complete figures by filling in the gaps or adding missing connections.
5. *Similarity:* We group items of similar shape, size, and color.

You can use these constructs to enhance audience understanding of your ideas: the speech outline can be cast in a pattern of thinking that is familiar to your audience. Consider the constructs for organizing subordinate points shown in the accompanying table.

These constructs also may assist you as you evaluate your outline, especially as you develop the technical plot. Are your most important ideas *near,* or *proximate,* to each other? Do they advance a chain of thinking in a coherent manner implying *continuity?* Are they linked together or *contiguous?* Are they sufficiently comprehensive to permit accurate *closure?* Are they *similar* enough to suggest they belong together as main points?

Further Reading

Jacob Beck, ed., *Organization and Representation in Perception* (Hillsdale, NJ: Lawrence Erlbaum, 1982); Stephen E. Palmer, "Gestalt Psychology Redux," in *Speaking Minds* eds. Peter Baumgartner and Sabine Payr (Princeton: Princeton University Press, 1995), 157–176; Barry Smith, ed., *Foundations of Gestalt Theory* (Munich: Philosophia Verlag, 1988); and Irvin Rock, ed., *The Legacy of Solomon Asch: Essays in Cognition and Social Psychology* (Hillsdale, NJ: Lawrence Erlbaum, 1990).

Strategies for Organizing Speech Information

Organizing Strategy	Main Construct	Explanation	Example
Parts of a Whole	Proximity	You help your audience perceive how the new information is all part of a whole.	"The grip, shaft, and head are the main parts of a golf club."
Lists of Functions	Continuity	You show your audience the connections between pieces of new information.	"The mission of a police department consists of meeting its responsibilities of traffic control, crime detection, and safety education."
Series of Causes or Results	Contiguity	You show your listeners the precise relationship between pieces of new information.	"The causes of high orange juice prices may be drought, frost, or blight in citrus-producing states."
Items of Logical Proof	Closure	You connect separate items of information along a coordinated line of reasoning.	"We need a new high school because our present building (a) is too small, (b) lacks modern laboratory and shop facilities, and (c) is inaccessible to handicapped students.
Illustrative Examples	Similarity	You help your audience accept your main point by grouping specific cases or examples.	Cite the outcome of experiments to prove that adding fluoride to your community's water supply will help prevent tooth decay.

of paper. On the blank sheet, opposite each outline unit, identify the corresponding supporting materials, types of motivational appeals, factors of attention, and other devices. For example, indicate on the blank sheet wherever you have used statistics; you might also include a brief statement of the function of the statistics. Then, examine the list of supporting materials, motivational appeals, factors of attention, and so on. Is there adequate supporting material for each point in the speech? Is the supporting material sufficiently varied? Do you use motivational appeals at key points in the speech? Do you attempt to engage your listeners' attention throughout the speech? Answering these questions with your technical plot outline can help you to determine whether your speech is structurally sound, whether there is adequate supporting material, whether you've overused any forms of support, and whether you have effectively adapted your appeals to the audience and content.

Sample Technical Plot Outline

What follows is the complete content of an outline with its technical plot. For illustrative purposes, all items in the outline are stated as complete sentences. In most cases, however, you will use a more precisely phrased speaking outline, provided that will fulfill your instructor's goals with respect to how detailed to make your outline.

Friends Don't Let Friends Drive Drunk

[The introduction and conclusion of this speech were developed in detail in Chapter 8, Beginning and Ending the Speech].

First topic: background on founders, helping create emotional identification

I. MADD and SADD were founded under tragic circumstances.
  A. MADD was founded in 1980 by Candy Lightner.
    1. One of her daughters was killed by a drunk driver.
    2. She wanted to protect other families from a similar tragedy.
  B. SADD was founded by Lightner's other daughter.
    1. The loss of her sister hurt her deeply.
    2. She knew the importance of peer pressure in stopping teenage drinking and driving.

Second topic: description
First subtopic: goals

II. You can understand MADD and SADD better if you know something about their goals, operations and effectiveness.
  A. MADD and SADD were organized the way they were because the Lightners have specific goals they wish to achieve.
    1. They want the general public to carry out the agitation necessary to effect changes.

Specific instances

      a. Members of the public can put pressure on government officials.
      b. They can write letters to the editor.
      c. They can campaign for state and local task forces.

      d. They can do all this for a minimal investment of money.

  2. They want to expose the deficiencies in current legislation and drunk driving control systems.

Statistics (segments)

      a. They want to toughen the laws on operating a motor vehicle when intoxicated [statistics on variations in state laws].

Specific instances

      b. They want to pressure judges to hand down maximum instead of minimum penalties [specific instances of light sentences].

Statistics (segments)

      c. They want to see more drunk driver arrests from city, county, and state law enforcement agents [statistics on arrest rates].

  3. They want to help the families of other victims.

      a. Most MADD and many SADD members have been victims themselves.

Testimony

      b. Families are taught to put their energy into getting something done [quotations from pamphlets] as well as into mourning.

  4. And finally, MADD and SADD want to educate the general public.

      a. They want to make people conscious of the tragedies of drunk driving.

      b. They want to focus media attention on the problem.

Second subtopic: action steps

B. MADD's steps for action demonstrate the thoroughness with which the organization understands the processes of public persuasion.

Throughout, extended hypothetical illustration exemplifies the steps

  1. First, a local chapter sets its goals.

  2. Second, it educates its organizers goal by goal so that everyone knows the reasons behind each step.

  3. Third, it sets research priorities.

      a. One group might check on local arrest records.

      b. Another might examine drunk driving conviction rates for various judges.

      c. A third might work with local media to find out how to secure time and space for a public service announcement on drunk driving.

      d. A fourth might talk with local schools and churches about safe prom nights.

  4. Fourth, once the research is complete, the local chapter can formulate its plans of action.

  5. Fifth, it can "go public" with action teams and task forces.

Testimony

  6. This five-step process parallels the campaign model for public persuasion devised by Herbert W. Simons in his book *Understanding Persuasion*.

Third subtopic: results of MADD/SADD work Statistics (magnitude)

C. Although still young, organizations such as MADD and SADD already have had significant effects.

    1. By 1984, there were 320 MADD chapters across the country.

    2. About 600,000 volunteers are now working on MADD projects.

    3. State laws already are changing.

Specific instances

        a. In 1982 alone, 25 different states enacted 30 pieces of drunk driving legislation as a result of MADD's lobbying.

        b. After petitions were submitted by the organizations, Congress raised the mandatory legal drinking age to 21.

        c. In Florida, convicted drunk drivers must have red bumper stickers on their cars reading, "CON-VICTED DUI."

Statistics (trends)

    4. Fatalities from drunk driving have decreased [quote pre-1980 and post-1980 statistics].

    5. MADD also takes credit for increasing the popularity of low-alcohol beer, wines, and wine coolers.

Third topic: local projects

III. You can work with MADD and SADD on local projects.

    A. Set up a workshop in local high schools for parent-child contracts.

Explanation

    1. In such a contract (which has no legal status) the teen agrees never to drive drunk, calling on the parent for a ride instead, while the parent agrees to ask no questions and to impose no special penalties for the teen's intoxication.

    2. The contract reinforces the importance of not driving drunk and makes the commitment to safety a mutual commitment.

    B. Set up a SADD "Project Graduation."

Example

    1. With the cooperation of the schools and, sometimes, local youth organizations or churches, a community can sponsor nonalcoholic postprom parties.

    2. They allow promgoers a chance to stay up late, have fun, and celebrate without alcohol.

    C. Work with local media to use public service announcements to halt teen and adult drunk driving.

Specific instances

    1. MADD chapters can order ads you may have seen on TV.

        a. Some oppose drunk driving.

        b. Some tell you to designate a nondrinking driver from among your group.

        c. Others urge hosts of parties to not let drunk guests drive.

Specific
instance

2. SADD chapters also can order ads and school posters, nonalcoholic party kits, and the like [show sample items].[2]

Developing a Speaking Outline

As you probably realize, a technical plot outline would be very difficult to use when you were actually delivering your speech on MADD and SADD. A technical outline is too detailed to manage from a lectern; you will probably be tempted to read it to your listeners because it includes so many details. If you read your outline, however, you'll lose your conversational tone.

Therefore you need to compress your technical plot outline into a more useful form. The speaking outline, like the full-sentence and technical plot outlines, use the same indention and symbol structure. The major difference is that each item in a **speaking outline** is referred to in shorthand—phrases or single key words. Developed in this manner, the previous full-sentence outline (pp. 238–239) looks like this:

A complex sentence outline can be distracting and confusing when used as a speaking outline. Use an outline that is easy to see as you stand in front of an audience.

Sample Speaking Outline

I. Determine general purpose
  A. Limit subject
    1. Fit available time
    2. Ensure unity and coherence
  B. Phrase in terms of listener response
II. Develop rough draft
  A. List main ideas
  B. Arrange main ideas
    1. Motivated sequence
    2. Traditional pattern
  C. Arrange subordinate ideas
  D. Add supporting materials
  E. Review rough draft
    1. Adequate coverage?
    2. Meet specific purpose?
III. Final outline form
  A. Complete sentences or key phrases
    1. Concise, vivid, parallel phrasing
    2. Address needs and interests of listeners
  B. Subordinate ideas—complete sentence or key word
    1. Under appropriate main head
    2. Coordinate with subordinate ideas of equal weight
  C. Add supporting materials
    1. Pertinent
    2. Adequate
    3. Varied
  D. Review outline
    1. Good form
    2. Adequate coverage
    3. Meets purpose

What you use in writing out your speaking outline will depend on your personal preference; some people like to work with small pieces of paper, others with notecards. Whatever your choice, however, your speaking outline should serve several functions while you're addressing your audience: (a) it should provide you with reminders of the direction of your speech—main points, subordinate ideas, and so on; (b) it should record technical or detailed material such as statistics and quotations; and (c) it should be easy to read so that it does not detract from the delivery of your speech. Each notecard or piece of paper should contain only one main idea.

FIGURE 9.1 Sample Speaking Outline on Notecards

FRIENDS DON'T LET FRIENDS DRIVE DRUNK

I. Background
   A. MADD 1980 Candy Lightner
   B. SADD her other daughter for hi-school kids

II. Description
   A. Goals
      1. public agitation (gov't. officials, letters to editor, task forces, all for little money)
      2. expose deficiencies in current legis. & control
         a. tougher laws state by state (STATISTICS)
         b. pressure judges (JUDGE NORTON, SANDERS, HANKS)
         c. more arrests (STATISTICS)
      3. public education
         a. more conscious
         b. media attention

   B. MADD's action steps
      1. goals (what community needs most)
      2. educate organizers
      3. set research priorities (arrest records, conviction rates, PSA's, prom nights)
      4. formulate plans of action
      5. go public
         (note on Simons's *Understanding Persuasion*)

   C. Results
      1. 320 MADD chapters by 1984
      2. 600,000 volunteers
      3. state laws changing
         a. 1982 25 states, 30 pieces of legis.
         b. Congress drinking age to 21
         c. Florida, red bumper sticker, CONVICTED DUI
      4. fatalities down (STATISTICS)
      5. popularity of low-alc beer, wines, coolers

III. Local projects
   A. contracts
   B. prom night (Operation Graduation)
   C. PSA's and publicity
      1. MADD TV ads
         a. after drunk driving
         b. sober group member
         c. host/guest—*Friends don't let friends d.d.*
      2. SADD projects
         a. school posters (SHOW POSTER)**
         b. non-alc party kits
         c. ads

Notecards for a speech on MADD and SADD

There are four main characteristics of properly prepared speaking outlines:

1. Most points are noted with only a key word or phrase—a word or two should be enough to trigger your memory, especially if you've practiced the speech adequately.
2. Ideas that must be stated precisely are written down fully, for example, "Friends don't let friends drive drunk."
3. Directions for delivery—for example, "SHOW POSTER"—are included.
4. Emphasis is indicated in a number of ways—capital letters, underlining, indention, dashes, and highlighting with colored markers. (Find methods of emphasis that will easily catch your eye, show the relationship of ideas, and jog your memory during your speech delivery.)

CHAPTER SUMMARY

Arranging and outlining do not have to be tedious tasks. If you've understood the fundamentals presented in this chapter, you now realize that outlines are both diagnostic tools and guides to delivering ideas. You are aware of the elements of a good outline:

• each item should contain only one idea;
• less important ideas should be subordinate to more important ones;
• logical relationships should be shown through proper indentation;
• a consistent set of symbols should be used; and
• in complete outlines, all main points and subordinate ideas should be written as full sentences.

You should also be able to work through the logical progression involved in developing ideas, from the construction of a *rough outline,* to the writing of a *full-sentence outline,* followed by the addition of a *technical plot,* and then the drafting of a final *speaking outline.* Should you desire, or your instructor approve, you might take some short cuts in the actual process by eliminating the full-sentence and technical outlines, or by writing out only the main and subordinate points and leaving the supporting materials in phrase form. Whether or not you risk using an abbreviated method, you should still be aware of the more comprehensive role that outlining can play in the speaking process.

KEY TERMS

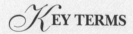

full-sentence outline (p. 238)
rough outline (p. 238)

speaking outline (p. 245)
technical plot outline (p. 239)

ASSESSMENT ACTIVITIES

1. Revise both (a) and (b) following the guidelines for correct outline form.
   a. The nuclear freeze concept is a good idea because it allows us to stop nuclear proliferation and it will help make us feel more secure.
   b. **I.** We should wear seatbelts to protect our lives.
   II. Studies indicate seatbelts protect children from serious injury.
   III. Studies indicate seatbelts reduce risk of head injury.
2. For a speech assigned by the instructor, develop a full-sentence outline and a technical plot in accordance with the samples provided in this chapter. Hand in your speech outline in time to obtain feedback before presenting your speech.
3. Working in small groups, select a controversial topic for potential presentation in class. Brainstorm possible arguments that could be offered on the pro and con sides. With these as a basis, develop a rough outline of the main points to be presented on both sides.

REFERENCES

1. Information taken from Vincent Marteka, "Words of Praise—and Caution—About Fungus Among Us," *Smithsonian* (May 1980): 96–104.
2. The material for this speech—including the statistics we haven't directly included—was drawn from the following sources: "MADD from Hell," *Restaurant Hospitality* (April 1990); "One Less for the Road?" *Time* (May 20, 1985); "Rascal, MADD Party with High Schoolers," *Advertising Age* (November 20, 1989); "War Against Drunk Drivers," *Newsweek* (September 13, 1982); "They're Mad as Hell," *Time* (August 3, 1981); "How to Get Alcohol Off the Highway," *Time* (July 1, 1981); "Health Report," *Prevention Magazine* (June, 1984); "Water Water Everywhere," *Time* (May 20, 1985); L. B. Taylor, *Driving High* (New York: Watts, 1983); Sandy Golden, *Driving the Drunk Off the Road* (Washington: Acropolis Books, 1983); and U.S. National Highway Traffic Safety Administration, *How to Save Lives and Reduce Injuries—A Citizen Activist Guide to Effectively Fight Drunk Driving* (pamphlet) (Washington: U.S. Government Printing Office, 1982).

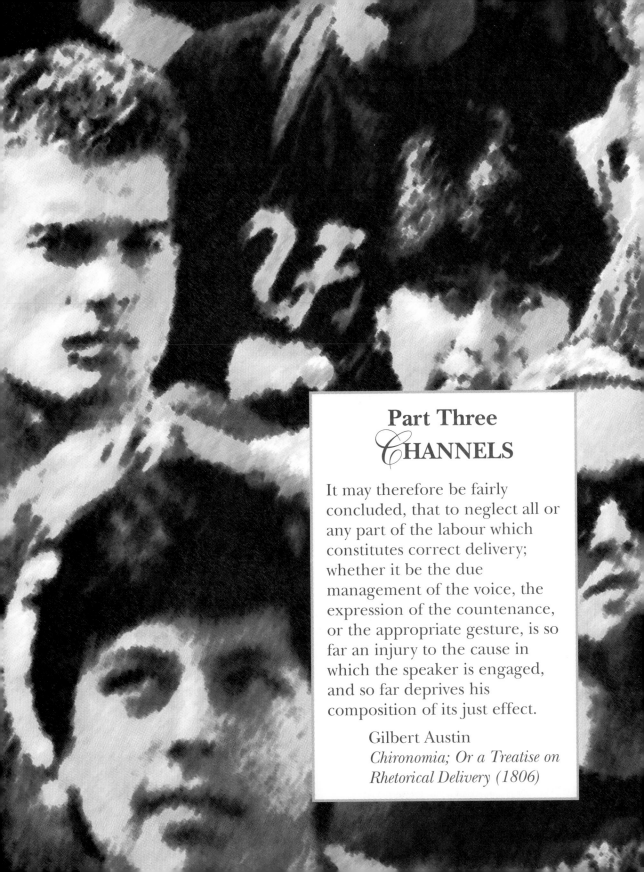

Part Three
CHANNELS

It may therefore be fairly concluded, that to neglect all or any part of the labour which constitutes correct delivery; whether it be the due management of the voice, the expression of the countenance, or the appropriate gesture, is so far an injury to the cause in which the speaker is engaged, and so far deprives his composition of its just effect.

Gilbert Austin
Chironomia; Or a Treatise on Rhetorical Delivery (1806)

CHAPTER

10

USING LANGUAGE TO COMMUNICATE

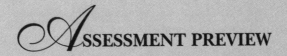

ASSESSMENT PREVIEW

After reading Chapter 10, the student with basic communication competencies will be able to

- present a speech in an oral style.
- employ basic techniques for achieving coherence.
- offer clear definitions of central terms.

The student with average communication competencies will also be able to:

- use at least five or six metaphors or images appropriately.
- use gender-neutral language consistently.
- employ language appropriate to the audience and to the speaker.

The student with superior communication competencies will also be able to:

- vary language intensity with the emotional atmosphere being created.
- maintain a consistent propositional or narrative form through a speech.
- control the seriousness of the rhetorical atmosphere being created.
- weave images and metaphors into the whole fabric of a speech appropriately.

*W*hen Neil Armstrong first set foot on the moon in 1969, millions of Americans heard him say, "That's one small step for man, one giant leap for mankind." It seemed an appropriate thing to say: a two-phrase speech captured in a simple, eloquent way the realization that another ball-of-rock in the universe had been traversed by an earthling. Yet, as people thought about Armstrong's words, at least some noticed that they formed a tautology; the distinction between a "step for man" and a "leap for mankind" was not clear at all. After Armstrong heard the rebroadcast, he was quick to say that a key word—the word "a"—had been lost in transmission. The words that he had actually intoned were, "That's one small step for *a* man, one giant leap for mankind." Then the two phrases actually asserted two different actions—those of an individual, and those of the people for whom that individual acted. Within another year or so, however, the astronaut faced still another question: Why did he talk only about the male half of the population? While the astronauts (at this point) were all male, the NASA team included both males and females, and all of "humankind," not just "mankind," took that leap into the future in late July of 1969. Neil Armstrong had no answer to that question, probably deciding to quit explaining his speech while he was still a hero.

As Armstrong discovered, language functions on multiple levels of meaning. Language is a **referential, relational,** and **symbolic** medium of communication. Through its referential or pointing abilities, language refers to aspects of the world: "dog," "cupcake," "man." Through its relational powers, it suggests associations or relationships between people; "Give me a cupcake" not only points to cupcakes but also indicates that one person has the power or authority to command another person. As well, Armstrong's little speech asserted that he was not only an individual, a man, but also a representative of all others, (hu)mankind, and thus related to his audience in a particular way. And, as we noted in the moon shot example, Armstrong's selection of the words "man" and "mankind" were taken to be signs of a gendered focus—perhaps symbolic of the male's penchant for seeing his half of the species as the achievers and as the lords of society. So, it's not enough to know words and what they abstractly mean when preparing speeches. You must also understand how language-in-use reflects human relationships and shared senses of reality—your culture and your thinking.

In the next three chapters, we'll turn our attention to the encoding of messages. **Encoding** is the activity of putting ideas into verbal and nonverbal codes so that an audience's **decoding,** or interpretative process, occurs in ways you'd like it to. The codes you use, the channels through which ideas are communicated to listeners, include verbal language, visual aids, and bodily and vocal behaviors—even movements, postures, and sound. In this chapter, we'll focus on word choices: using language strategically and giving an overall tone and force to speeches by making good stylistic choices.

*L*ANGUAGE USE IN ORAL COMMUNICATION

Before we tackle the questions of word choices and stylistic characteristics of effective speeches, we should stop and think about "speech" as a particular kind of language use. When you think of language, you probably think of printed words in magazines, books, and the like. The "language arts" that most people learned in school were the arts of written language—grammar, style, sentence structure, syntax, and the rational construction of paragraphs and whole essays.

But developing long before written language was speech, oral language. Written language is only about three thousand years old, give or take a century or two. Orality reaches into the unknowable preliterate ages; even with the coming of written language to the ancient world, it maintained its ascendency in the language world for centuries. Scribes *recorded* speech; speech still *created* ideas and guided human action. The power of oral rhetoric was at its greatest in ancient Greece precisely at the time—the fifth and fourth centuries B.C.E.—when Greek was being stablized as a written language.

Why all of this is important to you even now, at the dawn of a new millennium, is that *speech still retains, at least ideally, many characteristics it acquired in those years before writing.* Those characteristics taken together we identify as an **oral style**—language use recognizing that speech practices differ in significant ways from writing practices because of the kinds of social business people usually conduct through talk. We reviewed some of that business in Chapter 1, but let us go a bit further here. What determines how language should be used in face-to-face, oral communication? The following characteristics typify this sort of communication:

- Speech is *face to face*—that is, it involves people physically oriented to each other. The words and actions flow from the behavior of one person into the sensory equipment of another. Oral language thus is always specifically enveloped in actual persons who are aware of each other's presence and personages.
- Speech is strongly *social.* That is, in speaking, individuals bond with each other into concrete relationships. Speech is especially relational in its force because there is co-presence—that is, people who are directly apprehending each other and thus constructing or embodying relationships. Sometimes the relationship pre-exists, as when an employee talks with a boss. At other times, the relationship is built on the spot, as when two strangers start talking to each other on the bus.
- Speech is *ephemeral,* which is to say that the words disappear into nothingness as soon as they are uttered. Some of the sound waves strike the tympannus (eardrum) of people, but the rest dissipate completely. You can reread a paragraph, but you cannot hear oral words again unless you ask for a repetition. Speakers seldom repeat everything, so they have to find other ways to help listeners remember, especially when the speakers are

stringing together several ideas or arguments. This is why it's so important for oral language to be concrete or specific and why, as we shall see, connectives, metaphors, images, and so on are essential to public speaking.

- The best speech is *enthymematic,* built on ideas that the listeners generally accept. In ancient Greece, an **enthymeme** was an ideational structure, sort of like a syllogism, where the audience was presumed to be able to supply the missing premise. So, when an orator argued "We should go to war with Sparta because it will make us rich [feared/admired/safe]," the argument would make sense—and work—only if the listeners believed that wealth was good, that to be feared is a good thing for a country, that the admiration of others is to be sought out, or that collective safety is one of the goals every government should pursue. Building speeches enthymematically, on audiences' preexisting beliefs, attitudes, values, and interests is—as we've been noting all through this book—a key to success.

The fact, then, that oral public speech is face-to-face, socially bonding, ephemeral, enthymematic communication means that stylistically it's quite different from written language. When someone's written out a speech, it will probably begin something like this:

I am most pleased that you could come this morning. I would like to use this opportunity to discuss with you a subject of inestimable importance to us all—the impact of inflationary spirals on students enrolled in institutions of higher education.

Translated into an oral style, this speech might begin like this:

Thanks for coming. I'd like to talk today about a problem facing all of us— the rising cost of going to college.

Notice how much more natural (to the ear) the second version sounds. The first is wordy, filled with prepositional phrases, complex words, and formal sentences. The second addresses the audience directly, containing shorter sentences and a simpler vocabulary that make it easier to understand aurally. Oral style has other chararacteristics when used by the most competent speakers. We'll examine it in three ways in this chapter, looking first at effective oral word choices, then at appropriate style generally, and finally at specific linguistic-rhetorical strategies that give oral language more punch.[1]

*E*SSENTIALS OF EFFECTIVE WORD CHOICES

Before you can think strategically about language, you must be able to use it in understandable ways. You can clarify your messages if you keep in mind five features of effective word choice: accuracy, simplicity, coherence, language intensity, and appropriateness.

Accuracy

Careful word choice is an essential ingredient to effectively transmitting your meaning to an audience. If you tell a hardware store clerk, "I broke the do-hickey on my hootenanny and I need a thingamajig to fix it," you'd better have the hootenanny in your hand or the clerk won't understand. When you speak, one goal is precision. You should leave no doubt about your meaning.

Words are symbols that represent concepts or objects. Your listener may attach a meaning to your words that's quite different from the one you intended. This misinterpretation becomes more likely as your words become more abstract. *Democracy,* for example, doesn't mean the same thing to a citizen in the suburbs as it does to a citizen in the ghetto. *Democracy* will elicit different meanings from Americans who belong to the Christian Coalition than it will from those who belong to the American Socialist Party.

Students of general semantics, the study of words or symbols and their relationships to reality, continually warn us that many errors in thinking and communication arise from treating words as if they were the actual conditions, processes, or objects. Words are not fixed and timeless in meaning, nor does everyone use them in exactly the same way.

To avoid vagueness, choose words that express the exact shade of meaning you wish to communicate. You might say that an object *shines,* but the object might also *glow, glitter, glisten, gleam, flare, blaze, glare, shimmer, glimmer, flicker, sparkle, flash,* and *beam.* Which word allows you to describe the object most precisely?

Simplicity

"Speak," said Lincoln, "so that the most lowly can understand you, and the rest will have no difficulty." Because electronic media reach audiences more varied than Lincoln could have imagined, you have even more reason to follow his advice today. Say *learn* rather than *ascertain, try* rather than *endeavor, use* rather than *utilize, help* rather than *facilitate.* Don't use a longer or less familiar word when a simple one is just as clear. Evangelist Billy Sunday illustrated the effectiveness of familiar words in this example:

> If a man were to take a piece of meat and smell it and look disgusted, and his little boy were to say, "What's the matter with it, Pop?" and he were to say, "It is undergoing a process of decomposition in the formation of new chemical compounds," the boy would be all in. But if the father were to say, "It's rotten," then the boy would understand and hold his nose. "Rotten" is a good Anglo-Saxon word, and you do not have to go to the dictionary to find out what it means.[2]

Simplicity doesn't mean *simplistic;* never talk down to your audience. Just remember that short, direct words convey precise, concrete meanings.

Coherence

People listening to you speak don't have the luxury of reviewing the points you have made as they do when they are reading a written essay. Nor are they able to perceive punctuation marks that might help them distinguish one idea from another as you speak. In order to be understood, oral communication requires **coherence,** or the logical connection of ideas. To achieve coherence, you must use **signposts,** or words or phrases such as *first, next,* or *as a result,* that help listeners follow the movement of your ideas. Signposts such as "the history of this invention begins in..." also provide clues to the overall message structure.

Summaries, like signposts, provide clues to the overall speech structure. Preliminary and final summaries are especially helpful in outlining the major topics of the speech. **Preliminary summaries** (also called *forecasts* or *previews*) precede the development of the body of the speech, usually forming part of the introduction; **final summaries** follow the body of the speech, usually forming part of the conclusion. Consider the following examples:

Abraham Lincoln said, "Speak so that the most lowly can understand you, and the rest will have no difficulty."

Preliminary Summaries	Final Summaries
Today I am going to talk about three aspects of. . . .	I have talked about three aspects of. . . .
There are four major points to be covered in. . . .	These four major points—[restate them]—are. . . .
The history of the issue can be divided into two periods. . . .	The two periods just covered—[restate them]—represent. . . .

In addition to these summarizing strategies, signposts may be **connectives,** or transitions—linking phrases that move an audience from one idea to another. The following are useful connective statements:

- In the first place. . . . The second point is. . . .
- In addition to. . . . notice that. . . .
- Now look at it from a different angle. . . .
- You must keep these three things in mind in order to understand the importance of the fourth. . . .
- What was the result?
- Turning now to. . . .

The preceding signposts are neutral: they tell an audience that another idea is coming but don't indicate whether it's similar, different, or more important. You can improve the coherence of your speeches by indicating the precise relationships among ideas. Those relationships include parallel/hierarchical, similar/different, and coordinate/subordinate relationships. Here are some examples:

- *Parallel:* Not only . . . but also. . . .
- *Hierarchical:* More important than these. . . .
- *Different:* In contrast. . . .
- *Similar:* Similar to this. . . .
- *Coordinated:* One must consider X, Y, and Z. . . .
- *Subordinated:* On the next level is. . . .

Preliminary or final summaries and signposts are important to your audience. The summaries give listeners an overall sense of your entire message; if listeners can easily see the structure, they'll better understand and remember your speech. The signposts lead your listeners step by step through the speech, signaling specific relationships between and among ideas.

Intensity

You can communicate your feelings about ideas and objects through word choices. You can communicate your attitude toward your subject by choosing words that show how you feel. For example, consider these attitudinally weighted terms:

Highly Positive	Relatively Neutral	Highly Negative
Savior	G.I.	Enemy
Patriot	Soldier	Baby-killer
Freedom fighter	Combatant	Foreign devil

Those nine terms are organized by their intensity, ranging from the highly positive *savior* to the highly negative *foreign devil*. Notice the religious connotations present in the extreme examples of language intensity.

How intense should your language be? Communication scholar John Waite Bowers suggested a useful rule of thumb: let your language be, roughly, one step more intense than the position or attitude held by your audience.[3] For example, if your audience is already committed to your negative position on tax reform, then you can choose intensely negative words, such as regressive and stifling. If your audience is uncommitted, you should opt for comparatively neutral words, such as burdensome. And, if your audience is in favor of tax changes, you can use still less negative words, such as unfair, so as to avoid turning them off and to encourage them to keep an open mind. Intense language can generate intense reactions, but only if you match your word choices to your listeners' attitudes.

Appropriateness

Your language should be appropriate to the speech topic and situation. Solemn occasions call for restrained and dignified language; joyful occasions call for informal and lively word choices. The language used at the christening of a baby wouldn't work at a pep rally, and vice versa. Suit your language to the tone of the occasion.

FIGURE 10.1 Language Intensity Chart

		Subject	Verb	Object
➕	Positive	A Doctor of Philosophy at an institution of higher learning	discussed	dialectical perspectives on life and living.
➕➖	Neutral	The philosophy professor at State U	outlined	Karl Marx's economic and social theories.
➖	Negative	An effete intellectual snob at the local haven for druggies	harangued our children with	Communist drivel.

𝒜SSESSMENT CHECK

Rehearse your next speech by speaking into a tape recorder. Then listen to the speech, keeping in mind the following questions about your use of language:

- Did I speak accurately? Which language choices were not clear?
- Did I use simple language that my listeners will be able to decode easily?
- Did I use signposts and summaries so my listeners will understand the relationships among my ideas?
- Were my word choices appropriate for the intended audience and occasion?

Make sure that your language is appropriate to your audience. Before you use informal language, check to see who's listening. Informal language, including slang, quickly goes out of style. *Gee whiz, wow, good grief, far out, awesome,* and *radical* became popular at different times. *Far out* would sound silly in a speech to your peers, and *radical* would sound ridiculous to an audience of senior citizens.

𝒮ELECTING AN APPROPRIATE STYLE: STRATEGIC DECISIONS

Now, we can think more systematically about how oral style should guide the ways you talk with other people, or how you present yourself orally. The combination of stylistic decisions you have to make generally is called **tone,** the predominant effect or character of a speech. While tone is an elusive quality of speech, we can identify some of its primary features. There are four dimensions of tone that you should consider: serious versus humorous atmosphere; gendered versus gender-neutral language; speaker-, audience-, or content-centered pronouns; and propositional versus narrative form.

Serious Versus Humorous Atmosphere

You cultivate the atmosphere of the speaking occasion largely through your speaking style. In a graduation speech or an awards banquet address, you want to encourage the personal reflection of your listeners; but at a fraternity gathering or holiday celebration, you want to create a social, interactive atmosphere.

Sometimes the atmosphere of the occasion dictates what speaking style should be used. You don't expect a light, humorous speaking style during a funeral. Even so, sometimes a minister, priest, or rabbi will tell a funny story about the deceased. Yet the overall tone of a funeral eulogy should be somber. In contrast, a speech after a football victory, election win, or successful fund drive is seldom solemn. Victory speeches are times for celebration and unity.

Humorous speeches can have serious goals. As we'll see, even speeches designed to entertain have worthy purposes. These speeches can be given in grave earnestness. The political satirist who throws humorous but barbed comments at pompous, silly, or corrupt politicians aims to amuse the audience as well as urge political reform.

ℰTHICAL MOMENTS
DOUBLESPEAK

Advertisers, politicians, and military spokespersons often are accused of using words that deceive or mislead. The Bush and Clinton administrations didn't want to raise taxes, but they instead pursued *revenue enhancement* through *user fees*. The rush to **doublespeak**—the use of a technical jargon that sidesteps issues or distorts meaning—was accelerated during the Vietnam War, when "we got *pacification* for eradication, *strategic withdrawal* for retreat, *sanitizing operation* for wholesale clearance, *accidental delivery of armaments* for bombing the wrong target, *to terminate with extreme prejudice* for a political assassination, and many, many others" (Bryson, 302). Advertisers have given us *real faux pearls* and *genuine imitation leather*, and, of course, *virgin nylon*. The indiscriminate use of the phrases *low sodium, low cholesterol, low sugar,* and *low fat* has led to a governmental attempt to control the abuse of such labels. So how about you?

1. Suppose you notice biased language in an article you're going to quote in a speech. Should you cite it as supporting material in your speech?
2. Do you ever use big words and unnecessary technical language just to impress your listeners? Should we call "football players" by that sanctimonious phrase, "student athletes"? Do you feel better if someone calls a "test" an "hourly opportunity" or a "feedback session"? Is spanking a child any less onerous if it's called "corporal discipline"?
3. How about using language to avoid hurting someone or making them feel bad? Should you really call someone "vertically challenged" instead of "short," "visually impaired" instead of "blind"? In these sorts of cases, do the new words actually call more attention to the person's difficulties than the old ones?

Further Reading

On the matter of neologisms—new and often technical words coming into English—see Bill Bryson, *Made in America: An Informal History of the English Language in the United States* (New York: William Morrow, 1994).

The speaking **atmosphere** is the mind-set or mental attitude that you attempt to create in your audience. A serious speaker urging future professors to remember the most important things in life might say, "Rank your values and live by them." That same idea expressed by actor Alan Alda sounded more humorous:

> We live in a time that seems to be split about its values. In fact it seems to be schizophrenic.
>
> For instance, if you pick up a magazine like *Psychology Today,* you're liable to see an article like "White Collar Crime: It's More Widespread than You Think." Then in the back of the magazine they'll print an advertisement that says, "We'll write your doctoral thesis for 25 bucks." You see how values are eroding? I mean, a doctoral thesis ought to go for at least a C-note.[4]

Which atmosphere is preferable? The answer depends on the speaking situation, your speech purpose, and your listeners' expectations.

Gendered Versus Gender-Neutral Nouns and Pronouns

While words themselves are not intrinsically good or bad, as we noted at the beginning of this chapter, they can communicate values or attitudes to your listeners and they suggest relationships between you and your audience. Gender-linked words, particularly nouns and pronouns, require special attention. **Gender-linked words** are those that directly or indirectly identify males or females—*policeman, washerwoman, poet,* and *poetess.* Pronouns such as *he* and *she* and adjectives such as *his* and *her* are also obviously gender-linked words. **Gender-neutral words** do not directly or indirectly denote males or females—*chairperson, police officer,* or *firefighter.*

Since the 1960s and the advent of the women's movement, consciousness of gendered language has gradually surfaced. The question of whether language use affects culture and socialization still is being debated. However, as a speaker you must be careful not to alienate your audience or to propagate stereotypes unconsciously through your use of language. In addition to avoiding most gender-linked words, you've got to handle two more problems:

1. *Inaccurately excluding members of one sex.* Some uses of gendered pronouns inaccurately reflect social-occupational conditions in the world: "A nurse sees *her* patients eight hours a day, but a doctor sees *his* for only ten minutes." Many women are doctors, and many men are nurses. Most audience members are aware of this and may be displeased if they feel that you're stereotyping roles in a particular profession.

2. *Stereotyping male and female psychological or social characteristics.* "Real men never cry." "A woman's place is in the home." "The Marines are looking for a few good men." "Sugar 'n spice 'n everything nice—that's what little girls are made of." Falling back on these stereotypes gets speakers into trouble with audiences, both male and female. In these days of raised consciousness, audiences are insulted to hear such mis-

informed assertions. In addition, these stereotypes conceal the potential in individuals whose talents are not limited by their gender.

These problem areas demand your attention. A speaker who habitually uses sexist language is guilty of ignoring important speaking conventions that have taken shape over the last several decades.

Ultimately, the search for gender-neutral expressions is an affirmation of mutual respect and a recognition of equal worth and the essential dignity of individuals. Gender differences are important in many aspects of life, but when they dominate public talk, they're ideologically oppressive. Be gender-neutral in public talk to remove barriers to effective communication.[5]

Speaker-, Audience-, or Content-Centered Emphases

Because you use speeches to conduct different kinds of personal, social, and professional business, you can end up emphasizing various aspects of the communication process in your message. Sometimes, you're stressing *your* thoughts, *your* opinions—your position as a knowledgeable or sensitive person. On such occasions, much of the speech is constructed in the first person: "I." At other times, the focus is on the audience or on things that you and the audience can accomplish together; in those circumstances, you're likely to address the audience in the second-person ("you") or in the first-person plural ("we"). And then, there are times when it's the subject matter itself that's the center of attention—for example, in a class lecture. Then references to "I" and "you" or "we" all but disappear.

Sometimes, the emphasis of the whole speech is speaker-, audience-, or content-centered, though more often, the emphasis shifts from one section to another. That's something that clearly happened in a speech given by Allen H. Neuharth, chair of the Freedom Foundation. When he accepted the DeWitt Carter Reddick Award for Outstanding Achievement in Communication given him by the College of Communication of the University of Texas at Austin, Neuharth employed all three emphases:

> **"I" Directed:** In 1952, just two years out of the University of South Dakota, a classmate and I started a weekly statewide sports tabloid newspaper called *So-Dak Sports*. We begged, borrowed and stole all the money we could—about $50,000. Two years later, we had lost it all, our venture went belly-up and we were bloodied and bowed. I ran away from home, went to Miami, found a job as a reporter for $95 a week.
>
> There, when I wasn't working or having fun in the sun, I thought a lot about what went wrong with my plan to become rich and famous in South Dakota. Gradually, I got it. I didn't really have a plan. I only had an idea. I hadn't really considered the risk/reward ratio. I hadn't figured out how to pay the rent. My first venture went broke because of mismanagement. I had mismanaged it. Once you admit you're the one who screwed up, it's much easier to get up off the floor, dust yourself off and try again.

*H*OW TO
AVOID SEXIST LANGUAGE

- *Speak in the plural.* Say, "Bankers are often. . . . They face. . . ." This tactic is often sufficient to make your language gender-neutral.
- *Switch to "he or she" when you must use a singular subject.* Say, "A student majoring in business is required to sign up for an internship. He or she can. . . ." This strategy works well as long as you don't overdo it. If you find yourself cluttering sentences with "he or she," switch to the plural.

- *Remove gender inflections.* It's painless to say *firefighter* instead of *fireman, chair* or *chairperson* instead of *chairman* and *tailor* instead of *seamstress.*
- *Use gender-specific pronouns for gender-specific processes, people, or activities.* It is acceptable to talk about a mother as *her* or a current or former president of the United States as *him.* Men do not naturally bear children, and a woman has not yet been elected to the White House.

    "You/We" Directed: [W]e must overcome our reluctance to criticize ourselves or our co-workers or competitors. Most in the media are unbelievably thin-skinned. We spend most of our lifetime criticizing or analyzing everyone else—politicians, business people, academicians. But we seldom turn that spotlight on ourselves. Our egos are enormous.

"They/It" Directed: The media, thanks to instant satellite communication, is the glue that is bringing this globe together. Without the satellite—and instant global communication—there would have been no Tiananmen Square sit-in in Beijing. No breakdown of the Berlin Wall. No marches in Poland, Romania, and Czechoslovakia. And the hardliners would not have flunked revolution 101 in the old Soviet Union last August.[6]

In mixing self-revealing, audience-directed, and content-centered emphases, Neuharth achieved multiple purposes: he established a personal bond with his audience (relational communication), he gave them some messages to act on (referential communication), and he added to his expert credibility by talking clearly about the world of the journalists (symbolic communication). You, too, should decide whether to emphasize yourself (personal revelations), your audience (directives to your listeners), or the subject matter (ideas and arguments about the external world) in various combinations in your talks.

Propositional Versus Narrative Style

Finally, speaking styles can be largely propositional or narrative. Propositional styles emphasize a series of claims, with supporting evidence for each, that culminate in a general proposition. In this style, the claims suggest what action should be taken or what policy should be adopted or rejected. Narrative style, on the other hand, couches claims and evidence in a more informal, often personal, story that epitomizes the general claim being advanced. Thus both *argue*, in the sense that they're claims on an audience's attention, belief, and action; however, they do so in radically different ways. In the following illustrations of *propositional* and *narrative* approaches, assume that you, as the speaker, want to persuade your classmates to consult with their academic advisors on a regular basis.

Propositional Style

I. You ought to see your advisor regularly because he or she can check on your graduation requirements.
  A. Advisors have been trained to understand this school's requirements.
  B. They also probably helped write the department requirements for your major, so they know them, too.
II. You ought to see your advisor regularly because that person usually can tell you something about careers in your field.
  A. Most faculty members at this school regularly attend professional meetings and find out what kinds of schools and companies are hiring in your field.

Speakers consider the needs of the audience and occasion when deciding whether to use a propositional or narrative speaking style.

    B. Most faculty members here have been around a long time and, thus, have seen what kinds of academic backgrounds get their advisees good jobs after school.

III. You ought to see your advisor regularly to check out your own hopes and fears with someone.

    A. Good advisors help you decide whether you want to continue with a major.

    B. If you decide to change majors, they often will help you find another advisor in another department who can work with you.

Narrative Style

    I. I thought I could handle my own advising around this school, and that attitude got me into trouble.

        A. I could read, and I thought I knew what I wanted to take.

        B. I decided to steer my own course, and here's what happened.

    II. At first, I was happy, taking any course I wanted to.

        A. I skipped the regular laboratory sciences (chemistry, biology, physics) and took "Science and Society" instead.

        B. I didn't take statistics to meet my math requirement but instead slipped into remedial algebra.

    C. I piled up the hours in physical education so I could have a nice grade-point average to show my parents.

III. When I was about half done with my program, however, I realized that:

    A. I hadn't met about half of the general education graduation requirements.

    B. I wanted to go into nursing.

IV. Therefore, I had to go back to freshman- and sophomore-level courses even though I was technically a junior.

    A. I was back taking the basic science and math courses.

    B. I was still trying to complete the social science and humanities requirements.

V. In all, I'm now in my fifth year of college, with at least one more to go.

    A. My classmates who used advisors have graduated.

    B. I suggest you follow their examples rather than mine if you want to save time and money.

Either style can be effective, depending on the audience's expectations and the speaker's resourcefulness in generating an effective argument. The propositional form provides a concise, logical series of "should" statements to direct audience action. In the narrative form, your talent as a storyteller is put to the test. While the examples above suggest the use of either style as the structure for the body of an entire speech, speeches may combine both. Neuharth (see pages 264–266) used a narrative style in discussing his own life experience, then moved on to a propositional form in relaying his views on the kinds of reforms journalists must engage in.

Building an oral style appropriate to you, your audience, the occasion, and the subject matter takes some serious thought on your part. Think through the degree of seriousness, the gender focus, the I/you-we/it emphasis, and the use of propositional or narrative forms. Shaping them carefully is the mark of a sophisticated and talented speaker.

*R*HETORICAL STRATEGIES

Rhetorical strategies—the ways you use words to affect listeners' beliefs, attitudes, values, and behaviors—give power to your speaking style or tone and control the symbolic atmosphere within which your ideas are heard. There are countless strategies available to speakers; here, we'll concentrate on some of the simplest yet muscular ones: definitions, restatements of various kinds, imagery, and metaphor.

Definitions

Audience members need to understand the fundamental concepts of your speech. You can't expect them to understand your ideas if your language is un-

Definitions can help listeners grasp concepts that are important to their overall understanding of the speaker's key ideas.

familiar. As a speaker, you have several options when working to define unfamiliar or difficult concepts.

You're most familiar with a **dictionary definition,** which categorizes an object or concept and specifies its characteristics: "An orange is a *fruit* (category) that is *round, orange* in color, and a member of the *citrus family* (characteristics)." Dictionary definitions sometimes help you to learn unfamiliar words, but they don't help an audience very much. If you do use dictionary definitions, go to specialized dictionaries. You certainly wouldn't depend on *Webster's Third International Dictionary* to define *foreclosure* or *liability* for a presentation on real estate law. For this technical application, sources such as *Black's Law Dictionary* and *Guide to American Law* are more highly respected.

Occasionally, a word has so many meanings that you have to choose one. If that's the case, use a **stipulative definition** to orient your listeners to your subject matter. A stipulative definition designates the way a word will be used in a certain context. You might say, "By *rich* I mean. . . ." or you might use an expert's stipulative definition such as this one from former President Jimmy Carter:

Who is rich? I'm not talking about bank accounts. But I would say that everyone here is rich. And we don't deliberately discriminate. A rich person is someone with a home and a modicum of education and a chance for at least a job and who believes that if you make a decision that it'll have some effect at least in your own life, and who believes that the police and the judges are on your side. These are the rich people.[7]

You can further clarify a term or concept by telling your audience how you are *not* going to use the concept—by using a **negative definition.** So, Chicago police Sergeant Bruce Talbot defined "gateway drug" in this manner: "[F]or adolescents, cigarette smoking is a gateway drug to illicit drugs such as marijuana and crack cocaine. By gateway drug I do not mean just that cigarettes are the first drug young people encounter, alcohol is. But unlike alcohol, which is first experienced in a social ritual such as church or an important family event, cigarettes are the first drug minors buy themselves and use secretly outside the family and social institutions."[8] Defining negatively can clear away possible misconceptions. Using a negative definition along with a stipulative definition, as did Sergeant Talbot, allows you to treat a commonplace phenomenon in a different way.

Sometimes you may want to reinforce an idea by telling your listeners where a word came from. One way to do this is by using an **etymological definition,** as Everett Parker did when addressing the Church of Christ:

> Communication, communion and community spring from the same Latin root, *communis*—to have in common. The fundamental component of society is the community. Community devolves out of a communion of interests and experience. Communication develops out of a give-and-take communication process that is free, constant, and universal.
>
> Communication is the most fundamental human manifestation. But communication has hard sledding where there is a lack of communion, or worse, a breakdown in community.[9]

One of the best ways to define is by an **exemplar definition,** especially if the concept is unfamiliar or technical. Exemplar definitions are familiar examples, such as the following: "The building we're in today, the Administrative Center, is a perfect example of what I want to talk about—Bauhaus art and architecture. This style of architecture represented a redefinition of aesthetics that has affected many buildings, paintings, and plays with which many of you are familiar."

A **contextual definition** tells listeners how a word is used in a specific context. So, Professor Jonathan Mann was arguing that AIDS and other new diseases are changing our understanding of health—not as individuals but as a society. He captures that change by defining the word *solidarity* in terms of health:

> [S]olidarity describes a central concept in this emerging perspective on health, individuals, and society. The AIDS pandemic has taught us a great deal about tolerance and nondiscrimination, a refusal to separate the condition of the few from the fate of the many. Solidarity arises when people real-

John F. Kennedy's inaugural address is an example of the effect of skillful rephrasing to clarify a message and to make it more forceful.

ize that excessive differences among people make the entire system unstable. Charity is individual; solidarity is inherently social, concerned with social justice, and therefore also economic and political.[10]

Still another means of making technical or abstract notions easier to understand is the **analogical definition.** An analogy compares a process or event that is unknown with known ones, as in, "Hospitals and labs use cryogenic tanks, which work much like large thermos bottles, to freeze tissue samples, blood, and other organic matter." By referring to what is familiar, the analogical definition can make the unfamiliar much easier to grasp. But you've always got to be sure that the analogy, like the shoe, fits.

Overall, when thinking about kinds of definitions to use, remember that you have many different kinds of definitions to choose from when working with concepts an audience may find unfamiliar or difficult. Select a definitional strategy that makes sense for your subject matter, those listeners, and your purposes.

Restatement

As we've noted, listeners cannot reread speech; it flys into the stratosphere, never to be heard again—unless you learn to build redundancy into it. Three kinds of restatement are available to you: **rephrasing**—saying the same thing in different ways; **reiteration**—using different perspectives to describe or explain your meaning; and **repetition**—the articulation of the same ways as a kind of refrain or a structuring device.

Rephrasing. A most elegant example of skillful rephrasing is found in John F. Kennedy's inaugural address:

> Let the word go forward from this time and place, to friend and foe alike, that the torch has been passed to a new generation of Americans—born in this century, tempered by war, disciplined by a hard and bitter peace, proud of our ancient heritage—and unwilling to witness or permit the slow undoing of those human rights to which this nation has always been committed, and to which we are committed today at home and around the world.
>
> Let every nation know, whether it wishes us well or ill, that we shall pay any price, bear any burden, meet any hardship, support any friend, oppose any foe to assure the survival and success of liberty.[11]

Think what it would have sounded like had Kennedy only said "We'll do everything we can to protect human rights and assure the survival of liberty." That statement simply does not have the forcefulness of Kennedy's, which used rephrasing to enlarge his ideas and convey a sense of strong will.

Reiteration. An idea or claim can be illustrated from multiple viewpoints. Reiteration works rhetorically when you take several looks at a central theme. Henri Mann Morton used this approach to underscore society's need to balance concerns for cultural uniqueness and our common humanity by citing the words of a Cheyenne philosopher, High Chief:

> ["]In this land are many horses—red, white, black, and yellow. Yet it is all one horse.
>
> There are also birds of every color, red, white, black, and yellow. Yet, it is all one kind. So it is with all living things.
>
> In this land where once there were only Indians, there are different races, red, white, black, and yellow. Yet it is all one people.
>
> It is good and right.["]
>
> High Chief was a wise man. He knew that cultural uniquenesses have a strength of their own. At the same time, he recognized our common humanity.[12]

Repetition. A third form of restatement is brute repetition. Now, it's silly just to repeat; you can drive listeners crazy if you say everything twice. Repetition must always be purposive, often to provide a structure for a series of ideas or a rhythmic refrain that can catch up an audience in the excitement of the occasion. So, after talking about the Emancipation Proclamation's promise of freedom to African Americans, Martin Luther King, Jr., needed to drive home the point that 1963 was the moment in history when the 1863 order should be

---

𝒜SSESSMENT CHECK

Examine your speaking notes from a speech you have already delivered. How could you have improved your audience's understanding of the key ideas supporting your central idea or claim with definitions or restatements?

---

turned into reality. After talking about the "fierce urgency of *now*," King repeated the phrase "Now is the time" four times to achieve emphasis and to make his point about 1963 absolutely clear. And, of course, in the conclusion to this most famous speech, "I have a dream" and "Let freedom ring" were repeated multiple times each to create a refrain that left the audience in a frenzy, demonstrating the power of King's magnificent use of oral style.[13]

Restatement is important to the oral style because it provides emphasis, gives listeners a second chance to understand important ideas, and creates a rhythm that catches up an audience in the excitement of the occasion. Learn to use it strategically in spots where it'll do you the most good.

Imagery

People grasp their world through the senses of sight, smell, hearing, taste, and touch. To intensify listeners' experiences, you can appeal to these senses. The senses through which you reach your listeners *directly* are the visual and the auditory. Listeners can see you, your facial expressions, your movements, and your visual aids, and they can hear what you say.

You can stimulate your listeners' senses *indirectly* by using language to recall images they have previously experienced. **Imagery** consists of sets of sensory pictures evoked in the imagination through language. The language of imagery is divided into seven types, each related to the particular sensation that it seeks to evoke: visual (sight), auditory (hearing), gustatory (taste), olfactory (smell), tactile (touch), kinesthetic (muscle strain), and organic (internal sensations).

Visual Imagery. Visual imagery describes optical stimuli. Try to make your audience see the objects or situations that you're describing. Mention size, shape, color, and movement. Recount events in vivid visual language. Consider the conclusion from a speech by former Federal Communications Commissioner Newton N. Minow to the Gannett Foundation Media Center in 1991. He envisioned a past event, a look at primitive TV in 1938, to reintroduce some timeless problems. He played off the "vision" of television as well as the imagery of light (or dark, in the case of the Gulf War of 1991). Vision became a wonderfully ambiguous word referring both to light and to what we learn to see in the world:

I commend some extraordinary words to the new generation. E. B. White sat in a darkened room in 1938 to see the beginning of television, an experimental electronic box that projected images in the room. Once he saw it, Mr. White wrote:

"We shall stand or fall by television, of that I am sure. I believe television is going to be the test of the modern world, and that in this new opportunity to see beyond the range of our vision, we shall discover either a new and unbearable disturbance to the general peace, or a saving radiance in the sky."

That radiance falls unevenly today. It is still a dim light in education. It has not fulfilled its potential for children. It has neglected the needs of public television. And in the electoral process it has cast a dark shadow.

This year, television has enabled us to see Patriot missiles destroy Scud missiles above the Persian Gulf. Will television in the next thirty years be a Scud or a Patriot? A new generation now has the chance to put the vision back into television, to travel from the wasteland to the promised land, and to make television a saving radiance in the sky.[14]

FIGURE 10.2 The Types of Imagery

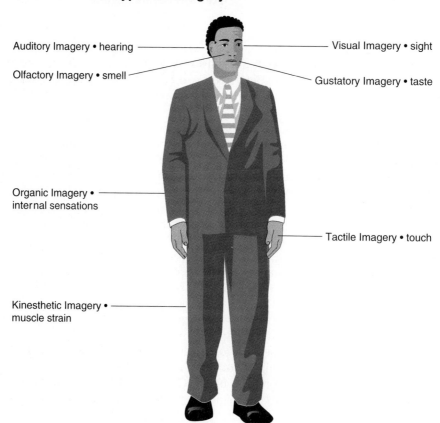

Auditory Imagery • hearing

Olfactory Imagery • smell

Visual Imagery • sight

Gustatory Imagery • taste

Organic Imagery •
internal sensations

Tactile Imagery • touch

Kinesthetic Imagery •
muscle strain

Auditory Imagery.   To create auditory imagery, use words that help your listeners hear what you're describing. Auditory imagery can project an audience into a scene. Author Tom Wolfe described a demolition derby by recounting the chant of the crowd as it joined in the countdown, the explosion of sound as two dozen cars started off in second gear, and finally "the unmistakable tympany of automobiles colliding and cheap-gauge sheet metal buckling."[15]

Gustatory Imagery.   Gustatory imagery depicts sensations of taste. Sometimes you may even be able to help your audience taste what you're describing. Mention its saltiness, sweetness, sourness, or spiciness. Remember that foods have texture as well as taste. While demonstrating how to make popcorn, you might mention the crispness of the kernels, the oily sweetness of melted butter, and the grittiness of salt. Such descriptions allow your listeners to participate in the experience through their imaginations.

Olfactory Imagery.   Olfactory imagery describes sensations of smell. Help your audience smell the odors connected with the situation you describe. Smell is a powerful sense because it normally triggers a flood of associated images. You can stimulate this process by describing the odor or by comparing the odor with more familiar ones. Elspeth Huxley remembered her childhood trek to Kenya at the turn of the century by recalling its smells:

> It was the smell of travel in those days, in fact the smell of Africa—dry, peppery yet rich and deep, with an undertone of native body smeared with fat and red ochre and giving out a ripe, partly rancid odour which nauseated some Europeans when they first encountered it but which I, for one, grew to enjoy. This was the smell of the Kikuyu, who were mainly vegetarian. The smell of tribes from the Victoria Nyanza basin, who were meat-eaters and sometimes cannibals, was quite different; much stronger and more musky, almost acrid, and, to me, much less pleasant. No doubt we smelt just as strong and odd to Africans, but of course we were fewer in numbers, and more spread out.[16]

Tactile Imagery.   Tactile imagery is based on the sensations that come to us through physical contact with external objects. In particular, tactile imagery gives sensations of texture and shape, pressure, and heat or cold. Let your audience feel how rough or smooth, dry or wet, or slimy or sticky modeling clay is (texture and shape). Let them sense the pressure of physical force on their bodies, the weight of a heavy laundry bag, the pinch of jogging shoes, the blast of a high wind on their faces (pressure).

Sensations of heat or cold are aroused by thermal imagery. General Douglas MacArthur's great speech to the Cadets of West Point on "duty, honor, and country" used vivid examples of tactile imagery as he described soldiers of the past, "bending under soggy pack on many a weary march, from dripping dusk to drizzly dawn, slogging ankle deep through mire of shell-pocked roads; to form grimly for the attack, blue-lipped, covered with sludge and mud, chilled by the wind and rain, driving home to their objective, and for many, to the judgment seat of God."[17]

Kinesthetic Imagery. Kinesthetic imagery describes the sensations associated with muscle strain and neuromuscular movement. Let your listeners experience for themselves the agonies and joys of marathon racing—the muscle cramps, the constricted chest, the struggle for air—and the magical serenity of getting a second wind and gliding effortlessly toward the finish line.

Organic Imagery. Hunger, dizziness, nausea—these are organic images. Organic imagery captures internal feelings or sensations. There are times when an experience is not complete without the description of inner feelings. The sensation of dizziness as a mountain climber struggles through the rarified mountain air to reach the summit is one example. Another is the way the bottom drops out of your stomach when a small plane tips sharply, then rights itself. Since such imagery is powerful, you shouldn't offend your audience by overdoing it. If you call attention to sheer technique, to description for its own sake, imagery will lose its power. And, too, overdone organic imagery becomes gruesome, disgusting, or grotesque when you get too far, say, into the description of blood and guts.

The seven types of imagery—visual, auditory, gustatory, olfactory, tactile, kinesthetic, and organic—directly involve listeners' sensory equipment in your speech. Sensations become avenues into their minds. Not every image will work with everyone, so use a variety throughout your speech to engage various segments of your listeners. And, too, well-crafted narratives can interweave multiple sorts of images in a single vision, as you can see here:

> The strangler struck in Donora, Pennsylvania, in October of 1948. A thick fog billowed through the streets enveloping everything in thick sheets of dirty moisture and a greasy black coating. As Tuesday faded into Saturday, the fumes from the big steel mills shrouded the outlines of the landscape. One could barely see across the narrow streets. Traffic stopped. Men lost their way returning from the mills. Walking through the streets, even for a few moments, caused eyes to water and burn. The thick fumes grabbed at the throat and created a choking sensation. The air acquired a sickening bittersweet smell, nearly a taste. Death was in the air.[18]

In this example, college student Charles Schaillol uses vivid, descriptive phrases to reach the senses of his listeners: visual—"thick sheets of dirty moisture"; organic—"eyes to water and burn"; olfactory and gustatory—"sickening bittersweet smell, nearly a taste." In telling the story of Donora, Pennsylvania, Schaillol works hard to position his listeners squarely in the middle of that town in 1948.

To be effective, such illustrations must be plausible and must keep listeners' attention focused on the subject matter, not the technique. The language must convey a realistic impression that the situation being described could happen. When imagaic language is used well, listeners' feelings are engaged in an almost experiential way. Had Schaillol simply said "Air pollution was the cause of death in Donora," he would not have been able to tie together his ideas and his audience's feeling-states nearly so well.

Metaphor

Images created by appealing to the senses are often the result of metaphors. A **metaphor** is a piece of language used in an unusual way, normally to transfer the meaning of one person, place, thing, or process to something else. "The man was a lion in battle" transfers characteristics we associate with lions—authority, power, commanding presence—to the person; "lion" is being used metaphorically in this sentence. We use metaphors when they'll help our listeners understand something more clearly; as rhetorical scholar Michael Osborn notes, good metaphors should "result in an intuitive flash of recognition that surprises or fascinates the hearer."[19] If the hearer is not jolted, informed, or given a clear orientation to whatever's being talked about, the metaphor probably is dead (as in "the legs of the table," where "legs" is a dead metaphor) or just plain ineffective. Once-fresh metaphors can turn into **cliches**— metaphors so far gone that they can have almost a reverse effect. Cliches can diminish your ideas rather than enhance or clarify them, unless they're used humorously, as in the advertisement for the book *The Dictionary of Cliches:* "Not to beat around the bush, or hedge the bet, this is a must-read for every Tom, Dick, and Harry under the sun!"[20]

Good metaphors can create new understanding and uplift an audience. Such metaphors even can be drawn from everyday experiences, which can give them wide audience appeal. For example, relying on our common experiences of lightness and darkness, Martin Luther King, Jr., intoned a solemn message that was driven by metaphor:

> With this faith in the future, with this determined struggle, we will be able to emerge from the bleak and desolate midnight of man's inhumanity to man, into the bright and glittering daybreak of freedom and justice.[21]

This basic light-dark metaphor allowed King to suggest (a) sharp contrasts between inhumanity and freedom as well as (b) the inevitability of social progress (as "daybreak" inevitably follows "midnight"). The metaphor communicated King's beliefs about justice and injustice and urged others to action now that daylight was upon us.

As we wind to a close, remember that words are not neutral pipelines for thoughts flowing from one person to another. Words not only reflect the world outside the mind but also help shape and create perceptions of people, events, and social contexts—referentially, relationally, and symbolically. Language and its effective use enables you to move others to believe, to think, and to act.

ASSESSING A SAMPLE SPEECH

William Faulkner (1897–1962) presented the following speech on December 10, 1950, as he accepted the Nobel Prize for Literature. His listeners might have expected a speech filled with the kind of pessimism so characteristic of his novels. Instead, he greeted them with a stirring challenge to improve humankind.

Notice in particular Faulkner's use of language. Although known for the tortured sentences in his novels, he expresses his ideas clearly and simply in his speech. His style suggests a written speech, yet his use of organic imagery and powerful metaphors keeps the speech alive. The atmosphere is generally serious, befitting the occasion. You might expect a Nobel Prize winner to talk about himself, but Faulkner did just the opposite. He stressed his craft, writing, and the commitment necessary to practice that craft; this material emphasis led naturally to an essentially propositional rather than narrative form. More than 40 years ago, William Faulkner offered a speech that is as relevant today as it was in 1950.

ON ACCEPTING THE NOBEL PRIZE FOR LITERATURE

William Faulkner

Even though he's accepting one of the most prestigous awards a human being can receive, Faulkner immediately tries to deflect attention from himself to his work.

The language of the whole speech is forecast in the first paragraph: agony, sweat, profit, anguish, and travail versus spirit, glory, acclaim, pinnacle comprise his vocabulary. Metaphors of struggle and childbirth are contrasted with images of soul and achievement.

I feel that this award was not made to me as a man, but to my work—a life's work in the agony and sweat of the human spirit, not for glory and least of all for profit, but to create out of the materials of the human spirit something which did not exist before. So this award is only mine in trust. It will not be difficult to find a dedication for the money part of it commensurate with the purpose and significance of its origin. But I would like to do the same with the acclaim too, by using this moment as a pinnacle from which I might be listened to by the young men and women already dedicated to the same anguish and travail, among whom is already that one who will some day stand here where I am standing./1

Our tragedy today is a general and universal physical fear so long sustained by now that we can even bear it. There are no longer problems of the spirit. There is only the question: When will I be blown up? Because of this, the young man or woman writing today has forgotten the problems of the human heart in conflict with itself which alone can make good writing because only that is worth writing about, worth the agony and the sweat./2

He attacks fear of the atomic bomb.

First, he suggests the presence of the fear and then via restatement comes back to it in the next three sentences. Second, he continues the linguistic contrasts between fear and spirit, human heart in conflict and the agony and the sweat.

Faulkner is now ready to expand his central ideas via a series of literal and metaphorical contrasts: love versus lust, defeats versus victories, value and hope versus pity and compassion. Body metaphors complete the paragraph: bones, scars, heart versus glands. A flood of imagery washes over the listeners in his conclusion: images are auditory ("the last ding-dong of doom," "his puny inexhaustible voice," and "the poet's voice"); visual ("the last worthless rock hanging tideless in the last red and dying evening"); tactile ("the pillars" that provide support for people to "endure and prevail"); and organic ("lifting his heart").

He must learn them again. He must teach himself that the basest of all things is to be afraid; and, teaching himself that, forget it forever, leaving no room in his workshop for anything but the old verities and truths of the heart, the old universal truths lacking which any story is ephemeral and doomed—love and honor and pity and pride and compassion and sacrifice. Until he does so, he labors under a curse. He writes not of love but of lust, of defeats in which nobody loses anything of value, of victories without hope and, worst of all, without pity or compassion. His griefs grieve on no universal bones, leaving no scars. He writes not of the heart but of the glands.[3]

Until he relearns these things, he will write as though he stood among and watched the end of man. I decline to accept the end of man. It is easy enough to say that man is immortal simply because he will endure: that when the last ding-dong of doom has clanged and faded from the last worthless rock hanging tideless in the last red and dying evening, that even then there will still be one more sound: that of his puny inexhaustible voice, still talking. I refuse to accept this. I believe that man will not merely endure: he will prevail. He is immortal, not because he alone among creatures has an inexhaustible voice, but because he has a soul, a spirit capable of compassion and sacrifice and endurance. The poet's, the writer's, duty is to write about these things. It is his privilege to help man endure by lifting his heart, by reminding him of the courage and honor and hope and pride and compassion and pity and sacrifice which have been the glory of his past. The poet's voice need not merely be the record of man, it can be one of the props, the pillars to help him endure and prevail.[4]

William Faulkner, "On Accepting the Nobel Prize for Literature," The Faulkner Reader (New York: Random House, 1954).

CHAPTER SUMMARY

Language is a *referential, relational,* and *symbolic* medium of communication, which means that speakers have to be most sensitive to the ways they *encode* their messages for the listeners who *decode* them. Central to effective speaking is the challenge of capturing an *oral style,* because public speaking is *face to face, social, ephemeral, enthymematic* communication. One of the keys to an oral style of language use is effective word choice: *accurate, simple, coherent, properly intense,* and *appropriate* language choices. In selecting language that creates an *oral style* appropriate to you, the occasion, the subject matter, and the audience, you must make good decisions about *serious* versus *humorous atmosphere, speaker-, audience-,* or *content-centered nouns* and *pronouns, gendered* versus *gender-neutral language,* and *propositional versus narrative form.* As far as rhetorical strategies are concerned, consider:

- *Definitions* (dictionary, negative, etymological, exemplar, contextual, and analogical)
- *Restatements* (rephrasing, reiteration, and repetition)
- *Imagery* (visual, auditory, gustatory, olfactory, tactile, kinesthetic, and organic)
- *Metaphors*

Language choices, and the resulting ways that the oral styles of speakers are created, comprise the speaker's most crucial channel of communication.

𝒦EY TERMS

analogical definition (p. 271)
atmosphere (p. 263)
auditory imagery (p. 275)
cliches (p. 277)
coherence (p. 258)
connectives (p. 259)
contextual definition (p. 270)
decoding (p. 254)
dictionary definition (p. 269)
doublespeak (p. 262)
encoding (p. 254)
enthymeme (p. 256)
etymological definition (p. 270)
exemplar definition (p. 270)
final summaries (p. 258)
gender-linked words (p. 265)
gender-neutral words (p. 265)
gustatory imagery (p. 275)
imagery (p. 273)

kinesthetic imagery (p. 276)
metaphor (p. 277)
negative definition (p. 270)
olfactory imagery (p. 275)
oral style (p. 255)
organic imagery (p. 276)
preliminary summaries (p. 258)
referential language (p. 254)
reiteration (p. 272)
relational language (p. 254)
repetition (p. 272)
rephrasing (p. 271)
rhetorical strategies (p. 268)
signposts (p. 258)
stipulative definition (p. 269)
symbolic language (p. 254)
tactile imagery (p. 275)
tone (p. 261)
visual imagery (p. 273)

𝒜SSESSMENT ACTIVITIES

1. Choose one of the items listed below and describe it, using seven types of imagery to create a portrait you could use in a speech.
   - Eating a tropical fruit in a tropical setting
   - A complicated machine of some kind

- One of the creatures from *Jurassic Park* (or any other popular movie)
- The oldest (or newest) building on campus

Highlight each of the images you use and label it for your instructor.

2. Read one of the sample speeches in this textbook. Identify the methods the speaker uses to make the language effective. Were the essentials of effective word choice observed? Did the speaker create what seems to you an appropriate style as defined here? Were rhetorical strategies of definition, restatement, imagery, and metaphor used well, or not? Grade the speaker's competence (minimal, average, superior) as an oral stylist, justifying your grade.

ℛEFERENCES

1. The principal work developing a full theory of oral style is Walter Ong's *Orality and Literacy: The Technologizing of the Word* (New York: Methuen, 1982), especially ch. 3, "The Psychodynamics of Orality." Important in understanding the sociocultural transitions that one makes when moving from oral to literate language is Eric Havelock's *The Muse Learns to Write* (New Haven, CT: Yale University Press, 1986). All these and many other ideas about orality and literacy are reviewed in Bruce E. Gronbeck, Thomas J. Farrell, and Paul A. Soukup, eds., *Media, Consciousness, and Culture: Explorations of Walter Ong's Thought* (Newbury Park, CA: Sage, 1991).

2. Quoted in John R. Pelsma, *Essentials of Speech* (New York: Crowell, Collier, and Macmillan, 1934), 193.

3. John Waite Bowers, "Language and Argument," in *Perspectives on Argumentation*, ed. G. R. Miller and T. R. Nilsen (Glenview, IL: Scott, Foreman, 1966), 168–172.

4. Alan Alda, "A Reel Doctor's Advice to Some Real Doctors," in Stephen E. Lucas, *The Art of Public Speaking* (New York: Random House, 1983), 364.

5. For overviews of gender and communication, see Judy C. Pearson, *Gender and Communication* (Dubuque, IA: Wm. C. Brown, 1985); Barbara Bate, *Communication and the Sexes* (New York: Harper and Row, 1987); Lea P. Stewart, Pamela J. Cooper, and Sheryl A. Friedly, *Communication Between the Sexes: Sex Differences and Sex-Role Stereotypes* (Scottsdale, AZ: Gorsuch Scarisbrick, 1986); Lana F. Rakow, ed., *Women Making Meaning: New Feminist Directions in Communication* (New York: Routledge, 1992); Margaret Gallagher and Lilia Quindoza-Santiago, *Women Empowering Communication: A Resource Book on Women and the Globalisation of Media* (New York: International Women's Tribune Centre, 1994); and Doug A. Newson and Bob J. Carrell, eds., *Silent Voices* (Lanham, MD: University Press of America, 1995).

6. Allen H. Neurath, "Acceptance Address," DeWitt Carter Reddick Award: *Address by the 1992 Recipient* [pamphlet] (Austin: College of Communication, University of Texas at Austin, 1992), n.p.

7. James E. Carter, "Excellence Comes from a Repository That Doesn't Change," *Vital Speeches of the Day* 59 (July 1, 1993), 548.

8. Bruce Talbot, "Statement," Hearings Before Senate Committee on Commerce, Science, and Transportation, *Tobacco Product Education and Health Promotion Act of 1991, S. 1008,* November 14, 1991, 102nd Congress (Washington: U.S. Government Printing Office, 1991), 77.

9. Everett C. Parker, "A Modest Proposal in Behalf of Democracy," *Vital Speeches of the Day* 52 (November 1, 1995): 47.

10. Jonathan Mann, "Global AIDS: Revolution, Paradigm, and Solidarity," in *Representative American Speeches, 1991–1992,* ed. Owen Peterson (New York: H. W. Wilson, 1992), 52–53.

11. From *Public Papers of the Presidents of the United States: John F. Kennedy* (Washington: U.S. Government Printing Office, 1961).

12. Henri Mann Morton, "Strength Through Cultural Diversity," in *Native American Reader,* ed. J. Blanche (Juneau, AL: Denali Press, 1990), 205.

13. For analyses of the oral style of "I Have a Dream," see John H. Patton, "'I Have a Dream': The Performance of Theology Fused with the Power of Orality," in *Martin Luther King, Jr., and the Sermonic Power of Public Discourse,* eds. Carolyn Calloway-Thomas and John Louis Lucaites (Tuscaloosa: University of Alabama Press, 1993), and Bruce E. Gronbeck, "Rhetorical Visions of America from the Margins, 1963–1988," in Christer Åsberg, ed., *Retoriska Frågor: Texter om Tal och Talere Från Quintilianus till Clinton Tillägnade Kurt Johannesson,* ed. Christer Åsberg (Stockholm: Norstedts, 1995), 267–295.

14. Newton N. Minow, "How Vast the Wasteland Now?" in *Representative American Speeches, 1991–1992,* ed. Owen Peterson (New York: H. W. Wilson, 1992), 52–53.

15. A selection from Tom Wolfe, *The Kandy-Kolored Tangerine-Flake Streamline Baby* (Thomas K. Wolfe, Jr., 1965). Reprinted by permission of Farrar, Straus and Giroux, Inc. and International Creative Management.

16. Elspeth Huxley, *The Flame Trees of Thika: Memories of an African Childhood* (London: Chatto & Windus, 1959), 4.

17. Excerpt from Douglas MacArthur, "Duty, Honor and Country," *The Dolphin Book of Speeches,* ed. George W. Hibbit (George W. Hibbit, 1965). Reprinted by permission of Doubleday & Company, Inc.

18. From Charles Schaillol, "The Strangler," *Winning Orations.* Reprinted by permission of Larry Schnoor, Executive Secretary, Interstate Oratorical Association, Mankato State University, Mankato, MN.

19. Michael Osborn, *Orientations to Rhetorical Style* (Chicago: Science Research Associates, 1976), 10.

20. Quoted on the cover of James Rogers, *The Dictionary of Cliches* (New York: Ballantine Books, 1985).

21. From Martin Luther King, Jr., "Love, Law and Civil Disobedience" (Martin Luther King, Jr., 1963). Reprinted by permission of Joan Daves.

CHAPTER
11
USING VISUAL AIDS IN SPEECHES

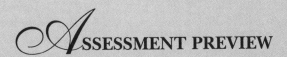

ASSESSMENT PREVIEW

After reading Chapter 11, a student with basic communication competencies will be able to:

- list the basic types of visual aids.
- understand the communicative functions of visual aids.
- make decisions regarding which aids might be used in a specific speech situation.

The student with average communication competencies will also be able to:

- understand the importance of integrating visual and verbal material.
- select visual aids that are appropriate to the topic and situation.
- use physical objects appropriately in demonstration speeches.

The student with superior communication competencies will also be able to:

- determine whether graphs, charts, and other visual aids are misleading.
- evaluate the communicative potential of visual aids.
- create visual aids that are appropriate to the topic and situation.

ue had everything ready to show slides as part of her speech—they were in the right order, none were upside down, and she had practiced timing the speech so she knew how long to show each slide before moving on. The classroom had a pull-down screen, so she didn't need to bring one. The windows had shades, so she could darken the room to enhance the visual effect. The day of the speech, she brought the slide projector and extension cord in; she'd gone home the previous weekend, brought it back, and set it up. All was going well until "pop" and the light went out on the projector. Sue had not thought to bring a spare. She had to finish the speech having gone through only three of the slides—all her preparation had gone for naught.

Sue's experience is that of other speakers; even with attention to preparation, one missed detail may be enough to ruin the use of visuals. We fully expect that you will repeat Sue's experience—perhaps not with the missing spare bulb, but in some other way. From a practical perspective, using visuals requires a great deal more thought and attention to detail than might at first meet the eye.

Given that, you might wonder—why use visuals at all? One answer to this question is to consider the general impact of visuals in our contemporary society. This has been called the **ocularcentric** [ocular = eye; centric = centered] **century.**[1] That is, ours has become a time when sight threatens to be the dominant sense. Television, film, transparencies, VCRs and videotape, videodiscs, the CD-ROM and related digital technologies, overhead and opaque projectors, billboards, poster art, banners trailing from airplanes, sidewalk tables with samples from a store's "today only" sale—our world is filled with visual communications. No time or place before yours has been so visually oriented. Entire companies—from famous media studios down to small-town graphics production shops in basements—exist because of our willingness to pay for good pieces of visual rhetoric.

The public speaker, of course, always has been in the visual communication business. A speaker's physical presence in front of an audience is a powerful visual statement. Body language, facial expression, eye contact, and gestures—all of these combine to make the visual channel of public speaking a carrier of significant messages. The use of *visual aids* makes the world of sight an essential part of oral communication transactions. From the objects a second grader brings to school for "show and tell" to the flipcharts that sales trainers use, speakers multiply and deepen their communication messages when they use visual channels well.

Research on visual media, learning, and attitude change has revealed helpful information about the impact of visual aids on audiences.[2] Much advice, however, still flows directly from veteran speakers to those new at public presentations. In this chapter, we'll mix advice from social-scientific research with wisdom from experienced speakers. First, we'll deal with the general functions of visual aids; then we'll examine various types and look at some advice on how to use them to greatest effect.

THE FUNCTIONS OF VISUAL AIDS

Visual materials provide punch for any presentation in two ways: (1) they help listeners comprehend and remember your material, and (2) they improve the persuasive impact of your messages.

Comprehension and Recall

While the old saying that "A picture is worth a thousand words" may be something of an exaggeration, its truths are reflected in research. Visual research has demonstrated that bar graphs, especially, make statistical information more accessible; simple drawings enhance recall; and charts and such human interest visuals as photographs help listeners process and retain data.[3] Pictures have significant effects on children's recall and comprehension during storytelling.[4] Your own experience probably bears this out. Recall the high school teachers who worked with models, maps, slides (transparencies) or overheads, and video; most likely you'll remember their presentations better than those in other classes where visual materials were rare or nonexistent.

Persuasiveness

In addition to improving comprehension and recall, visuals can heighten the persuasive power of your ideas because they engage listeners actively. If you watched any of the televised O. J. Simpson trial, for example, you are aware of the dramatic effects of a glove that didn't seem to fit, the use of graphs and charts to explain complex blood tests for DNA matching, and the slides showing a bruised and battered Nicole Brown years prior to her death.

Undeniably, credibility and persuasiveness are enhanced by good visuals.[5] Visual materials satisfy the "show-me" attitude prevalent in a vision-oriented or ocularcentric age; they provide a crucial means of meeting listener expectations.[6]

TYPES OF VISUAL AIDS

To give you the broadest possible look at visual aids, we'll divide them into two large classes: **physical objects** and **representations of objects and relationships.** Then we'll examine more particular types and give you some tips on how to use them in your talks.

Physical Objects

The objects that you bring to a presentation, including your own body, can be categorized under two headings: (a) *animate* (living) objects and (b) *inanimate* (nonliving) objects.

Animate Objects. Live animals or plants can, under some circumstances, be used to enhance your speeches. If your speech explores the care and feeding of gerbils, you can reinforce your ideas by bringing to the speech one or two gerbils in a properly equipped cage. Describing the differences between two varieties of plants may be easier if you demonstrate the differences with real plants. However, you might be stretching your luck by bringing a real horse into the classroom to show how one is saddled or by bringing in an untrained puppy to show how one is paper trained.

You want to use the actual object to focus audience attention on your speech, not to distract the audience with the object. A registered Persian cat may seem to be a perfect visual aid for a speech about what judges look for in cat shows until a person in the first row has an allergic reaction to your pet.

You also can use your own body as a visual aid: demonstrating warm-up exercises, ballet steps, or tennis strokes adds concreteness and vitality to presentations. In any case, make sure that members in the back rows can see the animal, plant, or demonstration. Demonstrate a yoga position from a sturdy table top rather than from the floor. Slow the tempo of a tennis stroke so that the audience can see any intricate action and subtle movements. One advantage of properly controlled visual action is that you can control the audience's attention to your demonstration. Discretion and common sense about what's possible and in good taste will help make animate visuals work for you rather than against you.

Inanimate Objects. Demonstrations are often enhanced by showing the actual object under discussion. A speech about stringing a tennis racket is enhanced by a demonstration of the process with an actual racket. A speech about the best way to repair rust holes in an automobile fender is clarified by samples of the work in stages. Cooking or house remodeling demonstrations are enlivened with samples prepared before the presentation, since the presenter usually doesn't have time to complete the actual work during the presentation. Take a tip from TV cooking shows—they work with several copies of a dish to illustrate different stages; you can do the same if your purpose is to illustrate a sequence of events in remodeling or making something.

Whether an object is animate or inanimate, you want to keep audience attention focused on the message of your speech. To do this, place the object between you and the audience as much as possible. If you stand in front of the object or to the side, you risk blocking the view, of at least some of your listeners, disrupting their focused attention and frustrating them.

Representations of Objects and Relationships

When you can't use actual objects or your own physical movement to clarify your message, you can resort to using representations, or images, that help to convey an understanding of what you are discussing. These **representations** may be relatively **concrete**—such as photographs, slides, film or videotape seg-

Representations convey information in various ways. For instance, a photograph of an in-line skate (top) gives an audience a realistic but complicated view of the object, whereas an abstract representation, such as a diagram (bottom), strips away unnecessary details to illustrate the parts of the object more clearly. Also abstract, yet highly visible, an action shot (center) provides a feeling of a three-dimensional image of the object, allowing a speaker to point out its parts and discuss their functions.

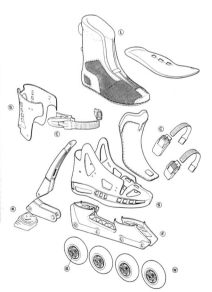

ℰTHICAL MOMENTS
CAN PICTURES LIE?

Can pictures lie? Aren't they each worth a thousand words because seeing is believing, showing is better than telling? Not really, especially in the ocularcentric age. Consider:

- Hopes for finding American soldiers missing in action (MIAs) in Vietnam often depended upon photos that seemed to show American soldiers standing with signs with current dates on them. Those pictures were faked.
- Thanks to electronic scanners, you now can easily add to or subtract from pictures, printing the altered photos so cleanly that the forgery is almost impossible to detect.
- During the 1992 presidential campaign, political action committees (PACs) ran ads that showed Bill Clinton holding hands in victory on the Democratic Convention stage with Ted Kennedy. What the PAC had done was put a picture of Kennedy's head on Vice President Al Gore's body.

Pictures can be altered to "say" something that isn't true. Or, they can add imaginings to words in order to intensify them, even focus them on a particular idea that someone doesn't want to say aloud; the 1992 PAC ad seemed to be saying that "Bill Clinton is much more liberal than you think."

The visual channel can be very helpful to both speaker and audience when it is used in morally defensible ways. It can be destructive of the truth when it's not.

ments—or more **abstract**—such as graphs, charts, and models. They may involve a simple chalkboard or a flipchart or equipment such as overhead transparencies, slide projectors, VCRs with television monitors, or computer-generated and controlled slides. There are advantages and disadvantages to each of these.

Photographs. With photographs, you can illustrate flood damage to ravaged homes or depict the beauty of a wooded area threatened by a new shopping mall. One problem with photographs, however, is that audiences may not be able to see details from a distance. You can compensate for this shortcoming by enlarging photos so that people can see them more easily. Avoid passing small photos through the audience because such activity is noisy and disruptive. The purpose of a visual aid is to draw the attention of all members of the audience simultaneously.

Slides.   Slides (transparencies) allow you to depict color, shape, texture, and relationships. If you're presenting a travelogue, you need slides to show your audience the buildings and landscape of the region. If you're giving a speech on the history of the steam engine, slides can help you to show various steam engines in operation. If you're speaking against the construction of a dam, you can enhance your persuasiveness by showing slides of the white water that will be disrupted by the dam. If you're discussing stylistic differences among famous artists, slides of artworks from the Baroque and Neoclassical periods can illustrate the distinctions you need to make. Using slides requires familiarity with projection equipment. Recall Sue's experience—attention to small, seemingly inconsequential details will make a major difference in how smoothly the presentation goes. Do you know how to change the projection lamp? Did you bring along a spare bulb just in case? Will you need an extension cord? Do you know how to remove a jammed slide? If you operate on the assumption that whatever can go wrong will, you'll be prepared for most problematic circumstances.

Videotapes and Films.   These aids can also be useful in illustrating your points. Two or three videotaped political ads can help you illustrate methods for packaging a candidate. Again, familiarity with the operation of a videocassette recorder and its television monitor or of a film projector ensures a smooth presentation. Too often, speakers assume that the equipment will be provided and a skilled technician will be available, only to find that no one knows how to run the machine properly. Such delays increase your nervousness and detract from your presentation. Slide and film projectors will require time to set up; you also may need to wheel in a monitor/VCR cart, hook it in, and get it running. Some classrooms are cable-ready, hence allowing you to show a "live" excerpt should the timing work out.

Models.   You can use models, reduced or enlarged scale replicas of real objects, to convey plans or to illustrate problems. Architects construct models of new projects to show clients. Developers of shopping malls, condominiums, and business offices use models when persuading zoning boards to grant needed rights-of-way or variances. You can use models of genes to accompany your explanation of gene splicing. As with other inanimate physical objects, models need to be manageable and visible to the audience. If you are using a model that comes apart so that different pieces can be examined, practice removing and replacing the parts beforehand.

Drawings.   Whether drawn in advance or as you speak, you will find it useful in some instances to construct rough line drawings or to provide the audience with more formally drawn pictures to represent ideas. How "finished" these are will depend on the formality of the situation. Flipchart drawings may be sufficient to explain cell division to a small group of classmates, but when presenting the same information to a large audience, you need refined visual support materials. The care with which you prepare these visuals will convey to your audience an attitude of indifference or concern.

Chalkboard Drawings. When you want to convey an understanding of a process step by step, chalkboard drawings are especially valuable. By drawing each stage as you discuss it, you can control the audience's attention to your major points. Coaches often use this approach when showing players how to execute a particular play or defend against an opponent's play. Take care, however, that you don't rely on the board so much that you spend the majority of your speech with your back to your audience.

Overhead Projectors. Speakers can use *overhead projectors and transparencies* just as they would use chalkboards—illustrating their points as they talk. However, overhead projectors offer some advantages over chalkboards. One advantage is that you can turn it off when you've made your point, thus removing any distraction from your message. Another advantage is that you can uncover one part of a transparency at a time, keeping the remainder covered so as to control the flow of information. Finally, you can prepare transparencies before the speech, giving them a more professional appearance than chalkboard drawings. During the speech, you can point to the transparency or add to it to emphasize your claims.

When you're using either a chalkboard or an overhead projector, keep the following points in mind: First, make your drawings large enough so that the audience can see them. Second, if you continue to talk to the audience as you draw, be brief; your audience's attention will wander if you talk to the board or to the light source for more than a minute or two. Third, consider the visual field while you draw—where you should stand to avoid blocking the audience's view of your visuals? Fourth, when you're through talking about the illustration, erase it or turn off the projector.

Graphs. *Graphs* show relationships among the various parts of a whole or variables across time. There are several types of graphs:

1. **Bar graphs** show the relationships between two or more sets of figures. If you were illustrating the difference between lawyers' and doctors' incomes or between male lawyers' and female lawyers' incomes, you would probably use a bar graph.
2. **Line graphs** show relationships between two or more variables, usually over time. If you are trying to explain a complex economic correlation between supply and demand, you would use a line graph.
3. **Pie graphs** show percentages by dividing a circle into the segments being represented. A charitable organization could use a pie graph to show how much of its income was spent on administration, research, and fund-raising campaigns. Town governments use pie graphs to show citizens what proportion of their tax dollars go to municipal services, administration, education, recreation, and law enforcement.
4. **Pictographs** represent size and number with symbols. A representation of U.S. and Russian exports of grain might use a miniature drawing of a wheat shock or ear of corn to represent 100,000 bushels; this repre-

FIGURE 11.1 Bar Graphs

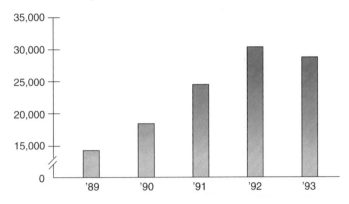

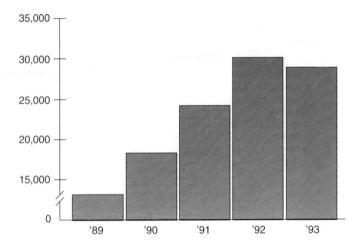

Bar graphs visually illustrate relationships. Changing the spacing and size of bars can affect the visual message.

sentation would allow a viewer to see at a glance the disparity between the exports of two countries.

Your choice of bar, line, pie, or pictorial graphs will depend on the subject and the nature of the relationship you wish to convey. A pie graph, for example, can't easily illustrate discrepancies between two groups, nor can it show effects of change over time.

Regardless of the type of graph you choose, when you are preparing a graph, you must be very careful not to distort your information. A bar graph can create a misleading impression of the difference between two items if one bar is short and wide while the other is long and narrow. Line graphs can por-

FIGURE 11.2 Line Graphs

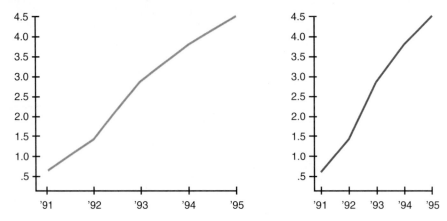

Line graphs can reveal relationships, but they also can deceive the unwary. These two graphs show the same data, but the use of different spacing makes the increase in hotel room prices seem much steeper in the second version than the first. Always look at the scales and their units when trying to interpret line graphs. Source: *Smith Travel Research, as reported in* USA Today, *October 27, 1995, B1.*

FIGURE 11.3 Pie Graph

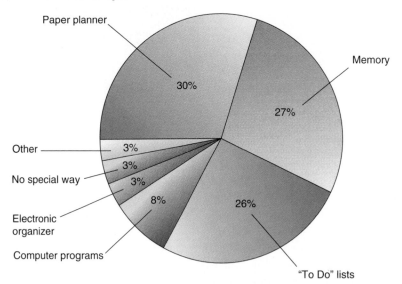

A pie graph shows percentages of a whole; this graph shows the percentage of persons using various forms of organizational reminders. (Note the total still relying on "paper" resources in today's computer age!) Source: *Opinion Research Corp. for Fuji Computer Products, as reported in* USA Today, *October 27, 1995, B1.*

tray very different effects of change if the units of measurement are not the same for each time period. You can avoid misrepresenting information by using consistent measurements and by using a computer to generate your graphs (see page 292 and below).

Charts and Tables.   **Charts** and **tables** condense large blocks of information into a single representation. If you want to discuss what products are imported and exported by Japan, you can break down imports and exports on a table. When you want to show the channels of communication or the lines of authority in a large company, your presentation will be much easier to follow if your listeners have an organizational chart for reference.

There are two special types of charts: **flipcharts** unveil ideas one at a time on separate sheets; **flowcharts** show the chronological stages of a process on a single sheet. Both flipcharts and flowcharts may include drawings or photos. If you present successive ideas with a flipchart, you'll focus audience attention on specific parts of your speech. If you present successive ideas with a complete chart, however, the audience may stray from your order of explanation to read the entire chart. You can use a flowchart to indicate what actions might be taken across time—for example, the sequential stages of a fundraising campaign.

FIGURE 11.4   Pictographs

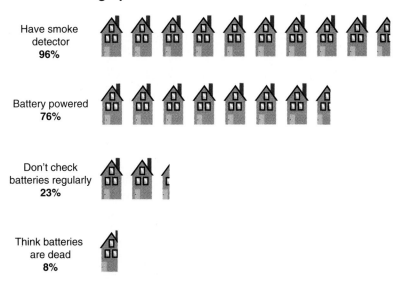

Have smoke detector
96%

Battery powered
76%

Don't check batteries regularly
23%

Think batteries are dead
8%

The speaker can use artistic skill to depict the number of homes with smoke detectors, those powered by battery, those not checked regularly (90% of the fires causing death were in homes with nonworking detectors), and those who think the batteries are dead. Source: *Angus Reid Group for American Sensors, as reported in* USA Today, *October 27, 1995, A1.*

As long as the information is not too complex or lengthy, tables and charts may be used to indicate changes over time and to rank or list items and their costs, frequency of use, or relative importance. Tables and charts should be designed so that they can be seen and so that they convey data simply and clearly. Too much information will force the audience to concentrate more on the visual support than on the oral explanation. For example, a dense chart showing all the major and minor offices of a company may simply overwhelm listeners as they try to follow your explanation. If the organization is too complex, you may want to develop a series of charts, each one focusing on a smaller unit of information.

Representing Textual Material.   You are not limited to these representational forms of displaying information. You also can utilize any of the above equipment to convey textual material: an outline of your talk, a list of the key items to be covered, a quotation from an authoritative source. All of these can be displayed on a chalkboard or through slides or overhead transparencies, etc. Corporate trainers, for example, will often use slides created through a computer program such as PowerPoint and displayed electronically from a ceiling-mounted projector to outline their presentation and convey key information. If you are giving a seminar on how to navigate the World Wide Web, for example, you might use visuals that duplicate what is seen on a computer screen. Saying "click the mouse here" is much easier if your audience can see where the cursor is on the screen at the front of the seminar room.

There are two things to consider when working primarily with text materials. First, keep enough "white space" on the page or slide so that the audience does not get lost among the verbiage. Second, make sure the type size is large enough for the audience to see; while you can magnify type to some extent by adjusting the distance between projector and screen, some type may yet remain too small to read.

Using Handouts.   All of the above information also can be put on handouts and worked with while you are speaking. Charts, graphs, outlines, rough drawings—all of theses can be photocopied and given to each audience member. Giving one to each member is better than passing only a few copies around—which will distract listeners as they get involved reading and passing things to each other. Often, giving each member a copy is the strategy of choice, if you want each person to have the material in their possession at the close of your talk. The primary difficulty you have to work against is the tendency of the audience to read ahead of where you are. If you have more than one handout, you can control this by sequencing the handouts—and by having someone handle the actual distribution while you talk. You also can control the audience's access to information, to some extent, by using an overhead transparency. Use a separate sheet to uncover the items as you go through; this won't stop all members from reading ahead, but at least it will focus attention on where you are at any given moment.

*A*SSESSMENT CHECK

As you prepare your next speech, draw some rough sketches of visual aids that would clarify your ideas for the audience. Discuss with a classmate or small group how you will coordinate them with the verbal materials.

You also can wait until the conclusion of your speech, and then distribute material relevant to your speech topic that you want the audience to take away with them.

*S*TRATEGIES FOR SELECTING AND USING VISUAL AIDS

To decide which visual aids will work best for you, take into account four considerations:

1. the characteristics of the audience and occasion;
2. the communicative potential of various visuals;
3. your ability to integrate verbal and visual materials effectively; and
4. the potential of computer-generated visual materials to help you with your communication tasks.

Consider the Audience and Occasion

Before you select specific visual aids, common sense will tell you to think about your listeners: Do you need to bring a map of the United States to an audience of college students when discussing the westward movement of population of this country? If you're going to discuss a football team's offensive and defensive formations, should you diagram them for your audience? Can you expect an audience to understand the administrative structure of the university without providing an organizational chart?

How readily an audience can comprehend *aurally* (by ear) what you have to say is another more difficult question to answer. It may be quite difficult, for example, to decide what your classmates know about the organization of such groups as the National Red Cross or what Rotary Club members know about the administrative structure of your college. Probably the best thing you can do is to speak with several of your listeners ahead of time. This and other forms of audience research can help you decide on how to use the visual channel.

As part of your preparation process, take into account the speaking occasion. Certain occasions demand specific types of visual support materials. The corporate executive who presents a report on projected future profits to a board of directors without a printed handout or diagram will probably put his or her credibility in jeopardy. The military adviser who calls for governmental expenditures for new weapons without pictures or drawings of the proposed weapons and printed technical data on their performance is not likely to be a convincing advocate. An athletic coach without a chalkboard at halftime on which to diagram plays will probably confuse some of the players. In short, if you speak in situations where speakers traditionally have used certain visual aids, meet those expectations in your own work. If an occasion doesn't appear to require certain visual supports, analyze the occasion and your topic further for different visual possibilities. Use your imagination. Be innovative. Don't overlook opportunities to make your speech more meaningful, more exciting, and more interesting for your listeners.

Well thought out computer-generated visual aids can give your presentation a level of professionalism and class and enhance your credibility.

Consider the Communicative Potential of Various Visual Aids

Keep in mind that each type of visual aid is best at communicating a particular kind of information. Each type also must blend with your spoken presentation as well as with your audience. In general, pictorial or photographic visuals can make an audience *feel* the way you do. For example, you can use slides, movies, sketches, or photographs of your travels in Thailand to accompany a speech on social conditions in equatorial Asia. Direct representations can be filled with feeling and show an audience what you experienced in another place or situation.

Visuals containing descriptive or written materials, on the other hand, are especially useful in helping an audience to *think* the way you do. Models, diagrams, charts, and graphs about the population and economy of Thailand or the increase in AIDS in that country could help you persuade your listeners to conclude that the United States should increase its aid.

Evaluate Computer-Generated Visual Materials

When considering visual aids, you can tap into the expanding world of computer graphics. While you may not be able to produce results similar to those on the latest televised football game, you can still use readily available **computer-generated visual materials.** Here are some suggestions for ways to use such materials:

- *Use computer graphics to create an atmosphere.* It's easy to make computer banners with block lettering and pictures. Hang a banner in the front of the room to set a mood or establish a theme. For example, a student urging her classmates to get involved in a United Way fundraising drive created a banner with the campaign slogan, "Thanks to you, it works, for all of us." Initially, the banner captured attention; during the speech the banner reinforced the theme.
- *Enlarge small computer-generated diagrams.* Most computer diagrams are too small to be seen easily by an audience. You can use a photo duplicating machine that enlarges images sometimes 140 to 200 percent of the original size to make a more visible diagram. Depending on the facilities available, you may be able to transfer your visual image to a large screen through the use of a projector wired to your computer; this will also enlarge the diagram so that it can be seen.
- *Consider enhancing the computer-generated image in other ways.* Use markers to color in pie graphs or to darken the lines of a line graph. Use press-on letters to make headings for your graphs. Convert computer-generated images into slide transparencies for projection during your speech. Mixing media in such ways can give your presentations a professional look. If you have access to the right technology, you can create three-dimensional images of buildings, machines, or the human body.
- *Know the limitations of computer technology.* Remember that you're the lead actor and your visuals are props. Choose the visuals that fit your purpose, physical setting, and audience needs. Computers are most effective when processing numerical data and converting them into bar, line, and pie graphs.

$\mathcal{H}$OW TO
EFFECTIVELY INTEGRATE VERBAL
AND VISUAL MATERIALS

Remember some key points about visuals that will help you save time, increase the impact of your speech, clarify complex relations, or generally enliven your presentation.

1. *Design representations with care.* Use contrasting colors (red on white, black on yellow) to highlight different kinds of information in a chart or to differentiate segments of a graph.

2. *Keep charts and other graphic aids clear and simple.* The more easily the audience can decipher the information, the more impact the visual will have. Make sure that your charts and graphs work for you: Do they make the essential information stand out clearly from the background?

3. *Make your visual large enough to be seen clearly and easily.* Listeners get frustrated when they must lean forward and squint in order to see detail in a visual aid. Make your figures and lettering large enough to be seen from the back of the room.

4. *Make your visuals neat.* Draw neatly, spell correctly, make lines proportional, and make letters symmetrical. Visual aids contribute to audience assessment of your credibility and competence.

5. *Decide how to handle difficult visual aids in advance.* Decide on a visual aid and practice with it well in advance, especially for demonstration speeches. Suppose you want to demonstrate tombstone dabbing or making paper casts of old tombstone faces. Tombstones are heavy. Do you bring one to class? Tombstone dabbing takes time and is very messy. How much of the process do you show? You could discuss in detail the chemicals used for cleaning stone surfaces, the different kinds of paper, various dabbing techniques, and locations of interesting tombstones. How detailed should you get? Unless you think through such questions in advance, you'll undoubtedly find yourself making some poor decisions in mid-speech.

6. *Be prepared to compensate orally for any distraction your visual aid may create.* Listeners may find the visual aid so intriguing that they miss part of your message. You can partially compensate for any potential distraction by building reiteration into your speech. As added insurance, you might also keep your visual aid out of sight until you need to use it.

7. *Be prepared to coordinate slides, films, overhead projections, or video-*

tapes with your verbal message. Mechanical or electronic messages can easily distract your listeners. If your audience concentrates harder on the moving images than on your words, you defeat your own purpose. You need to talk louder and move more vigorously when using a machine to communicate, or you can show the film or slides *before* or *after* you comment on their content.

8. *Hand your listeners a copy of the materials you wish them to reflect on after your speech.* If you're making recommendations to a student council, you should provide copies of your proposal for the council's subsequent action. Or, if you're reporting the results of a survey, your listeners will better digest the most pertinent statistics if you give each listener a copy of them. Few people can recall the seven warning signs of cancer, but they might keep a wallet-sized list handy if you provided them with it. Select only those items with lasting value. Time the distribution so it doesn't interfere with your speech.

CHAPTER SUMMARY

We asked a question in the introduction on to this chapter: Why use visuals at all? At this point, the reasons should be abundantly clear. We live in an *ocular-centric century*. Visuals aid listener *comprehension* and add *persuasive impact* to a speech. While we cannot, in a single chapter, make you proficient at all of the possibilities available, you should be able to consider your topic and occasion and make informed judgments about whether to use visuals, and which forms would be most appropriate in your situation. You also should be able to categorize potential visual aids as *physical objects* and *concrete or abstract representations*. You also should know a bit more about using *animate* (living) and *inanimate* (nonliving) objects and about using *representations* such as pictures, slides, video tapes, chalkboard drawing, graphs, charts, tables, handouts, and computer-generated materials. Just as important, you also should be able to select which visual aids, and in what form, to use in particular speeches after considering the following:

- The audience and occasion
- The communicative potential of various visual aids
- Ways to integrate verbal and visual materials effectively
- The best use of computer-generated materials
- How to coordinate verbal and visual channels for maximum impact

KEY TERMS

abstract representations (p. 288)
bar graphs (p. 290)
charts (p. 293)
computer-generated visual
   materials (p. 297)
concrete representations (p. 286)
flipcharts (p. 293)
flowcharts (p. 293)

line graphs (p. 290)
ocularcentric century (p. 284)
physical objects (p. 285)
pictographs (p. 290)
pie graphs (p. 290)
representations of objects and
   relationships (p. 289)
tables (p. 293)

ASSESSMENT ACTIVITIES

1. Think of several courses you have taken in high school and/or college. How did the instructors use visual aids in presenting the subject matter of these courses? Were such materials effectively used? Was there a relationship between the subject matter and the type of visual aid used? Give special consideration to proper and improper uses of the chalkboard by the instructors. When was the chalkboard use helpful, and when did it detract from the topic? Are there special problems with the use of visuals when audience members are taking notes while listening? Prepare a brief

written analysis of these or other questions that occur to you, including several illustrations from the classes, in answering this general question: What in your view constitutes appropriate and inappropriate use of visual materials?

2. Visual aids capture appropriate moods, clarify potentially complex subjects, and sometimes even carry the thrust of a persuasive message. Examine magazine advertisements and "how-to" articles in periodicals, look at store windows and special displays in museums and libraries, and observe slide-projection lectures in some of your other classes. Then (a) using the types of the visual materials considered in this chapter, classify those that you have encountered; (b) assess the purposes these materials serve—clarification, persuasion, attention focusing, mood setting, and others; (c) evaluate the effectiveness of each of the materials you have examined; and, finally, (d) prepare a report, paper, or journal entry on the results of your experiences and observations.

3. Prepare a short speech explaining or demonstrating a complex process. Use two different types of visual aids. Ask the class to evaluate which aid was more effective. The following processes might be used, or might stimulate your thoughts of others to use:
   a. The procedure for gene splicing.
   b. Tapping maple trees for the production of maple syrup.
   c. Navigating the World Wide Web.
   d. The pattern of jet stream movements.
   e. The genetic inheritance of color traits in flowers.

$\mathscr{R}$EFERENCES

1. Jacques Ellul, *The Humiliation of the Word,* trans. Joyce Main Hanks (Grand Rapids, MI: William B. Eerdmans, 1985). See also Martin Jay, "The Rise of Hermeneutics and the Crisis of Ocularcentrism," in *The Rhetoric of Interpretation and the Interpretation of Rhetoric,* ed. Paul Hernadi (Durham, NC: Duke University Press, 1989), 55–74.

2. Further information on the value of visual perception can be found in Larry Raymond, *Reinventing Communication: A Guide to using Visual Language for Planning, Problem Solving, and Reengineering* (Milwaukee: ASQC Quality Press, 1994); Chris Jenks, *Visual Culture* (New York: Routledge, 1995).

3. William J. Seiler, "The Effects of Visual Materials on Attitudes, Credibility, and Retention," *Communication Monographs* 38 (1971): 331–34.

4. For more specific conclusions regarding the effects of various kinds of visual materials, see James Benjamin and Raymie E. McKerrow, *Business and Professional Communication* (New York: HarperCollins, 1994), 175–179.

5. Joel R. Levin and Alan M. Lesgold, "On Pictures in Prose," *Educational Communication and Technology Journal* 26 (1978): 233–244.

6. For more information on visual communication, see Paul Messaris, *Visual "Literacy": Image, Mind, and Reality* (Boulder, CO: Westview Press, 1994).

$\mathcal{U}$SING YOUR VOICE AND BODY TO COMMUNICATE

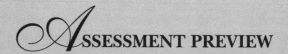

$\mathcal{A}$SSESSMENT PREVIEW

After reading Chapter 12, the student with basic communication competencies will be able to

- be heard intelligibly by his or her listeners.
- use enough vocal variety and stress to make most parts of the message comprehensible to listeners.
- take and maintain a direct, open stance in front of audiences.
- execute basic (especially descriptive) gestures firmly and effectively.
- maintain eye contact with the audience.

The student with average communication competencies will also be able to

- suggest the emotional atmosphere appropriate to the speech mood through vocal control.
- adjust vocal and physical activity to the amount of space between speaker and listeners.
- use physical movements as transitions between segments of speeches.
- reflect the emotional tenor of the speech in facial expressions and gestures.

The student with superior communication competencies will also be able to

- show a level of vocal control that makes the voice the complete instrument of intellectual, social, and emotional connections between speaker and listeners.
- vary the amount and pace of physical movement, the variety of facial expressions, and the range and shape of gestures to make the body the complete vehicle of oral communication, adapting nonverbal behavior to speaker needs, the setting, audience characteristics, and the subject matter of the speech.

he great Greek orator Demosthenes initially had such a weak and indistinct voice that he reputedly practiced speaking by shouting into the coastal winds of the Aegean Sea and loading his mouth with pebbles in order to practice articulating around them. Abraham Lincoln suffered from severe stage fright. Eleanor Roosevelt appeared awkward and clumsy, speaking with a high-pitched, hoarse voice; only after years of practice could she command an audience with her delivery. John Kennedy's strong regional dialect and his repetitive, wood-chopping gestures were parodied throughout the campaign of 1960, and became the objects of intense speech-training sessions. Robert Dole had such trouble with speech dynamism that his staff resorted to campaign ads made up of quick cuts from line to line to make him appear more animated in the campaign of 1996.

ORALITY AND HUMAN COMMUNICATION

That people with the stature of Greek orators, American presidents, internationally famous humanitarians, and candidates for high office took time to improve their speech delivery skills should not be surprising. These cultural heroes all realized that public service comes, yes, from thinking great thoughts, but also from forging strong interpersonal bonds that allow those great thoughts to become shared values and actions. Even in the age of electronic interconnectivity, it is still person-to-person contact that's the basis of social formations. We share ideas, values, and courses of action, most fundamentally, through speech.

In Chapter 10 we started to explain the idea of orality and the importance of cultivating an oral syle of speechmaking. Let's go further now. What are the characteristics of **speech delivery**—the use of voice and body to communicate with others in your presence—that enhance the importance and power of public speaking? Communication theorist and critic Walter Ong has devoted his life to answering that question in broad terms, by trying to understand the ways in which oral (preliterate) cultures worked. The characteristics defining oral connections between people, to Ong,[1] include the following:

1. *Aggregative.* The best human speech gathers together ideas—commonly shared notions—and relates the subject matter to them. Maxims, folk sayings, and even clichés often are accumulated or aggregated in speeches. So, when Bill Clinton campaigned in 1996, he ended many speeches with a political cliché: "the best America is yet to come." It is a phrase that Michael Dukakis had used before him in the 1988 campaign, and that Clinton had articulated occasionally in the 1992 effort. It's an almost perfect political slogan, because it captures the sense of exciting change that permeates most campaigns and it taps into what is known as American optimism or exceptionalism: The idea that the United States believes it can always grow and overcome any problem because it is a flexible democracy with problem-solving

skills provided by people assembled from all other countries.[2] The best speeches aggregate maxims, pieces of wisdom, even clichés, tying them to the subject matter—in Clinton's case, his legislative proposals. If you gather together *only* clichés, of course, the speech is empty. The maxims and pieces of wisdom are there to bond your ideas and yourself to other members of the community, not to take the place of new ideas.

2. *Agonistic.* Human speech is an inherently combative form of communication. This is not to say that speakers are always angry or vicious—not at all. But the best speakers know that they're struggling with ideas and with listeners, looking for ways to speak ideas in forceful and commanding ways and to engage listeners not only intellectually but also emotionally. Pat Buchanan during the 1996 presidential campaign was not only agonistic but also antagonistic, attacking his opponents even while wrestling to convert his listeners to his antiabortion, antigovernment, anti-foreign aid messages. At the other end of the scale is Crystal Cathedral preacher Robert Schuller, a smooth, witty, accommodating speaker; yet he too pleads with audiences and reaches out with sympathy, love, and the power of positive thinking to burrow into their psyches. Both Buchanan and Schuller know that agonism—struggle with others—is something that makes speeches work and that represents public talk's superiority over other modes of communication.

3. *Situational.* The best speech is always grounded in the concreteness of the here-and-now, the specific situation. Philosophical essays and poetry can try to be timeless; speeches should always be timely, made for now. The Greek idea of **kairos**—appropriateness for time and place—was a concept important to classical rhetoricians. That sense of timely specificity develops because (1) speakers are usually called on or expected to speak when something is in need of repair or celebration, and that something itself is concrete (you need help understanding a city council resolution, you feel anger and sorrow at the death of a friend, you want someone to express the joy you feel when winning a game), and (2) concreteness is important because of the sheer physicalness of person-to-person speech: words seem to flow on material sound waves from a speaker's mouth to listeners' ears; the bodies of the speakers and listeners are present; touch occurs when handshakes follow a talk; and the very ideas discussed flow from the total human body—mouth, yes, but also arms and legs, head and torso, the clothing and jewelry that adorn that body, and technologies that amplify sound and vision. The material situatedness of public speech gives it a sense of command and presence simply not possible with written language, radio or television broadcasts, or Internet chat lines.

To think about the kinds of interhuman connections that are established through vocal and bodily presence may seem a bit too theoretical and idealistic for your tastes. Yet, if you're going to understand why control of voice and body as channels of oral communication is so important, you must think about such matters. Sure, you've been talking all of your life and probably have gotten along all right. But when you grab onto a lectern to address a waiting audience, hoping to achieve your general and specific purposes, you must stop to think of how best to aggregate ideas, tone them powerfully, and situate yourself and your thoughts concretely enough among today's concerns to meet audience expectations and needs. If you do all of that well, you'll have the satisfaction of knowing that you've spoken in as competent and as socially successful a way as you can.

Let us now turn to the details, to more specific aspects of using voice and body as instruments fostering human relationships.

$\mathcal{U}$SING YOUR VOICE TO COMMUNICATE

The human voice is the physical instrument that shapes the meanings of words and ideas. Since preliterate times, when all cultures were oral, voice has been the primary connector between people, creating a sense of identification, of community. You must learn to control your vocal sound stream to make it central to your communication habits.

You communicate your enthusiasm to your listeners through your voice. By learning about the characteristics of vocal quality, you can make your ideas more interesting. Listen to a stock market reporter rattle off the daily industrial averages. Every word might be intelligible, but the reporter's vocal expression may be so repetitive and monotonous that the ideas seem unexciting. Then, listen to Al Michael doing a play-by-play of a football game or Dick Vitale covering a basketball game. The excitement of their broadcasts depends largely on their use of voice.

Our society prizes one essential vocal quality above all others—a sense of **conversationality.**[3] The conversational speaker creates a sense of two-way, interpersonal relationship, even when behind a lectern. The best hosts of afternoon talk shows or evening newscasts speak as though they're engaging each listener in a personal conversation. Speakers who've developed a conversational quality—Geraldo Rivera, Oprah Winfrey, Barbara Walters, Joan Lunden, and Regis Filbin, for example—have recognized that they're talking *with*, not *at*, an audience.

The Effective Speaking Voice

Successful speakers use their voices to shape their ideas and emotionally color their messages. A flexible speaking voice has intelligibility, variety, and understandable stress patterns.

Intelligibility. **Intelligibility** refers to the ease with which a listener can understand what you're saying and is dependent upon loudness, rate, enunciation, and pronunciation. Most of the time, inadequate articulation, a rapid speaking rate, or soft volume is acceptable because you know the people

A listener's judgment of a speaker's personality and emotional commitment often centers on the speaker's vocal quality, especially the sense of conversationality the speaker conveys.

you're talking with and because you're probably only three to five feet from them. In public speaking, however, you may be addressing people you don't know, often from 25 feet or more away. When speaking in public, you have to work on making yourself intelligible. Try the following techniques:

1. *Adjust your volume.* Probably the most important single factor in intelligibility is how loudly you speak. **Volume** is related to the distance between you and your listeners and the amount of noise that is present. You must realize that your own voice sounds louder to you than it does to your listeners. Obviously, you need to project your voice by increasing your volume if you're speaking in an auditorium filled with several hundred people. However, you shouldn't forget that a corresponding reduction in volume is also required when your listeners are only a few feet away. The amount of surrounding noise with which you must compete also has an effect on your volume, as illustrated in Figure 12.1.

2. *Control your rate.* **Rate** is the number of words spoken per minute. In animated conversation, you may jabber along at 200 to 250 words per minute. This rate is typical of people raised in the North, Midwest, or West. As words tumble out of your mouth in informal conversations, they're usually intelligible because they don't have to travel far. In large auditoriums or outdoors, though, rapid delivery can impede

intelligibility. Echoes sometimes distort or destroy sounds in rooms; ventilation fans interfere with sound. In the outdoors, words seem to vanish into the open air.

When addressing larger audiences, cut your rate by a third or more. Obviously you don't go around timing your speaking rate, but you can remind yourself of potential rate problems as you prepare to speak. Get feedback from your instructors and classmates regarding your speaking rate.

3. *Enunciate clearly.* **Enunciation** refers to the crispness and precision with which you form words. Good enunciation is the clear and distinct utterance of syllables and words. Most of us are "lip lazy" in normal conversation. We slur sounds, drop syllables, and skip over the beginnings

FIGURE 12.1 **Loudness Levels**

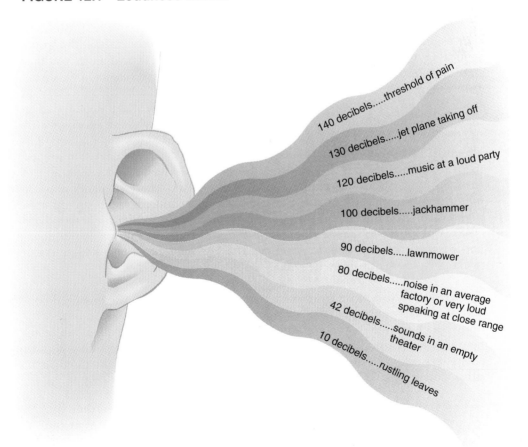

140 decibels.....threshold of pain

130 decibels.....jet plane taking off

120 decibels.....music at a loud party

100 decibels.....jackhammer

90 decibels.....lawnmower

80 decibels.....noise in an average factory or very loud speaking at close range

42 decibels.....sounds in an empty theater

10 decibels.....rustling leaves

As you can see, noise varies considerably. How could you adjust your volume if you were speaking to a "quiet" audience? What if you were competing with a lawnmower outside the building?

and endings of words. This laziness may not inhibit communication between friends, but it can seriously undermine a speaker's intelligibility.

When speaking publicly, force yourself to say *going* instead of *go-in,* *just* instead of *jist,* and *government* instead of *guvment.* You will need to open your mouth wider and force your lips and tongue to form the consonants firmly. If you're having trouble enunciating clearly, ask your instructor for some exercises to improve your performance. (See "How to Improve Your Voice.")

4. *Meet standards of pronunciation.* To be intelligible, you must form sounds carefully and meet audience expectations regarding acceptable pronunciation. Even if your words aren't garbled, any peculiarity of pronunciation is sure to be noticed by some listeners. Your different pronunciation may distract your listeners and undermine your credibility as a speaker.

A **dialect** is language use—including vocabulary, grammar, and pronunciation—unique to a particular group or region. Your pronunciation and grammatical or syntactical arrangement of words determine your dialect. You may have a foreign accent, a white southern or black northern dialect, a New England twang, or a Hispanic trill. A clash of dialects can result in confusion and frustration for both speaker and listener. Audiences can make negative judgments about the speaker's credibility—that is, the speaker's education, reliability, responsibility, and capacity for leadership—based solely on dialect.[4] Paralinguists call these judgments vocal stereotypes.[5] Wary of vocal stereotypes, many news anchors have adopted a midwestern American dialect, a manner of speaking that is widely accepted across the country. Many speakers become bilingual, using their own dialects when facing local audiences but switching to midwestern American when addressing more varied audiences. When you speak, you'll have to decide whether you should use the grammar, vocabulary, and vocal patterns of middle America. The language of your audience is the primary factor to consider.

Variety. As you move from conversations with friends to the enlarged context of public speaking, you may discover that listeners accuse you of monotony of pitch or rate. When speaking in a large public setting, you should compensate for the greater distance that sounds have to travel by varying certain characteristics of your voice. **Variety** is produced by changes in rate, pitch, stress, and pauses.

1. *Vary your rate.* Earlier, we discussed normal rates of speech. Alter your speaking rate to match your ideas. Slow down to emphasize your own thoughtfulness or quicken the pace when your ideas are emotionally charged. Observe, for example, how Larry King varies his speaking rate from caller to caller or how an evangelist changes pace regularly. A varied rate keeps an audience's attention riveted to the speech.

$\mathscr{H}$OW TO
IMPROVE YOUR VOICE

The instructor's manual that accompanies this textbook has several exercises for voice improvement; your instructor can get it from Longman Publishers. If you or others are concerned about the way you use your voice, those exercises can be most useful. Here's a sample of what you can do:

- *Breath control.* Say the entire alphabet, using only one breath. As you practice, try saying it more and more slowly so as to improve your control of exhalation.
- *Control of pitch.* Sing "low, low, low, low," dropping one note of the musical scale each time you sing the word until you reach the lowest tone you can produce. Then sing your way back up the scale. Now sing "high, high, high, high," going up the scale to the highest note you can reach. Sing your way back down. Go up and down, trying to sense the notes you're most comfortable with—your so-called optimum pitch. Give most of your speeches around your optimum pitch.
- *Articulatory control.* Pronounce each of the following word groups, making sure that each word can be distinguished from the others. Have someone check your accuracy: jest, gist, just;

thin, think, thing; roost, roosts, ghost, ghosts; began, begun, begin; wish, which, witch; affect, effect; twin, twain, twine. Or try the following tongue twisters:

The sixth sheik's sixth sheep's sick.
Three gray geese in the green grass grazing; gray were the geese and green was the grazing.
Barry, the baby bunny's born by the blue box bearing rubber baby buggy bumpers.

2. *Change your pitch.* **Pitch** is the frequency of sound waves in a particular sound. Three aspects of pitch—level, range, and variation—are relevant to effective vocal communication. Your everyday or **optimum pitch level**—whether it is habitually in the soprano, alto, tenor, baritone, or bass range—is adequate for most of your daily communication needs.

The key to successful control of pitch depends on understanding the importance of **pitch variation.** As a general rule, use higher pitches to communicate excitement and lower pitches to create a sense of control or solemnity. Adjust the pitch to fit the emotion.

Stress.   A third aspect of vocal behavior is stress. **Stress** is the way in which sounds, syllables, and words are accented. Without vocal stress, you'd sound like a computer. Vocal stress is achieved in two ways—through vocal emphasis and through the judicious use of pauses.

Use Vocal Emphasis.   **Emphasis** is the way that you accent or attack words. You create emphasis principally through increased volume, changes in pitch, or variations in rate. Emphasis can affect the meaning of your sentences. Notice how the meaning of "Tom's taking Jane out for pizza tonight" varies with changes in word emphasis:

1. "TOM's taking Jane out for pizza tonight." (Tom, and not John or Bob, is taking Jane out.)
2. "Tom's taking JANE out for pizza tonight." (He's not taking out Sue.)
3. "Tom's taking Jane OUT for pizza tonight." (They're not staying home as usual.)
4. "Tom's taking Jane out for PIZZA tonight." (They're not having seafood or hamburgers.)
5. "Tom's taking Jane out for pizza TONIGHT." (They're going out tonight, not tomorrow or next weekend.)

A lack of vocal stress not only gives the impression that you are bored but also causes misunderstandings of your meaning. Changes in rate can also be used to add emphasis. Relatively simple changes can emphasize where you are in an outline: "My s-e-c-o-n-d point is. . . ." Several changes in rate can indicate the relationship among ideas. Consider the following example:

We are a country faced with . . . [moderate rate] financial deficits, racial tensions, an energy crunch, a crisis of morality, environmental depletion, government waste . . . [fast rate], and - a- stif - ling - na - tion - al - debt [slow rate].

The ideas pick up speed through the accelerating list of problems but then come to an emphatic halt with the speaker's main concern, the national debt.

Such variations in rate emphasize for an audience what is and what isn't especially important to the speech.

Use Helpful Pauses. Pauses are the intervals of silence between or within words, phrases, or sentences. When placed immediately before a key idea or before the climax of a story, they can create suspense: "And the winner is [pause]!" When placed after a major point, pauses can add emphasis, as in: "And who on this campus earns more than the president of the university? The football coach [pause]." Inserted at the proper moment, a dramatic pause can express feelings more forcefully than words. Clearly, silence can be a highly effective communicative tool if used intelligently and sparingly and if not embarrassingly prolonged.

Sometimes, speakers fill silences in their discourse with sounds: *um, ah, er, well-ah, you-know,* and other meaningless fillers. Undoubtedly, you've heard speakers say, "Today, ah, er, I would like, you know, to speak to you, um, about a pressing, well-uh, like, a pressing problem facing this, uh, campus." Such vocal intrusions convey feelings of hesitancy and a lack of confidence. Make a concerted effort to remove these intrusions from your speech. Also avoid too many pauses and those that seem artificial, because they can make you appear manipulative or overrehearsed.

On the other hand, don't be afraid of silences. Pauses allow you to stress important ideas, such as the punch line in a story or argument. Pauses also intensify the involvement of listeners in emotional situations, such as when Barbara Walters or David Frost pauses for reflection during an interview.

Controlling the Emotional Quality

A listener's judgment of a speaker's personality and emotional commitment often centers on that speaker's vocal quality—the fullness or thinness of the tones and whether the sound is harsh, husky, mellow, nasal, breathy, or resonant. Depending on your vocal quality, an audience may judge you as being angry, happy, confident, fearful, sincere, or sad.

Fundamental to a listener's reaction to vocal quality are **emotional characterizers,** cues about a speaker's emotional state. These cues include laughing, crying, whispering, inhaling, or exhaling.[6] Emotional characterizers combine with your words to communicate subtle shades of meaning. Consider for a moment a few of the many ways you can say, "I can't believe I ate the whole thing." You might say it as though you were reporting a fact, as if you can't believe you ate it all, or as though eating the entire thing were an impossible achievement; or you might say it as though were expressing doubts about whether you actually did eat the whole thing. As you say the sentence to express those different meanings, you might laugh or inhale sharply, altering your emotional characterizers. Such changes are important cues to the audience as to how to take or understand what you're saying.

The vocal qualities you can control become prime determiners of your vocal style: intelligibility is a base characteristic, for without it you have no chance whatsoever of reaching anyone with your message; variety and stress help listeners pick out the especially important parts of it. Emotional characterizers add in the human dimensions, providing invaluable cues as to how your message is to be not only understood but also responded to—how are we to feel about your subject matter? These sorts of paralinguistic or vocal connections knit speaker and audience together.

Practicing Vocal Control

Don't assume that you'll be able to master in a day all of the vocal skills we've described. To attain them, you have to train your mind, convincing yourself to express certain kinds of feelings publicly before you can, for example, fully modulate multiple vocal qualities. You also have to work on your vocal instrument—to practice aloud. Ask your instructor to provide you with exercises designed to make your voice more flexible. And then practice some more. Work with as many different kinds of audiences as you can, working in intelligibility, variety, and stress in front of real people; this helps you engrain constructive changes in your speaking style into everyday conversation. Then you should be ready to seek the sense of conversationality so highly valued in this society in the enlarged context of public speaking itself. Good luck.

$\mathcal{U}$SING YOUR BODY TO COMMUNICATE

Just as your voice communicates and shapes ideas through the oral-aural channel, so your physical behavior in front of an audience helps control listeners' understandings of and reactions to what you're saying. The visual channel is so important that even our word "idea" is derived from the Greek word "to see."[7] Both the oral and the visual channels can be worked to create a common understanding of your ideas and how you want others to feel about them. Questions of physical behavior are usually talked about as **nonverbal communication.**

Dimensions of Nonverbal Communication

While some use the phrase *nonverbal communication* to refer to all aspects of interpersonal interaction that are nonlinguistic, we'll focus the discussion here on physical behavior in communication settings. In recent years, research has reemphasized the important role of physical behavior in effective oral communication.[8] Basically, three generalizations about nonverbal communication should guide your speechmaking:

1. *Speakers reveal and reflect their emotional states through their nonverbal behaviors.* Your listeners read your feelings toward yourself, your topic, and your audience from your facial expressions. Consider the contrast

between a speaker who walks briskly to the front of the room, head held high, and one who shuffles, head bowed and arms hanging limply. Communications scholar Dale G. Leathers summarized a good deal of research on nonverbal communication processes: "Feelings and emotions are more accurately exchanged by nonverbal than verbal means. . . . The nonverbal portion of communication conveys meanings and intentions that are relatively free from deception, distortion, and confusion."[9]

2. *The speaker's nonverbal cues enrich or elaborate the message that comes through words.* A solemn face reinforces the dignity of a wedding. The words "We must do either *this* or *that*" can be illustrated with appropriate arm-and-hand gestures. Taking a few steps to one side tells an audience that you're moving from one argument to another. A smile enhances your comment on how happy you are to be there.

3. *Nonverbal messages form a reciprocal interaction between speaker and listener.* Listeners frown, smile, shift nervously in their seats, and engage in many types of nonverbal behavior. The physical presence of listeners and the natural tendency of human beings to mirror each other when they're close together mean that nonverbal behavior is a social bonding mechanism. For this chapter, though, we'll concentrate on the speaker's control of physical behavior in four areas: proxemics, movement and stance, facial expressions, and gestures.

Proxemics. **Proxemics** is the use of space by human beings. Two components of proxemics, physical arrangement and distance, are especially relevant to public speakers:

1. *Physical arrangements.* The layout of the room in which you're speaking, including the presence or absence of a lectern; the seating plan; the location of chalkboards and similar aids; and any physical barriers between you and your audience.

2. *Distance.* The extent or degree of separation between you and your audience.[10]

Both of these components have a bearing on the message you communicate publicly. Typical speaking situations involve a speaker facing a seated audience. Objects in the physical space—the lectern, a table, several flags—tend to set the speaker apart from the listeners. This setting apart is both *physical* and *psychological.* Literally as well as figuratively, objects can stand in the way of open communication. If you're trying to create a more informal atmosphere, you should reduce the physical barriers in the setting. You might stand beside or in front of the lectern instead of behind it. In very informal settings, you might even sit on the front edge of a table while talking.

So, what influences your use of physical space?

FIGURE 12.2 Classification of Interhuman Distance

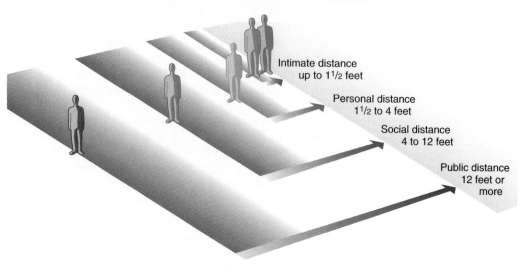

Intimate distance
up to 1¹/₂ feet

Personal distance
1¹/₂ to 4 feet

Social distance
4 to 12 feet

Public distance
12 feet or
more

Edward T. Hall, The Hidden Dimension *(New York: Doubleday, 1969).*

1. *The formality of the occasion.* The more solemn or formal the occasion, the more barriers will be used; on highly formal occasions, speakers may even speak from an elevated platform or stage.
2. *The nature of the material.* Extensive quoted material or statistical evidence may require you to use a lectern; the use of visual aids often demands such equipment as an easel, a VCR, or an overhead projector.
3. *Your personal preference.* You may feel more at ease speaking from behind rather than in front of the lectern.

The distance component of proxemics adds a second set of considerations. In most situations, you'll be talking at what anthropologist Edward T. Hall has termed a "public distance"—12 feet or more from your listeners"[11] (see Figure 12.2). To communicate with people at that distance, you obviously can't rely on your normal speaking voice or subtle changes in posture or movement. Instead, you must compensate for the distance by using larger gestures, broader shifts of your body, and increased vocal energy. By contrast, you should lower your vocal volume and restrict the breadth of your gestures when addressing a few individuals at a closer distance.

Movement and Posture.   The ways you move and stand provide a second set of bodily cues for your audience. **Movement** includes physical shifts from place to place; **posture** refers to the relative relaxation or rigidity and vertical position of the body. Movements and posture can communicate ideas about yourself to an audience. The speaker who stands stiffly and erectly may, without uttering a word, be saying, "This is a formal occasion" or "I'm tense, even afraid, of this audience." The speaker who leans forward, physically reaching out to the audience, often is saying silently, "I'm interested in you. I want you to understand and accept my ideas." The speaker who sits casually on the front edge of a table and assumes a relaxed posture may suggest informality and readiness to engage in a dialogue with listeners.

Movement and postural adjustments regulate communication. As a public speaker, you can, for instance, move from one end of a table to the other to indicate a change in topic; or you can accomplish the same purpose by changing your posture. At other times, you can move toward your audience when making an especially important point. In each case, you're using your body to reinforce transitions in your subject or to emphasize a matter of special concern.

But keep in mind that your posture and movements can also work against you. Aimless and continuous pacing is distracting. Nervous bouncing or swaying makes listeners seasick, and an excessively erect stance increases tension in listeners. Your movements should be purposeful and enhance the meaning of your words. Stance and movement can help your communicative effort and produce the impressions of self-assurance and control that you want to exhibit.

Facial Expressions.   When you speak, your facial expressions function in a number of ways. First, they communicate much about yourself and your feelings. Researchers Paul Ekman and Wallace V. Friesen call these **affect displays**—facial signals of emotion that an audience perceives when scanning your face to see how you feel about yourself and how you feel about them.[12]

Second, facial changes provide listeners with cues that help them interpret the contents of your message. Are you being ironic or satirical? Are you sure of your conclusions? Is this a harsh or pleasant message? Researchers tell us that a high percentage of the information conveyed in a typical message is communicated nonverbally. Psychologist Albert Mehrabian has devised a formula to account for the emotional impact of the different components of a speaker's message. Words, he says, contribute 7 percent, vocal elements 38 percent, and facial expression 55 percent.[13]

Third, the "display" elements of your face—your eyes, especially—establish a visual bond between you and your listeners. Our culture values eye contact. The speaker who looks people squarely in the eye is likely to be perceived as earnest, sincere, forthright, and self-assured. In other words, regular eye contact with listeners helps establish a speaker's credibility. Speakers who look at the floor, who read from notes, or who deliver speeches to the back wall sever the visual bond with their audiences and lose credibility.

Of course, you can't control your face completely, which is probably why listeners search it so carefully for clues to your feelings. You can, however, make sure that your facial messages don't belie your verbal ones: when you're uttering angry words, your face should be communicating anger; when you're pleading with your listeners, your eyes should be engaging them intently. In short, let your face mirror your feelings. That's one of the reasons it's there!

Gestures. **Gestures** are purposeful movements of the head, shoulders, arms, hands, and other areas of the body that support and illustrate the ideas you're expressing. Fidgeting with your clothing and notecards and playing with your hair aren't purposeful gestures. They distract from the ideas you're communicating. The effective public speaker commonly uses three kinds of gestures:

1. *Conventional gestures* are physical movements that are symbols with specific meanings assigned by custom or convention. These gestures *condense* ideas: they are shorthand expressions of things or ideas that would require many words to describe fully. A speaker can use the raised-hand "stop" gesture to interrupt listeners who are drawing premature conclusions or the "V for victory" sign when congratulating them for jobs well done.
2. *Descriptive gestures* are physical movements that describe the idea to be communicated. Speakers often depict the size, shape, or location of an object by movements of the hands and arms; that is, they draw pictures for listeners. You might indicate the size of a box by drawing it in the air with a finger or raise an arm to indicate someone's height.
3. *Indicators* are movements of the hands, arms, or other parts of the body that express feelings. Speakers throw up their arms when disgusted, pound the lectern when angry, shrug their shoulders when puzzled, or point a threatening finger when issuing a warning. Such gestures communicate emotions to listeners and encourage similar responses in them. Facial expressions and other body cues usually reinforce such gestures.[14]

You can improve your gestures through practice. As you practice, you'll obtain better results by keeping in mind three factors that influence the effectiveness of gestures: relaxation, vigor and definiteness, and proper timing.

First, if your muscles are tense, your movements will be stiff and your gestures awkward. You should make a conscious effort to relax your muscles before you start to speak. You might warm up by taking a few steps, shrugging your shoulders, flexing your muscles, or breathing deeply.

Second, useful gestures are natural and animated. They reflect your emotional state and help you to physiologically describe ideas in ways that others would. Exaggerated arm movements, repetitive chopping, and random twitches of your hands call attention to your body itself, not to the ideas being formed with its aid. The best gestures reflect important mental and emotional states.

Third, timing is crucial to effective gestures. The *stroke* of a gesture—that is, the shake of a fist or movement of a finger—should fall *on* or slightly before the point the gesture is emphasizing. Just try making a gesture after the world or phrase it was intended to reinforce has been spoken; if you do that regularly, people will think of you either as a drunk or a comedian. Timing gestures effectively demands that you be in a state of readiness: usually, arms by your sides, often with your hands resting on the lectern or held in a relaxed fashion in front of your bellybutton so that they're ready to move into action. Practice making gestures until they're habitual, and then use them when you want to visualize your ideas and feelings.

Adapting Nonverbal Behavior to Your Presentations

Although you'll never completely control your physical behavior, you can gain skill in orchestrating your gestures and other movements. You can make some conscious decisions about how you will use your body together with the other channels of communication to communicate effectively.

1. *Plan a proxemic relationship with your audience that reflects your own needs and attitudes toward your subject and your listeners.* If you're comfortable behind a lectern, use it; however, keep in mind that it's a potential barrier between you and your listeners. If you want your whole body to be visible to the audience but you feel the need to have your notes at eye level, stand beside the lectern and arrange your notecards on it. If you want to relax your body, sit behind a table or desk; but compensate for the resulting loss of action by increasing your volume. If you feel relaxed and want to be open to your audience, stand in front of a table or desk. Learn to be yourself while speaking publicly.

   Consider your listeners' needs as well. The farther you are from them, the more important it is for them to have a clear view of you, the harder you must work to project your words, and the broader your physical movements must be. The speaker who crouches behind a lectern in an auditorium of 300 people soon loses contact. Think of large lecture classes you've attended or outdoor political rallies you've witnessed. Recall the delivery patterns that worked effectively in such situations. Put them to work for you.

2. *Adapt the physical setting to your communicative needs.* If you're going to use visual aids—such as a chalkboard, flipchart, or working model—remove the tables, chairs, and other objects that might obstruct your audience's view. Increase intimacy by arranging chairs in a small circle or stress formality by using a lectern.

3. *Adapt the size of your gestures and amount of your movement to the size of the audience.* Keeping in mind what Hall noted about public distance in communication, you should realize that subtle changes of facial expression or small hand movements can't be seen clearly in large rooms or auditoriums. Although many auditoriums have a raised platform and a slanted floor to enhance visibility, you should adjust to the distance between yourself and your audience by making your movements and gestures larger.

4. *Continuously scan your audience from side to side and from front to back, looking specific individuals in the eye.* Your head should not be in constant motion; *continuously* does not imply rhythmic, nonstop bobbing. Rather, take all your listeners into your field of vision periodically; establish firm visual bonds with individuals occasionally. Such bonds enhance your credibility and keep your auditors' attention riveted on you.

   Some speakers identify three audience members—one to the left, one in the middle, and one to the right—and make sure they regularly move from one to the other of them. For those who don't have trouble moving from side to side, another technique is to do the same thing from front to back, especially if the audience isn't too big. Making sure that you are achieving even momentary eye contact with specific listeners in different parts of the audience creates the sense of visual bonding that you want.

5. *Use your body to communicate your feelings about what you're saying.* When you're angry, don't be afraid to gesture vigorously. When you're expressing tenderness, let that message come across your relaxed face. In other words, when you communicate publicly, use the same emotional indicators as you do when you talk to individuals on a one-to-one basis.

6. *Use your body to regulate the pace of your presentation and to control transitions.* Shift your weight as your speech moves from one idea to another. Move more when you're speaking more rapidly. Reduce bodily action and gestures accordingly when you're slowing down to emphasize particular ideas.

7. *Finally, use your full repertoire of gestures while talking publicly.* You probably do this in everyday conversation without even thinking about it; recreate that behavior when addressing an audience. Physical readiness is the key. Keep your hands and arms free and loose so that you can call them into action easily, quickly, and naturally. Let your hands rest comfortably at your sides, relaxed but ready. Then, as you unfold the ideas of your speech, use descriptive gestures to indicate size, shape, or relationships, making sure the movements are large enough to be seen in the back row. Use conventional gestures also to give visual dimension to your spoken ideas. Keep in mind that there is no right number of gestures to use. However, as you practice, think of the kinds of bodily and gestural actions that complement your message and purpose.

To see someone who adapted his nonverbal behavior to the requirements of the situation, secure a videotape of the second—the so-called Richmond— presidential debate of 1992, which included President George Bush and candidates H. Ross Perot and Bill Clinton. Watch Clinton in particular: he physically moved in on his audience when making his most important and personal points; his gestures were larger when he was seated on a stool than when he was wading into the audience; he visually took in the whole audience and focused intently on the people who asked him questions; his feelings were reflected in his stance; he shifted body positions to indicate shifts in topics. Through much of the 1992 campaign, and in the Richmond debate particularly, President Clinton demonstrated near-perfect coordination of the verbal and nonverbal channels of oral communication.

Using your voice and body as the actual instruments of communication—as the vehicles that inject mere ideas with the presence and emotions of actual human beings—will significantly enhance your chances for gaining audience support of those ideas. With practice, the vocal adjustments that now sound strange to your ears and the physical movements that feel a bit awkward will become second nature to you. You may not move with the grace of a ballerina, but everyone can learn to visualize and vocalize important dimensions of meaning in public speaking situations.

You live in a society that prizes great sound and great pictures—digitized audio and video experiences. Keep telling yourself that even more powerful than digitized reproduction is the compelling presence of a living, breathing human being. That's you behind the lectern. Unleash your vocal-visual potential for energized public talk.

CHAPTER SUMMARY

Speakers must learn to maximize the advantage of their face-to-face presence in oral communication, in part by understanding that oral communication processes are at their best when talk is *aggregative, agonistic,* and *situational*—that is, completely adapted to the particular time and place in which it is occurring. Speakers must learn to control their speaking voices and their physical behavior. A flexible speaking voice has *intelligibility, variety,* and understandable *stress* patterns. *Volume, rate, enunciation,* and *pronunciation* affect intelligibility, as do *dialects.* Changes in *rate, pitch, stress,* and *pause* patterns create variety in your presentations. *Emotional characterizers* communicate subtle shades of meaning to listeners. Regarding nonverbal (physical or bodily) communication, three generalizations are significant:

- Speakers reveal and reflect their emotional states through their nonverbal behaviors.
- Nonverbal cues enrich or elaborate the speaker's message.
- Nonverbal messages form bonds between speaker and listener.

Speakers knowledgeable about *proxemics* can use space to create physical and psychological distance or intimacy. A speaker's *movement and posture* can regulate thought and feeling states. *Facial displays* communicate feelings, provide important cues to meaning, establish a visual bond with listeners, and enforce speaker credibility. *Gestures* enhance listener reponse to ideas if they're relaxed, definite, and well timed. Speakers commonly use *conventional gestures, descriptive gestures,* and *indicators.* Practice is the name of the game; practice making your voice and body effective instruments of oral communication in a society that prizes good sound and good pictures.

KEY TERMS

affect displays (p. 315)
conversationality (p. 305)
dialect (p. 308)
emotional characterizers (p. 311)
emphasis (p. 310)
enunciation (p. 307)
gestures (p. 316)
intelligibility (p. 305)
kairos (p.304)
movement (p. 314)
nonverbal communication (p. 312)

optimum pitch level (p. 310)
pitch (p. 310)
pitch variation (p. 310)
posture (p. 314)
proxemics (p. 313)
rate (p. 306)
speech delivery (p. 303)
stress (p. 310)
variety (p. 308)
volume (p 306)

ASSESSMENT ACTIVITIES

1. Divide the class into teams and play charades. (For rules, see David Jauner, "Charades as a Teaching Device," *Communication Education* 20 (1971): 302.) A game of charades not only will loosen you up psychologically but should help sensitize everyone to the variety of small but perceptible cues you read when interpreting messages. Talk about those cues at the end of the game.

2. Select a poem and read it aloud. As you read, change your volume, rate, pitch, and emphasis, and use pauses. Practice reading the poem in several ways to heighten different emotions or to emphasize alternative interpretations. Record three or four readings and play them back for evaluation. Write a paragraph on each reading—describing the sound of your voice, emotional texture—and turn them in along with the tape.

REFERENCES

1. See especially Chapter 3 on the psychodynamics of sound in Walter J. Ong, *Orality and Literacy: The Technologizing of the Word* (London: Methuen, 1982).
2. Harold M. Zullow, "American Exceptionalism and the Quadrennial Peak in Optimism," in *Presidential Campaigns and American Self Images,* eds. Arthur H. Miller and Bruce E. Gronbeck (Boulder, CO: Westview Press, 1994), 214–230.
3. Thomas Frentz, "Rhetorical Conversation, Time, and Moral Action," *Quarterly Journal of Speech* 71 (1985): 1–18.
4. Mark Knapp, *Essentials of Nonverbal Communication* (New York: Holt, Rinehart and Winston, 1980).

5. Klaus R. Scherer, H. London, and Garret Wolf, "The Voice of Competence: Paralinguistic Cues and Audience Evaluation," *Journal of Research in Personality* 7 (1973): 31-44; Jitendra Thakerer and Howard Giles, "They Are—So They Spoke: Noncontent Speech Stereotypes," *Language and Communication* 1 (1981): 255–261; Peter A. Andersen, Myron W. Lustig, and Janis F. Andersen, "Regional Patterns of Communication in the United States: A Theoretical Perspective," *Communication Monographs* 54 (1987): 128–144.

6. Bruce L. Brown, William J. Strong, and Alvin C. Rencher, "Perceptions of Personality from Speech: Effects of Manipulations of Acoustical Parameters," *Journal of the Acoustical Society of America* 54 (1973): 29–35.

7. Chris Jenks, "The Centrality of the Eye in Western Culture," in *Visual Culture*, ed. Chris Jenks (New York: Routledge, 1995), 1.

8. Much of the foundational research is summarized in Mark L. Knapp, *Nonverbal Communication in Human Interaction*, 2nd ed. (New York: Holt, Rinehart and Winston, 1978).

9. Dale G. Leathers, *Nonverbal Communication Systems* (Boston: Allyn and Bacon, 1975), 4–5.

10. For a fuller discussion, see Leathers, 52–59.

11. Edward T. Hall, *The Hidden Dimension* (New York: Doubleday, 1969). The important matter here is not the exact distance, of course, but the idea that speakers must vary multiple aspects of their physical and vocal behavior as distances between them and their audiences grow.

12. Paul Ekman, *Emotion in the Human Face,* 2nd ed. (Cambridge, England.: Cambridge University Press, 1982).

13. Robert Rivlin and Karen Gravelle, *Deciphering the Senses: The Expanding World of Human Perception* (New York: Simon and Schuster, 1984), 98. Of course, such numbers are only formulaic estimates and are important only as rough proportions of each other. Even if Mehrabian is off by a considerable margin, his basic point—that voice and face are the primary vehicles for emotionally bonding speakers and their audiences—is indisputable.

14. For a more complete system of classifying gestures, see Paul Ekman and Wallace V. Friesen, "Hand Movements," *Journal of Communication* 22 (1972): 360.

Part Four
TYPES

All the ends of speaking are
reducible to four; every speech
being intended to enlighten the
understanding, to please the
imagination, to move the
passion, or to influence the will.
Any one discourse admits only
one of these ends as the
principle.

George Campbell
The Philosophy of Rhetoric (1776)

CHAPTER
13
$\mathscr{S}$PEECHES TO INFORM

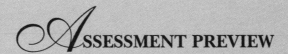

$\mathscr{A}$SSESSMENT PREVIEW

After reading Chapter 13, the student with basic communication competencies will be able to

- distinguish among the specific purposes of definitional speeches, instructional and demonstration speeches, oral briefings, and explanatory speeches.
- use at least a topical organizational pattern for informative speeches.
- employ at least one technique for making an informative speech topic relevant to the audience.
- employ at least one technique for achieving clarity through word choice.
- employ at least one technique of visualization.

The student with average communication competencies will also be able to

- make at least one association between new ideas and old ones.
- use two or three techniques for making the speech relevant, clear, and effectively visual.
- select organizational patterns besides topical patterns and specify why a particular pattern is being used on a particular occasion and for a particular audience.
- coordinate vocal patterns and bodily movements with informative language so as to help an audience see transitions, activities, and dimensions of the topic.

The student with superior communication competencies will also be able to

- employ mnemonic or other linguistic devices for helping listeners see how the points of a speech are structured.
- employ multiple techniques for achieving clarity through organization and word choice, association of new ideas with old ones and relevant visualizations.
- regularly build into a speech motivational appeals that gain and then sustain an audience's engagement with a speaker.
- engage an audience to such a level that all of the main ideas and most of the primary pieces of evidence and information are remembered by listeners.

A student, Ben, came in one day to ask his instructor how he could make an informative speech about the Vietnam War and its impacts on American life relevant to his listeners. "All that interests my classmates are bar hopping, sports, movies, dances, and television," he said. "Well, that's the key, Ben," said the instructor. "Bar hopping?" "No, the mass media! Think of all the television programs and films that have focused on Vietnam. For movies, we've had Coming Home, Apocalypse Now, The Deer Hunter, Full Metal Jacket, Platoon, Born on the Fourth of July, Heaven and Earth, The Killing Fields, *and all of the Rambo movies. On television we've had docudramas such as HBO's* "Vietnam War Stories"; *on PBS,* "Vietnam: The Documentary"; *on prime time television such series as* Magnum P.I., Hill Street Blues, Tour of Duty, *and* China Beach. *And there's more! Use these movies and TV programs as ways to reach your audience."*

Reaching your audience, as we've been saying throughout this book, is the bottom line. You can talk until the sun sets and then keep talking well into the night, but if you don't "reach your audience," you can forget it. Your listeners are aswarm in facts and information. You've got to find ways to grab them by the scruff of their psychic necks and the seat of their psychic pants, get them to sit up and take note, and then package facts and ideas in ways that they can understand and remember. That's what informative speaking is all about

First, we'll talk a bit about information and the processes whereby "facts" become usable human "knowledge." That will lead into a discussion of the essential features of informative speeches. We can then examine four types of speeches and deal with the ways of building them so as to maximize your chances for success.

FACTS, KNOWLEDGE, AND THE INFORMATION AGE

Our society seems to worship facts. A staggering amount of information is available to us, particularly because of such technologies as electronic media, photostatic printing, miniaturized circuitry, fax machines, and digitized data storage and retrieval sysems. Jumping onto Compuserve, Wow!, America Online, or your school's access to the World Wide Web puts you on an information highway with more and bigger lanes than the Santa Monica Freeway. The entire Indiana University library is available online, as are major collections of data from around the world. Detective Joe Friday from the old *Dragnet* television series would never dare say "Just the facts, Ma'am," today, for he'd immediately drown in data.

Furthermore, as Joe Friday knew, mere facts are not enough. Until he put those facts into a coherent order that turned them into elements of a scenario, a story of a crime, he had nothing but isolated factoids. Only after that information was patterned and hooked in cause-effect chains, and only after those chains were contextualized into the lives of particular people did the facts produce the story of crimes. Joe Friday had to not only gather the facts but

TABLE 13.1   Women on Active Duty in the American Armed Services[1]

Year	Percentage Women
1973	2.5
1975	4.6
1981	8.9
1983	9.3
1987	10.2
1992	11.5

humanize them—that is, use them to probe motivations, plausible human activities, and matters of opportunity and access to the means of crime. Without clarification, interpretation, and structuration, information is all but useless.

Information must be turned by competent speakers into knowledge. Think of **facts** as statements about the world upon which two or more people agree; "Gronbeck's house is forty-four feet long" is a fact, one that could be verified by some folks taking a tape measure to it. **Information** is a collection of facts associated with some topic. Consider the information shown in Table 13.1. There you have it: a collection of information. But to turn this into human **knowledge**—into information given human significance—you have to interpret and even extend it, perhaps, with additional facts: women were admitted to all of the military service academies in 1976. In 1993, the Department of Defense dropped most of its restrictions on women participating in aerial and naval combat, and, in that same year, the Clinton administration asked Congress to repeal the law barring women from serving on warships and ordered the services to justify their lists of all remaining jobs from which women were barred. Now you have information that you can turn into some knowledge claims: discussions of why the number and percentage of women in the armed forces has increased, the growing availabililty of military jobs (outside of medical and secretarial positions) for women, and the political dynamics of these processes. With some work, this information can be put into its human contexts that make it knowledge—in this case, knowledge about gender and military service.

And that's what informative speaking is about: turning facts into information and then information into knowledge. The challenge to all of us is to round up and bridle important parts of the information swirling around our environment, packaging it for human use and consumption.

ESSENTIAL FEATURES OF INFORMATIVE SPEECHES

Your goal as an informative speaker is to make it easy for your listeners to acquire and retain new information. There are five things you can do to help ensure that your listeners understand and remember what you say: You should strive for (1) clarity, (2) the association of ideas with familiar ones, (3) the effective packaging or clustering of ideas, (4) motivational appeals, and

(5) relevant visualizations; ultimately, you should communicate the sense that what you're saying is directly relevant to the lives of your listeners.

Clarity

Informative speeches achieve maximum clarity when listeners can follow and understand what you're saying. Clarity is largely the result of two factors: effective organization and word choice:

Effective Organization

Limit Your Points.   Confine your speech to three or four principal ideas, grouping whatever facts or ideas you wish to consider under these main headings. Even if you know a tremendous amount about your subject matter, remember that you can't make everyone an expert with a single speech.

Use Transitions to Show Relationships Among Ideas.   Word your transitions carefully. Make sure to indicate the relationship of the upcoming point to the rest of your ideas. You might say, "Second, you must prepare the chair for caning by cleaning out the groove and cane holes"; "The Stamp Act Crisis was followed by an even more important event—The Townshend Duties"; "To test these hypotheses, we set up the following experiment." Such transitions allow listeners to follow you from point to point.

Keep Your Speech Moving Forward.   Rather than jumping back and forth between ideas, charging ahead, and then backtracking, develop a positive forward direction. Move from basic ideas to more complex ones, from background data to current research, or from historical incidents to current events.

Word Choice.   The second factor in achieving clarity is being understood. You can develop understanding through careful selection of your words. For a fuller development of the use of language, see Chapter 10. For now, think about the following ways to achieve clarity.

Keep Your Vocabulary Precise, Accurate—Not Too Technical.   In telling someone how to finish off a basement room, you might be tempted to say, "Next, take one of these long sticks and cut it off in this funny-looking gizmo with a saw in it and try to make the corners match." An accurate vocabulary will help your listeners remember what supplies and tools to get when they approach the same project: "This is a ceiling molding; it goes around the room between the wall and the ceiling to cover the seams between the paneling and the ceiling tiles. You make the corners of the molding match by using a mitre box, which has grooves that allow you to cut 45-degree angles. Here's how you do it."

Simplify When Possible.   If your speech on the operation of a two-cycle internal combustion engine sounds like it came out of the documentation for computer software, then it's too technical. An audience bogged down in unnecessary detail and complex vocabulary can become confused and bored. Include only as much technical vocabulary as you need.

FIGURE 13.1   Association of New Ideas with Familiar Ones

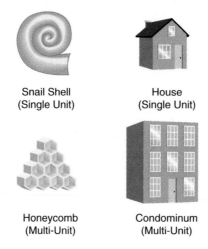

Snail Shell
(Single Unit)

House
(Single Unit)

Honeycomb
(Multi-Unit)

Condominum
(Multi-Unit)

Use Reiteration to Clarify Complex Ideas.   Rephrasing helps to solidify ideas for those who didn't get them the first time. You might say, for example, "Unlike a terrestrial telescope, a celestial telescope is used for looking at moons, planets, and stars; that is, its mirrors and lens are ground and arranged in such a way that it focuses on objects thousands of miles—not hundreds of feet—away from the observer." In this case, the idea is rephrased; the words aren't simply repeated.

Associating New Ideas with Familiar Ones

Audiences grasp new facts and ideas more readily when they can associate them with what they already know. In a speech to inform, try to connect the new with the old (see Figure 13.1). To do this, you need to know enough about your audience to choose relevant experiences, images, analogies, and metaphors to use in your speech.

Sometimes the associations you ought to make are obvious. A college dean talking to an audience of manufacturers on the problems of higher education presented his ideas under the headings of raw material, casting, machining, polishing, and assembling. He translated his central ideas into an analogy that his audience, given their vocations, would understand. If you cannot think of any obvious associations, you may have to rely on common experiences or images. For instance, you might explain the operation of the pupil in a human eye by comparing it to the operation of a camera lens aperture; you could explain a cryogenic storage tank by comparing it to a thermos bottle.

Clustering Ideas

You can help listeners make sense out of your speech by providing them with a well-organized package of tightly clustered ideas. Research on memory and organization has demonstrated that the "magic number" of items we can

How to
Use Psychological Principles for Clarity

Clustering items of information is often useful for speakers because it makes information much easier for listeners to grasp and retain. Psychologists throughout this century have been interested in discovering why things appear the way they do to us. Four principles of perception and cognition are still current in the literature:

1. *Proximity* suggests that elements close together seem to organize into units of perception; you see pairs made up of a ball and a block, not sets of blocks and sets of balls.

2. *Similarity* suggests that like objects are usually grouped together; you see three columns rather than three rows of items.

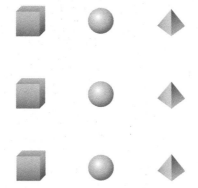

remember is seven, plus or minus two; more recent research has suggested that the number is probably five, again plus or minus two.[2] This research suggests that you ought to group items of information under three, five, or seven headings or in three, five, or seven clusters. You might, for example, organize a lecture on the history of the Vietnam War into three clusters—the 1950s, the 1960s, and the 1970s—rather than breaking it down year by year. College registration may be presented to freshmen as a five-step process: (1) secure registration materials, (2) review course offerings, (3) see an advisor, (4) fill out the

3. *Closure* is the tendency to complete suggested shapes; you see the figure of a tiger even though the lines are not joined.

4. *Symmetry* suggests that balanced objects are more pleasing to perceive than unbalanced ones.

These four principles suggest ways in which you can cluster ideas in your speeches: (1) Put your most important ideas close together so they can play off each other; (2) construct your main points in similar ways grammatically to make the structure stand out; (3) offer enough typical examples to allow for closure; and (4) balance your treatments of the main ideas to give a sense of symmetry—for example, use parallel sentences.

These principles can help you organize your speeches to take advantage of your listeners' natural perceptions.

References

For more information, see John R. Anderson, *Cognitive Psychology and Its Implications* (New York: W. H. Freeman, 1980), 53–56; Ronald H. Forgus and Lawrence E. Melamed, *Perception: A Cognitive-Stage Approach*, 2nd ed. (New York: McGraw-Hill, 1976), 177–182; and Michael Kobovy and James R. Pomerantz, eds., *Perceptual Organization* (Hillsdale, NJ: Lawrence Erlbaum Associates, 1980).

registration materials, and (5) enter the information into the computer. The American Cancer Society has organized the most common symptoms of cancer into seven categories to help you remember them.

Mnemonic devices in your outline also can provide memory triggers. CPR instructors teach the ABC of cardiopulmonary resuscitation: (a) clear the airwaves, (b) check the breathing, and (c) initiate chest compressions. A speaker giving a talk on the Great Lakes can show listeners how to remember the names of the lakes by thinking of HOMES: Huron, Ontario, Michigan, Erie, and Superior. These memory devices will also help you to remember the main points in your outline. Information forgotten is information lost; package your data and ideas in memorable clusters.

Motivating Your Audience

Fourth, you must be able to motivate your audience to listen. Unfortunately, many of us ignore this essential feature of good informative speeches. We blithely assume that because we are interested in something, our audience will also want to hear about it. You may be fascinated by collecting American commemorative stamps, but your listeners may yawn through your entire speech unless you motivate them. You need to give them a reason to listen. To get them enthused, you might explain how stamps reflect our heritage or you might tell them how competitions are held for stamp art.

Keep in mind what we've said about attention in Chapter 3. You can use the factors of attention to engage the members of your audience and to draw them into your speech.

Relevant Visualizations

Perhaps the bottom line when thinking of presenting information to others is the matter of relevance: Unless you find some way to make the information relevant to the needs, interests, anxieties, areas of known ignorance, or material conditions of people in your audience, they'll ignore you. You can't be clear unless you know what they already know; you can't associate new ideas with familiar ones if you don't know what's familiar to them; clustering ideas works only if the scheme you choose piques their interests; and motivational appeals are nothing without knowledge about motivational triggers of others—you've got to know what sets them off.

In the example that opened this chapter, what Ben was searching for was a way to make the Vietnam War relevant to a group of people born after it was over. The instructor's talk about movies and television shows was an attempt to make the war relevant to those people by calling up known **visualizations** of the war. Think back to the discussion of language in Chapter 10—to metaphor, imagery, and ostensive definitions. To visualize information is to depict its place in someone's life. For Ben's audience, the Vietnam war lived only in the mass media, where it could be seen by them. In seeking to make information relevant to audiences, you're going to have to draw them some word pictures, such as the following:

- "Picture this: You're walking down the street in Collegeville, enjoying a sunny afternoon, when you come across a man who looks desperate, and says "Ca-oo-elp-mee-plee-plee-ahm-hafin', ahm-ahm-ahm-hafin'." What do you do? Is this person drunk? Crazy? Sick? In diabetic shock? Having a heart attack? Or maybe just someone participating in a psych experiment? How are you going to handle this situation? Well, in my speech today, I'm going to tell you how to handle it. Today, I want to talk to you about. . . ."

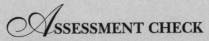

ASSESSMENT CHECK

After you outline your next speech, check it to make sure your audience will understand and remember the information. Ask yourself these questions:

- Have I related new concepts to ones my audience already knows?
- Have I organized all the information I gathered into three, five, or seven main groupings? Have I provided transitions among major points?
- Have I helped my audience visualize information so they will understand its relevance to them?
- Have I chosen words that are both precise and easy to grasp?

After you give your speech, evaluate the effect of any changes you made.

- "The initial attack on the destroyer Maddox, on August 2, was repeated today by a number of hostile vessels attacking two U.S. destroyers with torpedoes. The destroyers and supporting aircraft acted at once on the orders I gave after the initial act of aggression. We believe at least two of the attacking boats were sunk. . . . Air action is now in execution against gunboats. . . ."[3]

In the first example, the speaker tries to depict a familiar locale and a plausible event in that locale, so as to set up a speech on the new kinds of first-aid training currently offered to students at her school. In the second example, President Lyndon Johnson not only presents some facts about events in the Gulf of Tonkin in 1964, but goes on to use language—"unprovoked attack," the need to take "all necessary measures" to "prevent further aggression"— that tries to make those events relevant to Americans and their understanding of the Far East hostilities by clothing the facts in a vivid political story. Verbal depiction or visualization is a classic yet contemporary strategy for making information and viewpoints relevant to listeners' lives.[4]

TYPES OF INFORMATIVE SPEECHES

Now that we've looked at some of the essential features of competently executed informative speeches, we should examine some of the types of informative speeches you'll be asked to make during your lifetime. There are many different types of speech forms into which information is put, depending upon the situation and the level of knowledge possessed by listeners. Four of those forms—definitional speeches, instructional and demonstration speeches, oral briefings, and explanatory speeches—occur so frequently, however, that they merit our attention. They represent four different yet common ways in which people package or integrate information to meet the needs of others.

Definitional Speeches

"Dad, what's a 'latchkey kid'?" "Professor Delgado, what are the differences between copper wire phone connections, ISDN phone connections, and coaxial cable connections so far as modem operations are concerned?" "Now Jayne, I know this is a dumb question, but what's a 'dual-agency realtor' and what's in it for me?" You've been asking questions like this all of your life. A dictionary definition just doesn't help. A **definitional speech** seeks to present concepts or processes in ways that make them relevant to listeners. Once Sarina knows what a latchkey kid is, she'll understand what she's been called and will want to know whether that's good or bad. Once you know about different modem- computer connections, you'll be able to assess how much it's worth to you to pay for faster data transmission. Once you understand that Jayne's able to serve both you and a seller better if she's a dual-agency realtor, you'll know how to approach an offer you want to put in on a house.

Definitional speeches demand that you present ideas clearly and coherently, which means that the ways in which you structure them are very important.

Introduction. Because definitional speeches treat either unfamiliar or familiar concepts in a new light, their introductions must create curiosity and establish need in listeners. Creating curiosity is a special challenge in speeches on unfamiliar concepts since we're all tempted to say, "Well, if I've made it this far in life without knowing anything about black holes or carcinogens or trap blocking, why should I bother with learning more about these ideas now?" You need to make people wonder about the unknown. Use new information to attract attention and arouse curiosity.

Definitional speeches must also be attentive to the needs or wants of the audience. In other words, their introductions should include explicit statements that indicate how the information can affect the listeners, such as, "Understanding the dynamics of trap blocking will help you better appreciate line play in football and thereby increase your enjoyment of the game every Saturday afternoon in our stadium."

Body. Most definitional speeches use a topical pattern because such speeches usually describe various aspects of an object or idea. It seems natural, for example, to use a topical pattern for a speech on computer programming careers, organizing the body of the speech around such topics as "the duties of a computer programmer," "skills needed by a computer programmer," and "training you will need to become a computer programmer."

There are occasions when other patterns may serve your specific purpose even better than topical patterns. You might use an effect-cause pattern, for example, when preparing an informative speech on the laws of supply and demand. You could enumerate a series of effects with which people are already familiar—changing prices at the gas pumps—and then discuss the laws of supply and demand that account for such changes.

Informative speeches take many forms. A definitional speech presents concepts or processes in ways that make them relevant to listeners. An instructional speech explains a complex process verbally, and a demonstration adds a nonverbal illustration of such a process. A speaker giving an oral briefing assembles, arranges, and interprets information in response to a group's request. In an explanatory speech, the speaker clarifies the connections among concepts, processes, or events.

Conclusion. Conclusions for definitional speeches have two characteristics: (1) they usually include a summary of the main points, and (2) they often stress the ways in which people can apply the ideas that have been presented. For example, the speaker discussing diabetes could conclude by offering listeners the titles of books containing more information, the phone number of the American Diabetes Association, the address of a local clinic, or the meeting time and place of a diabetics' support group.

A speech defining diabetes could be outlined in a topical pattern as in the following sample outline.

Notice several features of this speech:

1. The speaker attempts early to engage listeners' curiosity and review listeners' personal needs to draw the audience into the topic. The use of a personal example is particularly good for this kind of speech.
2. The speaker offers statistics on diabetes early so that the audience knows that the disease is widespread and serious.
3. Three topics are previewed, then developed in the body of the speech to engage three aspects of listeners' thinking.
4. After offering a summary of the central idea, the speaker returns to the personal example, adding closure to the speech.

𝒮AMPLE OUTLINE FOR A DEFINITIONAL SPEECH

WHAT IS DIABETES?

Introduction

The speaker uses a vividly developed personal example to gain attention.
The scope of the problem is explained.
A motivation for listening is provided.

I. I never knew my grandmother. She was a talented artist; she raised six kids without all the modern conveniences like microwave ovens and electric clothes dryers; and my dad still talks about the time she foiled a would-be burglar by locking him in a broom closet until the police came. My grandmother had diabetes. It finally took her life. Now my sister has it. So do 13 million other Americans.

II. Diabetes threatens millions of lives, and it's one of nature's stealthiest diseases.

Supporting testimony shows the severity of the disease. Listeners are warned that ignorance of the disease makes the problem worse. The scope of the problem is expanded by pointing out that other medical conditions are complicated by diabetes.

III. It's important to understand this disease because, more than likely, you or someone you know will eventually have to deal with it.

   A. Diabetes is the third leading cause of death behind heart disease and cancer, according to the American Diabetes Association.

   B. Over one-third of those suffering from the disease don't even know they have it. That simple knowledge could make the difference between a happy productive life and an early death.

C. Furthermore, diabetes is implicated in many other medical problems: it contributes to coronary heart disease; it accounts for 40 percent of all amputations and most cases of new blindness.

The three main ideas of the speech are previewed.

The first main point is stated.

D. In the next few minutes, let's look at three things you should know about "the silent killer," diabetes—what it is, how it affects people, and how it can be controlled.

Body

I. What diabetes is.

Diabetes is defined in medical terms.

The symptoms of diabetes are explained.

A. Diabetes is a chronic disease of the endocrine system that affects your body's ability to deliver glucose to its cells.

B. The symptoms of diabetes, according to Dr. Charles Kilo, are weight loss in spite of eating and drinking, constant hunger and thirst, frequent urination, and fatigue.

The second main point is provided.

II. How diabetes affects people.

A. Type I diabetes occurs when your body cannot produce insulin, a substance that delivers glucose to your cells.

Type I diabetes is operationally defined.

1. Only 5 to 10 percent of all diabetics are Type I.
2. This type, also known as juvenile diabetes, usually shows up in the first 20 years of life.

Supporting statistics show the scope of this type.

3. Type I diabetics can be passed on genetically but is also thought to be triggered by environmental agents such as viruses.
4. Type I diabetics must take insulin injections to treat the disease.

Type II diabetes is operationally defined. Notice how this section of the speech parallels the preceding section in development.

B. Type II diabetics occurs when your body produces insulin but fails to use it effectively.

1. Of all diabetes 90 to 95 percent are Type II.
2. This type usually shows up after a person turns 40.
3. It often affects people who are overweight; more women are affected than men.
4. Insulin injections are sometimes used to treat the disease.

The third main point is provided.

The treatments for Type I are explained.

III. How to control diabetes.

A. Type I diabetes cannot be cured, but it can be controlled.

1. Patients must take insulin injections, usually several times a day.

2. Patients need to monitor their blood sugar levels by pricking a finger and testing a drop of blood.
3. According to *Science News,* several new treatments are available:
   a. One new device uses near-infrared beams to determine blood sugar level.
   b. Insulin can be taken through the nose or in pill form.
   c. Pancreatic transplants have been performed with limited success.

The treatments for Type II are explained.

B. Type II diabetes can be controlled through lifestyle modifications.
   1. Usually these diabetics are required to lose weight by exercising, according to Dr. JoAnn Manson.
   2. Changes in diet are also required.
   3. Some people take oral hypoglycemic medications that stimulate the release of insulin and foster insulin activity.
   4. If these modifications fail, Type II diabetics must take insulin injections.

Conclusion

I. Diabetes is a serious disease in which the body can no longer produce or use insulin effectively.
II. The two types of diabetes occur at different stages in life and require different measures for control of the disease.

Listeners are reminded of the definition of diabetes.
The three main ideas of the speech are reiterated.
The speech reaches closure by referring to the introductory personal example.
Listeners are warned that diabetes could affect them.

III. My grandmother lived with her diabetes for years but eventually lost her life to it. My sister has the advantages of new treatments and future research in her fight with diabetes.
IV. As we age, many of us will be among the 600,000 new diabetics each year. Through awareness, we can cope effectively with this silent killer.[5]

Instructional and Demonstration Speeches

"THIS IS NOT YOUR REAL LIFE; IF IT WERE YOU WOULD HAVE BEEN GIVEN BETTER INSTRUCTIONS." That sign testifies to the importance of instructions in daily life. You're bombarded by instructions in the classroom, at work, when purchasing or assembling a new product. Sometimes, the instructions are complicated enough so that you have to be shown: how a food processer works, what you need to do in lab to isolate oxygen, how to install a water filtration system on your cold-water pipes. An **instructional speech** offers a verbal explanation of a complex process; a **demonstration speech** goes further by providing a visual dimension, illustrating the actual product or process for the audience. To help with clarity and concreteness, both can use visual aids—pictures, graphs, charts, overheads, and the rest.

Flip through your television channels and you'll come across cooking demonstrations, home-improvement shows, sewing instructions, and painting lessons. Each presents the steps required to complete a project. Like successful television shows, your overall strategy with instructions and demonstrations should be to break down a process or procedure into a series of steps. Each step should be easy to understand and to visualize.

Introduction.   In some speaking situations, such as presentations in speech communication classrooms, listener attendance may not be voluntary. On these occasions, you'll have to pay attention to motivational matters. If your audience has invited you to speak or is attending your talk voluntarily, you can assume listener interest. When giving instructions or offering a demonstration, you'll usually need to spend only a little time generating curiosity or motivating people to listen. After all, if you're instructing listeners in a new office procedure or giving a workshop on how to build an ice boat, they already have the prerequisite interest and motivation; otherwise they wouldn't have come. When your audience is already motivated to listen, you can concentrate your introduction on two other tasks.

1. *Preview your speech.* If you're going to take your listeners through the steps involved in making a good tombstone rubbing, give them an overall picture of the process before you start detailing each operation.
2. *Encourage listeners to follow along.* Even through some of the steps may be difficult, urge everyone to listen. A process such as tombstone rubbing, for example, looks easier than it is: many people are tempted to quit listening and give up somewhere along the way. If, however, you forewarn them and promise them special help with the difficult techniques, they will be more likely to bear with you.

Body.   As we suggested earlier, most speeches of demonstration and instruction follow a natural chronological or spatial pattern. Consequently, you usually will have little trouble organizing the body of a speech of demonstration or instruction. Your problems are more likely to be technical and may include the following:

1. *The problem of rate.* If the glue on a project needs to set before you can go on to the next step, what do you do? You can't just stand there and wait for it to dry. Instead, you could have a second object, already dried, ready for the next step. You also need to preplan some material for filling the time—perhaps additional background or a brief discussion of what problems can arise at this stage. Preplan your remarks carefully for those junctures so you can maintain your audience's attention.

2. *The problem of scale.* How can you show various embroidery stitches to an audience of 25? When dealing with minute operations, you often must increase the scale of operation. In this example, you could use a large piece of poster board or even a 3- by 4-foot piece of cloth stretched over a wooden frame. By using an oversized needle, yarn instead of thread, and stitches measured in inches instead of millimeters, you could easily make your techniques visible to all audience members. At the other extreme, in a speech on how to make a home-made solar heat collector, you should work with a scaled-down model.

3. *The coordination of verbal and visual methods.* Both instructions and demonstrations usually demand that speakers "show" while "telling." To keep yourself from becoming flustered or confused, be sure to practice *doing* while *talking*—demonstrating your material while explaining aloud what you're doing. Decide where you'll stand when showing a slide so that the audience can see both you and the image; practice talking about your aerobic exercise positions while you're actually doing them; work a dough press in practice sessions as you tell your mythical audience how to form professional-looking cookies. If you don't, you'll inevitably get yourself into trouble in front of your real audience.

Conclusion. Conclusions for demonstration speeches usually have three parts:

1. *Summary.* Most audiences need this review, which reminds them to question procedures or ideas they don't understand.

2. *Encouragement.* People trying new processes or procedures usually get in trouble the first few times and need to be reassured that such trouble is predictable and can be overcome.

3. *Offer to help.* What sounded so simple in your talk may be much more complicated in execution. If possible, make yourself available for assistance: "As you fill out your registration form, just raise your hand if you're unsure of anything and I'll be happy to help you." Or point to other sources of further information and assistance: "Here's the address of the U.S. Government Printing Office, whose pamphlet X1234 is available for only a dollar; it will give you more details"; "If you run into a filing problem I haven't covered in this short orientation to your job, just go over to Mary McFerson's desk, right over here. Mary's experienced in these matters and is always willing to help." Such statements not only offer help but assure your listeners that they won't be labeled as dim-witted if they actually have to ask for it.

Thinking through requirements of instructional and demonstration speeches might result in a speaking outline like the following one.

$\mathscr{S}$AMPLE OUTLINE FOR A DEMONSTRATION SPEECH
HOW TO PLANT TOMATOES

Introduction

Listeners' interest is aroused by using questions and gustatory imagery.

I. Have you ever picked a luscious red tomato from the vine and bitten into it? Can you imagine the taste—juicy and sweet? What if I told you that you could have your very own tomatoes anytime you wanted them? And at a fraction of the cost of store-bought tomatoes?

Four steps for growing tomatoes are previewed.

II. Well, you can. With a little time and patience, you can grow your very own delicious tomatoes. In four easy steps, you can have your own tomatoes ready to eat in 65 days. Here's how.

Body

The first step is stated and a chart is displayed, showing varieties of tomatoes in columns along with their characteristics.
Soil requirements are developed. Notice how parallel development of characteristics rounds out this section of the speech.

I. First, you must select a variety of tomato seed that's suited to various geographical, climatological, agricultural, and personal factors.
   A. Some tomatoes grow better in hard soils; some in loose soils.
   B. Some varieties handle shade well; some need direct sunlight.
   C. Some are well suited to short growing seasons; others to long seasons.
   D. Each variety tends to resist certain diseases, such as blight, better than others.

The second step is stated.
Explanation of mixture is provided, and mixture is prepared, indicating proportions.
Germination trays are filled.
Half-grown and fully grown seedlings are brought out to demonstrate growth.
Technique of thinning seedlings is demonstrated.
Six-inch plants are shown.
Plants of different strengths are shown.

II. Once you have selected a variety (or maybe even two, so that they mature at different times), you must start the seeds.
   A. Prepare a mixture of black dirt, peat moss, and vermiculite as I am doing.
   B. Fill germination trays, pots, or cut-off milk cartons with the germination soil, and insert seeds.
   C. With water, sunlight, and patience, your plants will grow. I can't show you that growth here today, but I can use these seedlings to illustrate their care along the way.
      1. When the seedlings are about an inch or two tall, thin them.
      2. At about 6 inches [show them], you can transplant them safely.

3. But, you'll know more about which plants are strong if you wait until they are 10 to 12 inches tall.

The third step is stated.
Unpotting of seedlings is demonstrated.
Enlarged drawing that illustrates proper hole preparation and spacing of plants is shown.
Packing soil is demonstrated.
Amount of water per plant is shown.

III. Now you are ready to transplant the seedlings to your garden.
    A. Carefully unpot the seedlings, being sure not to damage the root network.
    B. Put each seedling in an already-prepared hole in your plot; this diagram shows you how to do that.
    C. Pack the garden soil firmly but not so hard as to crush the roots.
    D. Water it almost every day for the first week.
    E. Put some sort of mulching material—grass clippings, hay, black sheets of plastic—between the rows if weeds are a problem.

Sketches of various styles of cages are shown.

IV. Once you know that your plants are growing, cage or stake each plant.

Conclusion

The four steps of the process are summarized.

I. Growing tomatoes is a four-step process. First, you select the appropriate variety for your needs; next, you start the seeds in a special soil mixture; then, you transplant the seedlings; and, finally, you stake the plants.

The speaker's personal testimony is provided.

II. I used to settle for tough, dry, over-priced tomatoes in the supermarket until I discovered that I could grow them myself.

A final offer is made for the audience to sample garden tomatoes.

III. You can too! If my simple four-step process isn't enough to convince you, stop by my garden and pick a vine-ripened tomato. You'll never settle for less again.

Oral Briefings

An **oral briefing** is a speech that assembles, arranges, and interprets information gathered in response to a request from a particular group. Briefings may be designed to bring listeners up-to-date on the status of a project or new product, to preview or propose new initiatives for a group, or to orient audiences to the values and customs of others, as when a sales representative is prepared to work for forty-five days in the Thailand market.

Depending on the situation, the briefing can be *general* or highly *specific and technical*. So, an adviser may give a new student a general briefing about general education requirements without going into a lot of detail on particular courses. But, if you're speaking as one engineer to other engineers, listeners will expect more technical information. In this case, you'll need to be concerned with precise, subdivided numbers and a discussion of their implications: What do these data mean?[6] Whether you're working with general or technical briefings, however, you always must find a way to make your subject matter concrete and meaningful to your listeners.

Briefings are either *factual* or *advisory*. The factual briefing features the assembling, arranging, and interpreting of raw information, while the advisory briefing goes beyond that to make recommendations: What should be done as a result of the information?

Briefing audiences requires that you consider your role as an *expert*—as the source of predigested information for a group of people who, in turn, will act on what you have to say. That role carries with it the obligation to prepare with special care and the necessity to present ideas with clarity and balance. The success of a business, the government's legislative program, or a group's future may depend on your ability. Just as important, your job may depend on your ability to meet these demands. The following guidelines will be helpful in ensuring your concentration on the tasks at hand.

1. *The information you present must be researched with great care.* Although you may be asked to present statistical generalizations in only a five-minute report, your research must be extensive and solid. The audience will expect you to have at hand the concrete data on which the generalizations are based, especially if those generalizations are controversial or seem extraordinary. A quarterly report for a business that relies on material gathered from only one of several territories not only is incomplete; the conclusions drawn may be heavily skewed, especially if the territory isn't representative of the company as a whole.

2. *When making recommendations rather than merely reporting information, be sure to include a complete rationale for the advice you present.* Suppose, for example, that as a wheelchair-bound person, you have been called on to brief your student government on the status of access for the disabled on your campus and to make recommendations on how the assembly can help make the campus more accessible.

   First, you can use your own experience in listing the problems. Second, you will need to gather additional information about the current status of access. How well has the campus met the requirements specified in the 1991 American Disabilities Act? What plans does the campus have for remedying deficiencies? Beyond physical access, what is being done to ensure transportation? Are there enough volunteers to help students who may need assistance? How aware is the campus of the needs—would it help to have a seminar or awareness day sponsored by student government? How can students help students, either as individuals or through the collective resources of an organization such as student government?

Beyond gathering information and ideas relevant to a review of the situation and possible recommendations, you should consider a rationale for what is being advised. Why is it necessary to involve student government? What difference can student government make with respect to access for the disabled? If student government were to act as recommended, what other benefits might accrue besides making life on campus better? Would there be more action from other campus officials if the students got involved? In building the rationale, you also need to consider which recommendations are the most feasible, the least costly, the most essential. In ranking the recommendations from short-term–easy-to-enact to long-term–more-difficult-to-enact, you have applied distinct criteria: the time involved (now; later) and the ease with which change can be effected (easy; difficult).

3. *Make full use of visual aids when briefing audiences.* If your speech is short and to the point, yet contains information that may be complex and new to the audience, it will be to your advantage to use visual aids.

4. *Stay within the boundaries of the charge you are given.* Whether your briefing assignment is general or technical, you're the primary source of information at that moment. Thus, being sensitive to the audience's expectations and needs is essential. What's expected of you in this situation? Were you asked to gather information only, or were you charged with the responsibility of offering recommendations? Does the audience assume that you'll emphasize information from the past, current trends, or future prospects? Are cost implications expected in assessing a proposal?

Oral briefings require more attention to structural considerations than do the other informational speeches.

Introduction.   For the most part, you won't have to motivate your audience. In most cases, they already know why you're speaking and are already interested in the *content of the report.* You can begin an oral briefing, however, by briefly *reminding* an audience of the reasons or recapping the charge you were given. You also may wish to *describe the procedures* you used to gather information—where you went for information, how you obtained specific pieces, problems encountered in meeting your charge. Third, it's essential to *forecast* the ideas or issues to be covered in the presentation, because it prepares the audience to listen. Finally, *pointing ahead to any action* they are to take as a result of the information will help audience members place your remarks in the context of their potential future behavior. Thus, the key to a good briefing introduction is *orientation*—reviewing the past (their expectations and your preparation), the present (your goal in this presentation), and the future (their responsibilities following the presentation).

Body.   The principle underlying a choice of pattern is easy to state: *use a pattern that is best suited to the topic and audience expectations*. Have you been asked to provide a history of a group or of a problem? Have you been asked to review the current status of plans for a new building or new product? Then a chronological pattern will respond to topic needs and audience expectations. Does the audience want to know why they face a present situation? A cause-effect format might be more useful than a strict chronology, as the former points more directly to actions or events that influenced the current circumstances. Have you been asked to brief the audience on the new organizational structure being proposed for your group? If so, a topical approach might be best.

$\mathscr{S}$AMPLE OUTLINE FOR AN ORAL BRIEFING

Report from the Final Examination Committee

The reporter's "charge" is reviewed.

I. My committee was asked to compare and contrast various ways of structuring a final examination in this speech class and to recommend a procedure to you.
  A. First, we interviewed each one of you.
  B. Then, we discussed the pedagogical virtues of various exam procedures with our instructor.

Orientation is completed.

  C. Next, we deliberated as a group, coming to the following conclusions.

II. At first we agreed with many students that we should recommend a take-home essay examination as the "easiest" way out.

The deliberative process is summarized.

  A. But, we decided our wonderful textbook is filled with so much detailed and scattered advice that it would be almost impossible for any of us to answer essay-type questions without many, many hours of worry, work, and sweat.

Alternatives are eliminated.

  B. We also wondered why a course that stresses oral performance should test our abilities to write essays.

III. So, we reviewed the option of a standard, short-answer, in-class final.
  A. Although such a test would allow us to concentrate on the main ideas and central vocabulary—which has been developed in lectures, readings, and discussion—it would require a fair amount of memorization.
  B. And, we came back to the notion that merely understanding communication concepts will not

be enough when we start giving speeches outside this classroom.

IV. Thus, we recommend that you urge our instructor to give us an oral examination this term.

The recommended course of action is justified.

    A. Each of us could be given an impromptu speech topic, some resource material, and ten minutes to prepare a speech.

    B. We could be graded, in this way, on both substantive and communicative decisions we make in preparing and delivering the speech.

    C. Most important, such a test would be consistent with this course's primary goal and could be completed quickly and almost painlessly.

    Conclusion. Most often, oral briefings end with a conclusion that mirrors the introduction. The purpose or reason for the presentation is recalled, the main points are reviewed, and those who participated in data collection (if the effort was not yours alone) or made it possible for you to collect data are thanked publicly. Finally, a motion to accept the report may be offered, if appropriate in the setting, or the audience may be instructed as to their next actions based on the briefing. Questions from the audience also may be invited. Conclusions to briefings are best if they are quick, firm, efficient, and pointed.

Explanatory Speeches

An **explanatory speech** has much in common with the definitional speech because both share the function of clarifying a concept, process, or event. Normally, though, an explanatory speech is less concerned with the word or vocabulary involved than with connecting one concept with a series of others. For example, a speech of definition on political corruption would concentrate on the term, telling what sorts of acts committed by politicians are included by the term. An explanatory speech on corruption would go further into the subject, perhaps indicating the social-political conditions likely to produce corruption or the methods for eliminating it. The clarification involved in an explanatory speech is considerably broader and more complex than that of a definitional speech.

    The key to most explanatory speeches is the way in which the speaker constructs a *viewpoint* or *rationale*. Suppose, for example, that you want to explain the origins of U.S. involvement in Vietnam in the 1950s. You in fact could offer several explanations from varied viewpoints, depending upon which story of that country and the war you wanted to tell, with a focus on the French stronghold in what was then called Indochina. Or, you could focus on allied support, including $3 billion from the United States, and its impact on Euro-American foreign policy. You might tell the cultural story of

Indochina, its split between Western capitalism and Catholicism in the south and eastern (Chinese) communism and Buddhism in the north, leading to a clash of lifestyles supported by superpowers with vested social interests. Or, you might focus on the equally interesting military story: the French army with American support, holding the fort at Dien Bien Phu, absolutely convinced that it was invulnerable to a peasant army, only to find itself blown out in the seige of 1954. And, of course, the political story Vietnam might also be told: the Cold War, the American involvement with the French and with SEATO—the South East Asia Treaty Organization, which committed the United States to defend east Asian countries against Communist aggression.[7]

All of these approaches are "correct," and each gives you a significant explanation about the importance of Vietnam to western (including U.S.) interests as they were perceived at the time. But, if you tried to tell them all at once, you'd confuse your listeners. Your best strategy in most explanatory speeches, therefore, is to identify the viewpoint you will take—"Let me tell you the story of American involvement in Vietnam from an economic [cultural/military/political] point of view. If we look at it in that way, we'll see that. . . ." Such a statement signals your viewpoint, recognizes that you're not trying to offer every possible explanation, and tells your listeners what to listen for. Identifying a viewpoint helps you, and your listeners, keep the story straight.

Unlike definitional speeches, explanatory speeches can become complex and difficult to organize.

Introduction.   Introductions to explanatory speeches can use many of the techniques discussed thus far. You may have to raise curiosity in some instances: How many of your classmates are really concerned about the status of child care services on campus or the current status of social security benefits? You usually have to generate a desire to listen if your topic seems distant or only remotely connected to their actual day-to-day lives. If the explanation covers complex material, previewing the main points will help the audience follow your discussion. Encouraging people to follow along, especially with difficult material, also may be appropriate; you can indicate that you'll go into greater detail as you hit complex issues or that you'll be happy to elaborate on points after the speech.

Body.   The body of most explanations fits into either causal or topical patterns of development. If you are trying to explain how or why something exists or operates as it does, either cause-effect or its reverse works well. If you're trying to explain how a problem can be solved, addressing the problem and then the solution may be the most practical structure. These two organizational patterns are well suited to explanations because explanations emphasize the interconnection of events, phenomena, or ideas.

Conclusion.   Typically, the conclusion of an explanatory speech develops additional implications or calls for particular actions. For example, if you've explained how contagious diseases spread through geographical areas, you probably should conclude by discussing some actions listeners can take to halt the process of contagion. If you have explained the concept of children's rights by using the example of a young child who divorced his mother in order to be adopted by his foster family, you can close by asking your listeners to consider what these rights mean to them—how does it change their behavior or actions toward young children?

Suppose your major is archaeology, and you decide to discuss recent controversial claims regarding how the first "humans" acted in their environment. Consider the following outline to see how some of this advice can be put to work:

𝒮AMPLE OUTLINE FOR AN EXPLANATORY SPEECH

DID EARLY HUMANS "APE THE APES"?

Introduction

Raise your listeners' curiosity.

   I. When did we first become more "human" than "animal-like" in our behavior?

Tie new knowledge to their desire.

   II. That question can't really be answered, but the search for an answer highlights important characteristics of human beings' development.

Body

Using both spatial and chronological patterns, develop an understanding of the issues. Then work with a narrative to show the sequential development of ideas.

   I. The research of Louis and Mary Leakey, and more recently their son Richard, in Tanzania, Kenya, and Ethiopia resulted in an interpretation of "man as hunter" and "woman as gatherer."

     A. The major archaeological "finds" at Olduvai Gorge in Kenya, Koobi Fora in Kenya, and Hadar in Ethiopia are marked on the wall map to my left.

     B. The initial find was at Olduvai; Louis Leakey discovered what he termed "encampments" of men and women, with scattered bones and stone implements.

        1. He named these early humans *Homo habilis* or "handy man." They also are termed "hominids" to separate them from later humans.

2. Leakey argued that the males were the hunters and women the gatherers.

C. Louis and Mary's son, Richard, discovered even earlier remains in northern Kenya, at Koobi Fora. He followed the same interpretation in arguing the remains were sites of male hunters and female gatherers.

Transition

The interpretation of the Leakeys was initially applauded, but more recently has been challenged by others.

Interpret the facts so as to make knowledge claims.

II. The challenge to this interpretation asks, in effect, "How did the Leakeys know what hominids were doing millions of years ago—the evidence from the sites is insufficient to support their interpretation."

A. Using precise geological measures, Richard Potts of the Smithsonian Institution assessed the Olduvai sites and concluded that they were not encampments where men hunted and women gathered.

1. The sites give evidence of activity by both carnivores and hominids.

2. The sites were "caches" where implements were stored, rather than actual living sites.

B. There are several arguments which support Potts' conclusions.

1. The sites were concentrated in selected areas and represent deposits over time.

2. Bones that show evidence of being transported from an original place are marked by stone cuts.

3. Bones also show evidence of carnivore marks superimposed on those made by stone cuts.

4. Uncut and unformed stones were found with cut stones, indicating a "cache" where hominids might return.

Transition

C. A second conclusion, based on this finding, is that men and women were not definitely split in their duties, and in fact these early humans or hominids may have been more like their ape ancestors than like later hunters.

Enlarge the interpretations to make them relevant to today's issues.

III. In challenging Richard Leakey's interpretation, there are experts who believe that the *Homo habilis* were scavengers, not hunters.

A. The evidence suggests that the hominids chased carnivores, such as lions, away from a kill with stones, then proceeded to take what they wanted from the carcass.

B. The evidence also suggests that the "caches" were sites to which they returned with their meat to rest and eat; when night fell, they resorted to sleeping in trees rather than on the open ground.

Conclusion

I. These new interpretations suggest early hominids were more like apes than later humans.

    A. They did not have spears or fire, hence stalking and killing game was not as likely as scavenging.

    B. With this in mind, we can better appreciate the difference that fire and more advanced weapons made in their lifestyle.

II. The newer interpretations suggest how difficult it is to be certain about the lifestyle of our ancestors.

    A. As you read or hear new conclusions about our ancestors, keep an open mind.

    B. Newer findings may reveal even these conclusions to be premature.[8]

Finish with an undisputable knowledge claim.

ASSESSING A SAMPLE SPEECH

The following speech, "The Geisha," was delivered by Joyce Chapman when she was a first-year student at Loop College, Chicago. It illustrates most of the virtues of a competent informative speech: it provides enough detail and explanations to be clear to a Western audience; it works from images of geishas familiar to at least some audience members, adding new ideas or correcting old ones within the frames of reference listeners might have; its topical organization pattern is simple and easy to follow; and it gives the audience reasons for listening.

THE GEISHA

Joyce Chapman

A personal reference establishes an immediate tie between Ms. Chapman and her topic.

As you may have already noticed from my facial features, I have Oriental blood in me and, as such, I am greatly interested in my Japanese heritage. One aspect of my heritage that fascinates me the most is the beautiful and adoring Geisha./1

I recently asked some of my friends what they thought a Geisha was, and the comments I received were quite astonishing. For example, one friend said,

Ms. Chapman works hard to bring the listeners—with their stereotyped views of Geishas—into the speech through comments many might have made and references to familiar films.

"She is a woman who walks around in a hut." A second friend was certain that a Geisha was "A woman who massages men for money and it involves her in other physical activities." Finally, I received this response, "She gives baths to men and walks on their backs." Well, needless to say, I was rather surprised and offended by their comments. I soon discovered that the majority of my friends perceived the Geisha with similar attitudes. One of them argued, "It's not my fault, because that is the way I've seen them on TV." In many ways my friend was correct. His misconception of the Geisha was not his fault, for she is often portrayed by American film producers and directors as: a prostitute, as in the movie, *The Barbarian and the Geisha,* a streetwalker, as seen in the TV series, "Kung Fu," or as a showgirl with a gimmick, as performed in the play, *Flower Drum Song.*/2

The central idea is stated clearly.

A Geisha is neither a prostitute, streetwalker, or showgirl with a gimmick. She is a lovely Japanese woman who is a professional entertainer and hostess. She is cultivated with exquisite manners, truly a bird of a very different plumage./3

A transition moves the listeners easily from the introduction to the body of the speech via a forecast. The first section of the body of the speech is devoted to an orienting history which cleverly wipes away most of the negative stereotypes of the Geisha.

I would like to provide you with some insight into the Geisha, and, in the process perhaps, correct any misconception you may have. I will do this by discussing her history, training, and development./4

The Geisha has been in existence since 600 A.D., during the archaic time of the Yakamoto period. At that time the Japanese ruling class was very powerful and economically rich. The impoverished majority, however, had to struggle to survive. Starving fathers and their families had to sell their young daughters to the teahouses in order to get a few yen. The families hoped that the girls would have a better life in the teahouse than they would have had in their own miserable homes./5

A nice transition moves Chapman to her second point on the rigors of Geisha training. She discusses the training in language technical enough to make listeners feel that they're learning interesting information but not so detailed as to be suffocating.

During ancient times only high society could utilize the Geisha's talents because she was regarded as a status symbol, exclusively for the elite. As the Geisha became more popular, the common people developed their own imitations. These imitations were often crude and base, lacking sophistication and taste. When American GIs came home from World War II, they related descriptive accounts of their wild escapades with the Japanese Geisha. In essence, the GIs were only soliciting with common prostitutes. These bizarre stories helped create the wrong image of the Geisha./6

Today, it is extremely difficult to become a Geisha. A Japanese woman couldn't wake up one morning and decide, "I think I'll become a Geisha today." It's not that simple. It takes sixteen years to qualify./7

At the age of six a young girl would enter the Geisha training school and become a Jo-chu, which means house keeper. The Jo-chu does not have any specific type of clothing, hairstyle, or make-up. Her duties basically consist of keeping the teahouse immaculately clean (for cleanliness is like a religion to the Japanese). She would also be responsible for making certain that the more advanced women would have everything available at their fingertips. It is not until the girl is sixteen and enters the Maiko stage that she concentrates less on domestic duties and channels more of her energies on creative and artistic endeavors./8

The Maiko girl, for example, is taught the classical Japanese dance, Kabuki. At first, the dance consists of tiny, timid steps to the left, to the right, backward and forward. As the years progress, she is taught the more difficult steps requiring syncopated movements to a fan./9

The Maiko is also introduced to the highly regarded art of floral arrangement. The Japanese take full advantage of the simplicity and gracefulness that can be achieved with a few flowers in a vase, or with a single flowering twig. There are three main styles: Seika, Moribana, and Nagerie. It takes at least three years to master this beautiful art./10

During the same three years, the Maiko is taught the ceremonious art of serving tea. The roots of these rituals go back to the thirteen century, when Zen Buddhist monks in China drank tea during their devotions. These rituals were raised to a fine art by the Japanese tea masters, who set the standards for patterns of behavior throughout Japanese society. The tea ceremony is so intricate that it often takes four hours to perform and requires the use of over seventeen different utensils. The tea ceremony is far more than the social occasion it appears to be. To the Japanese, it serves as an island of serenity where one can refresh the senses and nourish the soul./11

One of the most important arts taught to the Geisha is that of conversation. She must master an elegant circuitous vocabulary flavored in Karyuki, the world of flowers and willows, of which she will be a part. Consequently, she must be capable of stimulating her client's mind as well as his esthetic pleasures./12

The third point of the speech—how a Geisha develops her skills in her actual work—is clearly introduced and then developed with specific instances and explanations.

The conclusion is short and quick. Little more is needed in a speech that has offered clear explanations, though some speakers might want to refer back to the initial overview of negative stereotypes in order to remind the listeners how wrong such views are.

Having completed her sixteen years of thorough training, at the age of twenty-two, she becomes a full-fledged Geisha. She can now serve her clients with duty, loyalty, and most important, a sense of dignity./13

The Geisha would be dressed in the ceremonial kimono, made of brocade and silk thread. It would be fastened with an obi, which is a sash around the waist and hung down the back. The length of the obi would indicate the girl's degree of development. For instance, in the Maiko stage the obi is longer and is shortened when she becomes a Geisha. Unlike the Maiko, who wears a gay, bright, and cheerful kimono, the Geisha is dressed in more subdued colors. Her make-up is the traditional white base, which gives her the look of white porcelain. The hair is shortened and adorned with beautiful, delicate ornaments./14

As a full-fledged Geisha, she would probably acquire a rich patron who would assume her sizable debt to the Okiya, or training residence. This patron would help pay for her wardrobe, for each kimono can cost up to $12,000. The patron would generally provide her with financial security./15

The Geisha serves as a combination entertainer and companion. She may dance, sing, recite poetry, play musical instruments, or draw pictures for her guest. She might converse with them or listen sympathetically to their troubles. Amorous advances, however, are against the rules./16

So, as you can see the Geisha is a far cry from the back-rubbing, street-walking, slick entertainer that was described by my friends. She is a beautiful, cultivated, sensitive, and refined woman.[9]/17

*C*HAPTER SUMMARY

Overall, informative speeches provide more interesting and greater challenges than most people realize. *Facts* and *information* aren't particularly useful to listeners until they're turned into *knowledge*—assembled and structured in ways that help human beings find those facts and that information relevant to their lives. In preparing informative speeches, you must be sensitive to certain matters:

- Clarity, through effective organization and word choice
- Ways to associate new ideas with old ones, so the audience can more easily understand the new ones
- Clustering ideas into three, five, or seven categories of related information

- Motivational appeals, especially when listeners are required to attend your presentation
- Relevant visualization, to show listeners how information is relevant to them.

The four kinds of informative speeches discussed in this chapter—*definitional speeches, instructional and demonstration speeches, oral briefings,* and *explanatory speeches*—occur often enough in your life to demand your attention. Evaluate the organizational strategies available to you in structuring these presentations so that they meet the needs of the situation and your listeners.

$\mathscr{K}$EY TERMS

definitional speech (p. 334)
demonstration speech (p. 339)
explanatory speech (p. 346)
facts (p. 327)
information (p. 327)

instructional speech (p. 338)
knowledge (p. 327)
oral briefing (p. 342)
visualizations (p. 332)

$\mathscr{A}$SSESSMENT ACTIVITIES

1. In a short essay, indicate and defend the type of arrangement pattern (chronological sequence, spatial sequence, etc.) that you think would be most suitable for an informative speech on five of the following topics. Do a brief outline of first-level headings to show your reader what that speech might look like.

   The status of minority studies on your campus
   Recent developments in genetic engineering
   The search for the origins of human life in the Olduvai Gorge
   How the stock market works
   Five World Wide Web sites every college student should visit
   Buying your first condo
   Ways parents can control television viewing by their children
   How the American presidential caucus and primary system works

2. Plan a two-to-five-minute speech in which you give instructions. You might explain how to calculate one's life insurance needs, how to program a VCR so that a person can watch one channel and record another, or how to do the Heimlich maneuver. Your instructor will grade you on the five essential criteria for all informative speeches: clarity, association of new information with old data, the way you clustered ideas, your selection of motivational appeals, and your use of relevant visualization

3. Describe an unusual place you've visited—for example, a church in a foreign city, a historical site, or a startling natural view. Deliver a three-to-five-minute speech to your class, describing the place as accurately and vividly as possible. Ask your listeners to envision it. After the speech, show them a picture of the situation you described: How accurately were they able to en-

vision the place? Have each of them offer you two or three suggestions for what you could have done to help visualize the place more accurately. Turn in your speech outline and your listeners' analyses to your instructor.

REFERENCES

1. Facts from *The World Almanac and Book of Facts 1994* (Mahwah, NJ: World Almanac, 1993), 704.
2. For background on information packaging, see G. Mandler, "Organization and Memory," in *Human Memory: Basic Processes,* ed. Gordon Bower (New York: Academic Press, 1977), 310–354; Mandler's articles in C. R. Puff, ed., *Memory Organization and Structure* (New York: Academic Press, 1976); and G. A. Miller, "The Magic Number Seven, Plus or Minus Two: Some Limits on Our Capacity for Processing Information," *Psychological Review* 63 (1956): 81–97.
3. President Lyndon Baines Johnson, "War: The Gulf of Tonkin," August 4, 1964, reprinted in *Presidential Rhetoric (1961–Present),* 4th ed., ed. Theodore Windt (Dubuque, IA: Kendall/Hunt, 1987), 65.
4. For studies dealing with rhetorical depiction and visualization, see Richard A. Cherwitz, "Lyndon Johnson and the 'Crisis' of Tonkin Gulf: A President's Justification of War," *Western Journal of Speech Communication* 42 (1978): 93–104; Donovan J. Ochs, "Rhetorical Detailing in Cicero's Verrine Orations," *Communication Studies* 33 (1982): 310–318; Michael Osborn, "Rhetorical Depiction," in *Form, Genre, and the Study of Political Discourse,* eds. Herbert W. Simons and Aram A. Aghazarian (Charleston: University of South Carolina Press, 1986), 79–107; Paul Messaris, *Visual "Literacy": Image, Mind, and Reality* (Boulder, CO: Westview Press, 1994); and Chris Jenks, "The Centrality of the Eye in Western Culture: An Introduction," in *Visual Culture,* ed. Chris Jenks (New York: Routledge, 1995), 1–25.
5. Information for this outline was taken from Phyllis Barrier, "Diabetes: It Never Lets Up," *Nation's Business* (November 1992): 77; David Bradley, "Is a Pill on the Way for Diabetes?" *New Scientist* (June 27, 1992): 406; Chales Kilo and Joseph R. Williamson, *Diabetes* (New York: Wiley, 1987); Mark Schapiro, "A Shock to the System," *Health* (July–August 1991): 75–82; Carrie Smith, "Exercise Reduces Risk of Diabetes," *The Physician and Sportsmedicine* (November 1992): 19; John Travis, "Helping Diabetics Shed Pins and Needles," *Science News* (July 6, 1991): 4.
6. For a discussion of oral briefings, see James Benjamin and Raymie E. McKerrow, *Business and Professional Communication: Concepts and Practices* (New York: HarperCollins, 1994).
7. For details on these stories, see David Halberstam, *The Fifties* (New York: Villard Books, 1993).
8. Outline adapted from Brian Fagan, "Aping the Apes," *Archaeology* 45 (May/June 1992): 16–19, 67; see also Richard Potts, *Early Humanoid Activities at Olduvai Gorge* (New York: Aldine de Gruyter, 1988).
9. Joyce Chapman, "The Geisha," in *Communication Strategy: A Guide to Speech Preparation* eds. Roselyn Schiff et al. (Glenview, IL: Scott, Foresman, 1981). Used with the permission of HarperCollins Publishers.

CHAPTER

14

$\mathcal{S}$PEECHES TO PERSUADE AND ACTUATE

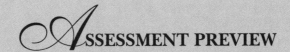

$\mathcal{A}$SSESSMENT PREVIEW

The student with basic communication competencies will be able to

- understand the three problems faced by persuasive/actuative speakers.
- distinguish between speeches of reinforcement, modification, and actuation.
- create a speech of reinforcement using the motivated sequence.

The student with average communication competencies will also be able to

- adapt the content and style of a persuasive or actuative speech to the listeners' psychological state.
- utilize reference groups to increase persuasive impact and enhance personal credibility.
- utilize the motivated sequence to create a speech of modification or actuation.

The student with superior communication competencies will also be able to

- critique a speaker's ability to adapt a message to the psychological state of the audience.
- critique efforts to enhance credibility in persuasive or actuative messages.
- understand the role of ethics in the use of specific appeals, including fear appeals.
- create messages that employ forewarning or inoculation strategies.
- know when to utilize two-sided messages with refutation.

lthough spring break was still months away, Sara Smyth knew her parents would need some persuading to allow her to spend a week in Aruba. The expense, among other factors, would be a hurdle to overcome. Sara thought about the arguments she might make, and considered her parents' resistance to each one. Finally, she settled on an approach that she felt was certain to work.

[Years later.] The Republican presidential convention was still months away, but Sara Smyth, a strong candidate for the nomination, felt that a "flat tax" proposal might be a distinctive feature of her campaign. Would the people in Iowa and New Hampshire, among other pre-convention states voting for delegates, buy the proposal? What if other candidates came forward with similar proposals? What arguments would entice people to see the proposal as unique, inviting, and thus aid in getting more delegates to cast their votes for her?

While these situations are vastly different, Sara's persuasive goal in each was influenced by her knowledge of the audience that would, ultimately, determine whether her idea was acceptable. The strategies that Sara might employ in each case may be different, but the general purpose is the same: *to ask that* other people *change their ideas or actions in a manner that accommodates the speaker's wishes.* Speakers also may seek to reinforce the ideas or values that people already are committed to.

The speaker or writer who persuades makes a very different demand on an audience from the speaker who informs. Informative communicators are satisfied when listeners understand what's been said. Persuaders, however, attempt to influence listeners' thoughts or actions. Persuaders request or demand that the audience agree with or act upon messages. Occasionally, persuaders seek to reinforce ideas or action, urging listeners to defend the present system and reject proposed changes. Whatever the specific purpose, the general purpose of all persuaders is to convince audiences of something. Broadly, persuasion encompasses a wide range of communication activities, including advertising, marketing, sales, political campaigns, and interpersonal relations. Given this book's focus on speechmaking, we'll narrow our thinking in this chapter to three types of speeches. Persuasive speaking is the process of producing oral messages that increase personal commitment, modify beliefs, attitudes, or values, or induce action.

Before we can talk about these three types of speech—which we will call speeches of *reinforcement, modification,* and *actuation*—we need to consider some general problems that you will face as a persuader: (1) the need for you to adapt your work to listeners' psychological states; (2) the requirement that you recognize the diverse populations in your audience and provide each listener with reasons for accepting your claims; and (3) the absolute need to enhance your credibility when selling ideas to audiences. These topics were discussed in a general manner in Chapters 4 and 5; as we reintroduce them here, the focus will be on how to use audience analysis and motivational appeals in

Persuasive speaking is the process of producing oral messages that increase personal commitment; modify beliefs, attitudes, or values; or induce action.

persuasive speaking. With this preview as a basis, we will then focus attention on speeches of reinforcement, modification, and actuation.

JUSTIFYING PERSUASIVE MESSAGES: THREE PROBLEMS FACED BY PERSUADERS

Persuading others is a challenging task. No matter what advertisers seem to assume, people don't change their long-standing beliefs, values, or behaviors on a whim; they need convincing rationales. The natural question, "Why should I believe or act as you desire?" must be met by "good reasons" for asking listeners to alter their thoughts or actions.[1] Reasons are not "good" simply because they are perceived as rational or logically reasonable; rather, their status is always determined by (1) listeners' psychological states, (2) sources of ideas (reference groups) acceptable to listeners, and (3) their assessment of the speaker's personal credibility. We will consider each of these problems in turn.

Adapting Messages to Listeners' Psychological States

The phrase **psychological state** refers generally to the complex of beliefs, attitudes, and values that listeners bring to a speech occasion. While there are hundreds of ways to talk about psychological states, in this chapter we'll limit ourselves to four.

Psychological Orientation and the VALS Program. A popular book of a decade ago was Arnold Mitchell's *The Nine American Lifestyles.*[2] He and some teammates set up the Stanford Research Institute's **Values and Lifestyles Program,** or **VALS,** in an attempt to understand motives, lifestyles, and governing values of groups of people. They set up the program because they understood that (1) people are governed by entire constellations of attitudes, beliefs, opinions, hopes, fears, needs, desires, and aspirations that are too complex to chart neatly on paper, but (2) they nonetheless have relatively consistent ways of acting at any given time of their lives. There are patterns to people's development and actions. These can be defined as **lifestyles,** relatively systematized ways of believing and acting in the world and the fairly consistent orientations people bring to their decision making.

The VALS program is an effort to capture those lifestyles in an analytically useful way. After considerable surveying and interviewing of Americans, Mitchell's team divided participants up into four comprehensive groups that in turn were subdivided into nine lifestyles. The categories (see Table 14.1) and the percentages of U.S. adults in each of them came from 1980 research, so the numbers may have changed by now, but the system itself is solid.

VALS defines groups of people who habitually respond to problems and their solutions in comparatively predictable ways.

TABLE 14.1   Mitchell's VALS Typology

Need-Driven Groups (11% of U.S. adults)

Survivor lifestyle (4%)
Sustainer lifestyle (7%)

Outer-Directed Groups (67% of U.S. adults)

Belonger lifestyle (35%)
Emulator lifestyle (10%)
Achiever lifestyle (22%)

Inner-Directed Groups (20% of U.S. adults)

I-Am-Me lifestyle (5%)
Experiential lifestyle (7%)
Socially Conscious lifestyle (8%)

Combined Outer- and Inner-Directed Groups (2% of U.S. adults)

Integrated lifestyle (2%)

- *Survivors* are the poverty-driven people—ill, depressed, withdrawn, under-educated, lacking self-confidence.
- *Sustainers* are closely related to survivors, although sustainers are more angry, distrustful, and anxious, and have the motive to advance economically, if possible.
- *Belongers* are the stereotypical middle-class Americans—traditional, conforming, family-oriented, "moral," mostly white, often female.
- *Emulators* are the great strivers, working hard to become richer and more successful than they are; members of this group are often young, competitive, and ambitious.
- *Achievers* are the more successful models of emulators, and are often professionals, comfortable, affable, wealthy.
- *"I-Am-Me's"* lead off the inner-directed group; they're highly emotional and flighty, both aggressive and retiring, conforming and innovative—always searching for their true selves.
- *Experientials* are adventure-seekers willing to experience life intensely; unlike I-am-me's, they are more involved with others.
- The *Socially Conscious* are driven by their concern for others, societal issues, trends, and events.
- *Integrated* people balance the strengths of the outer- and inner-directed people.[3]

These brief descriptions don't really capture the detail Mitchell offers in VALS on each group. He and his associates have been able to sculpt very specific profiles for members in each lifestyle, including attitudes toward others, consumption patterns, level of environmental concern, and so on. If you were a marketing analyst or political consultant, you'd want to explore each lifestyle's sets of beliefs, attitudes, values, and usual behavioral patterns carefully. As a speaker with few survey research resources, however, you'd use VALS in a different way.

As these examples attest, seldom are your audiences drawn purely from one group or another; hence the best approach is to *segment* the listeners, then *target* appeals to each segment in the ways that we discussed in Chapter 4. Even a general analysis of psychological orientation, therefore, helps you choose among the different ways you can urge change and even phrase the specific appeals you use.

Predisposition Toward the Topic.   Consider that an audience can have five possible attitudes toward a speaker's topic and purpose: (1) favorable but not aroused to act; (2) apathetic toward the situation; (3) interested but undecided about what to do; (4) interested in the situation but hostile to the proposed attitude, belief, value, or action; or (5) hostile to any change from the present state of affairs. Furthermore, such predispositions can be either relatively fixed or tentative and may vary from subgroup to subgroup within the audience. Given this sort of variability, consider the following suggestions as you design your speech:

How To

USE VALS TO CRAFT A PERSUASIVE MESSAGE FOR DIVERSE AUDIENCES

A cursory examination of your class-mates should reveal something like the following:

- There will be few representatives of the need-driven groups (Survivors and Sustainers).
- There will be several outer-directed students (Emulators and Achievers).
- There also will be several inner-directed students (especially from the Socially Conscious).

Based on this quick review, suppose you are proposing that your class-mates join in helping a neighborhood association clean up some nearby vacant lots in order to set up a park. For your classmates, you would want to feature appeals aimed at that particular psychological orientation.

I. We should help the neighborhood association clean the lots and build the park because:
   A. You would be demonstrating that even busy college students have the ambition to take on serious community projects. (Achiever)
   B. You would show the community that you have the leadership skills and technical abilities to carry it out. (Achiever)
   C. You would have done something of which you could be proud and which you could put on your résumé under "community service." (Socially Conscious)

If you were to shift your focus to the neighborhood association, a cursory examination may find:

- A larger percentage of "need driven" people would be found among the community members than might be the case in your college class.
- A majority of "Belongers" (outer-directed) would be found in the association.
- Some association members would be Socially Conscious.

For this audience, a different set of reasons would be appropriate:

I. You ought to be involved in the neighborhood cleanup and park construction because:
   A. The lots are now breeding grounds for rats and other vermin that make your life miserable. (Socially Conscious)
   B. Drug dealers might be driven out of the neighborhood if those lots are cleaned up. (Inner Directed and Socially Conscious)
   C. The presence of a park would increase your property value and even help those of you who are renters pressure your landlords to fix up your apartments. (Need Driven)
   D. A park would give you a free place to visit and enjoy on spring days and summer nights. (Inner and Outer Directed)

- *A message that incorporates both sides of an issue, and contains arguments refuting one side, will be more effective across diverse persuasive situations.* Thus, if your goal is to stimulate more favorable thoughts about your proposal, use a **two-sided message** with refutation. A **one-sided message,** which focuses on the arguments for your position only, can be effective, and is more effective than simply outlining both sides of an issue without adding refutative arguments.[4]

- *A message that recognizes the logical interdependence between ideas will target those people for whom beliefs are highly integrative.* There will be people in the audience for whom beliefs are interlocked—altering or affecting one belief will have a domino-like impact on other beliefs. Thus a listener might believe that a "flat tax" rate would cause higher taxes for the middle class and, in turn, that higher taxes would limit the saving potential and disposable income of a large number of people; this, in turn, will harm the stock market and will cause a reduction in spending for produced goods. For this listener, a speech favoring a flat tax would have to deal with all of these implications. Treating the flat tax as an isolated issue would be far less effective in this case as a persuasive strategy.

- *You must also deal not only with the strength of attitudes but also with their saliency.* **Saliency** refers to the relevance and "current" interest level of a belief, attitude, or value for an individual. For example, topics currently on the front page often are highly salient, as are topics of regular conversation. The saliency of an issue ought to affect your persuasive strategies in significant ways:

> *When topics are highly salient, listeners are more likely to be familiar with the central issues.*[5] You need to spend less time in providing a background for salient topics; on the other hand, audiences may well have certain expectations on salient topics. Be up to date.
>
> *On salient topics, listeners are more likely to resist changes in their beliefs and attitudes.*[6] This is an instance in which a two-sided message with refutation would be more helpful than a one-sided message. Acknowledge the audience's resistance in the need step, then demonstrate clearly in the satisfaction step how the solution is consonant with many related beliefs and attitudes.
>
> *When saliency is high, increase the number of strong arguments you offer; when saliency is low you'll be more effective if you increase the number of both strong and weak arguments.*[7] Those "in the know" won't put up with weak or frivolous arguments, although such arguments sometimes work on nonsalient issues.
>
> *The more central and salient the listeners' values are, the more likely the listeners are to be hostile.*[8] Issues such as the decriminalization of drugs or the rights of persons with alternative lifestyles are not only salient but, for some, a challenge to their most basic values about protection of the body or of family values. Your best bet in such situations is to go for small changes now—changes in the law to allow marijuana use in

cancer treatment programs or to legalize gay and lesbian marriages—
in hopes of pushing for more basic changes later.

Quote salient authorities. It makes a difference whether you cite Lyndon
LaRouche or Jesse Jackson on an issue concerning social welfare. Especially if listeners aren't ready to take the time to work on issues and consider information about them seriously, the saliency of authorities becomes crucial.[9]

- *Recognize that audience members will differ in their relative degrees of willingness
  to accept your ideas.* Audience members will have different ranges of acceptance or rejection, depending on how your proposal relates to their own
  views. Think in terms of not going too far in either direction from your
  proposal for a flat tax: A rate of 2 percent might be rejected by a moderate
  audience simply because it would seem to generate too little revenue; conversely, a rate of 35 percent might seem too high. A proponent of the flat
  tax will have a larger **latitude of acceptance;** conversely, an opponent
  would have a larger **latitude of rejection.**[10]

Degrees of Change.   Given the differences in degrees of willingness to accept and act on ideas, you also need to recognize that people will change only
so much as a result of your speeches. It's extremely difficult, except in rare circumstances such as radical religious experiences, to make wholesale changes
in people's beliefs, attitudes, and values. Generally, you ought to strive for **incremental change**—step by step movement toward a goal. As suggested above,
the distance you can move a listener is determined by (1) *initial attitude* and
(2) *latitude of change* the person can tolerate.[11]

Obviously, you cannot interview all audience members. Indeed, few speakers (political candidates are certainly exceptions here) scientifically assess the
psychological states of their listeners. But good audience analysis allows you to
guess shrewdly, then to adjust your appeals and plans of action accordingly.
Talk with people; check with civic attitude-testers such as the Chamber of Commerce; read local newspapers and other sources of information on community
problems, attitudes, and responses to those problems. All such sources of information on psychological states will help you maximize your chances for successful persuasion.

Drawing Upon Diverse External Reference Groups

Reference groups are collections of people and organizations that affect individuals' beliefs, attitudes, and values. They are collectivities "from which an individual derives attitudes and standards of acceptable and appropriate behavior and to
which the individual refers for information, direction, and support for a given
lifestyle."[12] You may or may not hold actual membership in such groups; you
might belong to the Young Republican Club and not to the Sierra Club (an environmental lobby), yet be influenced strongly by both. You voluntarily join some
reference groups; you might believe in the legal rights of everyone and so join
the American Civil Liberties Union. You are a part of other reference groups in-

How To
USE ATTITUDINAL VARIATION IN SELECTING A PERSUASIVE STRATEGY

Suppose that the possible attitudes toward the institution of a "flat tax rate" range from "extremely favorable" to "extremely unfavorable," as in the following scale:

1. extremely favorable toward a flat tax
2. moderately favorable
3. mildly favorable
4. neutral
5. mildly unfavorable
6. moderately unfavorable
7. strongly unfavorable toward a flat tax

Trying to convince someone who is strongly unfavorable (7) that a flat tax should be instituted would probably fail, even if you presented both sides of the argument. Those further removed from your position could be moved only a short way because of a single speech—to moderately or mildly unfavorable if you were a skilled arguer—if at all. Trying to change listeners too much can produce a **boomerang effect;** often, persuasive attempts backfire and create more rather than less resistance to ideas. In the face of a strong "1" speech, most "7s" become even more committed to their position. (See Figure 14.1.)

voluntarily—for example, you are born male or female and a member of an ethnic group. You share values with some of your reference groups; hence they have a positive effect on your attitudes and behavior, while those with values dissimilar to yours produce negative reactions in you. As a result, the National Right to Life Committee probably affects your thinking about abortion in either positive or negative ways; because it probably affects you, it is a reference group, even if you don't join or support it. Reference groups can be classified as *membership and non-membership groups, voluntary and involuntary groups,* and *positive and negative groups.*

With this background, consider some of the ways you can use reference groups in your persuasive and actuative speeches:

- *Make reference groups you want to use* salient *to your listeners.* You need to bring some group to a conscious level and make sure the group seems relevant to the topic at hand. You may, for example, be a regular participant in an e-mail group devoted to discussing pop culture. Drawing on conversations with other group members in a speech about the importance of studying pop culture may seem highly relevant but will not have as much impact if your audience is not familiar with the group or its purpose.

- *Cite the opinions of voluntary, positively viewed groups whose values coincide with positions you're taking.* This is a kind of testimony—useful, as we saw in Chapter 6, as orienting and probative supporting materials. Before invoking the National Rifle Association in a speech opposing gun control legislation, you will need to sense whether that group is viewed positively or negatively by your audience. If your speech were delivered at an NRA meeting, invoking the group's views would be naturally salient and positively regarded by the audience.

- *Cite voluntary, negative groups that the audience does not belong to when they **oppose** the position you're advocating.* Such groups are "devil-groups," groups people vilify and actively act against. Such references play into an "us versus them" orientation and, whether you like it or not, some listeners are as willing to act against something as for something else. They possess what are called *negative attribution styles.*[13] Drawing on the position of a Right to Life group in a speech delivered to a Pro-Choice gathering would be an example of this strategy.

- *The more significant a person's roles in any group, the more the group's norms and beliefs influence that person's thoughts and behavior.* The more committed you are to a group's goals, the more likely the values of the group will influence your attitude and behavior. Groups have a *normative* influence with respect to setting standards—the more active you are in the group, the more impact there will be on the group norms.[14]

- *Talk about reference groups to create a sense of security, of belongingness.* Aligning your views specifically with those of positive membership groups important to listeners not only helps you create acceptance but creates long-lasting acceptance.[15] If you are talking to students who are active members of student clubs and organizations, noting those reference groups and their position on issues will be helpful in gaining support for your ideas.

Beliefs, attitudes, and values are based, in part, on the traditions and customs of reference groups, although people differ in their degree of direct reliance.

Finally, as we've noted throughout this book, you're usually facing diverse audiences, which means that you must work many reference groups into most speeches in order to reach various segments of your audience. *You must aim for broad-based support of your position.*

Enhancing Personal Credibility

The issue of authority brings us to the third essential dimension affecting the persuasive process. A good deal of your potential effectiveness depends upon your perceived credibility, or *ethos*. In Chapter 1, we outlined several factors that can determine listeners' perceptions of your credibility—their sense of your expertise, trustworthiness, competency, sincerity or honesty, friendliness and concern for others, and personal dynamism. While you should work to maximize the potential impact of all of these factors whenever speaking, regardless of purpose, they are especially important when you seek to change someone's mind or behavior. The following guidelines can assist you in making decisions about the use of credibility as an effective tool in persuasion.

First, when speaking to people who are relatively unmotivated and who don't have enough background information to critically assess what they hear, *the higher your credibility the better your chances of being a successful persuader.* Conversely, if your credibility is low, even strong arguments will not overcome your

FIGURE 14.1 Incremental Approach to Attitude Change

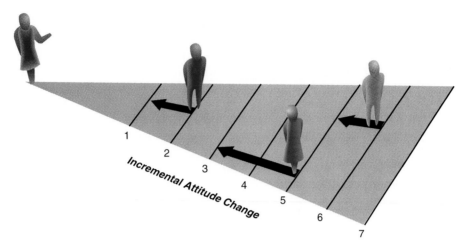

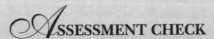

Incremental Attitude Change

1
2
3
4
5
6
7

initial handicap.[16] This guideline should give you a clear sense of why your own credibility is an important component in your chances for success.

Second, *you can increase the likelihood of being judged credible when seeking to persuade an audience by taking steps to enhance your image of competence and sincerity.* People who don't take the time to weigh your reasons and evidence are unlikely to change their beliefs and values if they think you've done a poor job of researching the issues or are insincere—they are less likely to judge you as trustworthy. There are several things you can do to increase the audience's perception of your *competence:* (1) carefully set forth all of the competing posi-

𝒜SSESSMENT CHECK

In developing a speech to change an audience's attitude, ask yourself these questions:

- Using VALS as a guideline, what is the dominant psychological orientation of the audience?
- Is the audience favorably or unfavorably predisposed toward my topic?
- Would a two-sided presentation with refutation be the best strategy in this situation?
- What major ideas are salient in the audience's mind?
- How willing might the audience be to change their views to accommodate my ideas?
- How much change can I ask for, or reasonably expect this audience to accept?

tions, ideas, and proposals relevant to a topic *before* you come to your own judgment; (2) review various criteria for judgment to show that your recommendations or positions flow from accepted and generally held criteria; and (3) show that the recommendations you offer actually will solve the problems you identified in the need step of your speech. You can increase the audience's sense of your *sincerity* by (1) showing yourself to be open to correction and criticism should any listener wish to question you (a calmly delivered, relevant response does more to defuse hecklers than responding in kind)[17]; (2) exuding personal warmth in your relations with the audience; (3) maintaining direct eye contact with listeners; and (4) recognizing anyone who has helped you understand and work on the issue or problem.

Third, *heighten audience members' sense of your expertise, friendliness, and dynamism, especially when seeking to move them to action.* People are unlikely to change their routines on your recommendation unless they feel that you know what you're talking about, that you have their best interests in mind, and that you're excited about your own proposal. *Expertise* can be demonstrated by (1) documenting your sources of information; (2) using a variety of sources as cross-checks on each other; (3) presenting your information and need analyses in well-organized ways; (4) using clear, simple visual aids when they are appropriate or necessary; (5) providing adequate background information on controversial issues; (6) competently separating causes from effects, short-term from long-term effects, hard facts from wishes or dreams, and one proposal from others; and (7) delivering your speeches in a calm and forthright manner.

A sense of *friendliness* and *concern* for others can be created by treating yourself and others as human beings, regardless of how controversial the topic is and how intensely you disagree with others, and depersonalizing issues, talking in terms of the "real-world" problems rather than in terms of personalities and ideologies. An audience's sense of your *dynamism* can be enhanced by speaking vividly, drawing clear images of the events you describe; using sharp, fresh metaphors and active rather than passive verbs; and expressing your ideas with a short, hard-hitting oral style rather than a long, cumbersome written style and using varied conversational vocal patterns, an animated body, direct eye contact rather than reliance upon your notes, and a firm upright stance.[18]

Finally, recognize that the audience's perception of you as a credible speaker will be, to some extent, dependent on their expectations—will they expect you to treat them fairly with respect to information being conveyed? The audience may perceive you to be a *biased* speaker, either in terms of distrusting the knowledge you convey—they may not believe you are in a position to possess or convey accurate information because your own views give you a warped sense of what is happening. A person who still maintains that the Nazi concentration camps were a hoax can be perceived as having **knowledge bias.** Further, a person may be perceived as knowing the information but not willing to divulge it in a complete or accurate manner. A person serving as a corporate spokesperson for Dow Chemical may not reveal the studies done on breast implants that suggested there were problems long before the issue become a

ETHICAL MOMENTS
USING FEAR APPEALS

Common sense would tell you that fear appeals would be among the most potent appeals to audiences. After all, if you can make your audience feel afraid for the future if a problem is not resolved, your proposal will be just the antidote. Unfortunately, a comprehensive review of decades of research on the impact of fear appeals suggests that this commonsense notion is not that well grounded, as "existing explanations of the effects of fear arousing persuasive messages are inadequate."* We are not able to offer clear advice about whether the use of fear appeals to gain acceptance of a message outweighs any harms caused by frightening people—perhaps needlessly. The inability to offer such advice raises an ethical question about the use, and potential misuse, of fear appeals. Consider the following scenarios:

1. You give a speech on the increase of date rape on college campuses. In order to convince your audience that date rape is wrong and extremely common, you create scenarios that appeal to the fears of your listeners. Your scenarios are so vivid that several of your listeners, who are rape survivors, are visibly overcome with emotion. One of the listeners is so upset that she must leave the classroom during your speech. Everyone in the audience sees her leave.

2. You feel very strongly that the college president is wrong to continue investing college money in countries where torture and imprisonment without trial are legal. You present a very persuasive speech about your feelings. In your speech, you appeal to your audience's fears by suggesting that the college president is actually propagating torture and corrupting the values of U.S. citizens to the point that someday torture and imprisonment without trial might be legal in the United States. Your listeners become so incensed, as a result of your speech, that they march to the president's house and set his car on fire.

3. You're preparing to give a speech on hate crimes in the United States. You want to make sure that you have your audience's attention before you begin, so you decide to present the details of a series of grisly murders committed in your town by a psychopath—even though these murders were not motivated by hate but by mental illness, and so they aren't examples of hate crimes.

*Frank J. Boster and Paul Mongeau, "Fear-Arousing Persuasive Messages," in *Communication Yearbook 8,* ed. Robert N. Bostrom (Beverly Hills, CA: Sage, 1984), 371.

legal quagmire for Dow. Such an individual may be perceived to have a **reporting bias.** In either or both cases, the legitimacy of a person's expertise or trustworthiness is called into question. Recognizing these negative audience perceptions may enable you to take steps to avoid being perceived as guilty of either bias in presenting your ideas.[19]

A public speaker's principal communicative virtue is the presence of a living, active human being behind the lectern—a person who *embodies* a message, whose own values are expressed in and through the message. People command more attention and interest than written words, and people, unlike films and videotapes, can feel, can react to audience members, and can create a sense of urgency and directness. Hence, personal credibility is an extremely valuable asset for the persuader and actuator.

TYPES OF PERSUASIVE AND ACTUATIVE SPEECHES

Although there are many ways to classify persuasive and actuative speeches, we'll examine them in terms of the *demands* each type makes upon an audience's psychological state and level of activity. We will examine speeches of reinforcement, modification, and actuation.

Speeches of Reinforcement

Americans are joiners. To get our political, economic, social, and personal work done, we constantly organize ourselves into groups and associations. Action-oriented groups gather and package the latest information, keep on top of issues that are important to the members of the group, and propose solutions to specific problems. Service groups organize charities, perform volunteer work, and provide support for other activities in communities. An inevitable fact of group life is that, as time goes by, members' interest in activities declines, membership drops, and the cause for which the group was formed gets lost in the myriad causes competing for the attention and support of the people in the community. Periodically, people need to be reminded of why they joined a group, what its services are, and how the group helps them meet their personal goals.

In public speaking, **reinforcement** is a process of calling up the original beliefs and values that caused people to join a group in the first place and of reinvigorating audience members so they once more contribute their time, energy, and finances to the tasks needing to be done. In a practical sense, reinforcement speeches are *epideictic*—they seek to increase adherence to, or rejection of, a particular set of values. As Perelman and Olbrechts-Tyteca observe:

> Epideictic discourse sets out to increase the intensity of adherence to certain values, which might not be contested when considered on their own but may nevertheless not prevail against other values that might come into conflict

with them. . . . In epideictic oratory, *the speaker turns educator.*[20] (Emphasis added.)

Reinforcement speeches are called for when people behave as though they are unconcerned about the problem and are unwilling to actively seek remedies. In cases in which apathy is less extreme, the committed still need an extra nudge to dip into their pockets and give assistance. Even those once very active in a group burn out and cease their involvement. These are the people that need to be recharged—a speaker needs to remind them of their initial reasons for being active, and why that activity is once again required of them. Whether the state of apathy and lethargy is extreme or moderate, the message is oriented toward reaffirming basic verities, reeducating audience members about the values that attracted them to the group in the first place. The key to reinforcement speaking is *motivation*. While people may say, "Sure, I support the Republican platform," or "Yeah, I agree with SADD's efforts to control drug and alcohol use in the schools," they may not be motivated to act upon the basis of their convictions. They need to have their original commitment resurrected. Keynote speeches often serve a reinforcing function; perhaps the most memorable in recent years is the late Barbara Jordan's keynote speech at the 1976 Democratic National Convention.

Speeches of Modification

Unlike speeches of reinforcement, speeches of **modification** seek specific psychological changes in one's belief state, attitudes toward an object, or basic values. Speeches of this type have been the central feature in the art of rhetoric since the time of the early Greeks. Whether your present or future role is that of a student, businessperson, lawyer, minister, sales clerk, doctor, or parent, the task of changing the views of others is a constant demand of your daily life. Using the categories of beliefs, attitudes, and values described in Chapter 4, we can examine three subtypes of speeches aiming at modifying the views of listeners.

Changing Beliefs. The psychological basis for most speeches aimed at changing someone's beliefs about the world is *differentiation*. That is, one can get you to change your beliefs about anything from eating seaweed to the U. S. response to the conflict in the former Yugoslavia by persuading you to perceive those matters in different ways. Persuaders who want you to differentiate between your old way of looking at something and a newer way of seeing it may use one or more of three basic strategies:

1. *Descriptive accounts.* A focus on specific characteristics of a product, an event, or issue is one means of providing "good reasons" for accepting a proposal. Someone might persuade you to consider tofu an acceptable food by assuring you that its vitamin and mineral content is superior to that of foods in your normal diet. To the extent that this remains a one-sided strategy, descriptive accounts are not always the

strongest move you can make. A stronger approach would be to build on this strategy by considering the negatives—questions that the audience might naturally have with respect to why tofu should be added to their diet—and offering reasons that make the negatives appear less influential or significant.

2. *Narrative.* A persuader may use narrative forms—for example, by telling a story about the United States preparedness level going into the Korean Conflict, ending with the moral that the country can never let its guard down. Two features of storytelling are essential if the narrative is to have persuasive force. First, listeners must perceive the story to be probable; it must make coherent sense to them. Second, the story must possess what Fisher terms "narrative fidelity"—it must appear consistent with other stories listeners have heard.[21] When both features are present, a story can function as a powerful image to move an audience.

3. *Appeals to uniqueness.* Someone attempting to get you to change your beliefs about a politician may convince you that the candidate is "not like all the others," pointing to unique aspects of that person's background, experience, public service, honesty, and commitment to action.

These three strategies are effective to the extent that listeners perceive the message to be important, novel, and plausible. The message must be one that isn't already well internalized by the audience members (they aren't already convinced), and the rationale for change must appear credible to them. Finally, the change itself must be seen as feasible or practical.[22]

Changing Attitudes. Attitude change is probably the most heavily researched psychological change of this century.[23] Given the previous discussion of attitude as predisposition, you're aware that this form of change involves modifying one's evaluation of an object from "good" to "bad," or at least to "neutral." Because attitudes are attached to beliefs ("Opportunities for women are increasing in this country [belief] and that is good [attitude]"), sometimes persuaders attempt to change an attitude by attacking a belief. If a speaker can show that the "glass ceiling" is still the norm for women's advancement, he or she then can link that assertion to a negative attitude ("The continued presence of the glass ceiling is harmful to women"). Because attitudes are organized into clusters around a value, they can sometimes be changed by getting people to think in different valuative terms.

Attitudes can be changed not only by attacking underlying beliefs or overarching values but also by direct assault. Parents attempt to instill any number of attitudes in their children by repeatedly offering short "lectures" (for instance, "Spinach is good for you" and "Don't give in to peer pressure—be an individual"). Repetition often has the desired effect, as children accept the attitude as their own and live by its creed. This is a risky strategy, as the repetitive nature of the assault can also be a cause for ignoring the advice ("I've heard that before"; "whatever"). Hence, if you seek to directly challenge the audience's views, be aware that you may increase rather than lessen their resistance toward change.

Changing Values. Perhaps the most difficult challenge for any persuader is to change people's value orientations. As noted in earlier chapters, values are fundamental anchors, basic ways of organizing our view of the world and our actions in it. They are difficult but not impossible to change. Three techniques often are used:

1. *Valuative shifts.* Like differentiation, this technique asks an audience member to look at an issue or a proposal from a different valuative vantage point. The person asking you to buy insurance, for example, tells you to look at it not simply as financial protection (a pragmatic value) but as family protection and a source of peace of mind (sociological and psychological values). Such appeals can persuade people to shift their valuative orientation and see an issue or proposal in a new way. While the issue remains unchanged, its relationship to the audience member is transformed from a negative one ("I don't need financial protection") to a positive one ("You're right, the *family* will need protection if something happens to me").

2. *Appeals to consistency.* When members of the Sierra Club hear appeals beginning with "We favor . . . ," they are being asked to approve a certain measure in order to remain consistent with others in their reference group. This will have an impact if approval of the reference group is a positive social value for them; if they are thinking of leaving the group, the "we" appeal will have less impact. When someone projects a value orientation from the present to the future ("If you like horror films, you'll positively love the Friday the Thirteenth series"), he or she is appealing to a logical consistency between horror films as a genre and the Friday series as a specific example of the genre.

3. *Transcendence.* This sophisticated method for getting you to change your values approaches the issue from the perspective of a "higher" value. President Clinton used such appeals in eulogizing the assassinated leader of Israel, Prime Minister Rabin. At a time of potential violence, Clinton's words counseled peaceful dialogue.

Thus, speeches of modification may seek a change in beliefs, attitudes, or values. Speeches designed to bring about these kinds of changes in listeners demand a higher level of communicative competence than most other types of speeches. As you know from experience, however, these competencies can be acquired by speakers willing to think through situations calling for such kinds of persuasion and willing to spend time on thorough speech preparation.

Speeches of Actuation

Moving uncommitted or apathetic people to action is a chore many prefer to avoid. For example, you may have heard such expressions from friends and acquaintances as "I don't like to ask people to contribute money to a cause, even if it's worthy," "Don't ask me to solicit signatures for that petition—I feel like I'm intruding on others' privacy," or "I'm just not persuasive enough to get people to volunteer to work at the Kiwanis Auction—ask Maria." If all of us felt this way, little would be accomplished. In some cases, simply making a living requires that we move others to action. Even if you take one of these positions, you've undoubtedly asked others to act on your behalf in other ways ("I need a ride to Columbus this weekend; would you take me up there?"). Though this request is an interpersonal encounter, it shares the same features as a more elaborate speech of **actuation**—the listener may well respond with "What's in it for me?" Getting people to see and accept the benefits that will accrue from acting as you desire is the primary purpose: *an actuative speech seeks, as its final outcome, a set of specifiable actions from its audience.* These actions may be as diverse as giving personal time to an activity (visiting a local nursing home), contributing money to a cause or product (donating to the Wildlife Fund), or changing a habit (stopping smoking).

There are two types of audiences for whom actuative speeches are generally appropriate: those who believe in the idea or action but are lethargic about doing anything and those who doubt the value of the action and are uninformed or uninvolved. The second situation is our concern here. Actuative speeches addressed to uninvolved listeners demand significant behavioral change. The goal might be as short range as making a profit the next quarter of the fiscal year or as long range as the sociopolitical transformation of society. Whatever the extent or loftiness of the goal, all actuative speeches depend upon making a set of needs salient for an audience, then demonstrating that a certain course of action will satisfy those needs.

As in the case of speeches of reinforcement and modification, *the key to effective actuation is motivation.* No matter how wonderful the new products, how exciting the political candidate, or how worthy the cause, unless a listener is personally convinced that the product, candidate, or cause will make a significant change in his or her life, your speech will fail to have its intended effect.

$\mathscr{S}$TRUCTURING PERSUASIVE AND ACTUATIVE SPEECHES

The overall structure of a persuasive or an actuative speech incorporates the features of the motivated sequence—attention, need, satisfaction, visualization, and action—relevant to the specific type of speech. Within each step, as appropriate to the topic and occasion, other patterns of organization can be used to bring a sense of coherence and cohesiveness to each step.

COMMUNICATION RESEARCH DATELINE

RESISTANCE TO COUNTERPERSUASION

In this chapter we've concentrated on the issue of persuading—increasing or otherwise changing people's acceptance of certain beliefs, attitudes, and values. We haven't, however, focused on the ways in which you can increase your listeners' *resistance* to ideas that run counter to your own. Besides persuading them to accept your beliefs or attitudes, you also may need to protect them against *counterpersuasion,* attempts by others to influence your audience away from your position.

As in taking vaccine to ward off a disease, you may *inoculate* your audience against your opponents' arguments. Studies by Michael Pfau and others of political advertising have found that voters who received prior messages that an opponent would attack the candidate, and voters who also received additional refutative arguments against the purported attack, were far more resistant to the opponent's message. This offers practical support for the view that forewarning an audience may be helpful. As Benoit's analysis of the research on inoculation study has suggested, it doesn't appear to matter whether the type of forewarning—letting audience members know in advance that they'll be exposed to a counterpersuasive attempt—is general, as in "an attack on me is imminent from my opponent" or is more precise with respect to the topic and position to be taken by the attacker. Nor does it appear to matter whether the attack really is imminent, or comes later.

Another strategy that increases resistance involves the amount of knowledge that people bring to a situation. For example, Hirt and Sherman found that individuals with greater knowledge are more resistant to refutational arguments.* Thus, you can increase potential resistance to messages that are contrary to your own by adding to the audience's knowledge about the issues involved.

For Further Reading

Pfau, M. "The Potential of Inoculation in Promoting Resistance to the Effectiveness of Comparative Advertising Messages." *Communication Quarterly* 40 (1992): 26–44; Pfau, M., and M. Burgoon, "Inoculation in Political Communication, *Communication Monographs* 15 (1988): 91–111; W. L. Benoit, "Forewarning and Persuasion," in *Forewarning and Persuasion: Advances through Meta-analysis,* eds. M. Allen and R. W. Preiss (Dubuque, IA: Brown and Benchmark, 1994), 159–184.

*Hirt, E. R., and S. J. Sherman. "The Role of Prior Knowledge in Explaining Hypothetical Events." *Journal of Experimental Social Psychology* 21 (1985): 591–643.

The Motivated Sequence and Reinforcement Speeches

The visualization and action steps are the crucial elements in most reinforcement speeches. This is because the listeners are already convinced of the importance of the problem and are predisposed to accept particular solutions. The most important goal in a reinforcement speech is to get listeners to renew their previous commitments and to charge once more into the public arena to accomplish a common objective. Thus, a typical reinforcement speech following the motivated sequence usually has a short attention step, a need step that documents recent gains and losses (especially losses, since they illustrate the desirability of reengagement), little or no satisfaction step, a more fully developed visualization step (which lets listeners "see" themselves as reengaged with the issues), and an action step that focuses on particular actions to take now or in the near future (as audiences for these speeches are usually ready to respond quickly to appeals for renewed efforts).

$\mathcal{U}$SING THE MOTIVATED SEQUENCE IN A REINFORCEMENT SPEECH

The situation: Your team has lost the last three games, in one instance by a lopsided margin. As you go into the final league game, the chance to gain home court for the playoffs is up for grabs—lose and you travel; win and you play the first game at home.

Putting "Athlete" Back into the Student-Athlete

Specific Purpose: To reinforce the listeners' previous commitment to the team.

Attention Step

    I. "Winning means we can look at ourselves with pride."
    II. "Winning means we meet the expectations of our supporters."

Need Step

    I. We've already won as students.
        A. You are proven student athletes with the highest academic average of any team on this campus.
        B. The seniors will graduate.
    II. What we need now is to win as athletes.
        A. "You play as you practice."
        B. Work ethic determines results.
        C. Only we, as athletes, should determine our destiny.

Satisfaction/Visualization Step (combined, as the solution [win the game] is accepted)

I. Given our last three losses, we could ask "Why not quit now?"
   A. It insults your commitment to excellence.
   B. It lets your fans down.
   C. Anyone who quits now lets the others down.
II. Renew commitment to hard work, fun, and a winning attitude.
   A. These are the ingredients that led to our past success.
   B. They will be sufficient to carry us through this week, into the game, and beyond.
III. What does winning this final game mean?
   A. It means being satisfied with your own participation as a player and team member.
   B. It means recognition for you and the university.
   C. It means home court advantage, and that is worth 10 points with our fans!!

Action Step

I. Now is the time to do what has to be done.
   A. Practice hard.
   B. Play this last league game as if it were your last.
II. Win or lose, be satisfied with your individual effort.
   A. Individual and team integrity and discipline count.
   B. Remember, "Winning is everything" only when done for the right reasons.

The Motivated Sequence and Speeches of Modification

Regardless of the nature or scope of the psychological modification you ask of your listeners, you can use the motivated sequence. When asking people to accept your judgments about a person, a practice, an institution, or a theory, you can seek to do these things:

- Capture the *attention* and interest of the audience.
- Clarify that a judgment concerning the worth of the person, practice, or institution is *needed* by showing (1) why such a judgment is important to your listeners personally and (2) why it is important to their community, state, nation, or world.
- *Satisfy* the need by (1) setting the criteria upon which an intelligent judgment may be based and (2) advancing the judgment you believe to be correct and showing how it meets the criteria.

- Picture the advantages that will accrue from agreeing with the judgment you advance or the evils that will result from failing to endorse it (*visualization* step).
- If appropriate, appeal for acceptance of the proposed judgment (*action* step).

$\mathcal{U}$SING THE MOTIVATED SEQUENCE IN A MODIFICATION SPEECH

Strength through Cultural Diversity

The situation: Henri Mann Morton presented a keynote speech at the Northwest's Colville and Okanogan National Forest conference on cultural diversity on March 23, 1989. As a Native American woman, she was in an excellent position to comment on the issues related to gaining workforce parity for all peoples. During the speech, she differentiates the Native American experience from that of others, in the hopes of modifying her audience's beliefs about the values and interests of Native Americans.

Specific Purpose: To modify audience beliefs about the values and interests of Native Americans.

Attention Step

I. "Thanks for honoring me with your gracious invitation to speak."

II. "We must never forget that American Indians were the first people to live in this beautiful country."

Need Step

I. The beliefs of the Native American are unique.
  - **A.** They believe in "the dualities of life . . . sky-earth; sun/moon; love-hate; wisdom-ignorance."
  - **B.** The most important duality is man-woman as together they are "part of the great sacred circle of life."

II. Tribal views also are unique—with different tribes holding different beliefs about women sacred.
  - **A.** The Hopi believe in the Spider Grandmother who made the four races of people.
  - **B.** The Iroquois give status to the Clan Mother.
  - **C.** The Cherokee give status to the Beloved Woman.
  - **D.** Each tribe grants respect to Indian women.

III. As a woman, I am part of that which has preceded me.
   A. "My grandmothers have been here for all time."
   B. "The land you strive to protect is my grandmother—my mother."
IV. Once the majority, we are now the "minority of minorities."
   A. We number less than one percent of the population.
   B. Due to our small number, policymakers are generally uninformed about our culture.
   C. "I would characterize American society as . . . 'culturally disrespectful.'"
V. Historically, American Indians have had three "agencies of oppression."
   A. Church: Christianize the pagans.
   B. Government: Assimilate them.
   C. Education: Civilize the "savages."

Satisfaction Step

I. Policy makers should acknowledge five basic truths.
   A. "Indians have been here for thousands of years.
   B. This is their homeland.
   C. Their own distinct cultures have evolved. . . .
   D. We were not forced into abandoning our cultures.
   E. Assimilation and acculturation occur on individuals terms."
II. The American Indian culture can contribute without changing.
   A. To the Iroquois, for example, "peace was the law."
      1. The same word is used for both 'peace' and 'law.'
      2. "Peace was a way of life."
   B. The allegory of the Great White Pine represents the unity of peace with law and land.
      1. For the Iroquois, the Tree symbolizes law
      2. The Tree's branches symbolize shelter within the law.
      3. The Tree's roots symbolize law's ability to stretch out and embrace all peoples.

Visualization Step

I. With recognition of the Indian's true nature and contribution can come change.
   A. Change is a cause for celebration.
   B. "With clarity of vision we can celebrate the natural diversity of our universe and our world."

II. The Indian values—patience, honest, acceptance, respect—can serve as the foundation for good interpersonal relationships in a culturally diverse world.

Action Step

I. I applaud your commitment to a culturally diverse workforce.

II. My tribute to you is to share with you a Cheyenne philosophical belief: "A nation is not conquered until the hearts of its women are on the ground. Then it is done, no matter how brave its warriors nor how strong its weapons."
   A. This is the power of women as equals.
   B. This is why the most powerful pairing is men and women working together.[24]

The Motivated Sequence and Actuative Speeches

Demands for action can be issued and defended very efficiently by using the motivated sequence. In fact, the desire to structure speeches that move people to action (to buy a product or to engage in another specified behavior) was the impetus behind Alan Monroe's development of this organizational scheme. The outline below is drawn from the sample student speech that follows. Read both the outline and the sample speech to get a clear sense of how the motivated sequence can be used in developing an actual speech.

USING THE MOTIVATED SEQUENCE IN AN ACTUATIVE SPEECH

Environmental Racism

The situation: you are presenting a speech to your classmates with the express purpose of convincing them that environmental racism is not only harmful but should be eliminated.

Specific Purpose: To persuade the class to believe that environmental racism should be eliminated.

Attention Step

I. "Every day I wake up and go dump my trash in the Oretaga's backyard."
   A. I really don't, but the expression is an apt summary of what our government does every day—dump-

ing garbage near the homes of the poor and dispossessed.

B. This activity has become known as Environmental Racism.

Need Step

I. Lower income and minorities suffer disproportionately higher exposure to hazardous waste.

II. Waste facilities are not the only cause of the problem

    A. Prisons are placed closer to lower income/minority populations.

    B. Freeways cut through these neighborhoods.

    C. Polluting industries are located nearer these areas.

III. The problem is not a small one

    A. A study found that three out of five African-American and Hispanic families live in communities with uncontrolled hazardous waste.

    B. In Houston, Texas, for example, all five landfills and three-quarters of the incinerators are in African-American neighborhoods.

    C. In East Los Angeles, for another example, five prisons and seven freeways cut through the area, home to predominantly Hispanic and African-American families.

Satisfaction/Visualization Steps

I. The solution is not an easy one to realize, as these areas generally are powerless to stop further encroachment.

II. Mainstream environmental organizations need to join forces with those organizations already in the affected communities, such as Victims of a Toxic Environment United (VOTE United).

III. Only through such efforts might the United States stop trying to hide its "third world" conditions in poverty stricken, powerless communities.

IV. Only through such efforts might ethnic and minority citizens cease to fear for their health and safety.

Action Step

I. I am asking you to sign a petition stating support for the merging of mainstream and local environmental organizations to battle this form of racism.

II. The petition will be sent to Earthshare, a coalition of mainstream environmental organizations dedicated to fighting environmental racism.

ASSESSING A SAMPLE SPEECH

The following speech was prepared by Kim Triplett of Western Washington University in Bellingham, Washington, for an Interstate Oratorical Association contest in 1994.[26] As you saw in the outline above, Triplett had to convince her audience that the problem actually existed, and that it was significant—it was not simply an isolated case. The relation between the motivated sequence and the actual speech should, by this point, be easy to see as you compare the outline with the presentation.

ENVIRONMENTAL RACISM

Kim Triplett

Attention

Every garbage day I wake up and go dump my trash in the Oretega's backyard across the street. You're probably thinking, "Really?" Of course not. But American government and industries don't think twice about dumping their trash in the backyards of minority communities across America, creating what environmentalists and civil rights activists call Environmental or Ecological Racism. Today, I will show you that environmental racism is entrenched in our minority communities and is silently torturing the residents of these cities and towns. It is time to awake from our slumber and stop the pain. /1

However, it is necessary to first establish exactly what environmental racism is. This will allow for an examination of existing environmental racism and its harms, which will enable us to look to a solution; and finally, envision the relief to be gained through the elimination of environmental racism. A lofty goal? Yes. But undeniably vital. /2

Need

In order to understand this vitality it is important to understand the issue at hand. Jay R. Hair, President of the National Wildlife Federation, explains in the February/March, 1993 issue of *National Wildlife* that environmental racism is a term that refers to the "documented findings that lower income and minority communities suffer disproportionately higher exposure to hazardous pollution." According to the March 2, 1992, issue of *The New Republic*, the battle against environmental racism began in 1982 when a chapter of the NAACP organized a protest against the placement of a PCB producing incinerator in 66 percent Black Warren County, North Carolina. As Peter Steinhart writes in the May, 1991, issue of *Audubon Magazine,* "It is a truism in America that freeways, prisons and waste facilities get foisted off on minority and poor communities." *Essence Magazine*'s July, 1991, issue adds incinerators and noxious industries to that list, making America's non-white communities some of the most lethal places to live in this country. /3

Because of the enormous prevalence of environmental racism, the scope of our examination will be limited to representative examples and a holistic overview. The harsh reality that many business owners and city planners refuse to face is that the placement of hazardous waste sites and polluting industries within a community can destroy a community. Robert Bullard explains in his book, *Dumping in Dixie,* that these establishments cause "environmental, social and economic disaster." He continues that these communities end up with "poison, pollution and poverty." These three "P's" translate into physical ailments. Linda Villarosa's July, 1991, article, "Showdown at Sunrise," explains that people report asthma, rashes, nosebleeds, eye irritations and bronchitis. Furthermore, an alarmingly high occurrence of cancer is found in these communities that most often cannot be attributed to lifestyle. /4

These ailments all stem from industrialization. Villarosa continues, "People of color pay the cost of the industrial treadmill." And it's not just a small fraction either. A 1987 study done by the United Church of Christ's Commission for Racial Justice found that three out of every five Black and Hispanic citizens live in communities with uncontrolled hazardous waste. /5

Example after example of environmental racism can be found. Robert Bullard tells the story of Houston, Texas, where all five landfills and six of the eight incinerators are located in Black neighborhoods. Houston's population is only 25 percent Black. East Los Angeles is one of the most blatant victims of environmental racism in our country. With five prisons, all of the maintenance yards for the city and county road departments and the bus and light rail systems, plus seven freeways that cut the city into sub-neighborhoods, East L.A. is one of the most dreaded places to live. Of course, the population is overwhelmingly Hispanic and African American. Peter Steinhart, in his *Audubon* article, "What Can We Do About Environmental Racism?", refers to a 4,500 bed, medium security prison that was built in East L.A. in

1985 after Lancaster had refused it because it would have been within one mile of a school. Now the prison is within two miles of 30 schools in East Los Angeles. /6

East Los Angeles has good company from the neighboring town of Vernon, with only 100 residents, but over 1,500 industries, including slaughter houses, meat packing plants and medical waste incinerators. /7

Another hot spot for environmental racism, and perhaps the most renowned, is an 85 mile stretch of 136 chemical companies between Baton Rouge and New Orleans. The pockets and makeshift communities of impoverished African Americans that dot this stretch of land are most commonly referred to as "Cancer Alley." /8

These plants pick their locations carefully, researching voting turnout and the number of English-speaking people off of census information. *Essence Magazine*'s July, 1991, issue explains that, "These plants locate in communities of people who are not empowered in the political process. Many of these communities are overwhelmed by social problems, so it's easy to dump on them." Furthermore, they are very earnest to stay right outside city and county lines so that minority citizens often have little or no jurisdiction over the toxic plants and industries, like Placid Refinery Company that sits right in Sunrise, Alabama's backyard. Placid admits to releasing 15,000 pounds of toxins into the air each year. The people of Sunrise, who live proudly in a town founded by a freed slave, suffer from mysterious rashes and other severe irritations, not to mention an inordinate rate of cancer. A big piece of the puzzle that creates this ugly picture, as *Essence Magazine* explains in their article about Sunrise, is that just because a company meets Environmental Protection Agency Guidelines, doesn't mean that they are safe to live near. Simply, because no one knows that quantity of emissions causes damage. No one knows what prolonged exposure to toxins really does and chances are the EPA is far too liberal in their regulations, but no one really knows. And not knowing in 1994 is equivalent to racist lynching in 1964. /9

Satisfaction and Visualization

Unfortunately, the solution to environmental racism is not as obvious as the problems. *Audubon Magazine* outlines the first step. People, especially those living outside of urban areas, must understand that these issues are lined with social issues of justice. Most urban activists form from existing churches and civil rights organizations who are already angered over other social injustices. Many of the organizations join forces with similar organizations to form larger groups, such as Victims of a Toxic Environment United or VOTE United. The main concern of these groups, however, is lack of money. They are poor communities joining together with poor communities who have trouble fighting against buyout plans and intimidation techniques. This is why the key to the solution is for mainstream environmental organizations to join forces with minority organizations in their battle against environmental racism. As Scott Douglas, a Professional Staff Member at Sierra Club, stated, "Environmental aggression is targeted toward areas where there is little or no effective political resistance." Mainstream environmental organizations can serve as the backbone to the urban organizations' anger over their victimization. Mainstream organizations are committed to lobbying for stronger regulations, placing limits on the amount of toxins that can be released into the air in relation to the number of surrounding citizens and how close inhabitants are. In addition, they must press for spreading these industries out and the elimination of overly hazardous institutions. Mainstream environmental organizations understand that these are the ultimate objectives and have the political and financial backing to see them through. /10

By enacting these various measures, the United States will start to look like a first world industrialized country, rather than trying to hide its Third World conditions behind its industrialization. Cultural and ethnic minorities will no longer fear for their existence, but perhaps one day flourish in their hard won battle. America will certainly hold stronger as it creates healthy, productive individuals, rather than having to support dying victims. And you and I will breathe easier knowing that our country has taken another step towards justice for all. /11

Action

I encourage you to be a part of that step in a simple but powerful way. After the round, or anytime during the tournament, come up and sign this petition to state your support for the merging of mainstream environmental organizations and urban minority protesters in their battle against environmental racism. I will be sending a copy of this petition to Earthshare, a newly formed group of over 30 mainstream environmental organizations, to the EPA and to VOTE United. Don't hesitate. Time truly is short, and someone's life may very well depend upon your signature. /12

By gaining an understanding of environmental racism, an exploration of its presence and disastrous impact was possible. The solution is desperately needed so the benefits can be reaped. /13

Perhaps the words of Albert Einstein are motivation to find a beginning to an end when he explained. "One hundred times everyday I remind myself that my inner and outer lives are based on the labors of other people, living and dead, and that I must exert myself in order to give in the same measure as I have received." Environmental racism is a product of the past still sold today. The time is now to exert ourselves and stop the pain. /14

CHAPTER SUMMARY

The rhetorical arts of persuasion and actuation are fundamental to any democratic society. Not only are they the heart and soul of capitalism, American mass media, and politics, but they are necessary to the operation of daily life. Effective persuasive speaking is a function of the following:

- Adapting to an audience's *psychological* states (psychological orientations, predispositions toward the topic, and degrees of change)
- Drawing upon diverse external *reference groups*
- Enhancing personal *credibility*

The strategies discussed under each of these topics are not exhaustive, but they suggest mental habits of audience analysis that speakers must employ each time they attempt persuasion. To increase your effectiveness, use them whenever you seek to *reinforce* an audience's commitment to shared values, to *modify* listeners' *beliefs, attitudes,* and *values,* or to move them to *action.* Using the motivated sequence will assist you in adapting your content and style to the audience.

KEY TERMS

actuation (p. 374)
boomerang effect (p. 364)
incremental change (p. 363)
knowledge bias (p. 368)
latitude of acceptance (p. 363)
latitude of rejection (p. 363)
lifestyles (p. 359)
modification (p. 371)

one-sided messages (p. 362)
psychological state (p. 366)
reference groups (p. 363)
reinforcement (p. 370)
reporting bias (p. 370)
saliency (p. 362)
two-sided messages (p. 362)
Values and Lifestyles Program (VALS) (p. 359)

$\mathscr{A}$SSESSMENT ACTIVITIES

1. Analyze the differences between an appeal to persuade and an appeal to actuate in relation to the one or more problems faced by speakers as discussed in this chapter for each of the following situations: (a) you want your parents to stop smoking; (b) you want to convince your best friend not to drop out of school; (c) you want a stranger to donate money to the local hospice program. In what ways do your appeals differ? What variables account for the differences? Which factors are the most difficult to analyze in each of these situations and why?

2. Develop and present to the class a five-to-seven-minute speech. Follow the steps in the motivated sequence appropriate to the type of speech chosen: reinforcement, modification, or actuation. As you construct your speech, keep in mind the strategies discussed in this chapter, both in terms of the essential features of all persuasive speeches and those specific to your speech. Adapt to the audience members as you deem appropriate from your analysis of their beliefs, attitudes, and values.

$\mathscr{R}$EFERENCES

1. For a discussion of the full range of rhetorical and narrative materials that count as "good reasons," see Walter R. Fisher, *Human Communication as Narration* (Columbia: University of South Carolina Press, 1987), chs. 2 and 3.

2. Arnold Mitchell, *The Nine American Lifestyles: Who We Are and Where We're Going* (New York: Macmillan, 1983).

3. Drawn from Mitchell, chs. 1 and 2, using many of his words for describing each category.

4. For background on the one-sided versus two-sided speeches, see James B. Stiff, *Persuasive Communication* (New York: Guilford Press, 1994), 117–119; see also Mike Allen, "Meta-Analysis Comparing the Persuasiveness of One-sided and Two-sided Messages," *Western Journal of Speech Communication* 55 (1991): 390–404 (1991).

5. Richard E. Petty and John T. Cacioppo, *Communication and Persuasion: Central and Peripheral Routes to Attitude Change* (New York: Springer-Verlag, 1986), 83.

6. Petty and Cacioppo, 129.

7. Petty and Cacioppo, 153.

8. Petty and Cacioppo, 87.

9. Petty and Cacioppo, 143.

10. For a review of Social Judgment Theory, see James B. Stiff, *Persuasive Communication* (New York: Guilford Press, 1994), 139–142, and Dierdre Johnston, *The Art and Science of Persuasion* (Dubuque, IA: Brown & Benchmark, 1994), 303–307.

11. Sarah Trenholm, *Persuasion and Social Influence* (Englewood Cliffs, NJ: Prentice-Hall, 1989), 58.

12. Philip Zimbardo, *Psychology and Life*, 13th ed. (New York: HarperCollins, 1992), 580–581.

13. Zimbardo, 640.

14. James B. Stiff, *Persuasive Communication* (New York: Guilford Press, 1994), 52–54.

15. Diane M. Mackie, "Systematic and Nonsystematic Processing of Majority and Minority Persuasive Communications," *Journal of Personality and Social Psychology* 53 (1987): 41–52.

16. Petty and Cacioppo, 205.

17. R. E. Petty and T. C. Brock, "Effects of Responding or Not Responding to Hecklers on Audience Agreement with a Speaker," *Journal of Applied Social Psychology* 6 (1976):1–17.

18. A complete summary of research on credibility, which supports these conclusions, is found in Stephen Littlejohn, "A Bibliography of Studies Related to Variables of Source Credibility," in *Bibliographical Annual in Speech Communication: 1971,* ed. Ned. A. Shearer (New York: Speech Communication Association, 1972), 1–40. Research showing that credibility tends to vary from situation to situation and topic to topic is represented by such studies as Jo Liska, "Situational and Topical Variations in Credibility Criteria," *Communication Monographs* 45 (1978): 85–92. For a contemporary account of the relationship between source credibility and attitude change, see Petty and Cacioppo and Stiff.

19. Alice H. Eagly and Shelly Chaiken, *The Psychology of Attitudes* (New York: Harcourt, Brace and Jovanovich, 1993), 357–358.

20. Chaim Perelman and L. Olbrechts-Tyteca, *The New Rhetoric: A Treatise on Argumentation,* trans. John Wilkinson and Purcell Weaver (Notre Dame, IN: University of Notre Dame Press, 1969), 51.

21. Fisher, ch. 5.

22. Donald Dean Morley and Kim B. Walker, "The Role of Importance, Novelty, and Plausibility in Producing Belief Change," *Communication Monographs* 54 (1987): 436–42. The theory is presented in Donald Dean Morley, "Subjective Message Constructs: A Theory of Persuasion," *Communication Monographs* 54 (1987): 183–203.

23. Kay Deaux and Lawrence S. Wrightsman, *Social Psychology,* 5th ed. (Pacific Grove, CA: Brooks/Cole, 1988), 160–209. See also Gerald R. Miller, Michael Burgoon, and Judee K. Burgoon, "The Functions of Human Communication in Changing Attitudes and Gaining Compliance," in *Handbook of Rhetorical and Communication Theory* eds. Carroll C. Arnold and John Waite Bowers (Boston: Allyn and Bacon, 1984), 400–474.

24. Adapted from a speech by Henri Mann Morton, "Strength Through Cultural Diversity," in *Native American Reader,* ed. J. Blanche (Juneau, Alaska: Denali Press, 1990). Portions of her speech are quoted verbatim.

25. Outline adapted from Kim Triplett, "Environmental Racism," *Winning Orations 1994,* ed. Larry G. Schnoor, Executive Secretary (Mankato, MN: Interstate Oratorical Association, 1994), 133–136.

26. Kim Triplett, "Environmental Racism," in *Winning Orations 1994.* Reprinted by permission of Larry Schnoor, Interstate Oratorical Association, Mankato State University, MN.

CHAPTER
15

$\mathscr{A}$RGUMENT
AND CRITICAL THINKING

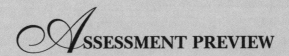

$\mathscr{A}$SSESSMENT PREVIEW

After reading Chapter 15, the student with basic communication competencies will be able to

- understand the social commitments one makes as an arguer.
- distinguish factual, valuative, and policy claims.
- understand and list the basic types of reasoning.
- employ at least three types of reasoning in an argumentative speech.

The student with average communication competencies will also be able to

- construct a sound policy argument with relevant evidence.
- employ all of the types of reasoning in an argumentative speech.
- apply the tests of reasoning to each type.
- recognize and evaluate at least five fallacies.

The student with superior communication competencies will also be able to

- evaluate a policy argument in terms of rationally and motivationally relevant evidence.
- determine whether reasoning is flawed either through tests of reasoning or critiquing fallacies of argument.
- apply the Toulmin model as a means of testing arguments.

*S*hould the United States continue supporting the United Nations? Should citizens endorse a "flat-tax" proposal? Should our university institute a new technology fee? Should we rent a movie tonight? These are very different questions, yet alike in a major respect. Each is debatable; none of the questions automatically suggests a "right" or "true" answer that all would agree with. Answering any of these with a simple "yes" or "no" will invite others to ask "why do you believe as you do?" You will be expected to provide reasons and evidence for your position. Your response, in turn, may well be challenged by your listeners. In short, this exchange involves you and your listener in **argumentation**—the give and take involved in advancing reasons for and against a particular claim that has been advanced. This process can be discussed in terms of **argument**—the actual "product" that results from the combination of a *claim* plus supporting *reasons* and *evidence*—as well as the act of **arguing** itself.[1] As you argue, you also engage in **critical thinking**—the process of examining the relationship between your own reasons and the claim you are advocating, and the reasons or evidence offered by those challenging your argument.[2]

If the questions raised above were capable of being answered truthfully, without any concern for being mistaken at some later point, there would be no cause for challenge. There are, however, few such questions that have such answers available. Hence, argument is a constant companion of those issues and ideas for which there are no certain answers. In arguing, our search is for the "best answer" we can offer given the knowledge available. We do not know for

Argumentation is inherently bilateral: It requires at least two competing messages. Reasons are given and refuted; claims are advanced and withdrawn.

certain whether supporting the United Nations will do us harm in the future, nor do we know whether a flat tax is the best solution to our economic situation, nor do we know whether a technology fee is the right way to raise money for new computer equipment. Finally, we cannot be certain that renting a movie is the optimum choice (especially if we have an exam tomorrow). Given this uncertainty, the best solution is to think critically about our choices by testing the evidence offered in support of reasons—is it reliable?—and examining the relationship between reasons and claims—do the reasons really support the claim? As we do so, two features of argumentation are worthy of comment. First, argument is a social process. Second, argument is aimed at justifying our beliefs and actions. We will begin with an examination of the social process involved in arguing with others. Then we will consider what is involved in justifying claims, with a focus on improving your effectiveness as an arguer.

ARGUMENT AND SOCIAL COMMITMENTS

Argument and critical thinking are bound together in public communication. Exchanging views in the social world automatically includes the critical assessment of those ideas. Engaging in argument commits you to social conventions governing deliberation, whether in private interchanges with close friends, or in public settings among friends and strangers.[3]

Commitment to Change Your Mind

You and those who challenge you must be willing to alter personal beliefs or actions when faced with strong counterargument.[4] You've experienced the frustration of arguing with someone who does not accept this social convention: a stubborn friend or other opponent who believes only what he or she is saying, and simply refuses to acknowledge the possibility that the position being advanced is wrong.

Commitment to Knowledge

Argument fails where ignorance prevails. As in accepting the possibility of being wrong, both parties to an argument must also accept a commitment to learn from each other, to search for new information, to test evidence in order to ensure that the best possible information is being used to support alternative positions. Those who are certain of their own beliefs ("Don't confuse me with facts. My mind is made up.") are closed to information counter to that which they already accept or which supports their position.

Commitment to Worthy Subjects

Ever been in a silly argument? Unfortunately, many arguments we engage in can be summarized in the following statement: "Argumentation concerns talk between the uninformed and the misinformed about the inconsequential."

COMMUNICATION RESEARCH DATELINE

ARGUMENTATIVENESS AND VERBAL AGGRESSION

Is being an arguer a positive or negative trait? How about the individual who argues by attacking the person rather than the substance of the argument? Isn't he or she violating the conventions of argumentation outlined in this chapter? Don't some people really like to engage in argumentation, while others seem to acquiesce in order to avoid an argument? Infante and his colleagues conducted a series of studies on *argumentativeness* and *verbal aggression*. They conceptualized argumentativeness in positive terms, as a socially desirable trait that predisposes an individual to assess reasons and to present arguments in accordance with appropriate social conventions. Students strongly oriented toward arguing with others were found to have experienced greater training in argumentation. They also reported a higher overall grade point, were born earlier in the family birth order (which is consistent with other research on the assertiveness of first-borns), preferred smaller classes (presumably because it is easier to engage in argumentation), and tended to be more liberal.

More importantly, Infante et al. found that "high argumentatives" are *not* less likely than "low argumentatives" to value the importance of maintaining general social relations or getting along with peers. Enjoying a good argument does not mean a person cannot respect others. In actual argumentation, those who scored high on an argumentativeness scale displayed less flexibility in the positions they advocated, appeared more interested in arguing and willing to argue, were perceived as more skillful arguers, and were more enthusiastic in their conduct of the argument.

The value of critical thinking, and the need to test ideas in private or in public is wasted on frivolous topics. There is a social need for argument about issues that matter, about causes that do in fact make a difference in how we treat each other, how we live with each other.

Commitment to Rules

Argument is a rule-governed process of arriving at a conclusion that is, to the best of one's knowledge, justifiable as a basis for belief or action. The rules

While argumentativeness is linked to assertive behavior, verbal aggressiveness is related to hostility and reflects a willingness to verbally abuse a person in the act of arguing. While argumentatively oriented people may resort to verbal aggression under some circumstances, the two "traits" are distinct psychological responses. People higher in argumentativeness are no more likely than others to engage in aggressive behavior. Two sources of verbal aggression are frustration with the way another person is arguing or with a recognition of one's own skill deficiencies and prior experience or social conditioning to respond aggressively. A person scoring high on the Verbal Aggressiveness scale is more likely to attack an opponent's competence, tease an opponent, use facial expressions and other nonverbal cues to attack the opponent's self-concept, and use profanity.

As this research suggests, argumentation can be a constructive, positive activity when it adheres to the social conventions. Arguing well with others can be personally enjoyable regardless of the outcome, but using verbal aggression is destructive to other people and diminishes the quality of any decisions that might be reached.

For Further Reading

Infante, Dominic A., "The Argumentative Student in the Speech Communication Classroom: An Investigation and Implications," *Communication Education* 31 (1982): 141–148; Infante, Dominic A. "Trait Argumentativeness as a Predictor of Communicative Behavior in Situations Requiring Argument," *Central States Speech Journal* 32 (1981): 265–272; Infante, Dominic A., and Andrew Rancer, "A Conceptualization and Measure of Argumentativeness," *Journal of Personality Assessment* 46 (1982): 72–80; Infante, Dominic A., and Charles J. Wigley III, "Verbal Aggressiveness: An Interpersonal Model and Measure," *Communication Monographs* 53 (1986): 61–69; Infante, Dominic A., J. David Trebing, Patricia E. Shepherd, and Dale E. Seeds, "The Relationship of Argumentativeness to Verbal Aggression," *Southern Speech Communication Journal* 50 (1984): 67–77. Infante, Dominic, Bruce L. Riddle, Cary L. Horvath, S. A. Tumlin, "Verbal Aggressiveness: Messages and Reasons," *Communication Quarterly* 40 (1992): 116–126.

may focus on the overall procedures for engaging in argument, as in using parliamentary procedure rules to govern who talks, when, and for how long. The rules also focus on the product itself: not any reason will support any claim— there needs to be some kind of logical, rational connection between a given reason and the claim being offered. Finally, as noted in Chapter 1, the rules may focus on conventions governing how to communicate in social or public settings.

The reliance on reasons given for belief or action constitutes the major difference between argumentation and mere fighting. As such, argumentation is a form of persuasion in that it seeks to change the beliefs, attitudes, values, and behaviors of others. At the same time, it's a form of mutual truth-testing, helping participants arrive at the best possible conclusions, given the information available at the time. Thus the process is more thoroughly *rule-governed* than other forms of public presentation.

These four commitments define the social parameters of argument in the social community. Whether you are engaging in private discussion or in public deliberation, the same conventions will apply. The process of thinking critically about how argument proceeds depends, in addition, on an understanding of how one arrives at a justifiable defense, or attack, of another person's position.

ARGUMENT AS JUSTIFYING BELIEF AND ACTION

The analysis of how one justifies a position begins with the **claim** being advanced, then examines the nature of **evidence** used in support of the claim and the major **reasoning patterns** (sometimes referred to as the warrants or inferences) used to connect evidence to claims.

Types of Claims

The majority of argumentative speeches assert that (a) something is or is not the case; (b) something is desirable or undesirable; or (c) something should or should not be done. The first step in constructing a successful argument is to determine clearly the nature of the claim you wish to establish.

Claims of Fact. If you are trying to convince your listeners that "Price controls on raw agricultural products result in food shortages," you're presenting a claim of fact—asserting that an audience is justified in believing that this state of affairs will occur. When confronted with a **factual claim,** two questions are likely to arise in the mind of a critical listener:

1. *By what criteria or standards of judgment should the accuracy of this claim be measured?* Some standards are rather obvious. If you were asked to judge a person's height, using a yardstick or other instrument would provide the answer. Listeners look for similar kinds of yardsticks when asked to evaluate more complex claims. Before agreeing that price controls will produce food shortages, critical thinkers will want to know exactly what "price control" means, as well as what constitutes a "shortage"; when is a shortage really a shortage—when food resources drop below expected levels or when food disappears completely? What standard is being used to define "shortage," thereby affirming the accuracy of the claim?

2. *Do the facts of the situation fit the criteria as set forth?* What kinds of food will count as part of the "shortage" being defined? Are we talking

about produce on grocery shelves, or unprocessed grain in elevators, or both? The criteria you advance for how "shortage" will be defined must appear reasonable to your audience, and your evidence then needs to fit the criteria—there must actually be a shortage of stored grain if that is part of the definition. Realize that the audience may choose to disagree with your criteria as well as with your evidence. Hence, you need to be prepared to defend both in response to possible attacks.

FIGURE 15.1 The Levels of Argumentation

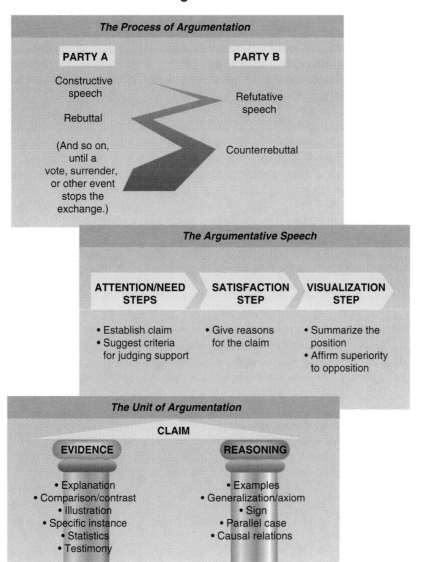

Claims of Value. A claim also may incorporate value judgments in asserting that your idea is worthy or that the idea of an opponent is undesirable or unjustified. In these cases, you are articulating a **value claim** that, as with a factual claim, is supported by (a) standards or criteria and (b) by the illustration of how your value term meets those criteria. In the preceding example, the claim that price controls cause shortages implies a value—things that cause shortages are not worthy of consideration. You must, however, do more than simply suggest a preference: "I don't like price controls." You need to know how price controls function, and what negative effects they create. This knowledge leads you to the criteria for judging the worth of price controls, and makes it easier to argue for their inadequacy due to the negative effects created.

Claims of Policy. A **policy claim** recommends a course of action you want the audience to approve. For example, you might claim that "The federal government *should* establish a flat tax rate." The policy claim incorporates fact and value claims as its primary "proofs":

Policy: The federal government should establish a flat tax rate . . . because. . . .
Value: A flat tax rate is an equitable tax policy because. . . .
Fact: A flat tax rate will simplify present IRS tax codes because. . . .
Fact: A flat tax rate will produce sufficient revenue because. . . .

The key term in the policy claim is *should*—it identifies a proposed policy or defends a policy or action that is currently the case. For our purposes, those policy claims examined will *challenge* the present system, procedure, or way of doing things. When establishing or analyzing a policy claim, four questions are relevant:

1. *Is there a need for such a policy or course of action?* If your listeners don't believe a change is called for, they aren't likely to approve your proposal. This doesn't mean you should avoid new ideas; rather, it suggests that the importance of establishing a *need for change* depends upon the audience's level of comfort with the status quo.
2. *Is the proposal practical or workable?* Can we afford the expenses it would entail? Will it meet the need as identified? Does such a policy stand a reasonable chance of being adopted? If the policy can't meet these basic tests, what chance does it have?
3. *Will the benefits of your proposal be greater than its disadvantages?* People are reluctant to approve a proposal that promises to create conditions worse than the ones it's designed to correct. Burning a building to the ground to get rid of rats may be efficient, but it is hardly desirable. The benefits and disadvantages must be carefully weighed in concluding that a proposal is indeed comparatively better than the present course.
4. *Is the offered proposal superior to any other plan or policy?* Listeners are hesitant to approve a plan if they have reason to believe that the current

policy is more practical and more beneficial. During the 1996 Republican campaign for the presidential nomination, Lamar Alexander, Pat Buchanan, Robert Dole, and Steve Forbes argued over flat tax proposals. Republican voters compared their plans to the current IRS tax code to determine whether the general idea was worthy of support, and to decide which tax plan was the best of the alternatives proposed.

The types of claims make different demands on you as an arguer (see Table 15.1). Your best strategy is to set forth claims, the criteria they are based on, and the evidence used to support the claim in a straightforward, honest manner. In that way, your audience can see what standard of judgment you are using, and decide whether it is appropriate, as well as how *you* see the evidence functioning in relation to the criteria and claim.

Previewing the underlying logic of your argument up front, unless there are solid reasons for delaying this information, enables your audience to follow your line of reasoning. You should say something on the order of "I hope to convince you that a flat tax rate is the best option for the American taxpayer. If the government takes this action, it will result in fair and equitable treatment for all taxpayers, regardless of income level."

Evidence

As you discovered in Chapter 6, supporting materials clarify, amplify, and strengthen the ideas in your speech. They provide evidence for the acceptance of a claim and its supporting points. Evidence is a crucial part of developing a

TABLE 15.1 Types of Claims

Claim	Description	Analysis
Fact	Assertion that something exists.	1. By what criteria is the accuracy of the claim measured? 2. Do the facts of the situation fit the criteria?
Value	Assertion that something is worthy/unworthy.	1. By what standards is something to be judged? 2. How well does the thing measure up?
Policy	Recommendation of a course of action	1. Is there a need? 2. Is the proposal practical? 3. Are the benefits greater than the disadvantages? 4. Is the proposal better than other courses of action?

clear, compelling argument, and it can be presented in any of the forms already discussed: explanation, comparison and contrast, illustration, specific instance, statistics, and testimony. As you conduct your search for information, the primary goal is to find supporting material that is both *rationally* and *motivationally relevant* to the claim being advanced.

Rationally Relevant Evidence. The type of evidence you select should reflect the type of claim you advocate. For example, if you are defending the claim that censorship violates the First Amendment guarantee of freedom of speech, you'll find testimony from legal authorities useful in supporting your argument. On the other hand, examples, illustrations, and statistics work better in those instances where you argue that a problem exists or a change in practices is needed. If you argue that shark fishing should be more heavily regulated, you'll find that examples of poor fishing practices and statistical evidence that relates to overfishing and potential loss to the ecosystem will be relevant to your purpose. Always ask yourself: "Given this claim, what evidence is naturally suggested by the subject matter?" What type of evidence is logically relevant?

Motivationally Relevant Evidence. Listeners often require more than logically relevant support. Your evidence also must create a compelling desire on their part to be involved, to endorse the belief, or to undertake a course of action. That is, to motivate your listeners you must answer the "So what?" question. To select motivationally relevant material, consider these two issues:

1. *What type of evidence will this audience demand?* To orient your thinking, turn this question around and ask, "As a member of the audience, what would I expect as support for this claim in order to accept it?" What motivates you to accept the argument may well motivate the audience. And, as noted above, some evidence seems naturally connected to certain subjects. A claim regarding relative costs of competing plans suggests things like statistical graphs or charts. If the audience is able to say "Yes . . . but. . . " after hearing your evidence, you haven't motivated them to accept your claim. Careful audience analysis and consideration of the occasion will help determine what will motivate your listeners.

2. *What evidence will generate the best response?* You should pose this question once you've determined the type of evidence required in your argument. For example, if you've decided to use expert testimony to support your argument, whom should you quote? If you're using an illustration, should you use a factual example from the local group or develop one of your own? Will your listeners be more moved by a personal story than a general illustration?

Forms of Reasoning (Inference)

You will make connections between claims, criteria, and evidence using different *forms of reasoning* or **inferences**. Forms of reasoning are habitual ways a

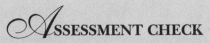

As you listen to claims asking for your belief or action, distinguish between claims of fact, value, and policy:

- Are the criteria clear, and is the evidence both rationally and motivationally relevant?
- Are there deficiencies in the evidence, such that you remain skeptical about either believing or acting as you are asked, or do you think you are justified in accepting the claim?
- What happens if you are wrong?

culture or society uses inferences to connect the material supporting a claim with the claim itself. In our culture, there are five primary patterns: reasoning from example, generalization, sign, parallel case, and causal relations.

Reasoning from Example. **Reasoning from example** (which is also often called **inductive reasoning**) is the process of examining a series of known occurrences and drawing a general conclusion, or using a single instance to reason to a future instance of the same kind. The conclusion is probable rather than certain: "In every election in our community over the past few years, when a candidate leads the polls by ten or more points with a month to go, he or she has won. Thus, my candidate will surely win next month." Maybe so— but maybe not. The inference in this case can be stated as "What is true of the particular cases is true of the whole class, or, more precisely, future instances of the same class." As this example suggests, most reasoning from example uses multiple instances in inferring a conclusion. However, a single instance can be a powerful illustration on which to base a conclusion. One can argue that one death at an intersection supports the need for a traffic light. Using relevant examples will ensure a high degree of probability and provide strong justification for the adoption of a claim.

Reasoning from Generalization or Axiom. Applying a general truism to a specific situation is a form of **deductive reasoning.** Where inductive reasoning is typified by an inferential leap on the basis of the evidence, deductive reasoning produces a conclusion that is true only if the premises are true. For example, you may know that generic drugs are cheaper than brand-name drugs. On the basis of this general truism, you ask your druggist for the generic prescription whenever possible as it will save you money. To the extent that the **generalization** holds true, your experience has to hold true as well.

Reasoning from Sign. This pattern uses an observable mark, or symptom, as proof of the existence of a certain state of affairs. **Sign reasoning** occurs when you note the appearance of a rash or spots on your skin (evidence) and

ℰTHICAL MOMENTS
THE USE OF EVIDENCE

The use of evidence generates several potential ethical dilemmas. Consider the following issues:

1. Should you suppress evidence that contradicts a point you are making? If your opponent isn't aware of the information, should you mention it?

2. What about the use of qualifiers? Should you leave in all of the "maybe's" and "possibly's" when you read or paraphrase a quotation? If you have to submit a written text or outline, you can use ellipses (the three dots that indicate something is missing from the original) where the qualifiers once were.

3. Does it make any difference if you overqualify a source? If you've discovered an article by a staff researcher at the National

Endowment for the Arts on the issue of funding controversial art, will it hurt to pretend the information is from an associate director of the agency? If it increases the credibility of the information, should it be used?

4. What difference does it make if a poll is conducted by the National Right-to-Life Committee or Planned Parenthood's Pro-Choice Committee? What if each organization asks polling questions in such a way as to encourage a response favorable to their position? Can you just say that "a recent national poll found that 75 percent of our citizens favor abortion rights?" You haven't really lied in suppressing the polling agency or the actual questions asked, have you? Is this acceptable?

---

conclude you have the measles (claim). Signs aren't causes; a rash doesn't cause measles, an ambulance siren doesn't cause the accident or crisis it responds to. Reasoning from sign is central to detective work, whether in your own investigation of a situation, a doctor's assessment of an illness, or a police detective's study of motives for a crime. However, isolating the signs and reasoning to a probable conclusion based on what they suggest may yield an erroneous conclusion. Sign reasoning doesn't produce certain evidence in all cases—motive, weapon, and opportunity don't prove a person committed a crime. Was O. J. Simpson really guilty? The inference that evidence is a sign of a conclusion is not always true. Nonetheless, we use sign reasoning as a means of projecting economic trends, as well as forecasting the weather or predicting how well a candidate will do in the coming election.

Reasoning from Parallel Case. Another common reasoning pattern involves **parallel case**—comparing similar events or things and drawing conclusions based on the comparison. The claim that your state should adopt a motorcycle helmet law might be supported by noting that a neighboring state, with similar characteristics, has one and has experienced lower death and head injury rates. In essence, you are claiming "What happened there can happen here." The political candidate's claim that what he or she has done for a community or state can be repeated in a larger arena, while not precisely parallel, draws strength from this type of argument. As the variables separating the cases grow in size and significance, this reasoning pattern will become less forceful.

Reasoning from Causal Relation. **Causal reasoning** assumes that one event influences or controls other events. You can reason from a specific cause to an effect or set of effects, or vice versa. For instance, assume that alcohol abuse on a campus appears to be increasing. Is the increase the result of lax enforcement of existing rules? Do loopholes allow for greater abusive situations to develop, in spite of best intentions? Are today's students more prone to abuse than in previous years? Pointing to one or more of these as the cause sets the stage for an analysis of potential solutions. The key is to point to connections between lax enforcement or loopholes and the resulting effect of increased alcohol abuse. The principle underlying this pattern is one of constancy: Every effect has a cause.

Testing the Adequacy of Forms of Reasoning

Central to thinking critically is testing the reasoning pattern for weaknesses, both as a user and as a consumer. Each pattern has its own unique set of criteria for establishing a valid, sound argument. Within the context of each pattern, apply the following questions to your own arguments and to those of others.

REASONING FROM EXAMPLE

1. *Have you looked at enough instances to warrant generalizing?* Just because you passed the last test without studying doesn't mean that not studying is the way to approach all future tests.
2. *Are the instances fairly chosen or representative?* Deciding never to shop in a store because a clerk was rude isn't exactly working on the basis of a representative, let alone sufficient, sample. You'll want to judge the store in a variety of situations. If you find that rudeness is the norm rather than the exception, your claim may be justified.
3. *Are there important exceptions to the generalization that must be accounted for?* While it is generally true, from presidential election studies, that "As Maine goes, so goes the nation," there have been enough exceptions

to that rule to keep candidates who lose in a Maine primary campaigning until the general election.

REASONING FROM GENERALIZATION OR AXIOM

1. *Is the generalization accepted?* Those who go on diets generally gain back the weight lost. People who marry young are more likely to divorce. Each of these is a generalization; you need to determine whether sufficient evidence exists to justify the claim if not already accepted as a general truism.
2. *Does the generalization apply to this particular case?* Usually, discount stores offer better deals, but on occasion one can find better prices at sales at local neighborhood stores. While "birds of a feather flock together" applies to birds, it may not apply to a group of humans.

REASONING FROM SIGN

1. *Is the sign error-proof?* Many signs constitute circumstantial evidence rather than absolute certain proof. Be especially careful not to confuse sign reasoning with causal reasoning. If sign reasoning were error-proof or infallible, weather forecasters would never be wrong.
2. *Is the observation accurate?* Witnesses sometimes testify to things that later prove to be wrong. People differ in their interpretations of events. Be certain that the observation is accurate—that the sign did exist as described or explained.

REASONING FROM PARALLEL CASE

1. *Are there more similarities than differences between the two cases?* Two items may have many features in common, but there also may be significant differences that would weaken your argument. Just because two states appear similar, they may also have many more differences that would weaken the effectiveness of the parallel being drawn.
2. *Are the similarities you've pointed out the relevant and important ones?* There are two students down the hall who dress in similar clothes, have the same major, and get similar grades; does this mean that if one is nice, so is the other one? Probably not, because the similarities you've noticed are relatively unconnected to niceness. Their personal values and their relations with others would be more important criteria on which to base a parallel case.

REASONING FROM CAUSAL RELATIONS

1. *Can you separate causes and effects?* We often have trouble with "Which came first?" kinds of issues. Do higher wages cause higher prices, or the reverse? Does a strained homelife cause a child to misbehave, or is it the other way around?

2. *Are the causes sufficient to produce the effect?* Causes must not only be *necessary* to produce an effect, they also must be *sufficient*. While air is necessary for fire to exist, it isn't all that's required or we would be in a state of constant fire.

3. *Did intervening events or persons prevent a cause from having its normal effect?* Causes do not always produce their expected effects; they may be interrupted by other factors. An empty gun does not shoot; droughts drive up food prices only if there is insufficient food on hand, the ground was already dry, or cheap alternatives are unavailable.

4. *Could any other cause have produced the effect?* Some effects may be produced by different causes; thus you need to search for the most likely cause in a given situation. Although crime often increases when communities deteriorate, increased crime rates can also be caused by many other changes. A sagging economy could also be a possible reason for higher crime. Perhaps crime only appears to have risen; in actuality, maybe people are just keeping better records.

5. *Is the cause really a correlation?* Correlations aren't necessarily causally related. Two phenomena may vary together without being related in any way. For example, since Abraham Lincoln's assassination, presidents elected in a year divisible by 20 (until President Reagan) died in office. However, the year was inconsequential in causing the death.

These patterns of reasoning and their tests are not the only means of evaluating the effectiveness of arguments. Arguments can be flawed in other ways as well. The following section describes common flaws or *fallacies* in reasoning.

Detecting Fallacies in Reasoning

In general, **fallacies** interrupt the normal process of connecting claims, criteria, and evidence. We will discuss ten of the most common garden variety fallacies; these are argument errors that you already have committed or have experienced as you listen to others provide reasons for their claims.

Hasty generalization (faulty inductive leap): This fallacy occurs when the conclusion is based on far too little evidence. If the answer to the question "Have enough instances been examined?" is no, a flaw in reasoning has occurred. Urging a ban on 747's because one was involved in an accident or on aerosol sprays because one blew up in a fire is insufficient support for the claim being urged.

Genetic fallacy: This argument rests on origins, historical tradition, or sacred practice: "We've always done it this way; therefore this is the best way." The fact that an idea or institution or practice has been around a long time may have little bearing on whether it still should be. Many people who defended slavery referred to the biblical practice of slavery. Times change, and new values replace old ones, suggesting that new practices may be more in tune with present values.

TABLE 15.2 **Distinguishing and Testing Types of Reasoning**

Form	Description	Example	Test
Example	Drawing a general conclusion from one or more examples.	I enjoy Bach, Beethoven and Ravel; I like classical music.	1. Sufficient instances? 2. Fairly selected? 3. Important exceptions?
Generalization or axiom	Applying a general truism to a specific example.	Bichons are friendly dogs; I'll buy a Bichon.	1. Generally accepted? 2. Applies to this instance?
Sign	Using a symptom or other observable event as proof of a state of affairs.	The petunias are dead. Someone forgot to water them.	1. Fallible sign? 2. Accurate observation?
Parallel case	Asserting that because two items share similar characteristics, they will share results.	Tougher enforcement of existing laws reduced drunk driving in Indiana; hence such laws will work in Iowa.	1. More similarities than differences? 2. Similarities are relevant, important?
Causal relation	Concluding that one event influences the existence of a second, later event.	The engine won't start; the carburetor is flooded.	1. Causes and effects separable? 2. Cause sufficient to produce effect? 3. Presence of intervening events? 4. Any other cause possible, important? 5. Cause or correlation?

Appeal to ignorance: The expression "You *can't* prove it *won't* work" illicitly uses double negatives. Incomplete knowledge also doesn't mean a claim is or isn't true: "We can't use radio beams to signal extraterrestrials because we don't know what languages they speak." In countering such claims, utilize arguments from parallel cases and from examples since they both transcend the "unknown" in providing support for a claim.

Appeal to popular opinion (bandwagon fallacy): "Jump on the bandwagon" and "Everyone is going" are appeals to group support. If others support the position, then you're pressured into supporting it as well: "But, Dad, everyone is going to the party!" While these claims may function as evidence of what people believe or value, they are not, for that reason, true. The world has witnessed hundreds of widely believed but false ideas, from the belief that night air causes tuberculosis to panic over an invasion by Martians.

Appeal to authority: Citing someone who is popular but nonexpert as the basis for accepting a claim is an inappropriate use of an appeal to authority. The critical question in using authoritative testimony is to ask: "Is the source an expert on this topic?" If not, why should you accept the claim?

Sequential fallacy: This phrase literally translates from the Latin (*post hoc, ergo propter hoc*) as "After this; therefore because of this." This is a primitive kind of causal argument because it is based on the sequence of events in time: "I slept near a draft last night and woke up with a nasty head cold" (the draft didn't cause the cold, a virus did). While the sequence may be appropriate ("The coach gave an inspirational half-time speech, and the players came out on fire"), there are often other circumstances (the players like the coach) that help produce the effect. Timing alone is not sufficient to draw causal connections.

Begging the question: This is circular or tautological reasoning: "Abortion is murder because it is taking the life of the unborn" rephrases the claim (it is murder) to form the reason (it is taking life). Nothing new has been said. In other cases, begging the question occurs in the form of a *complex question:* "Have you stopped cheating on tests yet?" assumes you have cheated in the past, when that may not be known. Saying "yes" admits past cheating; saying "no" admits to both past and present cheating. You can't win either way you go. Evaluative claims are especially prone to this abuse of reasoning.

Ambiguity: A word may have more than one meaning; using a term without clarifying its specific meaning can result in confusion and in inaccurate claims: "Some dogs have droopy ears. My dog has droopy ears. My dog is *some* dog!" The confusion rests with the word "some"—its first use suggests "not all" dogs, while the second word suggests "outstanding/exceptional." Such shifts in meaning can result in flawed claims.

Persuasive definition: Value terms and other abstract concepts are open to special or skewed definitions that are unique to the person or group offering them: "Liberty means the right to own military weapons"; "Real men don't wear cologne"; "A true patriot doesn't protest against this country while on foreign soil." Each of these definitions sets up a particular point of view that is capricious and arbitrary. You could say that persuasive definitions are self-serving, as they promote an argument at the expense of more inclusive definitions of the same terms. If you accept the definition, the argument is essentially over.[5] Substituting a definition from a respected, widely accepted source is a way of challenging this fallacy.

Name-calling: There are several forms of this fallacy; all involve attacking the person rather than the argument. You may attack special interests ("Of course you're defending her; she's your cousin") or personal characteristics ("No wonder you're arguing that way; dweebs [or "geeks"] always think that way"). In these two cases, being related is not proof of defense, and dweebs may have ideas as good as anyone else's. Claims ought to be judged on their own terms, not on the people or ideas with which they may or may not be connected.

These are some of the fallacies that find their way into causal and formal argumentation. A good basic logic book can point out additional fallacies.[6] If you know about fallacies, you'll be better able to construct sound arguments and to assess the weaknesses in your opponent's arguments. Also, thinking critically can protect you from being taken in by unscrupulous politicians, sales personnel, and advertisers. The process of protecting yourself from irrelevant appeals can benefit from the model for organizing and evaluating arguments that is presented below.

A Model of Organizing and Evaluating Arguments

Writing in 1958, the British philosopher Stephen Toulmin proposed that arguments be diagrammed in a visually clear pattern that would help ensure that all elements—implicit and explicit—were recognized. The following elements, and the visual model that illustrates the relationships among them, will aid you in analyzing and critiquing your arguments and the arguments of others.

1. *Claim:* Put simply, what are you proposing for audience consideration: fact, value, or policy?
2. *Data:* What materials, in the form of illustrative parallels, expert opinion, statistical information, research studies, and the like, can you advance to support the claim?
3. *Warrant:* What is the relationship between the parallel case, statistical data, or expert opinion and the claim? Upon what kind of assumption or inferential pattern does its acceptance as support for the claim depend? Materials don't function as evidence or support for no reason; *facts do not speak for themselves.* What makes an audience believe in the strength of the reasons as support lies in the following kinds of assumptions that warrant acceptance of the link between data and claim:
   a. An expert knows what he or she is talking about.
   b. Past economic, social, or political practices are reliable predictors of future occurrences.
   c. Inferential patterns (for example, cause, sign) suggest that the linkage is rational.
   We know, for instance, that an expert's credibility is a major determinant in gaining acceptance of the opinions being offered. In the development of the argument, this factor operates as an implicit *warrant* connecting the opinion to the claim. In matters involving economics, we know that the regularity of certain marketplace functions, such as supply and demand, exerts a powerful influence on events. Hence, when we claim that the prices of finished products will rise as a result of the increases in the cost of raw materials, we are tacitly assuming the normal operation of the marketplace. Likewise, the value of using parallel cases as support for a position rests on the regularity of an inferential pattern: when two cases are parallel, similar results can be expected.

4. *Backing:* Does the audience accept the relationship between the data and the claim as given? If not, what further data would help support the warrant? When the warrant linking a reason and claim is accepted by the audience, explicit development of this facet of the argument is unnecessary. If an audience already understands the logical pattern of an analogy and believes that the substance of the argument being presented is analogous, spending time to support the analogous nature of the relationship would be pointless. When a relationship between the reason and the claim isn't automatically accepted, the speaker will have to provide additional support focused on the warrant rather than the original claim. Thus, in supporting an argument claiming that price controls would cause food shortages with authoritative testimony

FIGURE 15.2   The Toulmin Model of Argument

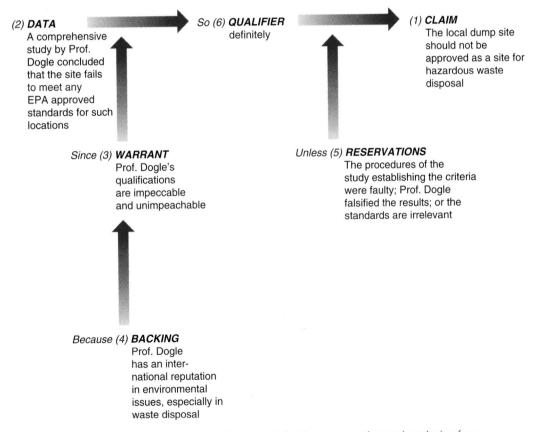

(2) **DATA**
A comprehensive study by Prof. Dogle concluded that the site fails to meet any EPA approved standards for such locations

So (6) **QUALIFIER**
definitely

(1) **CLAIM**
The local dump site should not be approved as a site for hazardous waste disposal

Since (3) **WARRANT**
Prof. Dogle's qualifications are impeccable and unimpeachable

Unless (5) **RESERVATIONS**
The procedures of the study establishing the criteria were faulty; Prof. Dogle falsified the results; or the standards are irrelevant

Because (4) **BACKING**
Prof. Dogle has an international reputation in environmental issues, especially in waste disposal

These six elements operate as a general framework for the construction and analysis of an argument. The interrelationships among the elements can best be displayed through a visual diagram. The numbers in the diagram correspond to the elements discussed.

from a politician, you may need to establish her expertise to increase audience acceptance.

5. *Reservations:* Can significant counterarguments be raised? In most cases, arguments on the opposite side are not only readily available but may even be as strong as your own reasons. Anticipating reservations in advance will help you strengthen your own argument. In general, these can be thought of as "unless" clauses in your argument.

6. *Qualifiers:* How certain is the claim? Note that we do not ask how certain *you* are; you may be absolutely sure of something for which you cannot offer verifiable support. How much can your listeners bank on the claim that you are putting forward as an acceptable basis for belief or action? Are you *sure* that price controls will have the claimed effect? Qualifiers such as *probably, presumably, virtually,* and *may* should be incorporated into the claim to reflect the strength of the argument.

The model has three principal uses in organizing your arguments. First, by setting forth the arguments' components in the manner indicated, you'll be able to capture visually the relationships among the components. How, for example, are the data you present linked to the claim? What sort of warrants (assumptions, precedents, rules of inference) are you using to ensure that the audience sees the connection between the data and the claim? Second, once you've written a brief description of the data and have identified the warrant on which its relationship to the claim rests, you can more clearly determine whether you wish to offer the claim as definite, or as only probable, likely, or possible. You'll also be reminded to reflect on the audience's grasp of the warrant. Is it a generally accepted relationship—will it be in this case?

Finally, by thinking through the possible reservations that others will have to your argument, you'll be in a better position to shore up weaknesses in advance and, where necessary, to build a stronger base from which to respond to issues that might undermine rather than directly refute your case.

Applying the elements also sharpens your ability to question an argument. The data may be misleading or in error, the relationship between the data and claim may be highly questionable (lacking a strong warrant); there may be so many reservations that the claim must be highly qualified; advocates may be pushing claims harder than the data will warrant. Using the model as a means of thinking about arguments can help you determine whether a claim goes beyond what can reasonably be supported by the evidence and available warrants.

$\mathcal{A}$SSESSING A SAMPLE SPEECH

Policies are supported by particular factual assertions as well as values. The advisability of an action is based on (1) the credibility of the facts offered in its support, and (2) on the audience's willingness to accept the value judgments being made.

In many cases, a speaker must reorient listeners' thinking, especially if they take something for granted, such as the safety of the water they drink every day. Athena Papachronis of Bradley University faced this problem in her analysis of the safety of common tap water.[7] She sets up the problem in paragraph 1, then proceeds to evaluate the potential causes of contamination in paragraphs 2 through 5. In paragraph 6, she forecasts the development of three reasons why these contaminants are not removed through normal purification processes (paragraphs 6 through 8) and then goes on to discuss possible solutions (paragraphs 9 through 12).

$\mathcal{C}$AN YOU DRINK THE WATER?

Athena Papachronis

Setup of the Argument

This year, the United States has experienced some of its greatest natural disasters: the catastrophic flooding in areas of the Midwest, and more recently, the Los Angeles earthquake. Although the severe damage has left thousands homeless, one of the most alarming results in both instances has been a lack of safe, sanitary drinking water. However, a study released September 27, 1993, by the National Resources Defense Council points out that it doesn't take a catastrophe to put us all at risk from our water supplies. Unfortunately, water, that is not contaminated by toxic waste, flooding or any type of extenuating pollution—water that has supposedly been purified and normally carried to our taps, is potentially deadly. According to the aforementioned study, 43 percent of all water purification systems do not meet federal guidelines. Quite simply, our nation's water purification process is not working. As Senior Attorney for the NRDC, Erik Olson notes, "This new information raises a huge warning sign that millions of Americans can no longer simply turn on their taps and be assured that their water is safe to drink." We need to take our

Policy Claim

own measures to ensure the safety of our water; and, considering that according to the *Washington Post* of July 20, 1993, over 90 percent of the American population gets their water supply from these community systems, we need to first, look at the specific contamination in our drinking water; second, understand why current EPA regulations fail to protect us; and finally, see what

*H*OW TO

DEVELOP ARGUMENTATIVE SPEECHES

Consider the following practical suggestions in developing an argumentative speech:

- *Organize your arguments, using the strongest first or last.* This takes advantage of a **primacy-recency effect.*** Presenting strong arguments at the outset sets the agenda for how listeners will think about your claim. On the other hand, your last argument will be retained more

Causes of the Problem

we need to do to ensure that when we turn on our water, our water isn't turning on us. /1

To fully understand the difficulties involved with our water purification process, we need to first, examine the potential contaminants in our tap water, and then the health risks they pose. The Safe Water Drinking Act of 1974 sets the federal standard for public water supplies, enforced by the Environmental Protection Agency. A total of 83 contaminants are required to be

easily, hence you may wish to build toward it, carrying your audience with you as you provide stronger and stronger reasons for adopting the claim.

- *Use a variety of evidence.* You can't bank on any one piece of material to move an audience toward your position; hence a broad variety of evidence appealing to relevance and motivation will strengthen your effectiveness. For example, if you wish to argue for restrictions on shark fishing, you can cite statistical evidence of overfishing that is depleting the population or you can present a graphic video clip showing de-finned sharks being dumped back into the ocean to die (shark fin soup is an expensive delicacy in some countries). The latter is a more moving illustration of the reason for restrictions on fishing.
- *Know the potential arguments of your opponent.* The best defense is a good offense, but it stands to reason that prior knowledge of the opponent's reasons will go a long way toward strengthening your own claims. Investigating your opponent's position as thoroughly as possible gives you a competitive advantage; you'll be less likely to be surprised or caught off guard by an argument.
- *Finally, practice constructing logical arguments and detecting fallacious ones.* Ultimately, arguing well depends on your understanding of logical reasoning. The common denominator of all arguments, despite their different content, is the patterns of reasoning people use. If you have a clear grasp of the basic building blocks, including the material presented in this chapter, your skill development will proceed at a much faster pace.

*Sarah Trenholm, *Persuasion and Social Influence* (Englewood Cliffs, NJ: Prentice-Hall, 1989), 242–243.

monitored and treated by utilities that provide drinking water. /2

However, there are two particularly critical items that are frequently overlooked: bacteria and microorganisms. Bacteria that are not from foreign sources or derived from accidents in the purifying process are naturally growing in water supplies. According to an American Water Works Association statement released July 20, 1993, on average each year, there are 250 to 500 incidents when local utilities must issue "boil orders" because the water is unsafe from bacteria. /3

Additionally, and more deadly, are chlorine-resistant microorganisms. Once again these microorganisms, known as cryptosporidium, are not entering the water supply from unusual sources. Cryptosporidium naturally thrives in source water, such as streams and lakes, before the purifying process, and too frequently are not removed. According to the *Bureau of National Affairs State Environment Daily* on March 7, 1994, the parasite is found in virtually all water sources. /4

The impact that these contaminants have on us can be tragic. The July 1, 1993, issue of *Money Magazine* reports that last year 60,000 New Yorkers had to boil their water and 13,000 people in Georgia became acutely ill when bacteria in the drinking water supply rose to unsafe levels. As recently as last month, the *Chicago Tribune* of March 15, 1994, reported that 120,000 people in Racine, Wisconsin, had to boil their water because it contained cryptosporidium. Worse, according to the January, 1994, issue of *Discover,* last year in Milwaukee over 370,000 people became ill, 4,000 were hospitalized and 54 people died from drinking water contaminated by cryptosporidium. Frighteningly, Kathleen Fessler, an epidemiologist for the Milwaukee Health Department, explains, "Some people got sick from a single sip of water at an airport fountain." And at best, the statistics are conservative. Situations like Milwaukee are occurring all over the country on a smaller scale, but because people don't realize that it is their water which is making them ill, they don't report it as such. The *ABC Evening News* of September 27, 1993, reports that the EPA estimates that on average each year nearly one million people become infected and at least 900 die from poorly purified water. /5

Rebuttal of the Opposing Arguments

But why is regular tap water, which most of us take for granted and assume to be safe, of such poor quality? The causes of poor purification are threefold: lax safety standards, an inability to implement them, and inadequate enforcement. It's interesting to note that Milwaukee's monitoring and filtration methods of water treatment met all state and federal standards when the outbreak occurred. The problem is that the standards are not stringent enough. For example, in July 1987 the EPA reset reestablished standards for water systems under the Safe Water Drinking Act but, according to the

February 21, 1994, Air and Water Pollution Reports, the EPA did not require testing or treatment for cryptosporidium, even though they knew as early as 1974 that the bug could be fatal. The July 20, 1993, issue of the *Washington Post* adds, that the Clean Water Act only requires water to be clean enough to be swimmable and fishable, but not necessarily drinkable. /6

However, even if the standards were strict enough to guarantee our safety, states do not have the financial capacity to implement them. The *Engineering News-Record* of September 20, 1993, reports that there is a $9 billion infrastructure gap which must be covered. As a result, according to *Time* of November 15, 1993, states do not conduct inspections frequently enough, fail to follow inspection guidelines, and often do not correct problems that are uncovered. Rather than pay those costs, many water systems have simply refused to comply with federal guidelines. /7

Finally, the reason that states can so easily evade these regulations altogether is due to an inadequate degree of enforcement. According to *Environmental Nutrition* of November 1993, during 1991 and 1992 the EPA logged nearly 300,000 state and federal violations, but only 1 percent resulted in any penalties—thus giving the states no incentive to even bother trying to comply. Unfortunately, the danger in this rests in the fact that according to a statement from the NRDC representative on March 15, 1994, the public is only notified of danger in their drinking water 11 percent of the time./8

Solution to the Problem

But what can be done to ensure that water, which is so vital to us, isn't actually damaging our health? We can take action nationally, locally and personally to guard our health. First, it is important to note that both the Clean Water Act and Safe Water Drinking Act are up for reauthorization in 1994. Although often it may sound trite to "contact your congressperson," we currently have an unparalleled window of opportunity. Because this legislation, by law, must come before Congress this year to be scrutinized and refinanced—and considering that 1994 is an election year we hold the attention of our representatives. If ever the citizenry had a chance to actually affect legislation, now is the time to demand stricter standards. Additionally, President Clinton is proposing a $599 billion revolving door fund to help the states pay for the implementation and enforcement of purification guidelines. Given the opportunity, we need to voice our support for these measures. But pending the actual passage of legislation, further steps need to be taken./9

On a local level, the company or municipal authority that supplies your water is required, by federal law, to give you an analysis of your tap water, and disclose any violation of health standards. However, it is up to us to take the initiative to ask. To find out how to contact your authority, you can call the EPA Drinking Water Hotline available in any public telephone directory. /10

However, ultimately, our safety is in our own hands. If you find that your water is substandard, you can buy a home water filter, certified by the National Sanitary Foundation, which is specific to the identified contaminant. Additionally, boiling water for 15 minutes is sufficient to destroy any dangerous contaminants. Another more simple, but more expensive alternative is to buy bottled water, but only if it bears the seal of NSF International, which guarantees its purity. /11

Although the natural disasters of the flooding of the Midwest and the California Earthquake were indeed tragic, at least people were aware of the potential dangers in their drinking water; and thus, could take measures to protect themselves. If we ignore the problems with our normal tap water, the catastrophe will remain hidden, and one that is just waiting to happen. /12

ℭHAPTER SUMMARY

Argumentation is a persuasive activity in which a speaker offers reasons and support for claims in opposition to the claims advanced by others. Arguing with others engages people in tasks central to *critical thinking:* assessing the reasons offered in support of claims. Within single argumentative speeches, particular arguments consist of the following:

- The *claim* to be defended
- The *evidence* relevant to the claim
- The *reasoning pattern,* or inference, used to connect the evidence to the claim.

Claims of *fact* assert that something is or is not the case, claims of *value* propose that something is or is not desirable, and claims of *policy* attempt to establish that something should or should not be done. Evidence is chosen to support these claims because it is *rationally* or *motivationally relevant*.

There are five basic reasoning patterns: *reasoning from example, reasoning from generalization or axiom, reasoning from sign, reasoning by parallel case,* and *reasoning from causal relation.* Each of the inferential, or reasoning, patterns can be tested by applying specific questions to evaluate the strength or soundness of the argument. Critical thinkers also should be on the alert for *fallacies* committed during an argumentative speech. The garden variety fallacies or flaws in the construction of arguments discussed in this chapter are *hasty generalization; genetic fallacy; appeals to ignorance, popular opinion,* and *authority; sequential fallacy, begging the question, ambiguity, persuasive definition,* and *name-calling.* Through the use of the Toulmin model of argument and its elements (*claim, data, warrant, backing, reservations, qualifiers*) you can better assess the quality of your arguments, as well as the quality of arguments addressed to you. If you are seeking to develop argumentative speeches, either to initiate support for a position or to offer a refutation of an opponent's position, you should consider the general strategies presented in this chapter. As you become more adept at constructing your own presentations, you also will increase your skill in critically appraising the arguments of your opponents.

$\mathcal{K}$EY TERMS

ambiguity (p. 405)
appeal to authority (p. 405)
appeal to ignorance (p. 404)
appeal to popular opinion (p. 404)
arguing (p. 390)
argument (p. 390)
argumentation (p. 390)
backing (p. 407)
begging the question (p. 405)
causal reasoning (p. 401)
claim (p. 394, 406)
critical thinking (p. 390)
data (p. 406)
deductive reasoning (p. 399)
evidence (p. 394)
factual claim (p. 394)
fallacies (p. 403)
generalization (p. 399)

genetic fallacy (p. 403)
hasty generalization (p. 403)
inductive reasoning (p. 399)
inferences (p. 398)
name-calling (p. 405)
parallel case (p. 401)
persuasive definition (p. 403)
policy claim (p. 396)
primacy-recency effect (p. 410)
qualifier (p. 408)
reasoning from example (p. 399)
reasoning patterns (p. 394)
reservation (p. 408)
sequential fallacy (p. 405)
sign reasoning (p. 399)
value claim (p. 396)
warrant (p. 406)

ASSESSMENT ACTIVITIES

1. How influential are political debates in campaign years? Locate studies of presidential debates, and present your critical summary in written form or as part of a general class or small group discussion.

2. Assume you're going to give a speech favoring mandatory military service to an audience of students hostile to your proposal. Outline your arguments using the Toulmin model of argument. What factors do you consider as you construct and frame your argument? Assume that several counterarguments are offered by your fellow students. What new factors must you consider in rebuilding your case for service?

3. Prepare a ten-minute argumentative exchange on a topic involving you and one other member of the class. Dividing the available time equally, one speaker will advocate a claim; the other will oppose it. Adopt any format you both feel comfortable with. You may choose from the following: (a) a Lincoln/Douglas format—the first person speaks four minutes; the second, five; and then the first person returns for a one-minute rejoinder; (b) an issue format—both speakers agree on, say, two key issues, and then each speaks for two and a half minutes on each issue; (c) a debate format—each speaker talks twice alternately, three minutes in a constructive speech, two minutes in rebuttal; and (d) a heckling format—each speaker has five minutes, but during the middle of each speech the audience or opponent may ask questions.

REFERENCES

1. For a summary of the senses in which the term can be employed, see Joseph Wenzel, "Three Perspectives on Argument: Rhetoric, Dialectic, Logic," in *Perspectives on Argument,* eds. Janice Schuetz and Robert Trapp (Prospect Heights, IL: Waveland Press, 1990).

2. Harvey Siegel, *Educating Reason: Rationality, Critical Thinking, and Education* (New York: Routledge, 1988), 1–47. The importance of critical thinking has been underscored in two recent national reports on higher education: The National Institute on Education's *Involvement in Learning: Realizing the Potential of American Higher Education* (1984); and the American Association of Colleges' report, *Integrity in the College Curriculum: A Report to the Academic Community* (1985). For a summary of research on critical thinking in the college setting, see James H. McMillan, "Enhancing College Students' Critical Thinking: A Review of Studies," *Research in Higher Education,* 26 (1987): 3–29.

3. For a discussion of argument as justification, see Raymie E. McKerrow, "The Centrality of Justification: Principles of Warranted Assertability," in *Argumentation Theory and the Rhetoric of Assent,* eds. David Cratis Williams and Michael David Hazen, (Tuscaloosa: University of Alabama Press, 1990), 17–32.

4. For a clear discussion of why one should acquiesce in the face of a stronger argument, see Douglas Ehninger, "Validity as Moral Obligation," *Southern Speech Communication Journal* 33 (1968): 215–222.

5. Charles L. Stevenson, *Ethics and Language* (New Haven: Yale University Press, 1944), ch. 9.

6. For further study of informal logic, see Irving M. Copi and Keith Burgess-Jackson, *Informal Logic*, 2nd ed. (New York: Macmillan, 1992).

7. Athena Papachronis, "Title Unknown," in *Winning Orations 1994*. Reprinted by permission of Larry Schnoor, Executive Secretary, Interstate Oratorical Association, Mankato State University, MN. Title created by authors.

CHAPTER

16

$\mathcal{B}$UILDING SOCIAL COHESION IN A DIVERSE WORLD: SPEECHES ON SPECIAL OCCASIONS

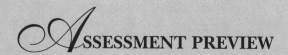

$\mathcal{A}$SSESSMENT PREVIEW

After reading Chapter 16, the student with basic communication competencies will be able to

- understand the significance of ceremony and ritual in a diverse community.
- distinguish between speeches of introduction, tribute, nomination, and goodwill.
- understand how and when to employ humor in relation to speeches to entertain.
- create a speech of introduction or nomination.

The student with average communication competencies will also be able to

- adapt content and style of a speech of tribute to an audience and occasion in an appropriate manner.
- create a speech to entertain that communicates a socially significant idea while remaining an entertaining address for an audience.
- utilize the motivated sequence to develop speeches of introduction, tribute, and goodwill.

The student with superior communication competencies will also be able to

- critique the ability of speakers to facilitate community building while retaining cultural diversity.
- develop speeches of tribute or goodwill that are memorable for their cogency and use of language.
- understand the critical importance of ritual and tradition in creating speeches that fit the occasion and the expectations of the audience.
- develop speeches that meet ethical commitments in community building.

*B*eing honored for achievement is a time to feel proud, a time to bask in the warmth of congratulations and praise from others. Being honored, as recipients of the Oscar, the Tony, and countless other awards in the music and entertainment industry know, is also a time to compose an acceptance speech. What should you say if you are the winner? Should you plan your acceptance in advance, or just "wing it" and hope for the best? What are the expectations of your audience?

Over the years, there have been several notable acceptance speeches given by celebrities—some notable because they violated the expectations of the audience. At the recent American Music Awards, for example, Garth Brooks was named the Artist of the Year. His acceptance speech was decidedly nontraditional, as he refused to accept the award, leaving it on the lectern as he left the stage. He attempted to cushion the nonacceptance by indicating he meant no disrespect to the AMA, but that he felt this kind of honor was not appropriate. Two decades earlier, three women were nominated for a National Book Award. As the following excerpt suggests, they too used the occasion to make a statement that violated audience expectations:

> We, Audre Lord, Adrienne Rich, and Alice Walker, together accept this award in the name of all the women whose voices have gone and still go unheard in a patriarchal world, and in the name of those who, like us, have been tolerated as token women in this culture, often at great cost and in great pain. We believe that we can enrich ourselves more in supporting and giving to each other than by competing against each other; and that poetry— if it *is* poetry—exists in a realm beyond ranking and comparison. We symbolically join together here in refusing the terms of patriarchal competition and declaring that we will share this prize among us, to be used as best we can for women.[1]

The three women had agreed in advance that, should one of them win, this acceptance would be delivered by the award recipient on behalf of all three. What's going on here? This is, after all, a **special occasion**—a time to thank the award sponsors, and to thank those whose assistance made it possible for one person to win. It's as if, instead of a stirring call to national pride on the Fourth of July, a speaker were to soundly berate Americans for small-mindedness and an unconscionably materialistic lifestyle.

What's going on in these instances cuts to the heart of what speaking on special occasions is about: presentations that uplift the human spirit, acknowledge humility in the face of adversity, and praise the generosity of others. At the same time, such occasions are open to the possibility of challenging an audience—such occasions may not represent what the community or nation needs at this moment in time.

On these and other special occasions, our consciousness of the role we should play as a representative of a select community, as in the case of entertainers, poets, or athletes, dictates the ground rules for speaking. Prior tradition—how speakers have handled their duties on previous occasions—at awards presentations, at Fourth of July commemorations, and other events specifies how we should perform. As presenters, we have a natural desire to do well, to earn the respect and admiration of the community on our return from the podium.

In this chapter, we'll look at several kinds of speeches you may give in the presence of or as the representative of such a select community. Before we discuss those speech types, however, we'll have to deal boldly with one of the major problems of our time—the fragmentation of society, *the challenge of communicating in an age of diversity*. Special-occasion speeches are absolutely crucial types of public talk. Unless we're willing to think about what holds us together—what makes us into a *community*—informative, argumentative, and persuasive speaking will produce no results.

CEREMONY AND RITUAL IN A DIVERSE COMMUNITY

The word "community" comes from the Latin *communis*, meaning "common," or, more literally (with the *-ity* ending), "commonality." A community is not simply the physical presence of people—say, those who live in the same town (a local community) or who worship together (a religious community). A **community** is a group of people who think of themselves as bonded together, whether by blood, locale, class, nationality, race, occupation, gender, or other shared experiences or attributes.

The phrase "who think of themselves" is key here. Of course, you share blood type with members of your family, but why is that important to your concept of family? While there are biological differences between males and females, why should gender become a factor in determining who gets paid more, who draws combat duty in time of war, or who's generally expected to raise the kids? Yes, skin comes in many different colors, but why have we made so much of that fact? To understand why, we need to recognize one fundamental truism:

> *While physiological, psychological, and social differences between people are real, the importance attached to those differences is socially constructed in arbitrary ways.*

Social Definitions of Diversity

A **social construction** is a mechanism used by group members to understand, interpret, and evaluate the world around them. There is no such thing, as Nelson Goodman notes, as "perception without conception."[2] Human beings cannot "see" their world without framing it, usually in language. Words store our experience of the world; just uttering "pit bull" brings to mind for most people frightening stories of their own or other people's experiences. Words encode our common attitudes; as we noted in Chapter 10, we have multiple words for the same object ("officer of the law," "cop") because our feelings about such people vary. Words express our evaluations; the difference between a "student-athlete" and a "jock" is a difference in how we value what the person does while at school. Saying that "we socially construct our world" isn't to say that we create it in some brute way; the physicality of the world is real, solid—and you'll literally hurt your toe when it bumps into a desk. Rather, we are saying that *human beings orient themselves to the world via language.* We see, interpret, and evaluate the world via language.

It follows, then, that at one level or another communication is always the attempt to get others to see, interpret, and evaluate the world as you do. The language you share within your social community builds a socially cohesive world. Unfortunately, that language may not have the same impact outside your own community. Words vary from time to time, from place to place, from context to context, and even from person to person. "Democracy" means one thing in the United States, another in the Russian republic, because of differing traditions, governmental institutions, and personal experiences. When a U.S. and Russian citizen talk to each other about democratic institutions, they must be careful to indicate very concretely how each is seeing, interpreting, and evaluating the world when using that term. Within our own communities such care is critical: building consensus across diverse ethnic, racial, and class groupings in our larger cities is not an easy task. One thing we have learned: *in an age of diversity, there is a tendency to fragment society rather than to share beliefs, attitudes, and values as a community.* One important means of self-definition is through special occasions. But, as we have seen in the experience of Garth Brooks and

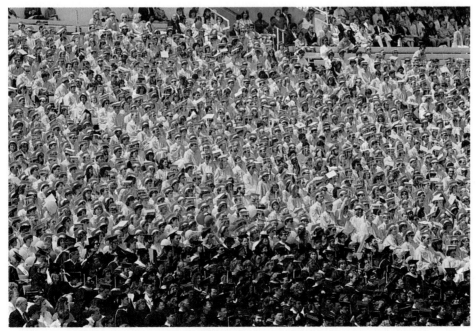

People tend to think of and identify themselves in terms of social groups and roles.

Adrienne Rich, such occasions also may challenge a community's sense of who they are and what they collectively should value. The great challenge of special-occasion speaking, therefore, is to get a society to live together while valuing their individual differences. We can become "one"—we can live in harmony with others—without sacrificing our own identity through the language that we employ in building social cohesiveness, a sense of togetherness as we struggle to define our common purpose.

Public Address as Community Building

Within your own community, the groups you belong to have a special influence on your beliefs and actions. Whether you are part of a religious group, a member of the university swim team, a fraternity or sorority member, or an active member of a residence hall council, the group functions as a reference point in your life—you draw self-definition from the groups you belong to and you use these same groups for reinforcement or for new information on problems. In this fashion, the **reference group** assists in defining who you are and your role in the community.

When seen as relevant to a problem or event, a group helps direct the choices you have, and may even dictate what should be done in order to remain in good standing within one or more of the groups. Just as your group memberships change over time, so does the power of particular groups to affect your thought and actions.[3] Yet, traces of groups from your youth follow you through life. The question we face in this chapter goes beyond that social-psychological truth: *Your sense of group identity, of community, is created largely through public talk.* The language of reference groups is inscribed in your memory. If you were a Boy Scout or a Girl Scout, you can still, to this day, recite the oath expressing your commitment to the group. Your civic education begins with pledging allegiance to the flag; it broadens when you participate in Memorial Day, Fourth of July, and Labor Day ceremonies (which include public addresses); and that education is reviewed every time the president appears on television or hopefuls campaign for local, state, and national office. Your sense of community undoubtedly is built out of bits and pieces of social constructions reinforced in you since your childhood.

As Michael Walzer puts it, "The state is invisible; it must be personified before it can be seen, symbolized before it can be loved, imagined before it can be conceived."[4] The same is true with most reference groups in your life. You cannot see group standards, only the behavior of individuals; you cannot feel the influence of groups outside of the words and other symbols they use to define their claim upon you.

While you may not be consciously aware of the influence of particular reference groups, their claim on your self-identity, your beliefs and actions, is brought home to you on special occasions, in special rituals. David Kertzer has described **ritual** as follows:

> Ritual action has a formal quality to it. It follows highly structured, standardized sequences and is often enacted at certain places and times that are

COMMUNICATION RESEARCH DATELINE

RITUALS AND POWER

We've discussed speeches for special occasions as community building. They're also important for community maintaining, and therein lies one of their great powers. We seldom think about our routine activities as "powerful," yet a whole line of research in cultural studies is working to substantiate that claim. Of recent vintage is Kertzer's *Ritual, Politics, and Power*. A professor of anthropology at Bowdoin College, Kertzer investigates the influence of ritual in politics. He defines "ritual" as "action wrapped in a web of symbolism," as "highly structured, standardized sequences . . . often enacted at certain places and times that are themselves endowed with special symbolic meaning" (p. 9).

Symbolization is the key here. Some highly standardized sequences of behavior, such as brushing your teeth or getting dressed, have little or no symbolic significance; they are simply habits or routines. Rituals are structured actions to which we attach particular collective significance, often about how the past is related to the present and how the present should affect the future. A political ritual, Kertzer notes, "helps us cope with two human problems: building confidence in our sense of self by providing us with a sense of continuity—I am the same person today as I was twenty years ago and as I will be ten years from now—and giving us confidence that the world in which we live today is the same world we

lived in before and the same world we will have to cope with in the future" (p. 10). As a community, we celebrate our pasts and construct our futures in the present; ritual is the mechanism of that celebration.

The notion of power comes into the picture when we consider politics as the process whereby vested interests in a society struggle for domination. Republicans fight Democrats for legislative or executive control; parents in a local school neighborhood come together to protest the school's closing; the Hispanic voters of Texas ask presidential candidates to take stands against the "English-language only" movement. Political struggle can be harsh, even fatal, in some societies. Citizens attempt to ritualize political fighting: they invent rules of "parliamentary procedure" to ritualize partisan debate; the transfer of power from one executive to another is ritualized in inaugural ceremonies. The power in such rituals, according to Kertzer, lies in their abilities (1) to control the actual struggles for power and (2) to help convince the witnesses (the populace) that authority is being wielded benevolently, in their name. The rhetoric of special occasions, thus, is a two-edged discourse of power and community maintenance.

Further Reading

Kertzer, David I., *Ritual, Politics, and Power* (New Haven, CT: Yale University Press, 1988.)

themselves endowed with special symbolic meaning. Ritual action is repetitive and, therefore, often redundant, but these very factors serve as important means of channeling emotion, guiding cognition, and organizing social groups. I have defined ritual as action wrapped in a web of symbolism.[5]

Confirmation or bat mitzvah services, the act of "hooding" a new Doctor of Philosophy during graduation, reciting the Pledge of Allegiance in school—these are kinds of ritual actions that Kertzer is talking about. All rituals are structured, standardized, and repetitive, with times and places set aside for ritual observances. Ritual is imbued with symbols and with public address to provide the means of channeling, guiding, and organizing that Kertzer mentions.

Speeches on special occasions are themselves, then, ritualized—they follow a set pattern and hence may seem trite or even uninteresting. If many nomination speeches sound alike from campaign to campaign, that's because few of us really want surprises in our campaign processes. Surprise could lead to change, and change in turn could upset our political system. In speeches for special occasions (except, as we shall see, speeches to entertain), you meet expectations by following the ritualized tradition—you invite revolutionary change when you violate those traditions. In one form or another, the goal of special-occasion speeches is always to socially construct the world in ways consonant with group traditions—to get you to see, interpret, and evaluate the world through the eyes of the group in which the public address is occurring.

The challenge that is set before us on special occasions is, in many ways, the most daunting of those faced by any speaker:

> *In an age of diversity, when each of us has been socialized into any number of specific ethnic, social, political, and religious groups, each of which makes demands upon our beliefs, attitudes, and values, how can we create a sense of shared community?*

Is it possible to share "community" when people are divided into two genders, innumerable religions, age groups ranging from the young to the elderly, multiple ethnic groups, a growing number of political parties, and Mac versus IBM users? How can public speakers reach across differences to create a sense of identity among listeners while respecting those differences? Or, if people do feel a sense of community, what can be done ritualistically and rhetorically to make them sensitive to the demands of community upon them?

Let's now look at some types of special-occasion talk: speeches to introduce, pay tribute, create goodwill, and entertain. How do we create unity while retaining our diversity? That is the challenge as we review the special occasions you may encounter.

✑PEECHES OF INTRODUCTION

The **speech of introduction** is usually given by the group's leader or by the person responsible for bringing the speaker before the group. These speeches are designed to prepare that group to accept the featured speaker and the speaker's message into the group's community and standards. In a sense, a speech of introduction paves the way, it gains *permission* to speak; in the case of a nonmember of the group or community, that permission is based upon what the person brings. What knowledge or skill, above and beyond what the group itself might already possess, does the speaker offer? If the speaker is a member of the group, the introduction should serve as a reminder of his or her role and accomplishments within the community.

Style and Content in Speeches of Introduction

Always, the speech should motivate the audience to listen to the presentation. Everything else must be subordinated to this aim. You aren't being called upon to make a speech yourself or to air your own views on the subject. You're only the speaker's advance agent; your job is to sell him or her to the audience. This task carries a twofold responsibility. First, you must arouse the listeners' curiosity about the speaker and/or subject, thus making it easier for the speaker to get the attention of the audience. Second, you must do all that you reasonably can to generate audience respect for the speaker, thereby increasing the likelihood that listeners will respond favorably to the message that's presented.

When giving a speech of introduction, your manner of speaking should be suited to the nature of the occasion, to your familiarity with the speaker, and to the speaker's prestige. It is never appropriate to tell a story that embarrasses or otherwise demeans the character or integrity of the person you are introducing—it makes no difference whether the person is a friend or stranger, or whether you think it is a "safe" story that the person should not find embarrassing or demeaning. If you are introducing a professor to your club or to student government, this is not the time to tell a presumably funny story about a class experience—don't even chance it! Match your introduction to the seriousness of the occasion.

As you consider the occasion, gauge the amount of time you need to spend talking by how well known the speaker is to the audience—a well-known

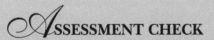
ASSESSMENT CHECK

In developing a speech that fosters community building, you should ask yourself these questions:

- How diverse an audience will be present for the presentation?
- What kinds of appeals, particularly for speeches of tribute or to secure good will, would be most appropriate, given the diversity of the audience?
- What particular words or phrases might others find offensive? How can I avoid appearing insensitive or using inappropriate language?
- Is the situation one where, knowing the expectations of audience and occasion, I should nonetheless stick to my principles and say what needs saying—keeping the language appropriate and in keeping with the occasion?

speaker does not need a long repetition of her accomplishments. For a lesser-known speaker, you may need to spend more time building her or his credibility for the audience. In general, however, observe these principles:

- *Talk about the speaker.* Who is he? What's her position in business, education, sports, or government? What experiences qualify him to speak on the announced subject? Build up the speaker's identity, tell what he knows or what she has done, but don't praise his or her ability as a speaker. Let speakers demonstrate their skills.
- *Emphasize the importance of the speaker's subject.* For example, in introducing a speaker who will talk about the budget cuts facing your university, you might say, "All of us pay tuition, and we know first-hand that budget cuts may mean a tuition hike for us. Knowing why the budget cuts are imperative, and what is likely to happen as a result is in our self-interest."
- *Stress the appropriateness of the subject or of the speaker.* If your town is considering a program of renewal and revitalization, a speech by a city planner is likely to be timely and well received. If an organization is marking an anniversary, one of the speakers may be its founder. As in the previous example, you could go on to note that the speaker is the university's vice president for finance and administration, and hence is in a position to know the reasons for the current crisis.

Organizing Speeches of Introduction

The necessity for a carefully planned introduction depends upon the amount of time available and the need to elaborate on the topic's importance or the speaker's qualifications. A simple introductory statement, "Ladies and gentlemen, the President of the United States," obviously requires little in the way of organization. For longer, more involved introductions, consider how much attention should be devoted to the background and expertise of the speaker and to the interest, importance, or urgency of the topic. A good way to start is to make an observation designed to capture the attention of the audience and then to proceed to develop topics that relate the speaker and message to group interests, desires, or needs. Remember that your introduction should not be longer than the speech it introduces. Aim for brevity.

$\mathcal{A}$SSESSING A SAMPLE SPEECH

The virtues of an excellent introduction, displaying tact, brevity, sincerity, and enthusiasm, are evident in the following introductory speech prepared by Benita Raskowski.

$\mathcal{I}$NTRODUCING A CLASSMATE

Benita Raskowski

We've all come to know Sandy Kawahiro in this class. When we introduced ourselves during the first week of the semester, you learned that Sandy was raised in Hawaii, later moving to the West Coast to live with an uncle. Sandy's first speech dealt with his experiences in California's Sonoma Valley as a minority person for the first time in his life and of the pressures those experiences put upon his values and behavior. In his second speech, Sandy offered an explanatory speech on his post-collegiate career, industrial relations./1

Today, Sandy's going to combine his personal and professional life. If you followed the state legislature's recent public hearings on discrimination on the job, or saw CBS' special report on work environments in Japan two nights ago, you know how important human relations training can be to a successful business operation. This morning, Sandy will continue some of those ideas in a speech arguing for further development of human relations programs in executive training packages. The speech is entitled "Human Relations Training on the Job: Creating Color Blindness."/2

SPEECHES OF TRIBUTE

As a speaker, you may be called upon to give a **speech of tribute,** to praise a person's qualities or achievements. Such occasions range from the awarding of a trophy after a successful softball season to dedicating a new recreational facility to delivering a eulogy at a memorial service. Sometimes tributes are paid to an entire group of people—teachers, soldiers, mothers—rather than to an individual. In all these circumstances, the focus is upon relationships between the community and the individual or group being paid tribute. Honorees are being held up for praise because of the ways in which they have contributed to or represented the community as a whole. If you enable your audience to realize the essential worth or importance of that person or group, you've succeeded, but you have to go farther than this. By honoring the person, you may also arouse deeper devotion to the cause or values he or she represents. Did the person give distinguished service to the community? Then others should serve as well. Was the person a friend and helper to young people in trouble? Then others should do youth work as well. Create a desire in your listeners to emulate the person or persons honored—that is community building. The following ceremonial occasions—farewells, dedications, memorial services—call for tributes of one kind or another.

Farewells

In general, the **speech of farewell** falls into one of three subcategories. When people retire or leave one organization to join another or when persons who are

ETHICAL MOMENTS
WAVING THE BLOODY SHIRT
AND THE BURNING FLAG

The phrase "waving the bloody shirt" dates from the year 1868, when tax collector and school superintendent A. P. Huggins was roused from his bed, ordered to leave the state, and given 75 lashes by members of the Ku Klux Klan. Huggins reported the incident to the military authorities, and an officer took his bloodied shirt to Washington and gave it to Radical Republican Congressman Benjamin Butler of Massachusetts. Later, when giving a speech in support of a bill permitting the president to enforce Reconstruction laws with military force, Butler waved Huggins's shirt. From then on, Republican orators regularly "waved the bloody shirt," blaming the South for starting the Civil War and accusing it of disloyalty to the Union and to its flag.

Similarly, in the late 1980s and early 1990s people have burned the U.S. flag to protest nationalism and to call attention to threats to freedom of speech and the Bill of Rights. In reaction, many people have "waved the burning flag," denouncing flag burning as unpatriotic and as a symbol of anti-American sentiment. "Waving the bloody shirt" and "waving the burning flag" represent particular persuasive strategies in special occasion speaking. In special occasion speeches, you're likely to hear patriotic recitals of the lives of martyrs who died that we might enjoy freedom, of traditional values and their symbols, and of the United States as the democratic bulwark, impervious to the assaults of all other political systems around the world.

Buried in this kind of public speaking are difficult ethical moments. Certainly as Americans we should know our history and who our martyrs were; we should be able to openly discuss values and the topics of patriotism and allegiance; and the United States, for better or worse, is expected to play a significant role in the international scene.

1. But what if our definition of patriotism begins to preclude discussion of alternative viewpoints?
2. What if references to traditional American values halt the examination of values of subgroups within our own society?
3. When does the defense of democracy become cultural imperialism—an attack on all other cultures, economies, and political systems?

Special-occasion speaking *is* a time for reflecting upon one's own culture and belief systems, but such situations can easily be used to batter someone else's culture and thoughts. What the Greeks called *epideictic* oratory, the oratory of praise and blame, is talk filled with ethical minefields. At what point does waving the bloody shirt or the burning flag stop, rather than encourage, dialogue?

admired leave the community where they've lived, the enterprise in which they've worked, or the office they've held, public appreciation of their fellowship and accomplishments may be expressed by associates or colleagues in speeches befitting the circumstances. Individuals who are departing may use the occasion to present farewell addresses in which they voice their gratitude for the opportunities, consideration, and warmth given them by co-workers and, perhaps, call upon those who remain to carry on the traditions and long-range goals that characterize the office or enterprise. In both situations, verbal tributes are being paid. What distinguishes them is whether the departing person is *speaking* or is being *spoken about.* More rarely, when individuals—because of disagreements, policy differences, or organizational stresses, for example—resign or sever important or longstanding associations with a business or governmental unit, they may elect to use their farewell messages to present publicly the basis of the disagreement and the factors prompting the resignation and departure from the community.

Dedications

Buildings, monuments, and parks may be constructed or set aside to honor a worthy cause or to commemorate a person, group, significant movement, historic event, or the like. At such **dedications,** the speaker says something appropriate about the purpose to be served by whatever is being set aside and about the person(s), event, or occasion thus commemorated.

At a dedication, the speaker says something appropriate about the purpose to be served by whatever is being dedicated or commemorated.

Memorial Services

Services to pay public honor to the dead usually include a speech of tribute, or **eulogy.** Ceremonies of this kind may honor a famous person (or persons), perhaps on anniversaries of their deaths. For example, many speeches have paid tribute to John F. Kennedy and Martin Luther King Jr. More often, however, a eulogy honors someone personally known to the audience and recently deceased. At other times, a memorial honors certain qualities that person stood for. In such a situation, the speaker uses the memorial to renew and reinforce the audience's adherence to ideals possessed by the deceased and worthy of emulation by the community.

Style and Content in Speeches of Tribute

When delivering a speech of tribute, suit the manner of speaking to the circumstances. A farewell banquet usually blends an atmosphere of merriment with a spirit of sincere regret. Dignity and formality are, on the whole, characteristic of memorial services, the unveiling of monuments, and similar dedicatory ceremonies. Regardless of the general tone of the occasion, however, in a speech of tribute avoid high-sounding phrases, bombastic oratory, and obvious "oiliness." A simple, honest expression of admiration presented in clear and unadorned language is best.

Frequently, in a speech of tribute a speaker attempts to itemize all the accomplishments of the honored person or group. This weakens the impact because, in trying to cover everything, it emphasizes nothing. Plan, instead, to focus your remarks, as follows:

- *Stress dominant traits.* If you are paying tribute to a person, select a few aspects of his or her personality that are especially likable or praiseworthy, and relate incidents from the person's life or work to illustrate these distinguishing qualities.
- *Mention only outstanding achievements.* Pick out only a few of the person's or group's most notable accomplishments. Tell about them in detail to show how important they were. Let your speech say, "Here is what this person (or group) has done; see how such actions have contributed to the well-being of our business or community."
- *Give special emphasis to the influence of the person or group.* Show the effect that the behavior of the person or group has had on others. Many times, the importance of people's lives can be demonstrated not so much by their particular material accomplishments as by the influence they exerted on associates.

ASSESSING A SAMPLE SPEECH

Harold Haydon offered the following remarks at the unveiling of *Nuclear Energy*, a bronze sculpture created by Henry Moore and placed on the campus of the University of Chicago to commemorate the achievement of Enrico Fermi and his associates in releasing the first self-sustaining nuclear chain reaction at Stagg Field on December 2, 1942.[6] The unveiling took place during the commemoration of the twenty-fifth anniversary of that event. Haydon was associate professor of art at the university.

Notice in particular how Haydon verbally controls the way the audience is to see—to understand, interpret, and evaluate—*Nuclear Energy*. The first three paragraphs ask the listeners to contemplate commemorative sculpture—its historical foundations and present-day functions.

Paragraphs 4 and 5 suggest that there's a spiritual side of scientific discovery that must always be honored. The sixth paragraph deals with the controversy involved with nuclear energy, but deflects that social-political debate by talking, instead, of the importance of artistic recognition. This allows Haydon in paragraphs 7, 8, and 9 to celebrate the union of science and art, the spirit of both people of science and people of art. Haydon thus asks the audience to see the heroic aspects of both science and art (while not looking at the possibly evil effects of science). He controls our vision masterfully.

THE TESTIMONY OF SCULPTURE

Harold Haydon

Historical significance of monuments

Since very ancient times men have set up a marker, or designated some stone or tree, to hold the memory of a deed or happening far longer than any man's lifetime. Some of these memorial objects have lived longer than man's collective memory, so that we now ponder the meaning of a monument, or wonder whether some great stone is a record of human action, or whether instead it is only a natural object. /1

There is something that makes us want a solid presence, a substantial form, to be the tangible touchstone of the mind, designed and made to endure as witness or record, as if we mistrusted that seemingly frail yet amazingly tough skein of words and symbols that serves memory and which, despite being mere ink blots and punch-holes, nonetheless succeeds in preserving the long human tradition, firmer than any stone, tougher than any metal. /2

We still choose stone or metal to be our tangible reminders, and for these solid, enduring forms we turn to the men who are carvers of stone and moulders of metal, for it is they who have given lasting form to our myths through the centuries. 3/

The spiritual dimension of commemoration

One of these men is here today, a great one, and he has given his skill and the sure touch of his mind and

How to
Organize Speeches of Tribute

Consider the following strategies in preparing your speech:

- *Direct the attention of the audience toward those characteristics or accomplishments that you consider most important.* There are two commonly used ways to do this: (a) make a straightforward, sincere statement of these commendable traits or achievements or of the influence they have had upon others, and (b) relate one or more instances that vividly illustrate your point.
- *Dramatize the impact of the persons' accomplishments by noting obstacles that were overcome.* Thus you might describe the extent of the loss to a family when their home burned before praising the Habitat for Humanity group that came to

their aid, with special mention of the college students who participated in rebuilding the home.
- *Develop the substance of the tribute itself. Relate a few incidents to show how the personal or public problems you have outlined were met and surmounted.* In doing this, be sure to demonstrate at least one of the following:

How certain admirable traits—vision, courage, and tenacity, for example—made it possible to deal successfully with these problems;

How remarkable the achievements were in the face of the obstacles encountered;

How great the influence of the achievement was on others.

eye to create for this nation, this city, and this university a marker that may stand here for centuries, even for a millennium, as a mute yet eloquent testament to a turning point in time when man took charge of a new material world hitherto beyond his capability. /4

As this bronze monument remembers an event and commemorates an achievement, it has something unique to say about the spiritual meaning of the achievement, for it is the special power of art to convey feeling and stir profound emotion, to touch us in ways that are beyond the reach of reason. /5

The union of art and science in the monument: The controversy

Nuclear energy, for which the sculpture is named, is a magnet for conflicting emotions, some of which inevitably will attach to the bronze form; it will harbor or repel emotion according to the states of mind of those who view the sculpture. In its brooding presence some will feel the joy and sorrow of recollection, some may

- *Synthesize the attributes of the person or group into a vivid composite picture of the accomplishment and its significance.* There are several ways to do this:

  Introduce an apt quotation. Try to find a bit of poetry or a literary passage that fits the person or group to whom you're paying tribute and introduce it here.

  Draw a word picture of a world (community, business, or profession) inhabited by such persons. Suggest how much better things would be if more people had similar qualities.

  Mention the sense of loss that will occur after the individual or group leaves. Show vividly how much he, she, or they will be missed. Be specific: "It's going to seem mighty strange to walk into Barbara's office and not find her there ready to listen, ready to advise, ready to help."

- *In closing, connect the theme of the speech with the occasion on which it is presented.* Thus, in a eulogy, suggest that the best tribute the audience can pay the person being honored is to live as that person did or to carry on what he or she has begun. In a dedication speech, suggest the appropriateness of dedicating this monument, building, or plaque to such a person or group and express hope that it will inspire others to emulate its accomplishments. At the close of a farewell speech, extend to the departing person or persons the best wishes of those you represent and express a determination to carry on what they have begun. If you are saying farewell, call upon those who remain to carry on what you and your associates have started.

dread the uncertain future, and yet others will thrill to the thought of magnificent achievements that lie ahead. The test of the sculpture's greatness as a human document, the test of any work of art, will be its capacity to evoke a response and the quality of that response. /6

One thing most certain is that this sculpture by Henry Moore is not an inert object. It is a live thing, and somewhat strange like every excellent beauty, to be known to us only in time and never completely. Its whole meaning can be known only to the ever-receding future, as each succeeding generation reinterprets according to its own vision and experience. /7

By being here in a public place the sculpture *Nuclear Energy* becomes a part of Chicago, and the sculptor an honored citizen, known not just to artists and collectors of art, but to everyone who pauses here in the presence of the monument, because the artist is inextricably part of what he has created, immortal through his art. /8

With this happy conjunction today of art and science, of great artist and great occasion, we may hope to reach across the generations, across the centuries, speaking through enduring sculpture of our time, our hopes, and fears, perhaps more eloquently than we know. Some works of art have meaning for all mankind and so defy time, persisting through all hazards; the monument to the atomic age should be one of these. /9

In summary, by isolating character traits that others can emulate, dramatizing accomplishments so that others will be inspired, illustrating the honoree's vision and courage, and synthesizing the person's significance in terms of group standards, you are not only honoring an individual's accomplishment but also pulling the listeners together in a community. Even a highly diversified audience can be galvanized into a collective if your topics and language help individual listeners to see the world of the honoree in a particular way.

$\mathscr{S}$PEECHES OF NOMINATION

The **speech to nominate** contains elements found in both speeches of introduction and speeches of tribute. Here, too, your main purpose is to review the accomplishments of an admired person. This review, however, instead of standing as an end in itself (tribute) or of creating a desire to hear the person (introduction), is made to contribute to an actuative goal—obtaining the listeners' endorsement of the person as a nominee for an elective office.

In our culture, one of the primary occasions for a speech of nomination is at the Republican and Democratic National Conventions. While it may be clear who the front-runner is for the nomination, tradition calls for each candidate still in the running to be placed in nomination before the assembled delegates. Speakers use this opportunity to extol the virtues of their candidate seriously. This may, in the case of unlikely winners, be the last chance to have a candidate's position aired before the delegates and, in turn, before a nationwide audience.

On these occasions, the manner of speaking is dignified, formal, and in keeping with the traditions of the respective conventions. In general, the content of the speech follows the pattern of a speech of tribute, but the illustrations and supporting materials are selected to highlight the nominee's qualifications for the office in question.

The steps outlined here assume that the candidate's interest in the position is well-known and positively received by many in the audience. In the event that you are introducing a relative newcomer, or a person whose nomination will alienate the audience, it may be better to refrain from naming the person at the outset. First, establish the qualities needed for the position and then, in naming your candidate, indicate how this nominee's qualifications will satisfy the requirements. Not all nominations, of course, need to be supported by a long speech. Frequently, especially in small groups and clubs, the person nominated is well known to the audience, and his or her qualifications are already appreciated. Under such circumstances, all that is required is the simple statement: "Mr. Chairman, given her obvious and well-known services to our club in the past, I nominate Marilyn Cannell for the office of treasurer."

$\mathcal{S}$PEECHES TO CREATE GOODWILL

The fourth type of special-occasion speech we will discuss is the **speech to create goodwill.** While ostensibly the purpose of this special type of speech is to inform an audience about a product, service, operation, or procedure, the actual purpose is to enhance the listeners' appreciation of a particular institution, practice, or profession. Thus the goodwill speech is also a mixed, or hybrid, type. Basically, it is informative but with a strong underlying persuasive purpose. There are numerous situations in which goodwill speeches are appropriate. The most common include luncheon meetings of civic and service clubs such as Rotary or Kiwanis, training programs such as those sponsored by schools or companies, and special demonstrations at conventions or product shows. In each case, speakers have the opportunity to show their appreciation for being invited to speak and to increase appreciation for the company or product they represent.

$\mathcal{H}$OW TO
PRESENT A NOMINATION

1. Since this is, fundamentally, a speech to actuate, begin with the declaration of intent: "I rise to place. . . in nomination for the office of. . . . "

2. Describe the qualifications required by the job, the problems to be dealt with, and the personal qualities needed in the individual to be selected.

3. Relate your candidate's qualifications—training, experience, success in similar positions, and personal qualities—to those required.

4. Urge audience endorsement of your candidate, and close by repeating your formal announcement: place the person's name into nomination.

An educational program provides the public with desired information, while creating goodwill for speaker's company or profession.

Style and Content in Goodwill Speeches

Three qualities—modesty, tolerance, and good humor—characterize the manner of speaking appropriate to goodwill speeches. On most occasions, you will find the audience well-disposed to hear you speak. The company you represent or the product you wish to introduce already is viewed positively by the audience—they simply want to know more about what is going on, or they want to know how to use the product in their own work. In other cases, the audience may be downright hostile. A state official coming into a community to indicate why a proposed school can't be built will likely have more difficulty creating goodwill. Speakers must be able to act not only as information sources on the company but also as persuaders who work to change uninformed beliefs and hostile attitudes. You must know and present the facts clearly and show a tolerant, patient attitude toward others. You also can communicate your awareness of the depth of feelings you face, and recognize that alternative opinions have merit.

On these occasions, you also will face the challenge of diversity as audiences will likely have stereotypical views that may make your task more difficult. If you are speaking to a local group about your fraternity's proposal to build a new house for members, you will face problems if they believe that all college students are lazy no-accounts whose only goal is to party. Overcoming such views is never easy. The challenge is to array information and valuable appeals in such a way as to attack those stereotypes. On most occasions, you must talk like a modest, tolerant, good-humored individual, not a person who is angered by the attitudes you hear. However, as implied at the beginning of this chapter, there will be occasions where you challenge those stereotypes far more directly, and with greater anger and frustration in your voice. You may not win your audience over in violating their expectations, but you may follow your own conscience in saying what you firmly believe needs saying at that moment. Choosing this posture is not one that is taken lightly, nor is it one that should mark every occasion; your indignation is felt far more strongly for its rarity than for its pervasiveness.

In selecting materials for a goodwill speech, keep three suggestions in mind. First, present novel and interesting facts about your subject. Make your listeners feel that you're giving them an inside look into your company or organization. Avoid talking about what they already know; concentrate on new developments and on facts and services that aren't generally known. Second, show a relationship between your subject and the lives of your listeners. Make them see the importance of your organization or profession to their personal safety, success, or happiness. Third, offer a definite service. This offer may take the form of an invitation to the audience members to visit your office or shop, to help them with their problems, or to answer questions or send brochures.

As is true of every type of speech, the style, content and organization of the goodwill speech must be adapted to meet the demands of the subject or occasion. You should, however, never lose sight of the central purpose for which you speak: to show your audience that the work you do or the service you perform is of value to them, that it will somehow make their lives happier, more productive, interesting, or secure.

${\mathscr S}$PEECHES TO ENTERTAIN

To entertain an audience presents special challenges to speakers. As you may recall, we identified "to entertain" as an independent type of speech in Chapter 3 because of the peculiar force of humor in speechmaking. Discounting slapstick (of the slipping-on-a-banana-peel genre), most humor depends primarily upon a listener's sensitivities to the routines and mores of society; this is obvious if you have ever listened to someone from a foreign country tell jokes. Much humor cannot be translated, in part because of language differences (puns, for example, do not translate well) and in even larger measure because of cultural differences.

Style and Content of Speeches to Entertain

Like most humor in general, a **speech to entertain** usually works within the cultural frameworks of a particular group or society. Such speeches may be "merely funny," of course, as in comic monologues, but most are serious in their force or demand on audiences. After-dinner speeches, for example, usually are more than dessert; their topics normally are relevant to the group at

How to
Organize Goodwill Speeches

Utilize the following advice in organizing your speech:

- *Attention Step.* Establish a friendly feeling and arouse the audience's curiosity about your profession or the institution you represent. You can gain the first of these objectives by a tactful compliment to the group or by a reference to the occasion that has brought you together. Follow this with one or two unusual facts or illustrations concerning the enterprise you represent.
- *Need Step.* Point out certain problems facing your audience—problems with which your institution, profession, or agency is vitally concerned. For example, if you represent a radio or television station, show the relationship of good communications to the social and economic health of the community. By so doing, you'll establish common ground with your audience. Ordinarily the need step is brief and consists largely of suggestions developed with only an occasional illustration; however, if you intend to propose that your listeners join in acting to meet a common problem, the need step will require fuller development.
- *Satisfaction Step.* Tell your audience about your institution, profession, or business and explain what it is or what it does. Relate interesting events in its history, explain how your organization or profession operates, or describe the services your organization renders. Tell what your firm or profession has done for the community: people employed; purchases made locally; assistance with community projects; or improvements in health, education, or public safety. Do not boast, but make sure that your listeners realize the value of your work to them.
- *Visualization Step.* Crystallize the goodwill that your presentation of information in the satisfaction step initially has created. Do this by looking to the future. Rapidly survey the points you have covered or combine them into a single story or illustration. To approach this step from the opposite direction, picture for your listeners the loss that would result if the organization or profession you represent should leave the community or cease to exist. Be careful, however, not to leave the impression that there is any real danger that this will occur.
- *Action Step.* Make your offer of service to the audience. For example, invite the group to visit your office or point out the willingness of your organization to assist in a common enterprise.

hand, and the anecdotes they contain usually are offered to make a point. That point may be as simple as deflecting an audience's blasé attitude toward the speaker, as group centered as making the people in the audience feel more like a group, or as serious as offering a critique of society.

Speakers seeking to deflect an audience's antipathy often use humor to ingratiate themselves. For example, Henry W. Grady, editor of the *Atlanta Constitution,* expected a good deal of distrust and hostility when, after the Civil War, he journeyed to New York City in 1886 to tell the New England Society about "The New South." He opened the speech not only by thanking the Society for the invitation but also telling stories about farmers, husbands and wives, and preachers. He praised Abraham Lincoln, a Northerner, as "the first typical American" of the new age; told another humorous story about shopkeepers and their advertising; poked fun at the great Union General Sherman—"who is considered an able man in our hearts, though some people think he is a kind of careless man about fire"; and assured his audience that a New South, one very much like the old North, was arising from those ashes.[7] Through the use of humor, Grady had his audience cheering every point he made about the New South that evening.

Group cohesiveness also can be created through humor. Politicians, especially when campaigning, spend much time telling humorous stories about their opponents, hitting them with stinging remarks. In part, of course, biting political humor degrades the opposition candidates and party; however, such humor can also make one's own party feel more cohesive. For example, Democrats created their own messages from bumper stickers in support of Richard Nixon's candidacy—taking "Nixon Now" stickers, and creating new ones saying "Nix on Nixon" or cutting of the *w* from "Now" to say "Nixon No" and putting them on their autos. As in the case of these creative reworkings of bumper stickers, speeches to entertain can be used to make a statement about current conditions and to urge the reform of social practices.

For a brief analysis of the following speech in terms of the motivated sequence, see the outline on page 193.

ASSESSING A SAMPLE SPEECH

A CASE FOR OPTIMISM

Douglas Martini

Most of you probably have heard some version of this poem:

Opening quotation

> Twixt the optimist and pessimist
> The difference is droll:
> The optimist sees the doughnut,
> The pessimist, the hole. /1

The longer I live, the more I'm convinced of the truth of that poem. Like a doughnut, life may seem full, rich, and enjoyable, or it can seem as empty as that hole

Claim

How to

ORGANIZE SPEECHES TO ENTERTAIN

The following sequence works well for speeches to entertain:

1. Relate a story or anecdote, present an illustration, or quote an appropriate passage.
2. State the essential idea or point of view implied by your opening remarks.
3. Follow with a series of additional stories, anecdotes, quips, or illustrations that amplify or illuminate your central idea. Arrange those supporting materials so they are thematically or tonally coherent.
4. Close with a restatement of the central point you've developed. As in step 1, you can use another quotation or one final story that clinches and epitomizes your speech as a whole.

---

in the middle. To the pessimist, the optimist seems foolish. But I'm here today to tell you it's the pessimist who's the foolish one. /2

Developmental materials: A series of humorous anecdotes

Another way of seeing the difference between an optimist and a pessimist is this way: an optimist looks at an oyster and expects a pearl; a pessimist looks at an oyster and expects ptomaine poisoning. Even if the pessimist is right—which is not very often—he probably won't enjoy himself either before or after he proves it. But the optimist is happy because he always has that expectation of future reward. /3

Pessimists are easy to recognize. They're the ones who go around asking "What's good about it?" when someone says "Good morning." If they looked around, they undoubtedly could find something good, as did the storekeeper after she was robbed. The day after the robbery she was asked about the loss. "Lose much?" her friend wanted to know. "Some," she said, "but then it would have been worse if the robbers had got in the night before. You see, yesterday I just finished marking everything down 20 percent." /4

There's another story about a happy-go-lucky shoemaker who left the gas heater in his shop turned on overnight, and upon arriving in the morning he struck a match to light it. There was a terrific explosion, and the shoemaker was blown out through the door to the middle of the street. A passerby rushed to help and asked if he were injured. The shoemaker got up slowly, jiggled his arms and legs, looked back at the burning shop, and said, "No, I'm not hurt, but I sure got out just in time, didn't I?" /5

Some writers have ridiculed that kind of outlook. The great French writer Voltaire made fun of optimism in *Candide*. "Optimism," he said, "is a mania for maintaining that all is well when things are going badly." A later writer, James Branch Cabell, did a turn on one of Voltaire's phrases when he quipped: "The optimist proclaims that we live in the best of all possible worlds; the pessimist fears this is true." /6

A lot of college professors, too, can't resist the urge to jab a little at optimists. But I, for one, refuse to take them seriously. I like the remark made by literary critic and journalist Keith Preston: "There's as much bunk among the busters as among the boosters." /7

Some may like the cynicism of Voltaire or *Doonesbury* cartoonist Gary Trudeau. But optimism is the philosophy I like to hear preached. There was a grandmother who complained about the weather. "But, Melissa," said her friend, "awful weather is better than no weather at all." So quit complaining. Change the bad things in the world that you can, to be sure, but then work within the rest. And stop expecting the worst. Be the optimist who cleans his glasses before he eats his grapefruit! /8

Summary and conclusion turn on the opening quotation

When you're tempted to grumble about your rotten future, remember the doughnut. And, as Elbert Hubbard advised: /9

As you travel through life, brother,
Whatever be your goal,
Keep you eye upon the doughnut
And not upon the hole. [8]/10

CHAPTER SUMMARY

Speeches on special occasions are grounded in the ceremonies or *rituals* that define and reinforce the fundamental tenets of a community. Speakers on such occasions face the special challenge of getting diversified audiences to see, interpret, and evaluate the world through the beliefs, attitudes, values, and rituals of the group observing the occasion. We define ourselves and live up to standards of behavior within *reference groups,* and yet, when those groups clash, unifying *social constructions* of the world must be built through language. Types of speeches on special occasions include *speeches of introduction, speeches of tribute* (farewells, dedications, memorial services), *speeches of nomination, speeches to create goodwill,* and *speeches to entertain.* Most of these forms are built so as to construct and reinforce community standards, although speeches to entertain often are used to critique group beliefs and practices in order to contribute to a better community.

KEY TERMS

community (p. 420)
dedications (p. 429)
eulogy (p. 430)
reference group (p. 422)
ritual (p. 422)
social construction (p. 420)
special occasion (p. 419)

speech of farewell (p. 427)
speech of introduction (p. 424)
speeches of tribute (p. 427)
speech to create goodwill (p. 435)
speeches to entertain (p. 437)
speech to nominate (p. 434)

ASSESSMENT ACTIVITIES

1. This chapter has argued that goodwill speeches usually are informative speeches with underlying persuasive purposes. Describe various circumstances under which you think the informative elements should predominate in this type of speech, and then describe other circumstances in which the persuasive elements should be emphasized. In the second case, at what point would you say that the speech becomes openly persuasive in purpose? If you prefer to work with advertisements, scan magazines to find public service ads that emphasize what a company is doing to help society with its problems or to promote social-cultural-aesthetic values. Then ask yourself similar questions about these advertisements.

2. In this chapter we have discussed speeches of introduction and tribute, but we have ignored speakers' *responses* to them. After you have been introduced, given an award, or received a tribute, what should you say? Knowing what you do about speeches of introduction and tribute, what kinds of materials might you include as attention, satisfaction, and visualization steps?

3. Your instructor will give you a list of impromptu special-occasion speech topics, such as the following:
   a. Student X is a visitor from a neighboring school; introduce him/her to the class.
   b. You are Student X; respond to this introduction.
   c. Dedicate your speech-critique forms to the state historical archives.
   d. You have just been named Outstanding Classroom Speaker for this term; accept the award.

e. You are a representative for a speechwriters-for-hire firm; sell your services to other members of the class.

You will have between five and ten minutes to prepare a speech on a topic assigned or drawn from the list. Present this speech in class, and be ready also to discuss the techniques you used in putting the speech together.

$\mathcal{R}$EFERENCES

1. Adrienne Rich, Andre Lord, & Alice Walker, "A Statement for Voices Unheard," in *Inviting Transformations,* eds. Sonya K. Foss and Karen A. Foss (Prospect Heights, IL: Waveland Press, 1994), 148–149.
2. Nelson Goodman, *Ways of Worldmaking* (Indianapolis, IN: Hackett, 1978), 6.
3. For a discussion of the kinds of group activity that reinforce the power of groups over your life, see James E. Combs, *Dimensions of Political Drama* (Santa Monica, CA: Goodyear, 1980), "The Functions of Ritual," 20–22. Cf. Philip G. Zimbardo, "Constructing Social Reality," *Psychology and Life,* 13th ed. (New York: HarperCollins, 1992), 595–607.
4. Michael Walzer, "On the Role of Symbolism in Political Thought," *Political Science Quarterly* 82 (1967): 194.
5. David I. Kertzer, *Ritual, Politics, and Power* (New Haven, CT: Yale University Press, 1988), 9.
6. Harold Haydon, "The Testimony of Sculpture," *The University of Chicago Magazine* (1968).
7. Henry W. Grady, "The New South," *American Public Addresses: 1740–1952,* ed. A. Craig Baird (New York: McGraw-Hill, 1956), 181–185.
8. Based in part on material taken from *Friendly Speeches* (Cleveland: National Reference Library, n.d.) all material developed for earlier edition of this book.

Index

PHOTO CREDITS

LITERARY CREDITS